THE NEW BOOK OF KNOWLEDGE ANNUAL

1974

HIGHLIGHTING EVENTS OF 1973

THE NEW BOOK OF KNOWLEDGE ANNUAL

THE YOUNG PEOPLE'S BOOK OF THE YEAR

Grolier
INCORPORATED
NEW YORK

ISBN 0-7172-0605-X
The Library of Congress Catalog Card Number: 40-3092

CONTENTS

CONTRIBUTORS

ASIMOV, Isaac
Scientist; author, *The Clock We Live On, Environments Out There*   LIVING THROUGH WINTER

BARBER, Alden G.
Chief Scout Executive, Boy Scouts of America
                    BOY SCOUTS OF AMERICA

BENNETT, Jay
Author, *The Long Black Coat* and *Shadows Offstage*
                    I DON'T UNDERSTAND

BISHOP, James G.
Executive Vice-President, Detroit Hockey Club; Member of the Canadian Lacrosse Hall of Fame
          LACROSSE: A NORTH AMERICAN SPORT

BLAIR, Barbara T.
Kent Fellow (in comparative religion), Danforth Foundation   JAINISM—2,500 YEARS OLD

BOHLE, Bruce
Usage Editor, American Heritage Dictionaries
          NEW WORDS IN DICTIONARY INDEX

CAVALLO, Mildred B.
Poet   CHRISTINE'S DREAM

COLBY, Constance Taber
Author, *A Skunk in the House;* Instructor, Barnard College (Columbia University)   RAISING A SKUNK

CRONKITE, Walter
CBS News Correspondent
                    OUR CHANGING WORLD

DAUER, Rosamond
Poet   DESIGNS

FLANDERS, Stephen C.
News Correspondent, WCBS News
     THE U.S. POLITICAL SYSTEM AND WATERGATE
          A NEW U.S. VICE-PRESIDENT

GARLOCK, George
Television Publicity Editor, Canadian Broadcasting Corporation (CBC)   THE BEACHCOMBERS

GOLDBERG, Hy
Co-ordinator of sports information, NBC Sports; frequent winner of New Jersey Sports Writer of the Year award   SPORTS

HAHN, Charless
Stamp Editor, *Chicago Sun-Times*
                    STAMP COLLECTING

HARP, Sybil C.
Editor, *Creative Crafts* magazine
                    MAKE A DÉCOUPAGE BOX

HINDS, Harold R.
Director, Earthskills Forum; co-author, *Wild Flowers of Cape Cod*   WILDFLOWERS

HINDS, Judy Adams
Co-manager, Maplevale Organic Farm
                    MAKING AN ORGANIC GARDEN

KATHMANN, Richard
Artist; Co-director of the environmental art project, Chicago River Spectacle Company
                    AIR STRUCTURES

KNOX, Richard G.
Director of Public Relations Department, Girl Scouts of the United States of America
                    GIRL SCOUTS OF THE U.S.A.

KUBLIN, Hyman
Professor of History, City University of New York
                    SINGAPORE

LAMBERT, Jean
Professor of French Language and Literature, Smith College; author and translator
A CHILD'S PARIS

LIDSTONE, John
Professor of Education, City University of New York; author, *Building with Wire*
WIRE SCULPTURE

LOFTING, Colin
National Publicity Director, Rodeo Cowboys Association; free-lance writer
RODEO TODAY

MACDONALD, M. A.
Author, *The Royal Canadian Mounted Police;* co-author, *Growing Up*
ROYAL CANADIAN MOUNTED POLICE

MARGO, Elisabeth
Author, *Taming the Forty-niner*
THE GHOST DANCERS

MASURSKY, Harold
Center of Astrogeology, U.S. Geological Survey
MARS

MENUEZ, Mary Jane
Poet
BIRTHDAY

MILNE, Robert Scott
Member, Society of American Travel Writers; free-lance writer
DRIVE-THROUGH ZOOS

MISHLER, Clifford
Editor, *Coins Magazine* and *Numismatic News*
COIN COLLECTING

O'MEARA, J. W.
Director, Office of Saline Water, U.S. Department of the Interior
WATER DESALTING

REINSTEIN, R. A.
Co-director, ISAR (Institute for Scientific and Artistic Research); free-lance science writer and editor
THE HOME ASTRONOMER

REUWEE, A. Daniel
Director of Information, Future Farmers of America
FUTURE FARMERS OF AMERICA

SHAW, Arnold
Author, *The Rock Revolution, The World of Soul, The Street That Never Slept, The Rockin' 50's*
THE MUSIC SCENE

STAPLETON, E. J.
Director of Public Information, Boys' Clubs of America
BOYS' CLUBS OF AMERICA

STASIO, Marilyn
Theater critic, *Cue* magazine; author, *Broadway's Beautiful Losers*
CHILDREN'S THEATER

TEDESCHI, Richard
Instructor in French and Italian Language and Literature, University of Massachusetts (Amherst)
THE HOUSES OF ALBEROBELLO

VAUGHAN, E. Dean
Director, 4-H and Youth Development Division, Federal Extension Service, U.S. Department of Agriculture
4-H CLUBS

VERTER, Leslie
Public Relations Co-ordinator, Camp Fire Girls, Inc.
CAMP FIRE GIRLS

WARBURTON, Ruth
Executive Director, Girl Guides of Canada
GIRL GUIDES OF CANADA

YOUNG, Sid
Executive Director, Communications Service, Boy Scouts of Canada
BOY SCOUTS OF CANADA

OUR CHANGING WORLD

At the beginning of 1973 it seemed as if the United States and the other nations of the world might be heading into a promising new year. President Richard M. Nixon and Vice-President Spiro T. Agnew took office after an overwhelming victory at the polls in 1972. It seemed as if the Administration had a strong mandate from the people. This hopeful note was sounded again in January, when a Vietnam cease-fire agreement was signed—a vital step in halting the war and American involvement in it. By March the last of the American prisoners of war held by North Vietnam and by the Viet Cong were released, and the last United States troops were withdrawn from South Vietnam.

However, even in January, dark clouds were already gathering. The trial of seven men involved in the break-in of the Democratic Party National Headquarters in the Watergate building in Washington, D.C., had begun. The Watergate matter rapidly emerged as a major issue in the minds of most Americans. As more and more information was brought to light in the nationally televised congressional hearings into campaign practices, what had begun as an examination of political "dirty tricks" became a major crisis: Could the American people trust the executive branch of their government or even the President himself? As a result of the crisis, there eventually were calls from some quarters for the President's resignation or impeachment.

The Administration was further shaken when an investigation into a bribery scandal threatened to involve Vice-President Agnew. In October Agnew resigned, and did not contest charges of income tax evasion. President Nixon nominated Republican Congressman Gerald R. Ford to succeed Agnew. Congress confirmed the appointment, and Ford became the 40th vice-president of the United States in December.

On October 6, smoldering issues between Israel and its Arab neighbors exploded in an all-out war that threatened the peace of the world. The United Nations was able to effect a cease-fire agreement between Israel and the Arab countries toward the end of October. As the year ended, peace negotiations between the nations involved had begun to show promise.

Under circumstances aggravated by war in the Middle East, the United States, Japan, and the nations of Western Europe were plunged into still another crisis—an energy shortage. Arab oil producers curtailed shipments of crude oil, especially to nations sympathetic to Israel. Japan and Western Europe were especially hard hit. Although at year-end there was some indication that Arab oil shipments might resume with the signing of an Arab-Israeli peace treaty, few experts believed that this alone would solve the problem of massive energy consumption in an increasingly industrialized world.

WALTER CRONKITE

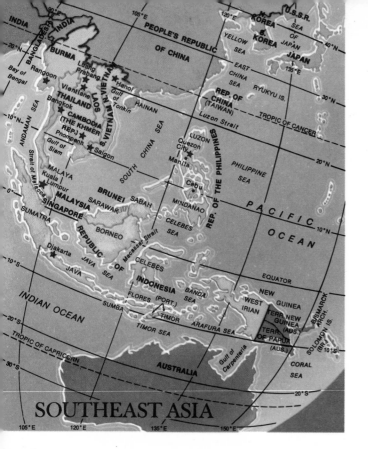

SOUTHEAST ASIA

Southeast Asia is so beautiful it sometimes seems a land of dreams. Long ago, travelers brought back tales of countries east of India and south of China where the air was filled with the scent of spices, lovely temples rose amid the jungle, and the rivers and coasts were bordered by shimmering terraces of rice.

In 1973 the attention of many people was focused on Southeast Asia in quite a different way. It was focused there because of the withdrawal of the United States from the Vietnam War. Peace agreements were reached in January among the warring parties—the South Vietnamese and United States governments on the one hand, and the North Vietnamese Government and the Vietcong forces on the other. Prisoners were exchanged by the end of March, and in the same month all United States troops remaining in South Vietnam left for home.

With their concern about Vietnam reduced, people are beginning to wonder about Southeast Asia as a whole. What are the nations of this vast region? What are its people really like and how do they live?

The nations of mainland Southeast Asia are Burma, Thailand, Laos, Cambodia, North and South Vietnam, and part of Malaysia. The island nations are Singapore, Indonesia, and the Philippines, the last two covering vast archipelagos. The island of Borneo is shared by Malaysia, Indonesia, and the British-protected state of Brunei. All these are independent countries. However, Portuguese Timor and Australian-governed eastern New Guinea are still administered by countries outside Southeast Asia. Southeast Asia as a whole is inhabited by some 280,000,000 people and has a land area of 1,738,000 square miles.

Long, long ago the peninsulas and islands of Southeast Asia were inhabited by small, dark-skinned people, who seem to have lived in a simple way. These people, a few of whom remain in remote mountain regions, were later overwhelmed by migrants who came down from southwestern China. The newcomers traveled along river valleys, heading into the warm lands of the Indochinese and Malay peninsulas and then across the seas to the islands of the Southeast Asian archipelagos. These migrants were the ancestors of

Rivers are the lifelines of Southeast Asia. The Mekong (*above*) is vital to rice production. Malaysian farmers (*below*) go to market by water.

Even the king's palace at Luang Prabang, Laos, is on the banks of the Mekong.

today's Malay and Indonesian peoples. Their great treks into Southeast Asia began about 2500 B.C. Other peoples came much later—chiefly Cambodians (Khmers), Burmese, Vietnamese, and Thais. They moved, in their turn, down from southwest China to settle in the Indochinese Peninsula. Each new group brought its own language, customs, and traditions into the region. Gradually the culture that each new group brought with it blended with the distinctly Southeast Asian life-style that had begun to develop in the region after the first migrations.

This way of life was based on rice growing, the use of metals, and seafaring. Most people lived in rural villages, with houses set around a central clearing—just the way 80 percent of all Southeast Asian people live today.

In ancient times and modern, the villagers would go each morning to work in the nearby fields, returning in the evening to their cool houses. A typical kind of Southeast Asian house is made of wood and has a peaked reed roof. It is built on stilts to protect it from floods, burglars, and wild animals. Often the wooden walls can be rolled up like blinds to let the breezes through, and a veranda, or porch, usually extends all around the house. Although the style of cooking varies from country to country, the family is likely to eat a supper of fish and rice with a spicy sauce, and drink tea with the meal. Later they fall asleep on soft woven mats. They hope that while they sleep the *phi* will not tweak their toes. The *phi* are spirits the Southeast Asians believe are everywhere, although their real homes are such places as rivers, hills, rocks, trees, and plants. Sometimes they torment a person who has not left sufficient

14

In the Philippines, rice is grown on terraces cut into the hillsides.

offerings of flowers or food. Such beliefs are called "animistic," and animism is the old religion of Southeast Asia. No matter what newer religion a person follows, he believes in the *phi* at the same time, for animism is a special way of looking at the world, and his people have held these beliefs for thousands of years.

Although his village, his fields, and his religious beliefs are the center of the average Southeast Asian's life, such modern devices as the radio keep him in touch with the outside world. Also, some of his children may have moved to the city, for such centers as Jakarta (Djakarta), Bangkok, Manila, Rangoon, Saigon, Hanoi, and Singapore have the same attraction for the young that cities do in other parts of the world. The young people bring back news of the city, to the fascination of some and the dismay of others.

Although the village way of life is common to all Southeast Asia, there are differences among the peoples and the countries of the region that must not be forgotten. For one thing, in almost every country, differences developed between the mountain and the lowland peoples. The mountain people often live in relative isolation, speaking their own languages and feeling little kinship with the people who live in the river valleys and along the seashores.

About the 1st century A.D., the great world religions, which were to take root in Southeast Asia and cause important differences, began to be introduced. The first of these was Hinduism, carried to Southeast Asia by Indian traders. Buddhism and Islam came later, by the same route. Today Burma, Thailand, Laos, and Cambodia are Buddhist countries. Most people in Malaysia and Indonesia

The center of Singapore, one of Southeast Asia's great port cities.

A Cambodian Buddhist wedding. Buddhism is a great force in Southeast Asia.

follow Islam. The Philippines is largely Roman Catholic, owing to a long period of Spanish rule. The culture and religion of Vietnam were influenced by China. The majority of people in the two Vietnams follow Mahayana Buddhism, but there is a powerful Roman Catholic minority in South Vietnam. Hinduism was long ago displaced by the other religions in Southeast Asia, except on the Indonesian island of Bali. There, a form of Hinduism blended with local Indonesian customs still prevails. Hinduism left another legacy to Southeast Asia—beautiful temple buildings in every country from Burma to Indonesia, representing one of the greatest architectural periods of the world.

With the coming of the Western powers to Southeast Asia after about 1500, more new ideas, new methods, and new peoples were introduced. Although Europeans ruled the region (except for Thailand) and brought Christianity to some areas, they did not settle in Southeast Asia in large numbers. However, many Indian and Chinese merchants, seeing economic opportunities, came in and settled. Singapore today is three-quarters Chinese as a result, and there are Chinese communities in many of Southeast Asia's other ports. A later need, for plantation workers and miners,

Silk fabric has become a major export of Thailand.

In Indonesia the ancient dance tradition of Bali continues today.

KHÔNG CÓ *i
QUÝ HƠ
ĐỘC LÀ TỰDO

Despite war and hardship, the people of Hanoi, North Vietnam (*above*), and Saigon, South Vietnam (*below*), in the great tradition of the Indochinese, go on with their daily lives.

brought Tamils from southern India and Chinese laborers into many parts of the region.

Southeast Asia is a much-divided land. Its peninsulas and islands are separated from one another by surrounding seas. And on land, high, jungle-covered mountains separate one region from another. In the lowland areas are economic riches. Southeast Asia is one of the major "rice bowls" of the Asian continent. Malaysia produces much of the world's rubber and tin. Indonesia and Burma have large oil deposits. The choice spices and woods that lured the ancient traders are still major products in some areas. The Moluccas, in Indonesia, once called the Spice Islands, produce cloves, nutmeg, and mace today just as they did long ago. And Burma's teak forests still provide a major export.

Southeast Asia's resources have often attracted outsiders, and the region's natural internal barriers have made it easy for them

North Vietnamese women (*above*) repair a war-damaged dike on the Red River. Vietnamese (*below*) light candles in a celebration marking the armistice in the Vietnam War.

to conquer it piece by piece. This is what occurred in the colonial period, from the 16th to the 19th century, and what happened again when Japan gained control in World War II.

The move toward nationalism, which has produced the present independent nations, was an aftermath of World War II, when Western control of Southeast Asia was interrupted by the Japanese occupation. The tragic war in South Vietnam arose partly from the drive for independence.

In North Vietnam, Communist leaders seized control of the independence movement and later tried to take over South Vietnam. In South Vietnam the leaders asked for United States support in their effort to hold on. It is to be hoped that, after so many years of fighting, all parties to the peace agreements signed in 1973 will keep faith and that all the nations of Southeast Asia will be able to pursue the development of their cultures and their resources without the threat of war.

A VIETNAMESE FOLKTALE

Song of the Silver Flute

The story I am going to tell you happened long ago, in a dim and fragrant past. It happened in a time of peace and serenity, in a season when the human heart was pure and love ran deep. There was a great and powerful ruler. He lived in a magnificent palace that was filled with many treasures. But the greatest treasure in all his kingdom, the one that the ruler cherished most of all, was his only child, his daughter. She was small, delicate, and beautiful. Her name, you ask? No one now alive can remember her name, she lived so long ago. But to this day, people remember the legend of her great beauty and of the mysterious song of the silver flute.

There was a wide stream that flowed by the palace of the King. Every evening the little Princess would sit on the riverbank and look out over the water. As she sat, alone and remote, she dreamed of love and romance. She dreamed of a fine and handsome prince who would one day come across the shimmering water of the river to her and say—in a vibrant voice: "I have come for you, my Princess. I have come to make you my bride." And when the Princess thought of that moment, tears of joy appeared in her lovely eyes.

One evening, just before nightfall, the Princess heard the sound of music as she sat in her usual spot on the riverbank. The sound was gentle, tender, and poignant. It was the voice of a flute, and it came from the middle of the river. The little Princess wrinkled her brow and tried to see better into the gathering darkness. But all she could make out was the outline of a small fishing boat and the dim figure of a man seated in the stern. The man was playing a flute that shone with a silvery gleam in the dim light of dusk. The Princess sat listening, her heart filled with joy, until finally the wonderful music faded away and the boat and the figure were lost in the darkness.

Evening after evening, the Princess sat on the bank of the river, and evening after evening, just as the shadows began to lengthen, she heard the exquisite music of the flute. Then, one sad evening, there was no sound of music at all. The boat, the mysterious figure, and the silvery gleam of the flute had vanished. It reminded the unhappy Princess of the fading of a lovely dream when one is waking from a deep sleep.

"Never, never, never," the Princess whispered to herself. "I know that it was all a dream."

The Princess began to grow pale. She would not leave the palace. She kept to her room, never once looking out of the window in the direction of the flowing waters of the river. Soon she grew too weak to walk, and her father, the King, began to despair of her very life.

One afternoon the King came into his daughter's room and sat down beside her. She lay on her couch, her eyes closed, and did not speak to her father. For a long, long time the King looked at his daughter, and he began to be afraid. Finally he spoke to her.

"My daughter," he said, "why do you keep the cause of your sadness from me, your own father?"

Her eyes remained closed.

"If you will tell me," the poor King pleaded, "I will grant your every wish."

Slowly the Princess opened her eyes and turned to her father. "Remember what you have promised, dear father," she said in a very soft voice.

"I will always remember," the King replied.

And so the Princess told the King about the unbearably sweet sound of the silver flute and about the figure in the stern of the boat.

"I must see the man again," the Princes said. "I must hear the marvelous music of the silver flute once more."

"You will, dear child," the King replied.

"I *must* see the man," she repeated.

"You will," said the King, "and I'm sure he is a true prince."

"I *must* see him," the Princess repeated once more so that her father would be sure to recall her words.

On hearing all of this, the King rose and sent messengers throughout his land to find the mysterious man who played the flute. And, wonder of wonders, the man was found and brought to the palace to see the sad and lovely Princess. But he was not a prince. He was a poor fisherman. And yet, looking at him, the Princess knew that she loved the fisherman dearly. And the fisherman, looking at the little Princess, knew for a fact that she was the loveliest person he had ever seen.

But the King made a grave mistake that many fathers have made in their time. He refused to let the Princess marry her fisherman.

"A fisherman may *never* marry a princess," the King ruled, using his most impressive, lawgiving voice.

"But you promised to grant me every wish I might make," the Princess replied.

"That is true," the King agreed, "I did."

"Then how can you refuse this wish to me?" she said.

"When you told me about him, your mysterious friend," he answered, "I thought he was a true and royal prince."

"But father—"

The King shook his head—firmly—no.

"I am sorry, my dear. A fisherman can never marry a princess. Never."

The Princess looked at her father but did not speak another word. The King ordered the fisherman to leave his silver flute behind and never, on pain of death, approach the Princess again. He then spoke sadly but firmly to his daughter.

"It was not the man you loved, my daughter. It was the sound of the amazing silver flute."

And so the King had the finest musician in the land play the silver flute for the Princess, evening after evening. And for a while it seemed to the King that his lovely daughter was happy once more. But he was quite wrong. For, one evening as the musician played the marvelous silver flute, the Princess closed her eyes, sighed once, and died.

And so the tragic tale seems to end.

But does it? I think not. For sometimes, just as the shadows begin to lengthen and soft darkness is about to fall, I think you can still hear the sound of a silver flute on the breeze that blows in off the river. And if you look very closely, you will see two figures appear in a ghostly boat that glides along the darkening stream—just out of reach. I think the figures are those of the Princess and her fisherman. They will probably sail together, as they wished, until the end of time.

Angkor Wat, the greatest building of the Khmer civilization.

CAMBODIA'S GREATEST TREASURE

Today almost any Cambodian can point the way to Cambodia's greatest treasure—the temple of Angkor Wat and the nearby royal city of Angkor Thom. In fact, Angkor Wat (the words mean "great temple") is so important to Cambodians that its outline forms the emblem on the national flag. But there was a time, a little over 100 years ago, when few Cambodians knew anything about the royal city and beautiful temples that their Khmer ancestors had built. Even though the seat of the old Khmer empire lay only about 150 miles northwest of Pnompenh, the modern capital, most Cambodians had heard of it only as a myth, a legend, or a rumor, scarcely to be believed. The jungle had swallowed it up.

Then one day in 1860 a French naturalist named Henri Mouhot was walking along a jungle path. He looked up and suddenly saw five tremendous gray towers shaped like lotus buds. He had discovered Angkor Wat, one of the architectural glories of the world. The sight of the soaring temple in the dimness of the jungle took his breath away. Mouhot and the archeologists who joined him soon found that the area for miles around was littered with temples from the greatest age of Khmer civilization. Thick jungle growth had covered and sometimes shattered them. Their carved shrines and galleries had become the homes of monkeys, snakes, birds, and butterflies.

Only a mile north of Angkor Wat the searchers found Angkor Thom ("great city"). The remains of the city walls enclosed a maze of royal palaces, paved terraces, broad avenues lined with statuary, remains of *baray*s (reservoirs), and, among several other temples, a great central temple called the Bayon. One feature of this city could not be

Vines still grip a temple near Angkor Thom.

overlooked: massive heads resembling those of the Buddha loomed everywhere. The city walls had five massive gates, each decorated with four of the gigantic faces. And in the Bayon rose many towers, each bearing the majestic image.

What they were seeing were the portraits of a god-king. And, as Angkor's story unfolded, it became clear that Angkor's history was bound up with the cult of the god-king.

The cult of the god-king goes back to Jayavarman II, who founded the Khmer kingdom in 802. Jayavarman practiced a form of Hinduism that lent itself to the worship of a god-king. And so, to assert and sanctify his rule, Jayavarman had a Brahman priest perform a rare ceremony that gave him the status of a god. From then on he was known as a *devaraja,* or "god-king," as were all but one or two of the Khmer kings who followed him.

The lands over which the god-king Jayavarman II ruled came to be known as Kambuja (the origin of the modern name "Cambodia"). The King moved his capital several times, at last settling close to present-day Angkor Thom. The site was chosen because it was near ample sources of food and water. Rich rice fields were nearby, and the Great Lake (Tonle Sap), teeming with fish, was just a few miles to the south. The Great Lake also flooded regularly, providing water for the Khmer reservoirs and irrigation systems. The capital remained in this general vicinity for the next 600 years—the whole period of Khmer greatness.

Nearly all the Khmer kings were builders, for each one wanted to add to the grandeur of his kingdom. Also, it was customary for each ruler to build his own great temple, which would house his ashes after he died. Usually the holy temple was placed in or near the center of the capital.

▶ ANGKOR WAT

In 1113 a ruler called Suryavarman II came to the throne. He decided to build his temple outside the city walls. Suryavarman's great temple, Angkor Wat, took most of his reign to complete (he died in 1150). When it was done, it proved to be one of the supreme creations of mankind. Angkor Wat is meant to represent the mythological Mount Meru, home of the Hindu gods. Mount Meru had five peaks, and they are symbolized by Angkor Wat's five grand lotus-bud towers. The towers rise from the center of three stepped terraces. The terraces are meant to imitate the rise of the sacred mountain.

Almost every inch of Angkor Wat's walls, pillars, and towers is decorated with lively carvings. On the walls of the covered gallery on the first terrace is a carved frieze, 8 feet high and a half mile long. It shows scenes from the Indian epic *Ramayana* (the story of the god Rama's search for his kidnaped wife), and vivid battle scenes from another Indian epic, the *Mahabharata.*

All around Angkor Wat is a large grassy courtyard 1 mile long on each side and bounded by a moat. A high wall stands inside the moat, with a magnificent gateway in the west side. A paved causeway crosses the moat, passes through the gateway, and leads across the grass to the temple.

▶ ANGKOR THOM

Angkor Thom, the royal city, stands a mile north of Angkor Wat. The city was built between 1200 and 1219 by Jayavarman VII, the most dynamic of the Khmer kings. He was a Buddhist, but was still able to fit his beliefs to the Hindu god-king cult, for he practiced a form of Buddhism that revered a being called Lokeshvara, Lord of the Worlds. The great heads of Angkor Thom represent Lokeshvara and the kingship of Jayavarman VII at the same time. Yet the Bayon and the other temples Jayavarman built all follow the basic Hindu, Angkor Wat design.

Jayavarman built his city on the ruins of an earlier city that had been largely destroyed. He followed a city plan made about the year 1000 by an earlier king. Some buildings remain from that time. One, the Phimeanakas, in which the rulers lived, was connected by a sacred road with the Ta Keo, a temple outside the city. Both these buildings have stepped terraces, a form later used at Angkor Wat. The Ta Keo has five receding terraces, the whole topped by five towers.

Before Jayavarman VII rebuilt the capital, he built a temple-monastery called Preah Khan nearby, which he lived in while the larger work went forward. Another temple he built on the outskirts of the capital was Ta Prohm, dedicated to his mother. It is a one-story building made up of a series of connected chapels.

Jayavarman's architects took only 19 years to rebuild Angkor Thom. Because the builders worked hastily, wind, rain, and the jungle have worn down and broken the masonry, and weathered the outlines of Angkor Thom's buildings far more than is the case with the massive buildings of Angkor Wat.

Like Angkor Wat, the Bayon, Jayavarman VII's great temple, has wall carvings on its interior galleries. The most memorable are the vast number of reliefs showing scenes of Khmer daily life: women giving birth, farmers sowing rice, slaves carrying bricks for

Closeup of a magnificent tower at Angkor Wat.

the temples—even a swimmer being bitten in two by a crocodile. The scenes have down-to-earth touches that are unusual in royal buildings.

Jayavarman's building frenzy produced fine works all over his kingdom, not just in Angkor Thom. But the effort to build so much magnificence used up his treasury and the energy of his people. After his reign the Khmer artists were worn out, and building gradually stopped. In the 1430's invading Thai armies drove the Khmers from their royal city. The beautiful buildings of the Khmer epoch were left to stand empty for most of the next 400 years, visited only by the birds and the beasts, the wind and the rain, and the creeping jungle.

The men at left perform in the *khon;* the women at right, the *lakon.*

THE DANCERS OF THAILAND

All over the world, in large countries and small, people love to dance. Whether to perform an act of religious worship, to celebrate a victory, or simply to express joy, the rhythmic movement of the human body has been used for centuries in various forms of dancing.

In the sunny, flower-filled country of Thailand, dance plays a major role in the performance of classical drama, known as *khon,* and the more informal drama called *lakon.*

Thai dancers train for many years, because the dances require strenuous, angular body movements. When the dancers assume the traditional postures of the dances, they appear to be almost chiseled in stone.

Traditionally, only male dancers were allowed to perform in the *khon,* and only female dancers in the *lakon.* But today this custom is no longer strictly followed.

The *khon* dance-drama is based on the

Ramakien, the Thai version of the Hindu epic the *Ramayana.* The *Ramakien* is written in lyrical verse, which is sung as an accompaniment to the dance. The dancers derive their rhythm from the music of an orchestra composed of drums, xylophones, gongs, wind instruments, and castanets.

Almost all the *khon* dancers wear highly stylized masks. The audience recognizes the various characters by the expression and the color of the mask. For instance, a nobleman-villain will wear a green mask; other characters may wear masks of red, yellow, purple, or white. Because the masks cover the face and prevent any facial expression from being seen, the dancing must express not only action but also thought and feeling: stamping a foot shows anger, and a stiff body with a special arm motion shows ambition.

The *khon* dancers wear beautifully embroidered costumes that sparkle with gold, silver, and twinkling stones on brocaded silk. The basic costume for men is a tight tunic with pointed, upturned epaulets, and calf-length tight pants with a bloomer-like drapery (called a panung) over the upper legs. Usually pointed gold crowns sit atop their heads, and bracelets encircle their ankles and wrists. The women in the *khon* usually wear shawls that leave only their arms bare, and wrapped skirts that are elaborately draped in front. Leg movements are restricted so as not to disturb the line of the costumes. For the most part, the dancers are barefooted.

The *lakon* is a more informal type of drama. Accompanied by singers and orchestra, the dances are usually based on local folktales and historical romances of kings, princes, giants, and lovely maidens who must be rescued from dreadful danger.

The women dancers of Thailand are especially famous for their intricate finger movements. These finger movements are as important to the performance of the *lakon* as the coordination of the feet and the rest of the body. Just as a French, Russian, or English child must practice five-finger exercises when learning to play the piano, so a Thai girl must learn the intricate finger movements of her dance. In the northern part of Thailand the girls may wear gilded brass fingernails that are 5 or 6 inches long. These shimmering extensions of their fingers give added emphasis to the delicate movements of their fingers.

Although the *lakon* dancers do not wear masks, stylized body movements are used instead of facial expressions. Like the dancers of the *khon,* the *lakon* dancers wear gold- and silver-embroidered brocade costumes and elaborate gold crowns.

Young children, many of whom come from families that have produced dancers for generations, begin their dance careers early. Many are trained from childhood in institutions sponsored by the Department of Fine Arts in Bangkok. These institutions are doing much to maintain the traditional and beautiful dances of the Thai people for future generations.

This graceful pair strike a pose in a dance based on the *Ramayana.*

Hardworking elephants take a refreshing bath at the end of the day.

WORKING ELEPHANTS OF BURMA

Nestled between the towering Himalayan mountains and the blue waters of the Bay of Bengal is the Southeast Asian country of Burma. This sunny, friendly land is known for its golden spired pagodas, or temples. It is also known for its lovely wood carvings, many of which decorate the lower portions of the pagodas.

Wood and wood carving are very important in Burma because almost three fifths of the land is heavily forested. The most important wood is teak: Burma is the world's leading exporter of this beautiful wood.

The forests of Burma are located in rough, hilly areas, and so it is almost impossible to use modern machines and transportation to harvest the trees. And this is why, many years ago, the English writer Rudyard Kipling wrote:

Elephints a-pilin' teak
In the sludgy, squdgy creek,
Where the silence 'ung that 'eavy you was
 'arf afraid to speak!
On the road to Mandalay . . .

Mr. Kipling's Cockney character was, of course, talking about those great, gray beasts that are the backbone of the Burmese lumber industry. Where tractors and trucks cannot go, the powerful elephant walks smoothly, lifting huge teak logs in his trunk. These giants of the animal kingdom roll logs down hillsides, and carry them into rivers where they are floated downstream to the seaports.

The Asian elephant is seldom more than 10 feet tall at the shoulder, and his ears are much smaller than those of his African cousin. His Latin name is *Elephas maximus.*

Almost 4,000 elephants work at lumbering in Burma. When new elephants are needed, it means a lot of labor because wild elephants must be caught and trained before they can be put to work. The new elephants should be between 15 and 20 years old so that they will be strong enough to do the heavy work.

Capturing elephants for work in the forests is similar to a cattle roundup in the American West. First a herd of elephants must be located. Hundreds of men join in the hunt and roundup, some as scouts and some as beaters. The beaters are men who drive the elephants from cover by shouting and making noise with bamboo clappers. When a herd is found, the men form a large rectangle around the elephants. This rectangle may cover an area of many square miles. The beaters and their helpers, tame elephants called *kumkies,* begin moving the wild herd toward a large corral, or *keddah.* This stockade covers many acres and contains a watering area and food. It has an opening shaped like a funnel, through which the elephants can enter.

Tree trunks form the walls of the corral, and more logs are used to make a curtain that is lowered over the opening after the elephants have been driven inside.

One by one, the elephants that have been chosen for work are secured by nooses on their hind feet and tied to trees. This dangerous job is done by trainers, or keepers, who are called *mahouts.* They are assisted by the *kumkies,* who work in twos and threes to bring their wild cousins under control.

A single *mahout* is usually assigned to a captured elephant, and it is he who will be responsible for training the animal. Like dogs, elephants can develop a great fondness for their masters. The *mahout* begins by trying to feed the tethered elephant. However, it may take several days before the wild animal will become hungry enough to accept food from the man. Finally the elephant will quiet down and accept his meals.

Next, he is escorted to a stall where his neighbors are the tame *kumkies.* He is left undisturbed and soon discovers that his neighbors are friendly and the food is good. This is not a bad life!

Once the elephant has begun to eat normally, his more formal training begins. The *mahout* is assisted by *kumkies* and their *mahouts,* and, with the help of a metal-pointed stick called a *hawkus,* or goad, the elephant is moved about. He is taken to bathe, with his tame companions as escorts. Elephants enjoy their baths very much, and within a few weeks the big animal will be looking forward to his daily swim with pleasure.

It takes almost 6 months to train the elephant, and the trainer must have a great deal of patience. The elephant will learn about 30 different commands from his master, and he will learn to respond to the pressure of the *mahout*'s toes behind his ears. Most of the words of command are monosyllables, and the same words are used in many countries, even though the trainers in different countries usually speak different languages. *Sum beit* means "kneel," and the words *doom rakh* mean "keep your tail still!"

The working elephants can be used for felling trees as well as for hauling logs. They press against a tree with their heads until it is at the proper angle and then complete the operation with a strong forefoot. Sometimes the elephant will even go around the tree to remove obstinate roots on the far side. A single elephant can pull a log of about 2 tons, and two working together can move about 5 tons of logs.

The elephants seem to adapt happily to their work and, like children, love to be rewarded with sweets.

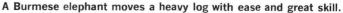
A Burmese elephant moves a heavy log with ease and great skill.

Dolls model Philippine dress. The men both wear the comfortable *barong tagalog*. The woman at left wears the *mestiza terno;* the one at right, the *balintawak*.

CLOTHES OF THE PHILIPPINES

From the largest island, Luzon, in the north, to the tiniest islands of the Sulu Sea, in the south, the Republic of the Philippines is one of the most varied countries in Southeast Asia. Composed of over 7,000 islands, the Philippines may appear to a visitor to have almost as many different peoples and languages, although, of course, there aren't nearly that many. There are, however, over 50 different ethnic groups, and they speak almost 90 different regional languages and dialects.

The Philippines is an especially interesting country precisely because it is so varied in so many ways. Of course, it is varied to begin with because it is a country made up of many scattered islands, not of one unified landmass. However, it is also varied because of its past. The islands have been invaded and influenced by people of many cultures. The invaders, over the centuries, have included the Chinese, Indonesians, Malays, Spanish, Americans, and Japanese. And, as you might expect, each of the invaders left a part of its own civilization. In addition, some of the inhabitants of the islands are descended from people who

originally lived in the area in ancient times. Some of these people still go hunting with bows and arrows, just as their ancestors did centuries ago.

The Filipino people, because they are so ethnically varied, dress differently in various parts of the country. Women in Manila, for instance, may be seen wearing the latest styles from the United States or Europe. On the other hand, in the mountainous northern reaches of Luzon Island, you might see a villager wearing a rain cape made of palm leaves. He is one of the Ifugao people, who live among the rice-terraced mountains. The Ifugao women wear heavy cotton skirts that they weave on ancient looms.

The Igorots, who are also native to Luzon, live in and around Bontoc, the capital of Mountain Province. They dress, farm, and hunt much as they have for generations. An Igorot woman may be tattooed from hand to elbow for decoration. Beads may be wound through her hair, and she wears a brightly woven striped skirt with a tasseled sash. The Igorot men wear tasseled loinclothes, and the elders often have tattoos on their chests and shoulders. The Igorot youths can be seen wearing small baskets, decorated with mirrors and buttons, on the backs of their heads. Once the young men get married they no longer wear these unusual basket-hats.

In the southern reaches of the Sulu Sea lives a group of Philippine islanders called the Samals. The Samal women use rice powder and spices to color their faces white, and they wear sarongs made of cotton. On the other hand, on the island of Jolo, the Moros, who are descended from Muslim invaders, wear short, brightly colored trousers. The Moro men wear tight jackets, and the women wear scarves in contrasting colors.

Filipino men have a national costume of their own that is often adopted by men from other countries who visit the islands. This garment is a loose shirt called a *barong tagalog*. The shirt may be made of cotton or of the more transparent, silky piña cloth, woven of a pineapple fiber. The *barong tagalog* is always worn outside the trousers, and it has long sleeves. When the shirts are made for formal occasions, they have beautifully embroidered panels down the front; for informal or everyday wear, the embroidery is simpler. In the warm, humid Philippine climate, the *barong tagalog* is as comfortable as it is beautiful.

Filipino women have two distinctive national costumes. The *mestiza terno* is one of them. In the *mestiza terno,* ruffled, sheer, butterfly-like sleeves fall to the elbow, and the *saya* (skirt) falls to the floor and flows in the back to a pointed train. The *balintawak,* the other national dress, has a *camisa* (bodice) and *pañuelo* (scarf) made of *sinamay* (sheer cloth made from abaca fiber). The sleeves of the *camisa* are full, crisp, and fairly short, usually to the elbow. The *pañuelo* is folded into a triangle with the point falling in back between the shoulder blades, and the front ends pinned low on the *camisa.* The *saya* is often made of silk and is sometimes partly covered by a three-quarter overskirt called a *tapis.* Embroidery, beading, and semiprecious stones are used to decorate the costume.

The men and women of the Philippines make a splendid sight when they wear traditional dress at a party or at a family or national celebration.

These lovely ladies wear modern versions of the *mestiza terno.* The costume at left is a Spanish adaptation; the version at right is American.

The graceful pair at left are dressed in costumes from central Luzon; the two at right wear the ancient dress of the Igorots.

Laotian women, on their way to fish, cross a flourishing rice field.

RICE FOR LAOS

In Southeast Asia the basic food is rice. In Laos the verb "to eat" literally means "to eat rice." Even when he dies, a Laotian needs rice, it seems. Laos, like its neighbors Cambodia and Vietnam, has suffered long years of war. Not long ago an American reporter noticed little heaps of grains of rice next to the field telephone at a Laotian army post. His curiosity aroused, the reporter asked the battalion commander what the rice was for. The commander hesitated a moment, then answered that the rice was an offering to the local spirits. The commander also said that if a soldier were killed, he would be buried with a little rice. The rice would help the soldier on his way into the afterlife.

As this story illustrates, spirits and ancient beliefs remain very much a part of Laotian life, even in the midst of a modern war. It is no surprise, then, that prayers and rituals remain very much a part of the growing of rice, the country's most important crop.

The official religion of Laos is Buddhism. But closely tied in with the official religion is the ancient folk religion of the Laotian people. The numerous spirits of this folk religion are called *phi*. Since the goodwill of the *phi* is considered vital to an abundant harvest, most rice fields contain in one corner a small altar, used for offerings to the *phi*.

The spirits are offered food and drink, and sometimes even cigarettes.

Virtually every stage of rice growing involves some kind of ritual. At the outset, the farmer plants his seeds on a day chosen by the local astrologer, a man who claims to predict the future by reading the meaning of the positions of the planets and stars. Then, about a month to 6 weeks after seeding, the time arrives for transplanting the young rice plants to give them more room to grow. A rice offering is placed on the altar. As he transplants the first seven shoots, the farmer chants this verse:

I plant the first shoot;
    May you be green as the Thao.
I plant the second shoot;
    May you be as green as the grass of
        the ninth month.
I plant the third shoot;
    May the gong of nine *kam* be mine.
I plant the fourth shoot;
    May 90,000 pounds of gold be mine.
I plant the fifth shoot;
    May 90,000 baskets of rice be mine.
I plant the sixth shoot;
    May I have a wife to sleep by my side.
I plant the seventh shoot;
    May a rare elephant saddled in gold
        and silver be mine.
Glory!
Prosperity!

(*Kam* are units of measure; the word literally means "handfuls.")

Once the chant is completed, the farmer and his family can go ahead with the hard work of transplanting.

Months later the rice is harvested. Perhaps the *phi* have blessed the farmer with a good harvest. Special rites are held for the opening of the sheds where the rice will be stored, ending the rice ceremonies until the next planting.

Laotians favor a sticky form of rice. They like to press it into lumps and dip it in a fish sauce spiced with pepper. Chicken and vegetable dishes add variety to their diet.

Rice is grown in one of two ways, depending on where the farmer lives. In the valley of the Mekong River, Southeast Asia's great waterway, farmers practice what is known as wetland farming. In the mountainous areas, the fields cannot be flooded, as they are in wetland farming, because the water runs off them. The rice cultivated in the mountains is therefore known as "dry rice," although it takes plenty of rain to grow it.

In wetland farming the land is flat. The farmer floods his land either by irrigation or simply by damming up his fields to keep the rainwater in. In May or June, just after the start of the rainy season, the farmers plow the land, trudging through their flooded fields behind a plow hitched to an ox or a water buffalo. The farmer chooses one corner of a field, and there he sows his rice seeds broadcast—scatters them around in somewhat the way your father seeds his lawn. In about a month the seeds have produced a lush green carpet of young plants, and it is time for transplanting. Men, women, and children carry thick clumps of rice stalks and carefully set the individual plants about 9 inches apart. In field after field the picture is one of tender young rice plants pushing up through the shining brown water.

In the mountains, things are done differently. Several months before seeding, the farmer goes out to a wooded area and hacks a clearing out of the underbrush. He gives the wood time to dry, then sets it afire. For weeks smoke hangs in the air over the Laotian countryside. Then the farmer clears the land of stones and any wood that is left, except for tree stumps, which are too much trouble to remove.

The onset of the rainy season, in May or June, signals the time for planting. A plow is seldom used to prepare the soil; many roots and stumps remain that would probably break a plow. Using a pointed stick, the farmer makes holes about a foot apart, drops in his seeds, and presses down with his naked heel. No transplanting will be needed, and the crop yield will almost certainly be less than in the lowlands.

After 2 or 3 years the fertility of these mountain plots is exhausted. In the lowlands, the river overflows its banks every year and deposits rich silt on the land. But the mountain farmer has no means of renewing the soil's fertility. He simply abandons the worn-out field and goes about the hard work of slashing out a new one from another stretch of woods.

After the rice is harvested—with either sickles or knives—comes the time for threshing, or removing the rice grains from the stalk. Threshing is done by beating the plants against boards or by flailing away with sticks. Then the rice has to be milled—that is, the coarse hull surrounding each grain must be removed. This is commonly done by means of a device operated by foot pedals. Finally, the farmer's work is done. The rice is stored away or taken to market, and for a few months the farmer and his family can turn to other things.

A Laotian farmer deftly plants a rice shoot.

Indonesian children listen to the music of the *gamelan* as the show begins.

SHADOW PUPPETS OF INDONESIA

For many hundreds of years, both children and adults all over the world have enjoyed watching puppet shows. Many countries have their favorite puppet-characters, such as Punch and Judy in England, Hanswurst and Kasperle in Germany, and Kukla and Ollie and the Muppets in the United States.

In tropical Indonesia, however, puppet shows are much more than entertainment for an hour or two. They are a form of a dramatic art called *wajang* or *wayang,* which means "shadow." While there are many different kinds of *wajang,* by far the most popular is the *wajang kulit*—the shadow puppet plays.

The puppets that perform in these plays are flat figures made from buffalo hide. They are rod puppets: they are held from below by a handle, and two rods extend from the puppets' arms. These two rods are used to manipulate the puppets.

Decorated with brightly painted and gilded costumes, jewelry, and headdresses, each puppet represents a specific character. The shape of the eyes, nose, mouth, and other physical features lets the audience know which characters are good and which are bad. The noble, good people have almond-shaped eyes and long, straight, pointed noses. Their heads may be slightly bowed to suggest modesty, and they won't have any chin whiskers. The evil or coarse characters have big, bulb-like noses and round eyes. And they wear more jewelry and are more exotically costumed than the good characters. The audience immediately recognizes the individual characters by their familiar features and dress.

The puppeteer is called the *dalang* and he is an extremely busy man, indeed. In a very long and involved play, he may handle as many as 350 different puppets. Not only does he manipulate the puppets, he also narrates the story, produces the sound effects, and conducts the orchestra (which is called the *gamelan*). Because many of the stories celebrate various religious events, the *dalang* may also perform religious rites before the play.

The *dalang* sits behind a white, cotton screen that is stretched on a bamboo frame. An oil lamp, or sometimes an electric light, shines above him. As the *dalang* works the puppets, shadows are thrown onto the screen. The audience sits on both sides of the screen. Those people sitting in front of the screen see only the flickering shadows of the puppets. The audience behind the screen sees the actual puppets, as well as the shadows.

As the performance of the evening begins, the audience quiets down. The first object to appear before their eyes is a carved-leather mountain or tree that symbolizes the entire *wajang* ritual. This symbol also appears at the end of each scene and act.

If you ever go to Indonesia to watch the *wajang kulit,* you must be prepared for a very long show. The performances of some of the legends may begin at nine o'clock in the evening, and they can last until six o'clock the next morning.

The *dalang* is regarded as a scholar. He must know many stories and legends, and he must be able to speak a number of Indonesian dialects in order to bring life to the many characters. He must also be able to insert local, humorous happenings into the narrative. He sometimes spends 3 hours on the prologue of the play. It may be midnight before the audience knows which particular tale it will be seeing that night.

The *dalang* taps signals to the orchestra to indicate which music they are to play to accompany the action he plans. He even sings the appropriate songs for the battle scenes or romantic stories he is portraying. The flickering shadow characters become larger and smaller as he moves the colorful figures closer to and farther from the screen. The noble or royal characters are never allowed to be lower than his own head.

Shadow plays telling of the Indonesian fight for independence from Dutch rule are just one part of the evolution of the *wajang kulit* stories and legends. Many of the plays, including some of the most popular, are based on Indonesian variations of Hindu and Muslim religious drama. The plots of these epic

The *dalang* works behind the shadow screen.

dramas become extremely complicated, so it is perhaps no wonder that the *dalang* spends almost 3 hours just introducing the main puppet-characters and letting the audience know who is good and who is evil. Moral and ethical advice is also offered for the education of the children.

During the second 3-hour period, which lasts until about three o'clock in the morning, clowns called *panakawan* are brought into action. They offer comic relief from the fierce battles and plot complications. In many respects the *panakawan* are similar to the comic characters in Shakespeare's plays, such as Bottom in *A Midsummer Night's Dream.*

The third period of the performance sees the plot come to a boil; the final fight in which good triumphs over evil; and perhaps a victory dance and a party. Finally, at dawn, the *dalang* places the leather mountain in the middle of the screen for the last time, and the shadow puppet show has ended.

A Tale Told at Midnight

Deep in the heart of the jungle there is a quiet little village of houses with thatched roofs. It is evening and a fire burns steadily in the open clearing. The people of the village are sitting around the warmth and glow of the fire. Above them the night broods, ready to settle down over the jungle. The people sit, quiet and expectant, waiting for the teller of tales to begin. He nods his old head once, then twice, and his voice is heard, soft and low like a murmuring stream. This is the tale he tells.

Once there was a great battle between all of the plants of the jungle. And this is how it all came about.

In those days all the plants had the power of speech, just as you and I have now. Sometimes it is good to know how to speak, and sometimes it is not good at all.

One sunny day the maize plant (we sometimes call it corn), the bean plant, and the jungle vine were having a friendly discussion. But like many friendly talks it began to change as it went along. It became a very heated discussion and not a friendly talk at all. Soon the three plants were no longer friends.

For the bean plant said, "All the world depends on me—that is, it would if there were no rice left growing."

"On you?" the maize exclaimed angrily.

"On me," the bean replied.

"Nonsense," snapped the maize. "Every single being on earth would starve to death if it weren't for me."

This statement made the jungle vine very furious indeed. "Oh, you two vain, proud fools," the vine said, "if there were no more rice, the people of the world would come to me in droves."

"Oh, you villain," shouted the bean plant.

"You conceited fool," shouted the maize plant.

"I am the most important plant," insisted the bean.

"I am," said the maize.

"Not true," said the bean, "I stand alone."

They were about to fling themselves on each other in their fury when Gadjah the elephant came lumbering by. He stood listening to the excited plants, horrified at their shouts and cries of anger and rage. When he had heard enough, he raised his trunk high and trumpeted for complete silence.

Then the elephant looked down upon the plants from his great height and spoke in a slow, solemn voice.

"I am Gadjah. I am the most powerful being in all the jungle. I shall judge you and you shall listen to me and abide by what I say. So listen, you foolish, quarreling plants!"

Gadjah trumpeted once more. Then he spoke again. "It is my considered decision that the maize plant is the most important of all plants—after rice, of course."

"Thank you, Gadjah. Thank you, O mighty and wise one," said the delighted maize plant, giving what passes with maize plants for a grin. And it was a triumphant grin, too, that he directed at the bean and the jungle vine.

"Now I must leave you," said Gadjah. "I have other matters to see to. Remember, no quarreling while I am away."

Gadjah trumpeted twice—once for emphasis and once because he liked the sound of his own trumpeting a good deal. Then Gadjah the great elephant went on his way. He was confident that he had settled the bitter argument that had raged among the plants.

But Gadjah had not accomplished the task. The instant he was out of sight the quarrel broke out again. In fact, a yam growing nearby, who had not been in the discussion before, heard the shouting and decided to express his point of view, too. He was quite sure that he was the most important of the plants and felt that the sooner the others knew it the better it would be.

"I am truly the most important of plants, you know," the yam said quite firmly.

"You?" the others chorused.

"I and I alone," replied the yam.

"Monster," said the maize.

"Fool," said the jungle vine.

"Villain," added the bean.

Things soon got quite out of hand again. The yam, who was small but aggressive, started hitting the bean plant. The maize plant kicked the vine. Before anyone, even the most nimble-tongued, could say "Gadjah," the plants were waging a truly bitter war among themselves.

The war of the plants proved to be an extremely fierce and savage conflict. It went on for days and days. Roots were pulled up, leaves torn off, blossoms thrown down—it was dreadful. All the animals of the jungle came to watch the fight. Even the trees, theoretically above it all, crowded close together, eager to see who would win the great battle.

And all this time Gadjah, the wise and powerful elephant, was many miles away, settling an argument in another part of the great forest. He had no idea what was going on among the plants.

There was much destruction and much injury. Even the innocent suffered. Just look about you at the trees the next time you are in the jungle. See how scarred some of their trunks are to this day from the arrows that the jungle vine shot from his mighty bow. Although the trees were not involved, the aim of the vine was not very good, and the trees got hit when he missed his true enemies— the yam, the maize plant, and the bean.

Finally, one of the birds of the forest grew so alarmed at what was happening that she flew off in search of Gadjah. When the bird found the elephant she told him what was going on among the plants. Gadjah trumpeted once in deep anger. Then he started off, crashing through the jungle as fast as his huge legs would carry him. The very earth trembled as he passed. When he reached the scene of the battle, the furious elephant pulled a big tree out of the ground—roots and all—swung it over his head and threw it into the midst of the struggling jungle plants. Then he trumpeted loudly.

"The war is over," he proclaimed. "It is officially over! From now until the end of time I, Gadjah, shall rule, so that there may be peace among the plants of the jungle. I once said that the maize plant was the most important plant—after rice, of course— of all of you. But now, maize, you have made me very angry. I hereby banish you from the jungle forever. From now on you will only grow in the open fields away from the jungle plants. And I warn the rest of you plants, too! I will not hesitate to banish any of you who start quarrels and fights."

And so it was and so it is to this very day. Have any of you ever seen maize (or corn) growing in a jungle? I'm sure you haven't. And have you seen or heard of plants fighting among themselves since the great Gadjah's time? I doubt that very much, too.

SINGAPORE

Singapore, one of the youngest countries in the world, is an island nation lying off the southern tip of the Malay Peninsula in Southeast Asia. Singapore covers only 224 square miles. Some of the great cities of the world, such as New York, London, and Tokyo, are larger in area than this tiny country. Singapore's neighbors are Malaysia to the north and east and Indonesia to the south and southeast. Singapore has long been known as one of the crossroads of world trade.

▶ **THE PEOPLE**

The more than 2,000,000 people of Singapore are mostly migrants or descendants of migrants who have come there from other parts of Asia. Malayans are now a minority. Most of the population are descendants of the Chinese. The rest are Indians, Pakistanis, and some Europeans.

However, the varied peoples of Singapore have held to their traditional customs even while living and working with others who follow different ways of life. As a result their customs have been changed and enriched. But now that they have become an independent country, the many different peoples of Singapore share a common goal—to become Singaporeans.

In many households all members of the family dress, eat, and find recreation much as their ancestors did. They observe the customs, festivals, and holidays of their parents. Yet something new has been added to the style of living, especially among the younger generations. Goals in life have changed and hopes for more satisfying jobs and careers have been aroused. Modern apartments and electrical gadgets are now commonplace. Television sets and transistor radios provide family entertainment. Public sporting events are now more popular, as are other educational and cultural events. One may choose to live as his ancestors did or enter fully into modern life.

Religion. The people of Singapore follow the faiths of their ancestors. Buddhism, Taoism, and Confucianism are the leading religions among the Chinese. The Malays and Pakistani

SINGAPORE

are generally followers of Islam. Most of the Indian people are Hindus, but small numbers of them are Buddhists, Sikhs, or Christians. Westerners in Singapore belong to various denominations of the Christian faith. A visitor to Singapore soon sees an astonishing number of temples, shrines, mosques, and churches. He will observe a broad architectural view of the world's major religions.

Language. A wide variety of languages is

FACTS AND FIGURES

REPUBLIC OF SINGAPORE is the official name of the country.

CAPITAL: Singapore.

LOCATION AND SIZE: Southeast Asia. **Latitude** — 1° 15′ N to 1° 28′ N. **Longitude** — 103° 40′ E to 104° E. **Area** — 224 sq. mi.

PHYSICAL FEATURES: Highest point — Mount Timah (581 ft.). **Lowest point** — sea level.

POPULATION: Over 2,000,000 (estimate).

LANGUAGES: Malay (official), Chinese, Tamil, English.

RELIGIONS: Buddhist, Taoist, Confucian, Hindu, Muslim, Christian.

GOVERNMENT: Republic. **Head of state** — president. **Head of government** — prime minister. **Legislature** — parliament. **International co-operation** — Commonwealth of Nations, United Nations.

NATIONAL ANTHEM: Majulah Singapura ("Forward Singapore").

ECONOMY: Agricultural products — fruits, vegetables, coconuts, tobacco, poultry. **Industries and products** — shipbuilding, petroleum refining, steel and metal products, electronics, chemicals, rubber products and processing, lumber processing. **Chief exports** — various manufactured goods, raw materials, fuels and lubricants. **Chief imports** — food, chemicals, machinery, manufactured goods. **Monetary unit** — Singapore dollar.

Footbridge over Raffles Quay in downtown Singapore.

Children attending class in primary school.

in constant use in Singapore and may be heard in every street, park, school, and outdoor market. Malay is the official language of the state. While it is not spoken by everyone, for many Singaporeans it is a second language. As a result many Malay words and expressions have been adopted by the people who speak other languages. Chinese is spoken by a large majority of the people. The tongues of India, notably Tamil (a language of southeastern India), have been spoken for many years. The most commonly used Western language has long been English. It is widely spoken by people in government and business, and is studied in the schools where knowledge of a second language is now required.

Education. The government and the people of Singapore have a high regard for schooling. Although education is not compulsory, every child is entitled to have at least 6 years of primary school education at public expense. Schooling is carried on in the principal language of the student, and at an early age students begin to study other languages commonly spoken in Singapore. Approximately a quarter of the primary school graduates go on to a 4-year secondary school program. Here the students may take academic, technical, vocational, or commercial subjects.

Most secondary school students go to work after graduation, but a small number continue their education at a university. The best-known of these institutions are the University of Singapore and Nanyang University (primarily attended by Chinese-speaking students).

▶ **THE LAND**

Singapore, located between the South China Sea and the Indian Ocean, is made up of a main island and a few offshore islets. The narrow Strait of Johore separates the island from the mainland of Malaysia. They are connected by a causeway over which passes a road and a single railroad track. Along the causeway runs a large waterpipe that supplies much of the freshwater needs of the islands.

The island itself is rather flat, broken only by a few rolling hills. Much of the land area is taken up by swamps and jungles.

▶ **ECONOMY**

Singapore owes its prosperity to its strategic location for trade and its natural deep-water harbor. The constant flow of raw materials, industrial machinery, and manufactured products creates work for many thousands of people. While trade is the backbone of the economy, the government in recent years has sought to develop local manufacturing. The Jurong Industrial Estate is a complex of more than 250 factories in which a wide variety of goods are now manufactured.

Only a small part of the island of Singapore is used for farming. The main products are rubber, coconuts, fruits, and vegetables, but most of Singapore's food must be

Singapore's modern skyline contrasts with the sampans that crowd the harbor.

imported. During the past few years progress has been made in expanding the shipbuilding and fishery industries.

▶ CITIES

The state of Singapore is dominated by the capital city, also called Singapore. Well over half the state's population lives in the city and suburban communities. The city of Singapore is the center of the government, as well as the center of commerce and industry. The broad clean boulevards of the city provide a striking contrast to the maze of small winding streets along which are crowded rows of homes and shops. In the downtown area swarms of people may be seen from early morning to evening. All kinds of vehicles—cars, motorcycles, bicycles, and animal-drawn carts—crowd the streets leading to the harbor. The port and harbor area is a beehive of activity, as ships from all over the world load and unload their cargoes.

▶ GOVERNMENT

Singapore has been an independent republic since September 16, 1963. A member of the British Commonwealth of Nations, the republic has a president as its head of state and is directed by a prime minister. He is assisted in his duties by a cabinet of appointed ministers. The island's principal legislative body is a parliament whose more than fifty members are elected by the people. Lee Kuan Yew, a dynamic leader of Chinese ancestry, has been prime minister since 1959. Under his direction a wide range of public welfare programs have been started.

▶ HISTORY

In 1819 Sir Stamford Raffles, an agent for a British trading company, took the lead in establishing British rule over Singapore. Gradually the small trading post became important to the British Empire. Singapore became a colony in 1867, and with the opening of the Suez Canal in 1869, the harbor became the shipping crossroads of Southeast Asia. The British developed Singapore into a commercial center. They also constructed a powerful naval fortification that served as a main base of strength of the Empire in Asia and the Pacific.

In 1959 Singapore ceased being a British colony and became a semi-independent country. Granted complete independence in 1963, Singapore joined other Malaysian states to organize the Federation of Malaysia. Conflicts between the different peoples created unrest and mistrust, so after two years Singapore withdrew from the Federation.

Now fully independent, the Republic of Singapore continues to prosper and win worldwide praise for its development as a politically and economically stable republic.

HYMAN KUBLIN
City University of New York

The executive branch speaks: President Nixon makes a statement on Watergate.

THE U.S. POLITICAL SYSTEM AND WATERGATE

The concept of the separation of powers was made the basic principle of the American system of government by the men who framed the United States Constitution in 1787. According to this idea, the three main branches of government—the executive, the legislative, and the judicial—operate separately and independently of one another. However, in order to prevent any one branch of government from becoming too powerful, a system of "checks and balances" was included in the Constitution.

Each of the branches of government has the means to "check" abuses of power by one or both of the other branches. For example, the Congress can check presidential power by refusing to confirm presidential appointments or by not appropriating funds for an agency of the executive branch of government—such as the Department of Defense. The president can check the legislative branch by vetoing a bill passed by Congress. The Supreme Court can check both by declaring unconstitutional a law passed by Congress and approved by the president. In this way all three branches of government are balanced off, one against the other. The checks and balances system is also designed to prevent any branch of government from using its power to undermine the rights of an individual.

These concepts have been tested many times in the history of the United States. One of the greatest tests of the system of separation of powers is still going on. The test has been provided by the so-called Watergate affair, stemming from the break-in of Democratic Party headquarters located in the Watergate complex in Washington, D.C. This scandal has forced the American people to question the most fundamental workings of the constitutional system.

The Watergate break-in, which developed into a three-way struggle involving the courts, Congress, and the President, took place on June 17, 1972. But the full force of the scandal did not sweep over the United States until nearly a year later.

The Senate ordered an investigation into the matter in February, 1973. Until that time, most of the probing had been carried on by John Sirica, the Chief Judge of the U.S. District Court for the District of Columbia; by a federal grand jury; and by the press. The press contributed most dramatically through the investigative work into the affair done by two *Washington Post* reporters.

The legislative branch acts: The Senate Watergate committee is in session.

▶ THE SYSTEM STARTS TO MOVE

In the United States, the unofficial but active role of the press in constitutional matters is as unique as the system of separation of powers itself. The press is not officially part of the constitutional system of the United States. However, it does play a vital role in the system. The First Amendment to the Constitution, guaranteeing freedom of the press, indicates this clearly. It was the digging for facts by the *Post* reporters, combined with Judge Sirica's tough questioning of the defendants in the Watergate burglary, that kept the case alive and eventually led to a demand for congressional action.

On June 22, 1972, President Richard Nixon made his first public comment on Watergate. He said: "This kind of activity . . . has no place whatever in our electoral process or in our governmental process. And as Mr. Ziegler [Nixon's press secretary] has stated, the White House has had no involvement whatever in this particular incident."

The Watergate trial began in January, 1973. Judge Sirica indicated that he did not believe the Watergate defendants had acted on their own in the break-in. He asked the defendants at one point whether they had not been under great pressure to plead guilty. The trial resulted in the conviction of all seven defendants.

Subsequently, defendant James McCord admitted in a letter to Judge Sirica that he and other defendants had been under "political pressure" to stay silent, and that

perjury had been committed during the Watergate trial.

A number of serious charges were subsequently laid at the door of the White House. They included a charge of an elaborate cover-up attempt by top White House officials; a charge of the payment of "hush money" to silence the Watergate Seven; and charges that the Nixon administration had promised government favors to big campaign contributors.

On May 18, 1973, the executive branch of government took a step of its own. Attorney General designate Elliot Richardson appointed Archibald Cox, a distinguished member of the Harvard Law School faculty, as special prosecutor in the Watergate case.

▶ CONGRESS ACTS

Under the United States Constitution, both the Senate and the House of Representatives have full power to authorize investigations by committees, looking toward possible action within the scope of the powers of Congress. These committees have the right to examine witnesses and to take testimony.

Congress entered the Watergate picture on January 3, 1973. At that time, Mike Mansfield, the Senate majority leader, told a caucus of Democratic senators: "The so-called Watergate affair appears to have been nothing less than a callous attempt to subvert the political process of the nation in blatant disregard of the law." Mansfield said he believed the Watergate break-in and the charges that false letters had been circulated against some of the Democratic candidates in the 1972 Florida presidential primary "warrant attention."

In February the Democrats named Senator Sam Ervin of North Carolina to be chairman of a committee to examine 1972 presidential campaign practices. The committee was told to investigate particularly the planning and circumstances of the Watergate break-in. It was also asked to determine whether there was any evidence of a subsequent cover-up. The committee was also empowered to look into any "dirty tricks" that might have been played during the 1972 presidential campaign. The televised hearings began on May 17, 1973. Now all three branches of government were involved in investigating the Watergate affair.

▶ EXECUTIVE PRIVILEGE

The power of the president of the United States to protect the men who work for him from questioning by people from other branches of government has played an important part in the Watergate affair. It is all bound up with such terms as "executive privilege" and "confidentiality." These terms mean that what a president and his aides write or say to one another is privileged matter. It is not available for examination by Congress, the judiciary, or the general public.

This question of executive privilege has important effects in regard to Watergate and to a number of other subjects as well. On May 22, 1973, President Nixon issued a long defense of his administration. The President said that in June, 1971, when *The New York Times* printed the stolen Pentagon Papers, he had "approved the creation of a special investigations unit within the White House . . . which later became known as 'the plumbers' . . . to stop security leaks."

President Nixon added that some of those individuals had engaged in specific activities in the course of his re-election campaign that "I would have disapproved had they been brought to my attention."

In the same statement, Mr. Nixon denied that he had sought to cover up possible connections between the seven men convicted in the original Watergate case and the White House. He also said: "Executive privilege will not be invoked as to any testimony concerning possible criminal conduct or discussions of possible criminal conduct in the matters presently under investigation, including the Watergate affair and the alleged cover-up."

But later a struggle developed over White House tape recordings of conversations between President Nixon and his aides that may have involved aspects of Watergate or of the misuse of campaign funds. Mr. Nixon invoked executive privilege. In August the President

The judicial branch is heard: Judge Sirica ponders the evidence.

told Judge Sirica that to make the tapes and related documents available to the court would violate the separation-of-powers doctrine and the principle of presidential confidentiality. On August 15, 1973, President Nixon made another Watergate report to the American people. He again declared that he had had no prior knowledge of the Watergate break-in and the cover-up that followed.

In the same speech, the President pointed out that the courts had long upheld the privilege of confidentiality of lawyer and client, husband and wife, priest and penitent. Mr. Nixon asserted: "It is more important that the confidentiality of conversations between a President and his advisers be protected."

▶ THE COURTS

The battle over the tapes continued in the courts. On October 12, 1973, the United States Circuit Court of Appeals for the District of Columbia made what it called an "unavoidable" and "extraordinary" ruling in regard to the disputed White House tapes. The court held, five to two, that President Nixon must turn over to the federal District Court the tape recordings possibly bearing on Watergate crimes.

The Court of Appeals put a definite curb on how far a president could go in invoking executive privilege. The ruling declared: "Though the President is elected by nationwide ballot, and is often said to represent all the people, he does not embody the nation's sovereignty. He is not above the law's commands."

On October 23 President Nixon responded to the Court of Appeals ruling and agreed to surrender the tapes to federal District Judge John Sirica. The President acted after a dramatic series of events the preceding weekend. First he had fired Archibald Cox, the special prosecutor in the Watergate case, for allegedly disobeying a presidential directive to limit the scope of his investigation. The President also had fired Assistant Attorney General William Ruckelshaus for refusing to carry out the Cox dismissal. Attorney General Elliot Richardson had resigned at the same time in protest over the Cox firing.

By surrendering the White House tapes, President Nixon avoided a confrontation between the presidency and the United States Supreme Court on the issues of executive privilege and confidentiality. However, the Justice Department purge of Cox, Richardson, and Ruckelshaus raised serious talk of impeaching President Nixon.

▶ IMPEACHMENT

The Constitution provides that "the President, Vice President and all civil Officers of the United States, shall be removed from Office on Impeachment for, and Conviction of, Treason, Bribery, or other high Crimes and Misdemeanors." An impeachment differs from an indictment (a formal statement charging someone with having committed a crime) because it is not a criminal proceeding. Impeachment and conviction leads to dismissal from office, not imprisonment.

The power of impeachment is conferred exclusively on the House of Representatives. The Senate has the sole power to try an official who has been impeached. An impeachable offense is any misbehavior that shows an official's disqualification—whether moral, intellectual, or physical—for holding and exercising an office. The power to impeach is a great one, and is potentially dangerous.

The only greater danger than having the power to impeach is not to have that power. Benjamin Franklin pointed out during the debate on the Constitution that if there were no provision for impeachment the only recourse would be assassination. In that case, he noted, a president would be "not only deprived of his life but of the opportunity of vindicating his character."

Whether or not President Nixon will be impeached will be determined by future developments. In the meantime, the painful questions raised by Watergate have troubled Americans of all walks of life. Most Americans have a deep respect for the institution of the presidency and resent having the integrity of its occupant called into question. The Watergate scandal has brought the presidency under a cloud. But an independent judiciary, the Congress, and a free press—together with executive agencies—are working to lift that cloud.

STEPHEN C. FLANDERS
WCBS News

Gerald R. Ford proudly displays the documents that proclaim him vice-president of the United States.

A NEW U.S. VICE-PRESIDENT

The resignation of Spiro T. Agnew as vice-president of the United States on October 10, 1973, set in motion constitutional machinery that had never been used before. The Agnew resignation meant that the provisions of the Twenty-fifth Amendment to the United States Constitution would govern the selection of a new vice-president.

Section 2 of the Twenty-fifth Amendment says: "Whenever there is a vacancy in the office of the Vice-President, the President shall nominate a Vice-President who shall take office upon confirmation by a majority vote of both houses of Congress." The Twenty-fifth Amendment was proposed in 1965 and ratified by the states in 1967.

Except for the provisions of Section 2, the Twenty-fifth Amendment was really an effort to resolve the problem of what to do when a president is disabled. The question of presidential disablement has arisen a number of times in the 20th century. Two presidents—Woodrow Wilson and Dwight D. Eisenhower—lay gravely ill while in office. A mortal illness shadowed the final months of President Franklin D. Roosevelt. There was a brief

period of confusion after President John F. Kennedy was fatally shot by an assassin.

It was the murder of President Kennedy that brought demands for changes in the presidential succession. These demands—in Congress and from national leaders—resulted in drafting and ratification of the Twenty-fifth Amendment.

President Nixon moved quickly to fill the number two post in his administration. Two days after Agnew resigned, President Nixon named the House minority leader, 60-year-old Gerald R. Ford, a Republican from Michigan, as vice-president designate. On November 27, Ford was confirmed by the Senate, and on December 6 by the House of Representatives. Thus Ford became the 40th vice-president of the United States.

The smoothness with which the new amendment passed its first test was somewhat deceptive. Congress had acted at a time when emotions about the Watergate scandal were running high. Mr. Nixon's credibility in the eyes of many members of Congress and other American citizens was at a low point. The Democratic members of Congress were especially wary of the President. Since the Democrats were the majority party in Congress, Democratic votes were needed to approve Mr. Nixon's vice-presidential choice. Congress as a body was also aware that it was entrusted with the task of seeing that the will of the people, as reflected in the overwhelming victory of the Republicans in the 1972 presidential election, was not set aside. In other words, Congress knew that there could be no hint of extreme political or party partisanship in carrying through the provisions of the Twenty-fifth Amendment.

Senator Edward Kennedy of Massachusetts touched on this problem of political loyalty when he urged his fellow Democrats to permit President Nixon to name the strongest man of his own choice as the new vice-president. Kennedy also said that whether or not the person named by Mr. Nixon would be a strong presidential contender in the 1976 election was not and could not be the issue— the key issue was that the man next in line for the presidency be the best man possible.

Other Democrats did not necessarily agree with Senator Kennedy. There were indications that the choice of a prominent Republican might well cause a floor fight in Congress.

President Nixon indicated, after he had chosen Gerald Ford, that he had been considering five men for the vice-presidency. They were Governor Ronald Reagan of California; John Connally, former secretary of the treasury; Governor Nelson Rockefeller of New York; United States Attorney General Elliot Richardson; and Congressman Ford. When he named Ford, Mr. Nixon said he had chosen a man "who can work with members of both parties in the Congress. . . ."

When the Twenty-fifth Amendment was drafted, under the leadership of Emanuel Celler, of New York, in the House and Birch Bayh, of Indiana, in the Senate, the real concern was to find a way to fill a vice-presidential vacancy caused by death or by a serious illness. The resignation of a vice-president under the threat of criminal charges being brought against him, as happened in the case of Vice-President Agnew, had not been anticipated. The possibility of a struggle between the two parties in Congress had not been anticipated.

Thus, Section 2 of the Twenty-fifth Amendment avoided setting any time limit within which a president must name a new vice-president. Nor was a time limit placed on how long Congress could take to confirm the presidential choice. When questioned on the intent of the amendment after the Agnew resignation, Celler said: "We wanted to give the President freedom of choice, no strings attached, beyond the conditions that his choice would be a man of honor, integrity, and intelligence. We never expected anyone to balk at the possible choice of a new Vice-President on the grounds that he might thereby run for President himself at the end of the unexpired term."

After weeks of interrogation of Ford by its rules committee, the Senate finally confirmed him. Senator Howard Cannon, the chairman of the committee, told his committee colleagues that Ford had undergone an investigation more exhaustive than that of any other vice-presidential nominee in history. Cannon bluntly stated that his committee had been "gravely cognizant that its investigation of Congressman Ford might offer greater significance than its stated purpose"—in other words, Ford might become President Nixon's successor if the President for any reason should fail to complete his term.

During the nearly two months of investigation of Ford's life and career, the United States was without a vice-president. Under the rules of succession in effect during this period of investigation, the Speaker of the House of Representatives, Carl Albert of Oklahoma, was next in line for the presidency. After him came the president pro tempore of the Senate, James O. Eastland of Mississippi. The order of succession after that is determined by cabinet rank.

The symbolism of the office of Vice-President of the United States was not lost on Gerald Ford. Vice-President Ford told Congress, after his confirmation in December, that "In exactly eight weeks we have demonstrated to the world that our great Republic stands solid, stands strong upon the bedrock of the Constitution."

STEPHEN C. FLANDERS
News Correspondent
WCBS News

WORLD OF SCIENCE

A Skylab III crewman works outside the space station.

"Adventuring in the world of wildflowers . . ."

WILDFLOWERS

Let me be your guide along a woodland path—perhaps on a cool spring morning when the trees are full of birds returning from the south and the vegetation is sparkling with heavy dew. Along a noisy brook you might dig a pepperroot and taste its spiciness. Not far away a skunk cabbage might lure you to test its pungent smell, and show you the secret of its purple-mottled hood. You might well find the red trillium, with its leaves and flower parts in threes. The red trillium is sometimes called birthroot, since the Indians of North America believed that it was useful as a medicine for women in childbirth. It has a strange smell. Because of this smell, some people call it the "wet dog" trillium.

Of course, I can't literally lead you along nature's pathways, but I can introduce you to a wonderful hobby. Adventuring in the world of wildflowers can be a fascinating pastime, making your vacations more meaningful and your outdoor rambles and hikes truly exciting expeditions into a new and beautiful natural world.

▶ VOYAGE OF DISCOVERY

Jumpseed, green dragon, silver and gold, squirrel corn, goldclub, feather-fleece, fireweed, blue-eyed Mary, fat hen, and turkey beard—these are some of the strange and beautiful folk names given to certain wildflowers. No one will ever know exactly where these names came from. But they are often appropriate and descriptive names, and learning them is one of the most interesting parts of learning about wildflowers.

Learning the precise name of a wildflower can be difficult, since there are about 4,000 different flowering plants in North America. You must learn to look carefully at the plants you discover. You should examine the structure of the flower, the way the flowers and leaves are arranged, and the sort of place where you find the plant growing. For really serious and accurate identification, you will want to learn the scientific names of wildflowers. Although the common or folk names are fascinating, they are also sometimes misleading and vary greatly from one place to another. As an example, the great mullein in different places is called velvet dock, Aaron's rod, Adam's flannel, blanket leaf, bullock's lungwort, candlewick, feltwort, hare's-beard, and stamp-pad leaf. However, the plant's real, scientific name, *Verbascum thapsus,* sets it apart from all other plants. If you had a pen pal in France who was interested in wildflowers and you wanted to tell him that the leaves and roots of the great mullein are considered by some people to be useful in producing sleep and relieving pain, you would use the scientific name for the plant. From his guide to the wildflowers of France he would know that what he calls *molène bouillon-blanc* or *tabac du diable* ("the devil's tobacco") is the same plant. Botanists the world over use scientific names in their studies so that there will be no confusion about what organisms they are referring to.

In order to learn to identify wildflowers, you should become familiar with the parts of a flower, the characteristics and arrangement of the leaves, and the different ways the flowers are displayed on a stem. All the common guides to wildflowers have diagrams that will help you learn the necessary botanical terms. Obtain a flower from somewhere, even from a local florist, so that your study of flower parts will be more interesting. It is best to use a flower that has only a few petals, because in many of the cultivated flowers some of the flower parts have disappeared or have been replaced by many petals.

In order to learn about the different parts of flowers you should have a few pieces of simple equipment. This is what you'll need: a pocket magnifying glass of about 10 power; a penknife with a small blade, for opening flowers; a dissecting needle (you can make one by holding a sewing needle with a pair of pliers and pushing it into the head of a small dowel); a small notebook to record your observations and identifications; and a guide to the wildflowers found in your area.

A word of caution! When you go out to gather wildflowers for identification or transplanting be sure, before you gather one, that there are several plants of the same kind nearby. Some wildflowers are becoming uncommon in certain areas and if they are picked or uprooted there will be no seeds formed to increase the number of plants. When you do come upon a plant all by itself or in a small group and suspect that it might be uncommon, do not transplant it right away. First make careful notes, with simple drawings, of the flower parts and their color, the arrangement of the leaves, and the habitat of the plant and use this information later to make a positive identification.

Once you have discovered the fascinating world of wildflowers you will want to pursue your interest in every season. Here is a list of wildflower projects arranged by season.

▶ WINTER

(1) Visit the scientific collections of flowering plants at your state university. Arrange for someone to meet you and give you a tour of the facilities. Botanists are usually pleased to show you how plants are preserved for study.

(2) Visit a greenhouse in your area and study the different types of flowers and leaves on the plants grown there. Make sketches. You will soon become familiar with the characteristics of each plant family you observe, and thus increase your ability to identify wildflowers.

(3) Build a plant press so you can make a dried-plant collection. You will need two pressing boards, 12 by 18 inches, made either of a lattice of slats within a frame or of solid plywood. To hold your specimens and to serve as blotters prepare many 16-by-23-inch pieces of newspaper. Also useful are pieces of cardboard the same size as your pressing boards. These pieces of cardboard will allow air to circulate through the press and carry away the moisture. For pressure, two straps or pieces of clothesline should be wrapped around the press and tightened.

(4) Many wildflowers are easy to grow. Begin plans for a wildflower garden. You could start by experimenting with a method of making several plants from one: cuttings. Snip three or four leafy shoots, about 3 inches long, from a large house plant such as a coleus, a geranium, or a philodendron. Have some moist sand ready in a durable container. Remove a few of the lower leaves from each shoot and insert the cut end to a depth of about 2 inches into the sand. Firm the sand around the cuttings. Cover them with a plastic bag and keep in bright light but not in full sun. Water them frequently enough to keep the sand moist. After 2 weeks carefully

Yellow Lady's-Slipper

Threadleaf Sundew

Wood Lily

Round-lobed Hepatica

Trumpets

52

Cardinal Flower

Fragrant Water Lily

Queen's-Slipper

Bloodroot

Blue Jasmine

53

lift each cutting from below with an old table fork to see if roots have developed. Transplant each rooted cutting into an individual pot of garden soil.

(5) Winter is the best time for browsing through wildflower guides at home or at the library. Note some of the differences between the flowers, especially the characteristics that set each family of plants apart from every other. This is also a good time to order pamphlets and other literature that would be useful in your new interest.

▶ SPRING

(1) Discovering the names of the different wildflowers you find on your rambles can be fun. Most popular guides to wildflowers are arranged by color. Carefully compare the pictures of flowers with the flower you wish to name. There are more technical guides (floras) available for identifying the plants in your area, but to use them you must develop your scientific vocabulary and increase your understanding of plant anatomy (the positions, names, and functions of different plant parts). Contact the botany department of your state university or ask your librarian about these guides.

(2) Study a single type of wildflower over a full season, and prepare a life-history report that could be used in your science classes in school or for a science fair. You should note where the plant grows, the type of soil, how the leaves and flowers unfold, how the flowers are pollinated, how the seeds are carried from the parent plant. Record everything that might be useful in the final write-up of your observations.

(3) Contact a local garden club or your librarian to find out if there are other people in your area interested in wildflowers. They can tell you of areas where interesting wildflowers can be found.

(4) Start filling your plant press with whole specimens of the wildflowers you collect on your hikes. Shake or wash the soil from the roots and place the plant between folded pieces of newspaper. Give each plant a number, and record the number in your notebook and on a newspaper folder for the specimen. Arrange each plant in your press so that there are several pieces of newspaper on each side.

Place the pieces of cardboard over the newspaper blotters. In your notebook, record the location of the plant and anything else about the fresh plant that might help you to identify it later. Be sure to get permission before you dig up any plants, and beware of poison ivy and poison sumac. Contact the Wildflower Preservation Society (3740 Oliver Street N.W., Washington, D.C. 20015) for names of protected plants in your state.

(5) Choose a spot for your wildflower garden and prepare the soil. Work to duplicate as much as possible the habitat of the plants you wish to grow. For instance be sure to give meadow and pasture plants full sun and dry or moist conditions. Woodland plants need complete or partial shade and considerable moisture. The only piece of equipment you have to have for planting your wildflower garden is a trowel or a small spade.

(6) Prepare a wildflower calendar to show when each flower blooms in your area. Use your notebook to record what you observe on your field trips and transfer the information to your calendar when you return home. Also record the general weather conditions at the time of your field trips. Compare information over several seasons to see how weather influences time of blooming.

(7) Collect and prepare an early spring salad using leaves and flowers of woodland violets; young flower buds and leaves of oxeye daisy; and young leaves of purslane, sheep sorrel, peppergrass, pennycress, shepherd's purse, mustard, winter cress, clover, and plantain. All are common, "weedy" wildflowers, and used alone or in combination with garden lettuce they make a wholesome and interesting tossed salad. Many wildflower plants are useful as salad ingredients, cooked as potherbs, as beverage plants, and as seasonings in many dishes.

▶ SUMMER

(1) Try to name at least one new wildflower each day of summer. Your days on vacation, on camping trips, visiting friends and relatives, at summer camps, or at home will seem to fly when you take your wildflower hobby with you. Be sure to carry along your wildflower guide, hand lens, notebook, and plant press. Collecting whole plants to add to your wild-

flower garden is possible only if you will be returning home within a few days. Carefully wrap each plant in several thicknesses of damp newspaper and pack it closely in wooden boxes or plastic-lined cardboard ones. Keep the plants moist and plant them in your garden as soon as you can.

(2) If your wildflower garden does well—and wild plants are sometimes as difficult to raise as wild animals—there are ways to increase the number of plants in your garden. If you are able to produce more plants from the ones you have, you can give them to friends, or perhaps set them out in the wild to replace the ones you transplanted to begin with. Plants that grow in compact clumps can be divided into several plants with a sharp knife or spade. Making cuttings of the young, leafy shoots of wildflowers is an excellent method of increasing the number of plants.

(3) Wildflower bouquets will add a colorful decoration to your room, the dining table, or any spot needing a bright splash of color. Give bouquets of wildflowers to friends and relatives. Most of the wildflowers of the open fields and meadows are numerous enough not to be endangered by your collections. Always ask permission before picking flowers on someone else's land, and never pick flowers near public pathways or hiking trails. Leave them for others to enjoy!

(4) During the hot days of summer gather the leaves of wild mints such as mountain mint, American pennyroyal, bee balm, and field mint. Steep the leaves in hot water for about 10 minutes in a covered teapot or similar container. Pour the brew into a pitcher filled with ice cubes. A little honey can be added to make a delightfully cool drink.

▶ AUTUMN

(1) As you learn the names of wildflowers you will want to know more about them. Such wildflower lore includes use of different parts of wildflower plants for herbal remedies or medicines. Several of the plants used by ancient and modern herbalists (those who grow or collect herbs, especially medicinal ones, or specialize in their use) have been found by scientists to contain useful medicines. In place of aspirin for pain relief, try a cupful of strong peppermint tea. If you should suffer from stomach cramps or heartburn, try a weak tea of calamus (sweet flag). This is made from a piece of the root about 1 inch long boiled for a few minutes in 1 pint of water and sweetened with honey. There are many recently published books on the healing power of herbs.

(2) Many plants are useful in making dyes. You might enjoy experimenting with a small article of unbleached, natural wool. You can achieve such vivid colors as pokeberry red, apple-bark yellow, elderberry blue, choke-cherry purple, and sassafras brown.

(3) The seeds of plants you want to increase should be collected and scattered where you want them to grow. Crushed limestone should be spread among plants that thrive best in soil that is not too acid, such as wild ginger, liverwort, columbine, Dutchman's-breeches and grass-of-Parnassus. Steamed bone meal and well-rotted cow manure are useful fertilizers for the wildflower garden. The best way to use them is to scratch them into the surface of the soil around your plants.

(4) Photographing or drawing and painting wildflowers is another way of collecting them. Closeup photographic slides of wildflowers that completely fill the screen when projected are beautifully striking. This is a special type of photography and requires considerable skill. Your collection of wildflower slides could provide an entertaining program for a meeting of your Scout troop or some other organization. If you have the interest and talent you should sketch and paint the wildflowers you like best. A collection of wildflower portraits is a memorable gift.

Your interest in the study of wildflowers may direct your path toward a career in botany, ecology, forestry, conservation, nature recreation, horticulture, or agriculture. A lifetime career often begins with an interest developed in early years. Wildflowers are like bright-colored road signs that read, "Here is Sweet Nectar and Nutritious Pollen for Bees, Beetles, and Butterflies, for Moths, Wasps, and Hummingbirds." But for you the sign should read, "Here is Color to Please the Eyes and an Enjoyable Hobby to Last a Lifetime."

HAROLD R. HINDS
Director, Earthskills Forum

WATER DESALTING

Our lives depend on a constant supply of fresh water, yet less than 1 percent of the water on the earth is fit for our use. All the rest is salt water.

Until the 1950's people in most parts of the world were able to get enough fresh water for their needs. There is as much fresh water today as there was then. But the world's population has been increasing very rapidly. More fresh water is needed for the greater number of people, and for their crops, domestic animals, and industries. It takes 37 gallons of fresh water to produce and process the materials that go into one slice of bread. More than 2,000 gallons of fresh water are needed in making the synthetic rubber used in one automobile tire. About 365,000,000,000 (billion) gallons of water are used in the United States every day, and the demand for water is rising at the rate of 25,000 gallons per *minute*. The enormously increased demand has left some places seriously short of fresh water.

Luckily fresh water can be made from salt water. There are more than 300 **desalination** (desalting) plants in the United States, and more than 400 in the rest of the world. Some of these plants desalt water from the sea, and others work with brackish water. This is salt water that is less salty than seawater. Brackish water is found in salt marshes, in some rivers, and underground in many areas.

Actually the "ordinary" fresh water we use has been desalted by nature. The heat of the sun warms the water on the surface of the oceans. Some of the water changes into water vapor, in the process called **evaporation.** The vapor rises, leaving behind the salt and other substances dissolved in the water. High in the air some of the vapor cools and turns back into fine droplets of water, in the process called **condensation.** The droplets form clouds and may later fall as rain or snow, far from the ocean. In this way streams and lakes receive fresh water.

Nearly 98 percent of artificially desalted water is produced by **distillation.** To distill a liquid such as salt water, it is heated to drive off some of the water as water vapor. The vapor is trapped and cooled. The cooled vapor condenses, turning to liquid again. The device in which the distillation is carried out is called a **still.**

One of the simplest ways to desalt water is in a **solar still.** Like natural desalting, this method depends on the heat of the sun. The top of the still has a glass roof, like a greenhouse. The sun shines through the glass onto a shallow pool of salt water. The water heats up and some of it evaporates, leaving the salt behind. The rising vapor condenses on the underside of the glass, forming drops of fresh water that run down into collecting channels.

Solar stills are built easily and cheaply. They also have the advantage of using free sunlight instead of expensive fuel for heating the salt water. But solar stills take up a great deal of space on the ground and are of little use when it is cloudy.

In most distillation plants the salt water is heated to boiling in a great metal tank. The steam that is produced passes into a second tank, where it cools, condensing into fresh water. The fresh water is pumped to a storage tank. The salt water left behind is called **brine.** It is pumped into another heating tank, producing more steam. In some plants the brine may be passed through as many as 12 tanks. In each one more water is separated from the salt.

Several types of distillation plants are used. Each type has some special advantage, but all of them share the disadvantage of needing coal, oil, nuclear material, or some other expensive fuel to keep the distillation process going. Another disadvantage in distillation comes from the strange behavior of calcium, which is one of the many substances dissolved in seawater. Most substances dissolve more easily in hot water than in cold.

DESALT IT YOURSELF

You can do an easy experiment to desalt water by freezing it. Mix a teaspoon of salt into a glassful of water. Taste a drop of the salty mixture. Pour into a bowl and place in the freezer. Wait until a cake of ice about ½ inch thick is at the top. Remove the ice cake and rinse it in running cold water. Taste the ice. If you rinsed the cake properly there should be no salt taste. Compare with the taste of the unfrozen water in the bowl.

SOLAR STILL

SUNLIGHT · GLASS ROOF · VAPOR · SALT WATER · FRESH WATER COLLECTING TROUGH

Calcium does the reverse. When seawater is heated in the distillation process, the calcium dissolved in the water comes out of solution. It forms **scale,** a solid material that clings to the pipes, clogging them and interfering with the heating up of the salt water.

A few desalting systems use freezing, rather than heat. When salt water freezes, the ice that forms does not contain any salt. The salt is left behind in the unfrozen water. If the ice is rinsed off and allowed to melt, it becomes fresh water. The freezing process has some advantages over distillation. Less energy is needed. Also, because the temperature of the seawater remains low, the calcium in the water does not form much scale in the pipes.

A third type of desalting system is called **electrodialysis.** It is used mainly for brackish water. An electric current provides the needed energy. Salt is made up of two elements—sodium and chlorine. The atoms of these elements are electrically charged particles called ions. The ions can move about freely in water. When an electric current passes through the salty water the sodium ions are pulled in one direction and the chlorine ions in the other.

Electrodialysis is carried out in a chamber whose walls are made of thin films called membranes. The electric current draws off the ions of sodium through the membrane on one side of the chamber. The chlorine ions are drawn off through the membrane on the opposite side, leaving the water in the chamber free of salt. In another membrane-using process, called **reverse osmosis,** salt water under pressure is freed of its salt.

Several other kinds of electrical and chemical desalting systems have been tried on a small scale, mainly by the Office of Saline Water (O.S.W.). This government agency is a part of the U.S. Department of the Interior. It conducts research in desalting methods and has built and operated several large desalting plants of various kinds.

The great problem in desalting is not whether it works, but how much it costs. Building the plants is costly, and so are the fuels or electricity that they use. But progress is being made. In 1952, when the O.S.W. was set up, it cost $7 or more to produce 1,000 gallons of fresh water from seawater. Twenty years later the cost was down to about $1. This is a great improvement, but it is still over three times as high as the cost of "ordinary" fresh water in most places.

One solution to the problem of fresh water may be plants with two purposes—making fresh water at the same time that they generate electricity. Power plants use oil, coal, or nuclear fuel to make the steam that runs the generators. As this steam finishes its work, there is still some heat left in it. In the dual-purpose plant this heat would be used for the distillation process. Perhaps such plants will provide man with ever-increasing amounts of fresh water at low cost.

J. W. O'MEARA
Director, Office of Saline Water
U.S. Department of the Interior

The moon in the third quarter, when it is half visible from earth.

THE HOME ASTRONOMER

Astronomers study the skies with giant telescopes on the tops of high mountains, and with huge, sprawling radio telescopes in the middle of the desert. Sometimes they send rockets high above the earth's atmosphere to gain information about space and the billions and trillions of objects in it. Often the information they gather is processed by complicated electronic equipment and then analyzed by a computer.

Most of us can't afford the instruments used by astronomers. But there is a great deal we can learn about the heavens by just going out in our backyards or onto our rooftops at night and looking up. And there are many more things we can see with the aid of a simple, inexpensive hand telescope or a pair of binoculars. The trick is in knowing what to look for. Let's see what's there on an average clear night.

▶ THE MOON

The most obvious and brightest object in the night sky is usually the moon. The moon is our nearest celestial neighbor and is the easiest to study because it is so close. As we see it from the earth, the moon goes through a regular series of changes every month, approximately. After the new moon, when we can't see it at all, we first see it as a thin crescent near the western horizon just after the sun has set. Each night it appears higher in the sky. About a week later, we see half the moon's surface; this is called the first quarter. In another week the moon is full and is nearly overhead about midnight. As the moon continues to rise later in the eastern sky each night, it grows smaller, passing through the third quarter. At the third quarter, half of the moon is again visible. The moon disappears again from the view of people on earth about 4 weeks after the preceding new moon. These changes, or phases, which mark the passage of each lunar month, are caused by the moon's orbit around the earth. Because the moon's orbit is not a perfect circle and because it is not in the same plane with the earth's equator, the time between moonrise one night and moonrise the next night is not always the same. For example, at the time of the harvest moon—the full moon nearest the change of season from summer to fall, about September 23—the full moon rises at nearly the same time for several nights in a row. In fact it is called the harvest moon because it provides farmers with light for working longer in the fields before the first frost.

With the unaided, or naked, eye, you can see vague markings on the moon's surface— "the man in the moon." With a pair of binoculars or a small telescope, you can see these more clearly. The darker, rather smooth areas are lunar plains called maria, which is Latin for "seas" (astronomers once thought these areas were oceans). The lighter areas are covered with mountain ranges and other earth-like features.

The best times to view the moon with binoculars or telescopes are before the first quarter and after the third quarter. At these times you can see the bright half lighted from the side. The lunar features are highlighted by shadows. Near the full moon, there are fewer shadows on the moon and the features are harder to see. In addition, the glare from reflected sunlight at full moon makes it harder to see moon features clearly.

▶ THE PLANETS

After the moon, the brightest object in the night sky is usually the morning or evening "star." Actually this is not a star at all, but a planet, usually Venus. The planets also have orbits around the sun that are close to the sun's path, or ecliptic. If you see a bright star near the ecliptic where you are not used to seeing one, it is undoubtedly a planet rather than a star (unless it is a man-made satellite or a balloon). Planets do not twinkle like stars but shine steadily. Through a telescope, a planet appears to be a small disk. To be sure which planet you are seeing, it is necessary to consult a table listing what part of the sky each planet is in, on or about that particular date, since the planets move through the sky —although much more slowly than the moon.

Two of the planets, Mercury and Venus, have orbits closer to the sun than the earth's orbit is. Therefore they are always seen near the sun. This is why Venus is so often the morning or evening star. Both planets show phases like the moon's when viewed through a telescope. But they are actually brighter when they are in a crescent phase than when full, because they are nearer the earth at the crescent stage. At its brightest, Venus is the brightest object in the night sky after the moon. It is sometimes even visible by day. Mercury is seldom seen by many observers because it stays so close to the sun. However, Mercury is also very bright and can be seen as the morning or evening star if one knows when and where to look.

Mars, Jupiter, and Saturn are also sometimes seen as the morning or evening star. These planets, which are bright enough to be seen easily with the naked eye, and the other three planets—Uranus, Neptune, and Pluto —all have orbits farther from the sun than the earth's is. They show only the full phase to the earth. Mars is one of the brightest objects in the sky at its maximum brightness, and is noticeably red. In fact, it is often called the "red planet." Jupiter, the largest planet in our solar system, is almost as bright as Mars at maximum. It has 12 satellites, or moons, four of which are visible in a small telescope or binoculars. Saturn is not as bright as Jupiter or Mars, but is still prominent compared to the stars. The most famous feature of this yellow planet is its ring system, which is visible through a small telescope.

▶ STARS AND CONSTELLATIONS

Now that we've gotten to know the moon and the planets a little better, let's take a look at the stars. They provide the glittering backdrop for the gliding motions of the celestial objects nearer to earth. Everyone knows the Big Dipper and the Little Dipper. Each is a part of a recognizable grouping of stars called a constellation. The sky is filled with constellations. They are the landmarks or signposts not only of the astronomer but also of the sailor, the airplane pilot, or anyone for that matter who is out at night and takes the trouble to get to know these "sky pictures."

Let's suppose you live in the Northern Hemisphere at the latitude of the United States. You can see some constellations, like those including the Big Dipper and the Little Dipper, all year long. Other constellations can be seen only at certain times of year. Still others can't be seen at all from the northern latitudes.

As the earth makes its annual trip around the sun, the side of the earth that faces away from the sun (where it is night) points toward a different part of the sky, depending upon where the earth is in its orbit. In a year, we people of earth move past a whole range of constellations and back to where we started. The constellations that are above the earth's North Pole, or around the sky's north pole (called the celestial pole), stay above the horizon all year and turn in a circle around the celestial pole as the seasons change. These constellations and the stars in them are called circumpolar. The other constellations we see are associated with particular times of year. Let's find out a little about some of these constellations and stars, beginning with the circumpolars and those of the summer sky.

▶THE SUMMER SKY

Summer is the easiest time to learn some of the stars because the weather is warm enough for one to spend some time out of doors at night. In midsummer the Big Dipper

The familiar, bright stars of the Big Dipper.

is in the northwest sky, with its cup right side up and its handle tipping upward. The stars of the Big Dipper all have Arabic names, starting with Alkaid, at the end of the handle; then Mizar; Alioth; and Megrez, where the handle meets the cup; Phad and Merak, along the bottom of the cup; and Dubhe, at the cup's outer "corner." Merak and Dubhe are called the Pointers because an imaginary line through them points upward to Polaris, the North Star. Polaris practically coincides with the celestial north pole. Polaris marks the end of the handle of the Little Dipper; this handle extends in a concave curve from Polaris to the cup, in contrast to the convex curve of the Big Dipper's handle. At the outer rim of the Little Dipper's cup is the bright star Kochab. The Big Dipper and the Little Dipper are not actually constellations themselves but are parts of the constellations Ursa Major and Ursa Minor—the Big Bear and the Little Bear. On the side of Polaris opposite to the Big Dipper side is the circumpolar constellation Cassiopeia, which looks like a W, an M, or a 3, depending on the time of year.

In the summer, there is a bright orange star in the western sky that can be found by continuing along a curving line that would be the extension of the Big Dipper's handle. This orange star is Arcturus, in the constellation Boötes, one of the five brightest stars in the entire sky. The name "Arcturus" is from a Greek word, meaning "watcher of the Bear"— that is, of the Big Dipper. Near Arcturus but a little upward from the curve leading from the Dipper's handle is a small semicircle of stars forming the constellation Corona Borealis, the Northern Crown. The brightest jewel in Corona Borealis is Alphecca, a bluish star.

Almost directly overhead in midsummer is Vega, a bright blue star in the constellation Lyra and another of the five brightest stars in the sky. Vega forms a very large triangle with the bright stars Deneb, to the east, and Altair, to the south. Altair, in the constellation Aquila (the Eagle), has one dimmer star in front of it, in line with Vega, and another behind it. If the line from Altair to Vega is continued north, it leads first to Eltanin, about half as far from Vega as Vega is from Altair, then runs west of the Little

Dipper and into the cup of the Big Dipper. The side of the triangle connecting Deneb to Vega is almost at right angles to the Altair–Vega line. Deneb is in the constellation Cygnus (the Swan), sometimes called the Northern Cross. Although blue Deneb does not appear any brighter than the other bright stars, it is an intensely bright star, 60,000 times more luminous than our sun. The reason Deneb does not seem especially bright to us on earth is its relatively great distance from earth, 1,600 light-years, as compared to Vega's distance of 26 light-years.

If the night is particularly clear, the Milky Way can be seen as a hazy band of light running through Altair, Deneb, and Cassiopeia. The Milky Way is actually a huge, disk-shaped collection of stars—a galaxy—that includes not only the sun but all other stars visible from the earth as individual stars.

In the Milky Way and far to the south is the constellation Scorpius, with bright red Antares, whose name means "similar to Mars." Antares is at the Scorpion's head, and Shaula at its tail. To the west of Scorpius is the smaller, faint constellation Libra (the Scales). Libra forms a sort of box shape in the heavens, whose southwest corner is marked by Zubenelgenubi, and whose north-west corner is marked by Zubeneschamali.

▶ THE AUTUMN SKY

As summer passes and autumn sets in, Vega and Deneb move into the western sky. A new group of constellations becomes visible in the east. The autumn stars are not as bright as those of summer. The main part of the sky to the south is dominated by a large square of stars known as the Great Square of Pegasus. Three of these stars—Algenib at the south-east corner, Markab at the southwest corner, and Scheat at the northwest corner—are in the constellation Pegasus. Pegasus is the famous winged horse of myth. The fourth star, Alpheratz at the northeast corner, is in the constellation Andromeda. Andromeda stretches out to the northeast, toward the bright star Mirfak in the constellation Perseus. Almost directly to the east of the Great Square is the bright orange star Hamal in the constellation Aries (the Ram). A line continuing the eastern side of the Great Square

The amazing burst of stars in the Milky Way.

(Algenib and Alpheratz) leads north through the western star of Cassiopeia's W and on to Polaris.

Far to the south, below the Great Square, are two bright stars lying near the horizon. The lower one, Fomalhaut, in the constellation Piscis Austrinus (the Southern Fish), is almost in line with the imaginary extension of the western edge of the Great Square. The other star, Diphda, in Cetus (the Whale), is slightly higher in the sky and more to the east.

▶ THE WINTER SKY

Winter brings not only crisp, sparkling weather, but also the most glittering array of stars of any of the seasons. The central constellation of the winter sky is Orion (the Hunter). Orion strides along the celestial equator, sporting seven bright stars. The three stars of his belt—Alnitak, Alnilam, and Mintaka—are framed by four stars marking Orion's arms (or shoulders) and feet. Brilliant blue Rigel at his left (western) foot and cool, red Betelgeuse at his right arm are the brightest of these stars. Saiph, at Orion's right foot, nearly the dimmest of the seven stars, is comparable in brightness to Polaris, the North Star. A line of dimmer stars dangles from the belt of Orion, marking his sword. One of these stars is actually a glowing cloud of luminous gases, the Great Nebula, visible if you use binoculars or a telescope.

To the southeast of Orion, on a curving line down from his belt, is Sirius (the Dog Star), the brightest star in the entire sky. Sirius is in the constellation Canis Major (the Big Dog), which also includes a small

The Great Nebula in the constellation Orion.

triangle of bright stars just below and to the left of Sirius. To find the Little Dog (Canis Minor), swing upward and eastward from Sirius to yellow Procyon, its brightest star, almost even with Orion's shoulders.

Sirius and Procyon begin a large loop of bright stars that arches around Orion. Continuing from Procyon, we reach Gemini (the Twins)—first Pollux and then Castor. Castor is specially interesting because, although it looks like a single star, it is actually a system of six stars, all revolving around one another. A small telescope will show it as a double star, but a more powerful telescope is needed to see all six stars. From the Twins, the loop runs to gleaming Capella, in Auriga (the Charioteer), then down to bright orange Aldebaran, in Taurus (the Bull), before swinging through Orion's belt and down to Sirius again. In Taurus and to the northwest of Aldebaran are the Pleiades (or Seven Sisters), the most famous open cluster of stars in the sky. Six of the seven stars can be seen easily with the naked eye. With a telescope, hundreds of Pleiades become visible.

▶ THE SPRING SKY

As the snow melts and the first signs of spring appear, winter's dazzling display of stars slips off to the west. By mid-spring, the Twins, Pollux and Castor, are low in the northwest sky, and the spring constellations hold center stage. Like the autumn constellations, they do not contain as many bright stars as the summer and winter skies do. The dominant feature is the Big Dipper. The Big Dipper has been swinging around the pole all winter and is now directly over Polaris, high in the sky. If the line through the Pointers to Polaris is extended in the opposite direction, southward, it leads to Leo (the Lion). The brightest star in Leo is Regulus. Regulus marks Leo's front paws, slightly to the west of the line from the Pointers. Regulus and Leo's shoulder and head form a sickle, or backward question mark. The body curves back the other way to Denebola, at Leo's tail.

The stars of the eastern sky in spring are those that were fading in the west in summer, so we've already seen many of them. Arcturus is on the curve of the extension of the Big Dipper's handle. This extension continues on to Spica, a bright star in Virgo (the Virgin), near the southern horizon, and to Corvus (the Crow), a small group of four stars just beyond Spica. A line from Regulus, in Leo, through Spica points to Zubenelgenubi, in the constellation Libra, which we saw earlier in the summer sky.

Now that you've been around the sky once with the passage of the seasons, you may find that you recognize some of the stars easily on second meeting. Others, which you had trouble finding before, may have become somewhat easier to spot with practice. After you've learned all the stars we've talked about here, perhaps you'll find some others, on your own, through other books and star charts. As the years pass, you may even come to look upon some of the stars and constellations as old friends, and welcome their return each year as the sign that a new season is arriving and another is passing. And once you know the landmarks and signposts of the sky, all the other celestial objects and events become that much easier to follow—the wanderings of the planets; the phases of the moon; the broad band of the Milky Way; annual meteor showers; comets; and all the rest. And all this is waiting for you right in your own backyard.

R. A. REINSTEIN
Codirector, ISAR
(Institute for Scientific and Artistic Research)

PICTURES IN THE SKY

Connect the stars and you will see some of the constellations.

CAPRICORN THE GOAT
He is hard to see because he is close to the horizon. In the drawing, the three little stars below the goat's tail are counted as one.

ORION THE HUNTER
He is a big constellation and is easy to see if you look for his belt, which is made of three stars. He carries a club in his right hand.

CYGNUS THE SWAN
This is a big constellation. The swan's wings are spread and he has a long neck. His feet trail behind as he flies down the Milky Way.

LEO THE LION
He lives right under the bear. His short front foot is formed by a very bright star called Regulus. If you find Regulus, you'll find Leo.

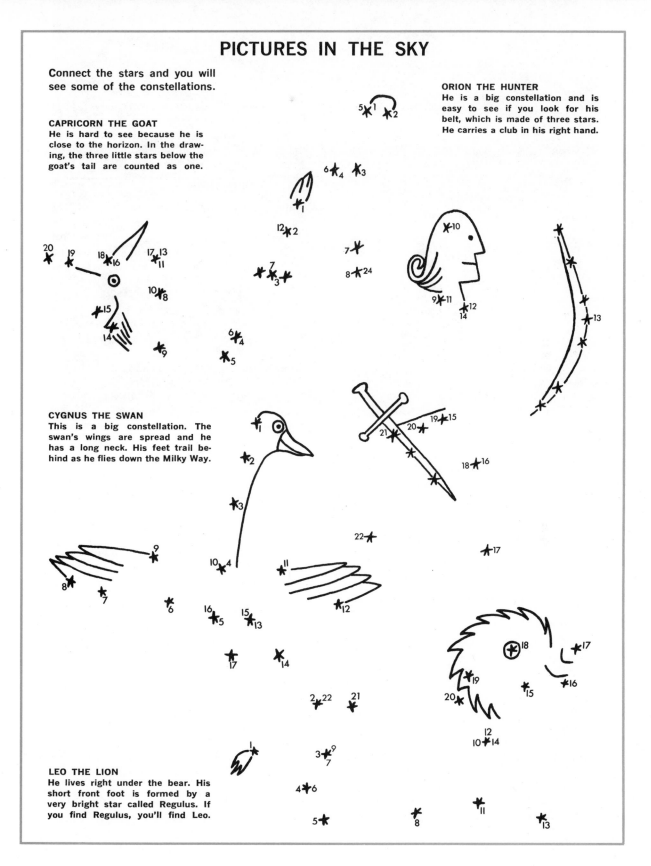

Health food stores are springing up all over the country.

THE HEALTH FOOD BOOM

The enormous popularity of "health foods" has made them a topic of endless discussion and much controversy. Just what are health foods? Some people think that these foods are "different," taste bad, and are sold only in special health food stores. Other people think that health foods are the best of foods, and wouldn't dream of eating anything else. Today the term "health food" has taken on a special meaning. It usually refers to those foods that are sold in the specialized health food stores that are springing up all over the country. What is sold in these health food stores? Do these products contribute to your health?

Nutritionists claim that many of the foods sold in health food stores can be found in local supermarkets for less money. They say, too, that although some of the foods do contribute to good health, some of the more specialized foods add nothing to your diet. Health food stores also feature such non-food items as cosmetics. They are often the same as those sold in department stores or drugstores at a cheaper price.

Many of the items in these health food stores have labels reading "organic" or "natural." "Organic" has come to mean that these fruits, vegetables, and grains have been grown in soils that have not been treated with chemical fertilizers or weed and insect killers. It also refers to meats that come from animals that have not been treated with hormones, antibiotics, or other chemicals. Organic meat comes from animals that have been fed only organic grains and feed. Many scientists do not believe that there is any real difference between organic and nonorganic foods. Scientists can't tell whether a vegetable or fruit has been fertilized organically or not. And no one has proved that organically fertilized foods are better for you.

The term "natural" has come to mean that no chemical additives (such as preservatives

64

and food coloring) were added to the food in processing. Fresh fruits and vegetables; fresh meats, poultry, and fish; and canned and frozen foods that contain no additives, are all natural foods. Little is known about the long-term effects of chemical additives. But the big danger at the moment is still old-fashioned food poisoning, and some chemicals are added to foods to help prevent this illness.

▶ ON THE HEALTH FOOD SHELVES

The following products are sold in health food stores. Some have been vastly over-rated, while others really do contain valuable nutrients.

Sea Salt

Sea salt is a controversial item sold in health food stores. It is much more expensive than ordinary salt, but it has not been proved to be any better. Nutritionists recommend that most people use iodized salt to ensure that they get enough iodine. The amount of iodine in sea salt varies, but there is usually either too much or too little.

Granola

Granola is one of the most popular foods sold in health food stores. It is an oat cereal, to which almonds, raisins, sesame seeds, coconut, and honey are sometimes added. Although it tastes good, it is more expensive and usually has more calories than other cereals.

Raw Sugar

Raw sugar is nutritionally almost the same as white sugar. It contains a few more minerals, but they are not present in sufficient amounts to justify the higher price it carries. Most nutritionists believe that we eat far too much sugar of all types. They suggest that we train our taste buds away from this potentially dangerous habit.

Brown Rice

This is rice from which only the outer shell has been removed. The bran and the germ, along with the starch, remain. In regular rice, the bran and the germ (which contain most of the vitamins and minerals) are removed in the milling, leaving only the starch. Brown

Granola and Raw Sugar

Brown Rice

rice is somewhat richer in protein, minerals, and some B vitamins than regular white rice. But unless rice forms the major part of your diet, the difference between the two types is not great enough to be important. Vegetarian diets based on brown rice and few other foods are lacking in many vital nutrients, and can be extremely dangerous. "Converted" rice, which is treated before it is milled to preserve the vitamins and minerals, has the same nutritional value as brown rice.

Honey

Yogurt

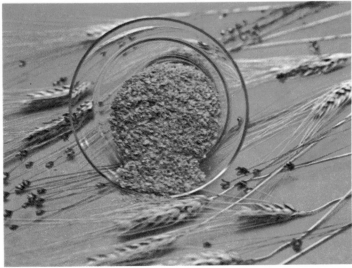

Wheat Germ

Honey

Honey is the nectar of various flowers that has been collected by bees. It is one of the oldest means of sweetening foods, and is an easily digested source of energy. Honey is nearly twice as sweet as regular sugar, so smaller amounts are needed to sweeten foods. Honey contains minerals and vitamins, but not in very large amounts.

Yogurt

Yogurt is a fermented milk product. It has been eaten in the Balkan countries and the Middle East for centuries. It is rich in calcium and protein, and is easily digested. It also contains acid that aids in digestion. Yogurt also helps the body absorb vitamins and minerals from other foods. Plain yogurt (without added gelatin, sugars, or fruits) purchased in the supermarket is exactly the same as the yogurt sold in health food stores.

Wheat Germ

The dark speck at the end of each wheat kernel is the germ. The germ is not used when wheat is milled into white flour. But it is the most valuable part of the wheat. It is a rich source of protein, B vitamins, and iron. Wheat germ contains as much protein as meat, but it is much less expensive. It can be eaten as a cereal, added to meat loaf, or sprinkled like bread crumbs on casseroles.

Whole Wheat Bread

Whole Grain Breads

Breads made from whole grain flours (which include the bran, germ, and starch) are often preferred to regular white bread by nutritionists, especially when bread is a major part of the diet. Regular white bread is made from flour that contains only the starch; the germ and bran are removed in the milling. "Enriched" white bread is made from flour that has had vitamins and minerals removed in the refining process, and has had only some of these nutrients restored. Whole grain breads can also be purchased in regular stores.

Nuts and Seeds

Seeds (such as sunflower, sesame, and pumpkin) and nuts are used as snacks. They may replace cake, cookies, and potato chips. Nuts and seeds have more vitamins (including B vitamins), minerals, and protein than regular snack foods, but they are also high in fats and calories. While nuts and seeds can be used as good snack foods, they are no substitute for protein-rich meat, eggs, milk, fish, cheese, or poultry.

Dried Fruits

Fruits dried without the use of sulfur as a preservative are found in health food stores. Most brands of dried apricots, pears, nectarines, and peaches sold in local super-

Nuts and Seeds

Unsulfured Dried Fruit

Organic Eggs and Carrot Juice

can. Fruit and vegetable juices contain many more vitamins and minerals and fewer calories than soft drinks, however.

Soybeans

This health food staple is used most often in the form of flour, and is added to breads, soups, meat loaf, and other such dishes. It provides twice as much protein as the same amount of meat, and is much cheaper. Soybeans contain no cholesterol, which is present in protein sources such as meat and eggs and is believed to contribute to heart disease. Although the United States is the world's largest soybean grower, most of the soybeans are exported or used to feed livestock. In many countries soybeans are a major protein source in the diet.

Sprouts

Alfalfa, mung bean, wheat, and soybean sprouts are eaten in soups and salads, on sandwiches, or as a vegetable. The sprouts are not generally available, but you can buy the seeds, which are very inexpensive, at health food stores and grow them yourself. They are rich in vitamin C.

Organic Eggs

These are eggs that come from hens that have been fed organic feed, and have not been treated with antibiotics or other chemicals.

markets are treated with sulfur in the form of sulfur dioxide to keep them bright and attractive. Sulfur also helps preserve the vitamin A and vitamin C content. Although sulfur dioxide is a poisonous gas, only small amounts are present in the fruit. Because no one knows exactly what these small amounts of sulfur do to the body, health food advocates feel it is better to eat fruits dried without sulfur.

Juices

Vegetable and fruit juices are good for you, but they can't cure ulcers or blood disorders, as some health food advocates imply that they

Mung Bean Sprouts and Avocado Oil

They are supposed to contain more nutrients than regular eggs, but there is no real difference between the two types. Organic eggs are also more expensive than the regular eggs sold in a supermarket.

Cosmetics

Other popular items sold in health food stores are cosmetics. Avocado oil is often suggested for dry skin and hair. It is not to be used as a cooking oil. Cosmetics made from cucumbers, strawberries, lemons, and tomatoes, or those containing vitamin E, smell nice and look good. They are usually very expensive, and no one has proved that they have any long-range beneficial effect.

PEANUT BUTTER COOKIES

INGREDIENTS

1 stick of margarine	1 cup chunky peanut butter
1½ cups whole wheat flour	¼ cup molasses
½ cup wheat germ	¾ cup honey
1 teaspoon baking soda	2 eggs
¼ teaspoon salt	1 teaspoon vanilla

NOTE: Unbleached white flour may be substituted for whole wheat flour.

DIRECTIONS

Mix the flour, wheat germ, baking soda, and salt in a large bowl. In another large bowl mix the eggs, vanilla, and margarine. They must be mixed very well, or creamed together. Then add the honey, molasses, and peanut butter to the egg mixture. Next add the dry ingredients, a little at a time, to the liquids. You will have a sticky, but delicious, dough. Shape the dough into balls about 1 inch thick. Put the balls of dough on a cookie sheet, and flatten them out with a fork. You can dip the fork into a glass of cold water from time to time to prevent the dough from sticking to it. Bake the cookies for about 12 minutes in a 350-degree oven. You should get about 4 dozen cookies altogether.

THE FIRST HUMAN BEING?

When did man first stand on his own two legs and begin to walk the earth?

Scientists have been asking that very question for centuries. For some time, it was believed that *Homo erectus,* a species that lived 1,000,000 years ago, was the earliest man to have walked upright. Among the *Homo erectus* specimens discovered in the past are the famous Java Man and Peking Man.

But skull fragments found in Africa in 1972 indicate that a form of life similar to today's man may have lived over 2,500,000 years ago. The startling new development is the result of discoveries made by Richard Leakey, administrative director of the National Museum of Kenya, Africa.

Leakey was one of the leaders of an archeological expedition that was working in a desert area near Lake Rudolf in East Africa. While exploring that region, the scientists uncovered bone fragments. After thorough investigation, they concluded that these may be the oldest known relics of early man.

The skull fragments were found covered by volcanic ash, and tests established that the ash was some 2,500,000 years old. According to Leakey, the skull is different from that of our own species, *Homo sapiens,* but it is also different from those of all other forms of early man. Thus it does not fit into any of the currently held theories of human evolution.

In addition to the skull fragments, other bones were found. Included were two intact thighbones. There were also parts of lower leg bones. The shape of these bones provides further evidence that, even at this early stage, man had begun to walk erect and not stooped over. Previously it was believed that man did not start to walk erect until much later. The bones have astonished scientists because "they are practically indistinguishable from the same bones of modern man."

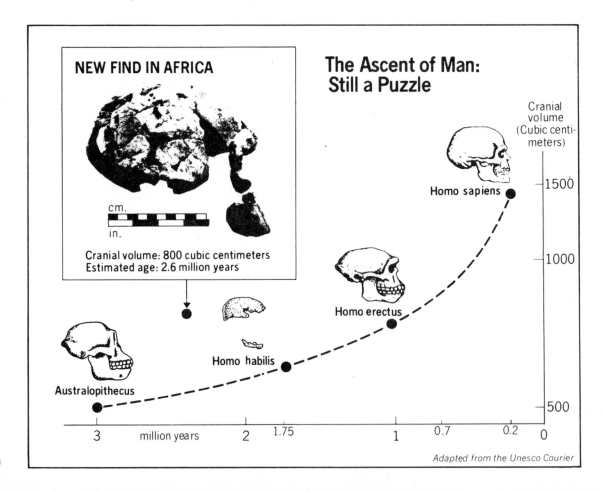

NEW FIND IN AFRICA

cm.

in.

Cranial volume: 800 cubic centimeters
Estimated age: 2.6 million years

The Ascent of Man:
Still a Puzzle

Cranial volume
(Cubic centimeters)

Homo sapiens — 1500

— 1000

Homo erectus

Homo habilis

Australopithecus

— 500

3   million years   2   1.75   1   0.7   0.2   0

Adapted from the Unesco Courier

A Mayan temple, hidden by jungle growth for 60 years, is rediscovered.

MYSTERY OF THE MAYA

On a hot afternoon in May, 1973, an expedition of seven men and two women struggled through the dense jungle at Río Bec, in southeastern Yucatán in Mexico. Five *chicleros* (Mexican woodsmen) led the way, hacking at the foliage and thick vines with their sharp machetes. And then suddenly it loomed before them—a shadowy, mysterious building. An ancient temple built by the Mayan Indians about 1,200 years ago had been rediscovered.

This relic of the great Indian civilization that once flourished in Mexico and Central America had first been discovered in 1912. But the notes left by one of the original discoverers were confusing. During the next few decades, the structure was covered by jungle growth. For 60 years, archeologists searched in vain for the building. Temple B, as it had been called by the original discoverers, just seemed to have disappeared.

In 1972, the husband and wife team of Hugh and Suzanne Johnston were commissioned by a public television station to go to Yucatán to make a documentary film on the subject of "The Mystery of the Maya." One part of the film was to deal with the long-lost temple. But this first attempt to rediscover the ancient ruin ended in failure.

The Johnstons went back to the United States and studied the notes of the 1912 expedition. The description of the location was unclear, but it did provide a general idea of where the temple might be found. The Johnstons set out again in the spring of 1973.

Luck was with them. Aided by their Mexican woodsmen-guides, they found the lost temple. Although it was wrapped in vines and other jungle growth, the building had remained in an excellent state of preservation. It had withstood damage from forest fires and the eroding effects of heavy rains.

The temple is an imposing structure. Built of limestone, it is 85 feet long and 55 feet high. Two large towers stand at the front corners. There are six large rooms, and steep, ladderlike steps leading up to the towers. Sections of the stucco-covered walls contain engraved designs.

Once the moss and other vegetation had been cleared, the members of the expedition could marvel at the skill of the ancient stoneworkers who had put together the building without mortar.

A CHINESE TORAH

Sometime in the 12th century, a small band of Jews journeyed from their homeland in the Middle East deep into China. There they founded a small Jewish community at Kaifeng, in eastern China near the Hwang Ho, or Yellow River. Over the years, scholars have pieced together information about Kaifeng and other Chinese-Jewish communities that have long since faded into history.

Recently, an ancient Torah from Kaifeng was discovered in the religious book collection at Southern Methodist University (SMU), in Dallas, Texas. "Torah" is a name for the first five books of the Bible, and for the hand-lettered Hebrew religious scroll containing those books.

The discovery that the Torah (written in Hebrew) was actually of Chinese origin was the result of detective work by Biblical scholars. Mainly it was the result of the continuing curiosity of Dr. Decherd Turner, Jr., of SMU. Whenever visiting Biblical scholars came to Dallas, Dr. Turner asked them to try to determine the Torah's origins. He got as many answers as there were scholars.

Copies of the Torah were sent to the head librarian at the Jewish Theological Seminary in New York City. As it happened, the seminary had an original Torah from Kaifeng in its own collection of rare books. The two Torahs were alike.

It was observed that the Torah in Dallas was written in a "flowing and rather graceful style." This contrasted sharply with the squarish, formal style of Western Torahs. In addition, the Dallas Torah was stitched together with silk threads rather than with threads made of animal tendons, which were used in the West. This was further evidence that the Torah might be of Chinese origin. Finally, the knobs on the rods used to roll up the Torah scroll were covered, in Chinese style, with a gold lacquer.

And so a mystery appears to have been solved. As for the Jewish community in Kaifeng, it had gradually disappeared in the 19th century. Its members intermarried with local people and were absorbed into the Chinese population. But before the community withered away, a number of its Torahs were purchased by Christian missionaries and brought to Europe. The whereabouts of five were known, including the one at the Jewish Theological Seminary and one in the British Museum, in London. Now, it would seem, another has been found in Dallas, Texas.

The Torah at SMU in Dallas, Texas—one of the five Chinese Torah's known to exist today.

A PHOENICIAN GODDESS

It was probably a stormy day, some 2,500 years ago, when a Phoenician ship went down off the coast of present-day Israel. (Phoenicia was an ancient seafaring kingdom that extended over parts of what is now Lebanon, Syria, and Israel.) There was nothing special about this ship. It was just another cargo vessel carrying the usual assortment of Phoenician trade goods. There were vases and jars made out of baked clay, and many small figures of Tanit, the Phoenician goddess of fertility.

At the time, the loss probably aroused very little interest. Ships often sank in rough seas. But for modern-day archeologists, the discovery of the wreck is of major importance.

The sunken ship was discovered by a spear-fishing skin diver in 1971, just north of Haifa, Israel. Since then a great many archeological treasures have been salvaged from the wreck.

The most important of these are the clay figurines of the goddess Tanit. The goddess was the only female deity known to have been worshiped by the Phoenicians. But until the discovery of the clay figurines, the only likenesses of the goddess that had been found were in ancient drawings and on ancient bronze coins. The fact that the ship was carrying the figurines indicates that worship of the goddess may have been more widespread than scholars have previously believed.

The clay figures vary in height. Some are as small as 6 inches, while others are about 15 inches. They appear to have been produced in great numbers from master molds. The majority of the figurines show the goddess with her right hand upraised, as if giving a blessing. Her left hand is placed over her breast. The goddess stands on a pedestal, which bears the symbol of the goddess—a disk on top of a triangle, with a horizontal line between them.

More of the well-preserved artifacts lie under 30 to 40 feet of water, scattered over a very large area. Divers have scooped up more than 200 figurines since the wreck was found. They are being carefully studied by marine archeologists. The work of probing around the sunken ship goes on, and it is hoped that other important discoveries will be made there as well.

A statue of the goddess Tanit.

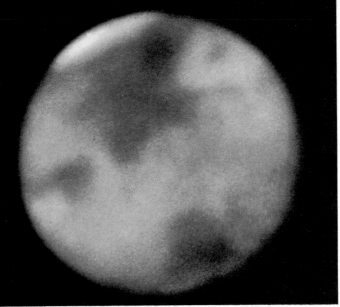

Photograph of Mars shows polar cap at upper left.

MARS

The earth is one of nine planets in the solar system. For centuries men have wondered what the other planets were like and whether life existed on any of them. Of all the planets, Mars always aroused the greatest curiosity, because conditions there seemed to be the best for the support of living things. This interest in Mars was greatly increased by the work of two astronomers, one Italian and one American.

The Italian was Giovanni Schiaparelli (1835–1910). In 1877, like many other astronomers, Schiaparelli turned his atten-

When at opposition, Mars is lined up directly with the earth and sun. Oppositions occur about every 780 days—slightly under 2 years, 2 months.

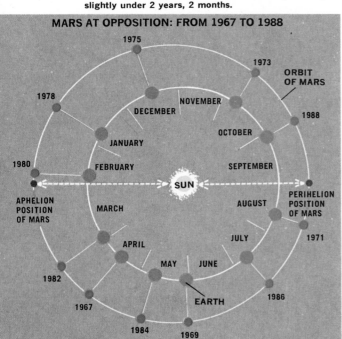

tion to Mars, because it was especially close to the earth that year. Schiaparelli observed straight dark lines on the planet's surface and drew maps showing these lines. Most astronomers, then and later, were unable to see the lines. Schiaparelli called the lines *canali,* the Italian word for "channels." But the word was wrongly translated into English as "canals." The straightness of the lines and the use of the word "canals" caused many people to assume that Schiaparelli had seen structures made by intelligent beings.

Schiaparelli thought the lines were long ditches of some kind, but he did not insist that they had to be the work of intelligent creatures. However, many people, including some astronomers, were convinced that the channels were artificial. One such astronomer was the American Percival Lowell (1855–1916). He drew maps of the planet, showing the canals in great detail. He insisted that the canals were there and that they had to be the work of intelligent beings.

Arguments over the existence of the canals went on for a long time, helped along by the exciting idea that there could be intelligent life on another planet. Popular interest in Mars rose to a new peak in 1965, when the American space probe Mariner 4 flew past Mars, coming within several thousand miles of the planet. It was the first of several successful probes launched by the United States. These probes sent back photographs of the surface of Mars and information about conditions there. Mariner 7 flew by Mars in 1969, and in November, 1971, Mariner 9 was put into orbit about 1,100 miles above the planet. The probe continued to operate for nearly a year, sending back an enormous amount of information. It measured temperatures, pressures, altitudes, and gravity on Mars. Mariner 9 also radioed back amazingly clear pictures of Mars, leaving no part of the planet unphotographed.

The pictures made by Mariner 9 show some straight channels, but not where Schiaparelli and Lowell had mapped the canals. What had they seen, then? There are many small, dark-colored areas on the Martian surface. Scientists of the Mariner project think these

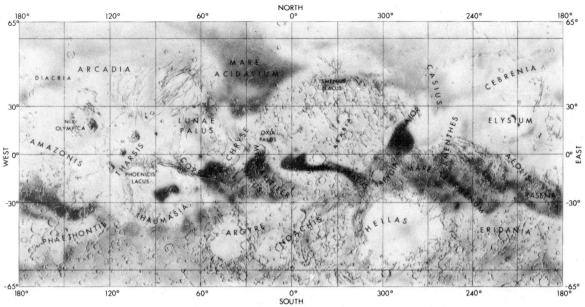

Map of Mars, based on photographs taken by Mariner 9. The polar regions are not shown. This is the first finely detailed map ever made of another planet.

areas caused an optical illusion, in which lines seemed to connect the dark spots. These lines were "canals."

▶THE RED PLANET

Like all planets, Mars has no light of its own. We can see it glowing brightly in the night sky because some of the sunlight that strikes it is reflected toward us. The planet is easy to recognize because of its red color. In fact it is sometimes called the Red Planet. Scientists believe that rust-colored substances, called iron oxides, give the surface of Mars its color. The color led the ancient Romans to name the planet Mars, after their god of war.

The Orbit of Mars

Counting outward from the sun, Mars is the fourth planet of the solar system. The path, or **orbit,** that Mars follows around the sun lies between the orbits of the earth and Jupiter. The planets follow orbits that are elliptical, like flattened circles. However, with Mars the flattening is greater than with most of the other planets. As a result, the distance between Mars and the sun can change a great deal. The planet sometimes comes within 128,500,000 miles of the sun. This nearest approach is called **perihelion,**

meaning "near the sun." When it is at **aphelion** ("away from the sun") the distance is 154,500,000 miles. The average distance is 141,500,000 miles. The large difference between perihelion and aphelion means that there is a large difference in the amounts of light and heat that Mars gets from the sun at different times of the year.

The planets revolve around the sun at different speeds. Planets near the sun move faster than those farther out. The earth makes one complete revolution around the sun in about 365 days. This is our year. A year on Mars is longer, because Mars is farther from the sun, so it moves more slowly. It also must go a longer distance to make one revolution. As a result, a year on Mars is 687 earth days.

The earth moves faster than Mars, so that it regularly catches up to that planet and passes it in a little over 2 years. Each time this happens there is a close approach of the two planets, called **opposition.** Astronomers welcome an opposition with Mars because it gives them the chance to study Mars in more detail. The distance between Mars and the earth is not the same in all oppositions. The planets come closest in years when Mars is closest to the sun. These especially close oppositions take place once

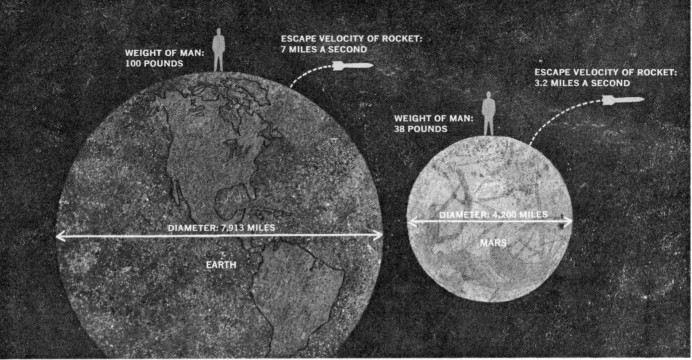

WEIGHT OF MAN:
100 POUNDS

ESCAPE VELOCITY OF ROCKET:
7 MILES A SECOND

ESCAPE VELOCITY OF ROCKET:
3.2 MILES A SECOND

WEIGHT OF MAN:
38 POUNDS

DIAMETER: 7,913 MILES

EARTH

DIAMETER: 4,200 MILES

MARS

Diagram shows earth's size and gravitational pull compared with those of Mars.

every 15 or 17 years. The planets are then only about 35,000,000 miles apart. Such an opposition occurred in 1971. At that time astronomers all over the world made observations of Mars, knowing that such an opportunity would not come again until 1988.

The Rotation and Size of Mars

Mars and the earth are very different kinds of worlds, but they are very much alike in two ways. The earth turns on its axis, in a motion called **rotation.** It takes 23 hours and 56 minutes to rotate once. Mars rotates in 24 hours and 37 minutes, so a day on Mars is only a little longer than a day on the earth.

Mars and the earth are also very much alike in the way the axis of each planet is tilted. The earth's axis is tilted at an angle of 23½ degrees. Because of the tilt, the northern and southern hemispheres receive unequal amounts of the sun's heat and light as the earth follows its yearly orbit around the sun. As a result, we have seasons. Mars also has seasons for the same reason. Its axis is tilted 25 degrees, about the same amount as the earth's. The Martian seasons are longer than ours, because Mars takes nearly two earth years to orbit the sun.

If you have seen motion pictures of astro-

nauts on the moon, you know they move with long, bounding steps. They can do this because the moon's gravity is much weaker than the earth's gravity. The strength of gravity depends on the mass, or amount of matter, of a planet or a moon. The moon's mass is much less than the earth's, so the pull of gravity there is weaker. Mars, too, has less mass than the earth, so gravity there is also weaker than on earth.

The diameter of Mars is 4,200 miles, only about half of the earth's diameter. And the rock material of Mars is less dense. The smaller size and lower density of Mars mean that an astronaut who weighs 150 pounds on earth would have a weight of only 57 pounds on Mars. The rocket that launched him from the earth would have to reach a speed of 7 miles per second to overcome the earth's gravitational pull. This speed is known as **escape velocity.** But to leave Mars, with its lower gravity, the rocket would have to move only 3.2 miles per second.

The earth has a magnetic field. The field is caused by the liquid metal that makes up the center, or core, of the earth. Scientists reasoned that a magnetic field around Mars could mean that Mars, like the earth, has a core of molten metal. When Mariner 4 flew past Mars in 1965, it did not detect any magnetic field. Some scientists believe this is proof that Mars does not have a liquid metal core, but other scientists do not agree.

▶ THE SATELLITES

Two satellites, or moons, move in orbit around Mars. They are nothing like our moon, whose diameter is one fourth the size of the earth's diameter. The Martian moons are tiny, each one being only a few miles in length. But scientists have been interested in them for a long time. One of these men was Johannes Kepler, the great German astronomer who worked out the laws of motion of the planets. Kepler believed that Mars had satellites. He was proved right more than 200 years later, when the satellites were finally seen in 1877 by Asaph Hall, an American astronomer. Mars was unusually close to the earth that year, and Hall decided to carry on a search for satellites. He found the two tiny moons on two successive nights. Because they moved with Mars, Hall named the moons after the servants of Mars. He called one of them Phobos, which means "fear," and the other Deimos, meaning "terror."

The Mystery of Phobos and Deimos

Phobos and Deimos are a puzzle, because they are so small and so close to their parent planet. Several theories have been suggested to explain how they arose. One theory is that the satellites are actually **planetoids.** Many thousands of these objects travel in orbits between Mars and Jupiter, like miniature planets (their name means "like a planet"). They range in length from a mile or so to nearly 500 miles. According to the theory, two planetoids came too close to Mars and were captured by its gravitational pull, becoming the satellites Phobos and Deimos.

Another theory states that Mars, Phobos, Deimos, and our own moon all came into being when the earth was very young. At that time the earth spun much faster than it does today, and its crust was much softer. The fast spinning caused masses of crust to be thrown out into space, to form the moon, Mars, and its satellites.

Still another theory suggests that the satellites are artificial, placed in orbit by in-

habitants of Mars, in the same way that artificial satellites now circle the earth, placed there by man. But the Mariner 9 photographs make this idea seem unlikely. Also, measurements of the size and density of Phobos and Deimos have convinced most scientists that the artificial satellite theory is wrong.

During its hundreds of orbits of Mars, Mariner 9 gathered information that took some of the mystery away from Phobos and Deimos. Its cameras showed that the two satellites are very much alike. Both are thickly covered with craters. These were made by collisions with tiny meteoroids that streak through space at great speeds.

The large numbers of craters on the satellites shows that the Martian satellites are probably more than 4,000,000,000 (billion) years old. The color of both is dark enough to suggest that they are made up largely of iron or carbon. Finally, both satellites are elongated and irregular in shape, rather than spherical like the earth. Phobos is about 13 miles long, and the smaller Deimos stretches about 8 miles.

For every rotation of Mars, Phobos orbits the planet three times. Therefore Phobos, as seen from Mars, would appear to rise in the west and set in the east.

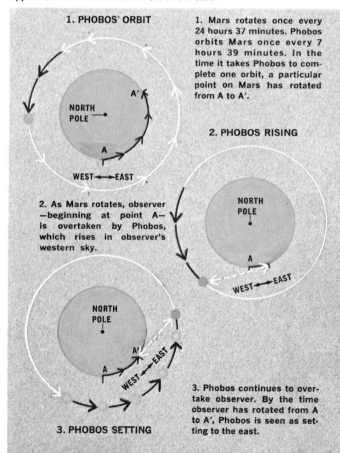

1. PHOBOS' ORBIT

1. Mars rotates once every 24 hours 37 minutes. Phobos orbits Mars once every 7 hours 39 minutes. In the time it takes Phobos to complete one orbit, a particular point on Mars has rotated from A to A'.

NORTH POLE

WEST ← → EAST

2. PHOBOS RISING

2. As Mars rotates, observer —beginning at point A— is overtaken by Phobos, which rises in observer's western sky.

NORTH POLE

WEST ← → EAST

NORTH POLE

WEST ← → EAST

3. PHOBOS SETTING

3. Phobos continues to overtake observer. By the time observer has rotated from A to A', Phobos is seen as setting to the east.

Knowing the small size of Phobos, you might not expect to be able to see it if you were on Mars. But it could be seen easily, because it is only 3,700 miles above the surface of the planet. At that distance Phobos would appear to be a disk, rather like our moon. It would even go through phases, or apparent changes of shape, like our moon. But because it is so close to Mars, Phobos travels very fast. It circles Mars once in less than 8 hours. The length of one day on Mars is a bit over 24 hours, so a visitor on Mars would see Phobos rise in the west and set in the east three times per day.

Deimos is smaller than Phobos, and it is more than 12,000 miles above the surface of Mars. It would appear to be no bigger than a bright star in the Martian sky. Deimos takes a little more than 30 hours to orbit Mars. Mars takes only a few hours less to make one turn on its axis, so Deimos would appear to move very slowly through the sky, taking more than 60 hours from its rising in the east to its setting in the west.

▶ THE ATMOSPHERE OF MARS

Long before space probes were developed, astronomers knew that Mars has an atmo-

Phobos, the larger satellite of Mars, photographed by Mariner 9 from a distance of about 3,500 miles. Part at upper right is not missing but is in deep shadow.

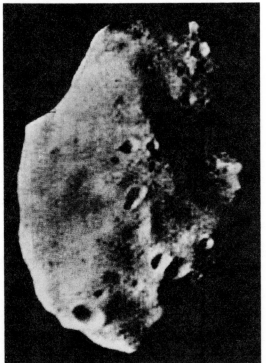

sphere. At times the surface of the planet became hazy, as dust storms swept over it. This meant that there must be winds on Mars. Winds are movements of air, so the dust storms were one proof of the existence of an atmosphere. Scientists believe Martian winds reach 100 miles an hour or more.

A great dust storm was raging when Mariner 9 began to send its first pictures to earth. The storm continued for weeks, so the pictures were very hazy. When the storm ended the pictures cleared up.

What kind of gases make up the atmosphere of Mars? On the earth an astronomer can learn a good deal about a distant planet and its atmosphere by using an instrument called a **spectroscope.** This instrument, attached to a telescope, breaks up the light from the sun, a planet, or a star into a rainbowlike pattern called a **spectrum.** Every substance has its own pattern, unlike the spectrum of any other substance. When an astronomer studies the spectrum of a planet, he can get a good idea of what substances are present there.

Before the Mariner flybys, scientists knew that there is carbon dioxide on Mars. They could not be sure whether there is any nitrogen. Instruments on the Mariners detected carbon dioxide, but no nitrogen and almost no oxygen were found. The Mariner cameras were able to photograph some thin clouds above a few places on Mars. Some of the clouds were made up of carbon dioxide and others contained water vapor.

The absence of nitrogen raised a question about life on Mars. All living things on the earth contain nitrogen. Any living things on Mars would therefore have to be chemically very different from those on earth.

The lack of nitrogen brought up a new mystery. Most of the nitrogen in the earth's atmosphere comes from within the earth, usually from volcanoes. The lack of nitrogen on Mars could mean that the volcanoes there are not active now. Or it could mean that any nitrogen present is taken out of the Martian atmosphere in some way.

▶ THE SURFACE OF MARS

Mars has always been a special challenge to man's curiosity because it is the only planet whose surface is visible from the earth. Seen through a telescope, large parts of Mars appear reddish-yellow. It was thought that these areas might be great sandy deserts. But the photographs made by the Mariners revealed a surface far more varied than scientists had expected. It is like the surface of the moon in many ways.

Craters of all sizes pit about half of the Martian surface. One of the biggest of these craters is about 1,200 miles in diameter, while the smallest that the Mariner 9 could photograph were about as big across as the length of a football field. Probably there are many smaller craters as well. Some craters are dug by meteorites that crash onto the surface of the planet. Materials thrown up by the impact fall back to form smaller craters. Other craters are formed by volcanic eruptions. Some craters have clear outlines, while older craters show a smoothing down caused by the wearing action of winds.

There are many level areas on the surface of Mars. Great mountains arise from some of these areas. One volcanic mountain, named Nix Olympica, is over 300 miles wide at its base and 16 miles high, with a crater more than 40 miles wide. This is a far bigger mountain than any on the earth. Three other great volcanoes are near Nix Olympica.

Are the Martian volcanoes erupting, or are they dead? Mariner 9 photographs show lava flows with sharp, unworn outlines, indicating that the flows are young in a geological sense. Clouds are seen over some volcanoes. Clouds often form when gases rise from an active volcano. But clouds can also form when water vapor in the atmosphere is swept up over high mountains of any kind.

Canyons longer, deeper, and wider than any on earth were photographed. One canyon is over 2,500 miles long. There are many **faults,** which are almost-straight cracks. There are also twisting features called **rilles,** like those seen on the moon by the Apollo 15 astronauts. Some of the Martian rilles may be ancient riverbeds. Other rilles may be lava channels.

The Polar Caps

Through a powerful telescope white areas can be seen at the north and south pole re-

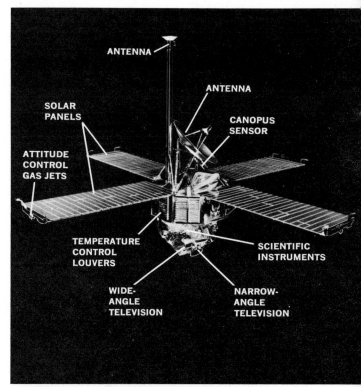

Mariner 6. Sensor uses light from the star Canopus as guide to point craft in the right direction.

Nix Olympica, a huge volcano on Mars. Picture was assembled from several Mariner 9 photographs.

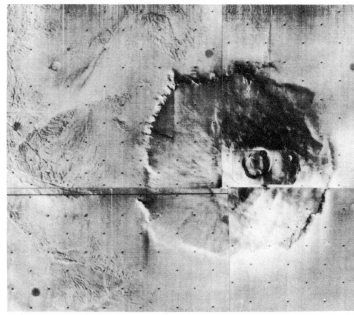

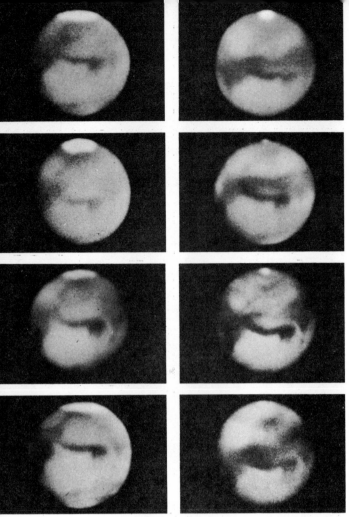

In spring (*left column*) polar caps are fairly large; the dark areas are greenish. During summer (*right column*) size of polar cap shrinks; areas around the tropics darken.

Rilles on Mars. Photograph by Mariner 9 from distance of about 1,100 miles. Rilles are about 1 mile wide.

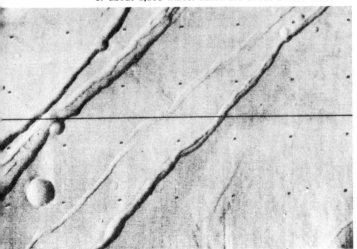

gions of Mars. The white areas, called polar caps, grow and shrink as the seasons change. For example, the south polar cap is at its largest as winter is drawing to an end in the southern hemisphere. At that time the cap may extend nearly halfway toward the equator of Mars. In spring the cap shrinks back toward the south pole.

What are the polar caps made of? The Mariner probes found very little water vapor in the atmosphere of Mars. So it seems unlikely that the caps are thick ice like that at the earth's poles. Some scientists think that the caps may be a very thin coating of ice covering the ground. However, the ice may not be frozen water, but frozen carbon dioxide, the substance we call dry ice. Other scientists believe the caps may be a mixture of frozen carbon dioxide and a small amount of frozen water.

Instruments on Mariner 9 measured ground temperatures on different parts of Mars. The polar temperature is about −190 degrees Fahrenheit, cold enough to freeze carbon dioxide gas. At the equator temperatures reach 60 degrees or more in the daytime but fall to −130 degrees at night.

The planets of the solar system are lighted and warmed by the sun. Temperatures on Mars are lower than on the earth because Mars is farther away from the sun. Even when Mars is nearest to the sun, it is about 35,000,000 miles farther away than earth is.

The Dark Areas

The dark areas on the surface of Mars are perhaps the most puzzling of the planet's features. They have been of great interest because they were thought to have a connection with living things on Mars. Some of these huge areas change their shape slowly, taking years to do so. Sometimes, after an area has changed so that it is hard to recognize, it changes back to its original form. One of the areas especially known for changes of shape is Solis Lacus, which means "lake of the sun." Astronomers once thought the dark areas might be seas and lakes. But the scientists of the Mariner project point out that it is very unlikely there ever was enough liquid water on Mars to form large bodies of water.

Changes in the color and brightness of

Scale model of the Viking probe. Part of the craft is designed to land on Mars, while the other part continues in orbit around the planet.

Mars could be caused by the seasonal growth and fading of lichens and mosses. You may have seen these plants growing on rocks or in moist shady places. Such plants can endure great extremes of heat and cold. It is exciting to think that living things, even if they are only simple plants, exist on another planet.

But recent observations of Mars have suggested new reasons for the changes. These reasons have nothing to do with living things. Thin clouds drift over Mars. They are composed of crystals of water ice and carbon dioxide ice. The movement of the clouds causes changes in color and brightness. Also, long-range and seasonal changes cause regular shifts in the wind pattern. Sands on the surface of the planet are blown regularly from place to place by the winds. The moving light- and dark-colored sands cause the changing pattern of color and brightness.

▶ IS THERE LIFE ON MARS?

The very small amounts of oxygen and water vapor in the atmosphere of Mars make it very unlikely that the planet could support living things of the kind we know on earth. But it is possible that some kind of life exists that does not depend on water and oxygen, but on some other substances.

Scientists of the United States and the Soviet Union are planning to launch probes that may shed more light on the possibility of life on Mars. The American probe, named the Viking, will be released from a spacecraft in orbit around the planet. After the probe lands, cameras on board will take photographs. Instruments will measure temperature, atmospheric pressure, and ultraviolet radiation. Special devices will analyze the soil for chemicals, including certain kinds of chemicals that are connected only with living things. These measurements and analyses may give the answer to the questions that man has been asking for so long, "Is there life on Mars?" and "Was there life on Mars in the past?"

HAROLD MASURSKY
Center of Astrogeology
U.S. Geological Survey

SCIENCE EXPERIMENTS

Day or night, whether you are awake or asleep, the cells of your body need a steady supply of oxygen. Each breath you take brings oxygen-containing air to your lungs. There the oxygen is absorbed into the blood. Then it is carried by the blood to cells throughout the body. When you are asleep or resting quietly, you need much less oxygen than when you work or exercise hard.

Scientists use a device called a spirometer for measuring the amounts of air breathed in and out of the lungs. You can make your own spirometer. With it you can roughly measure the amount of air in a single breath.

HOW MUCH AIR DO YOU BREATHE?

You will need a glass gallon jug, a ruler, a large basin, a rubber tube, and two wooden blocks.

1. Fill the jug with water. Cover its mouth with your hand. Place the jug upside-down on the blocks in the basin, which you have half filled with water.

2. Slip one end of a rubber tube into the neck of the jug.

3. As you sit quietly, exhale one full breath through the rubber tube. Measure the distance that the water in the jug goes down. The space above the water contains the air that you exhaled in that one quiet breath.

4. Refill the jug, and set it up as before. Now do some heavy exercise, such as deep knee bends, for several minutes.

5. While you are still puffing and panting, exhale one full breath through the tube. Measure again. Compare this measurement with the first one. How does exercise affect your breathing? If other people wish to try the experiment be sure to sterilize the end of the rubber tube: Dip it into boiling water, or wet it with alcohol and allow it to dry.

Is the moon larger at moonrise?

How heavy is that box? How big is the ball field? Questions like these are answered with numbers. Sometimes only an estimate is needed: "Oh, I guess the field is about 300 feet long and 200 feet wide." That answer might be good enough if you were just curious about the size of the field. But if you had to pay for building a wire fence all around the field, you wouldn't be satisfied with a rough guess. You would measure the field carefully, using an accurate steel measuring tape.

We use tapes and other measuring instruments because our senses are not usually accurate enough to tell us what we need to know. In fact, they can be badly fooled, as the following example shows.

Have you ever noticed how big the full moon seems to be as it comes up over the horizon, and how it seems to get smaller as it moves higher in the sky? The moon's size doesn't change. Neither does its distance from us change enough to account for the difference. We are fooled because we are used to seeing most things nearly on a level with ourselves. Through experience, we learn to judge horizontal distances fairly well. But vertical distances fool us, because we have less experience in judging them. That's why your senses fool you into thinking that the moon's size changes. But a simple measuring device that you can make will tell you the truth about the moon's size.

HOW TO MEASURE THE MOON

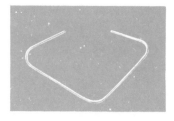

You will need a paper clip. Bend it open to the shape you see in the picture. Have it ready to use when the moon has just risen over the horizon. Hold the clip at arm's length, and look toward the moon. Squeeze the clip until the points seem about to pierce the outermost parts of the moon. Used in this way, your clip is a caliper. Calipers are instruments used to measure the diameter of objects such as pipes. After one hour, use your calipers to recheck the moon's size. Check again an hour or two after that. Since the size of the moon remains the same, the "change" must be in something we *think* happened.

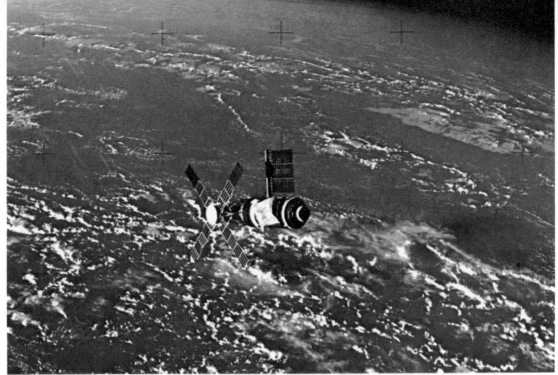

Skylab, the United States' first space laboratory, orbits the earth. The spacecraft sports a yellow "parasol" and its one remaining solar wing.

A WORKSHOP IN THE SKY

In recent years the world has watched in fascination as men have landed and walked on the moon. But now manned flights to the moon have ended, probably for a long while. In 1973 a new phase of space exploration began, when the United States launched Skylab, an earth-orbiting space station as big as a 10-story building.

During 1973, three teams of American astronauts lived and worked in Skylab as it circled the earth every 93 minutes. Although the three missions lacked the high drama of a moon landing, they presented their own challenges and provided some hair-raising moments. But the challenges were met, and the major work of the project was carried out. The teams of Skylab astronauts ended up by logging more time in space than had any previous space travelers. They also brought back a wealth of scientific photographs and information.

What were the main objectives of the Skylab missions? The primary purpose of Skylab was to test man's ability to remain in space for long periods. During space flights men do not experience the force of gravity as they do on earth: their bodies are weightless. The astronauts "swam" around in the Skylab spacecraft as if they were in a big fish tank. What would be the effects of such weightlessness during prolonged flights—a trip to Mars, for example? A trip to the moon and back takes less than 2 weeks, but a round trip to Mars would take almost a year. Much needs to be learned about the medical effects of prolonged weightlessness if men are ever to travel to Mars or other planets.

The second major objective of Skylab was to explore the practical and scientific value of having men orbit the earth. The Skylab astronauts performed a great range of experiments and studies as they circled 270 miles above the earth. They made studies of the sun and stars, studies that could not have been made from earth because of the interference of the atmosphere. The men also collected a vast amount of information about the earth's resources, ecology, and weather.

▶THE FIRST SKYLAB MISSION

Skylab, the space station itself, was launched from Cape Kennedy (now Cape Canaveral), Florida, on May 14. The first crew of astronauts was scheduled to be sent up the next day. But trouble forced a change of plan.

Barely a minute after Skylab had been launched, a thin aluminum shield tore off as the space station roared into the upper atmosphere. This mishap caused major problems. First, it disabled two great solar wings, which were to open after Skylab achieved orbit. The two wings were to convert sunlight into electricity, and without them Skylab was deprived of its major source of electrical power. The accident also caused the spacecraft to overheat. The aluminum shield was designed to reflect the sun's intense rays, and without its protection, temperatures in Skylab rose to over 125 degrees Fahrenheit. Some way had to be found to cool off Skylab or the entire mission would have to be abandoned.

The launching of the first crew was postponed several times, while scientists worked feverishly on a number of possible procedures to be tried by the astronauts. Finally, on May 25, the first Skylab crew, consisting of Captain Charles Conrad, Jr., Commander Joseph P. Kerwin, and Commander Paul J. Weitz, was launched from Cape Kennedy. Their mission was labeled Skylab II.

The crew, blasting off in a small spacecraft similar to the craft used in the Apollo moon program, was to dock with the orbiting space station. As the astronauts approached Skylab, they saw that one solar wing had been ripped away entirely, but that the other one was only jammed and unable to open. Standing in the hatch of the Apollo craft, Weitz used a long shepherd's crook to try to free the jammed wing. No luck. Then more troubles developed—the astronauts couldn't dock with Skylab. It took 10 tries before they overcame the difficulty and made a firm docking.

After a night's sleep in the Apollo capsule, the astronauts entered Skylab the next day. They found it as hot as expected and immediately set about solving the overheating problem. The solution was a space "parasol." Scientists on the ground had improvised a great parasol-like device of metal and fiber.

While the device was still closed, it was pushed out through a hatchway. It was then opened, much the way you would open an umbrella. The parasol worked. Temperatures began to fall inside Skylab, and within a few days the astronauts were able to move into their spacious Skylab quarters and get to work on their many experiments.

Later in the mission these ingenious space travelers were able to free Skylab's jammed solar wing. In a daring space walk, Conrad and Kerwin used shears to cut a metal strip that was preventing the solar wing from opening. Now there would be enough electrical power to complete their scheduled 28 days in space.

On June 22, Conrad, Weitz, and Kerwin returned to earth and splashed down in the Pacific Ocean. How would the men react to earth's gravity after 28 days in space? After shorter flights some American astronauts and Soviet cosmonauts had experienced great weakness and fatigue. It was therefore considered significant that the Skylab astronauts walked out of their capsule on their own after it had been lifted to the deck of the aircraft carrier *Ticonderoga*. However, the three men did suffer from some dizziness, nausea, fatigue, and low blood pressure after landing. Because of this, physicians recommended more exercise for the astronauts of the Skylab III and IV missions.

The opening of the space parasol.

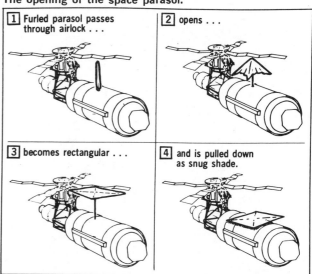

1 Furled parasol passes through airlock . . .

2 opens . . .

3 becomes rectangular . . .

4 and is pulled down as snug shade.

From Skylab the Chicago metropolitan area looks like this.

▶ THE SKYLAB III FLIGHT

The second team of astronauts to live and work in Skylab consisted of Captain Alan L. Bean, Major Jack R. Lousma, and Dr. Owen K. Garriott, a civilian scientist. They were launched from Cape Kennedy on July 28 and splashed down in the Pacific Ocean on September 25. The mission was highly successful, and the Skylab III crew spent a record-smashing 59 days in space.

During their 2 months in orbit, the astronauts circled the earth 859 times. They brought back about 77,000 photographs of the sun, taken through an array of telescopes mounted outside Skylab. Scientists hope these photos will greatly increase their understanding of the sun. The astronauts also brought back a great deal of data about the earth and its environment, including about 17,000 photographs.

Some of the Skylab III experiments were suggested by students. The National Aeronautics and Space Administration chose the experiments from among thousands of suggestions made by high school students across the country. One interesting experiment tested whether spiders could weave webs in the weightless environment of space. Two spiders, Anita and Arabella, were carried into space with the astronauts. For 2 days Anita and Arabella seemed confused by the absence of gravity. Then they adapted to their new surroundings and began to weave webs, just as they do on earth. The experiment seems to indicate that animals have a basic ability to adapt to weightlessness, a finding that seems to bode well for man's future in space.

On their doctors' orders the Skylab III astronauts did more exercise during their mission than the Skylab II astronauts had

Jack Lousma does a chore outside Skylab.

Arabella spinning a space web.

Alan Bean weighing himself on a special scale.

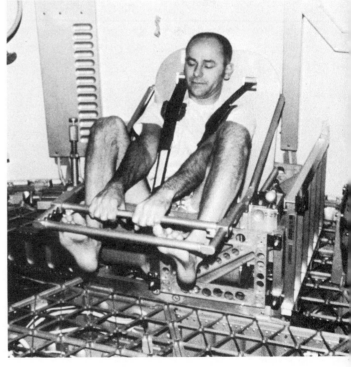

done. They spent hours working out on exercise machines to help their muscles and blood circulation. Apparently the increase in exercise worked. When the crew returned to earth, doctors pronounced them in better shape than the Skylab II crew had been.

▶THE SKYLAB IV MISSION

The third mission to Skylab, labeled Skylab IV, was scheduled to be the longest of all— a whopping 84 days. Lieutenant Colonel Gerald P. Carr, Lieutenant Colonel William R. Pogue, and Dr. Edward G. Gibson, a solar scientist, blasted off from Cape Canaveral on November 16, 1973. As 1974 began, they were more than halfway through their mission, with high hopes of completing the full 84 days. In addition to their other work, the astronauts were busy observing and photographing comet Kohoutek as it rounded the sun.

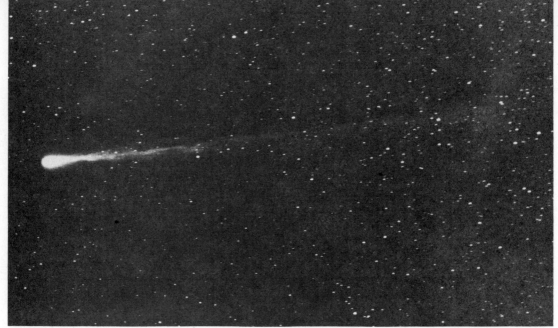

Photograph of comet Kohoutek, taken in mid-December, 1973.

COMET KOHOUTEK

"A plague is coming! It will kill us all."

"There will be a war."

"The King will die soon."

During the Middle Ages, terrified cries such as these went up when a comet appeared, its long tail streaming across the sky. At that time people thought that comets were omens of death and destruction. Even today a few superstitious people believe that comets are heralds of coming disaster.

But at the end of 1973 hundreds of millions of people throughout the world looked up, unafraid, for their first glimpse of comet Kohoutek. Early evidence indicated that the comet would be spectacular, but it did not live up to scientists' expectations.

Luboš Kohoutek, a Czech-born astronomer working in an observatory in Hamburg, West Germany, discovered the comet. Kohoutek was photographing asteroids—small, planet-like bodies that travel in orbits around the sun. He noticed a dim spot on two of the photographs taken in March, 1973.

The spot was the image of a comet that was moving between the orbits of Jupiter and Mars. The comet was then only about $\frac{1}{10,000}$ as bright as the faintest star visible to the unaided eye. Early calculations showed that it would be at its closest to the sun—about 13,000,000 miles from it—on December 29. At this very short distance from the sun, the comet could be expected to glow brightly. It seemed to offer a rare chance to see a comet even brighter than Halley's comet.

By mid-November a few early rising amateur astronomers had gotten a view of the comet with the help of binoculars or small telescopes. Its dimly glowing tail could be seen in the east about 3 hours before dawn. The comet brightened with each passing day, but it never came near reaching the brilliance that had been predicted for it.

The comet made its closest approach to the earth, a distance of about 75,000,000 miles, in early January, 1974. At that time it should have appeared at its brightest. Yet it was barely visible, even under good observing conditions, away from city lights. As a spectacle the comet was a failure, but scientists still felt that it would provide much new information about the solar system.

Comets are one of the greatest mysteries of the solar system. Scientists use instruments called spectrographs to study the light that comes to us from the sun, stars, and other objects in the heavens—including comets. In this way they can learn which chemical elements are present in these bodies. It looked as if especially good spectrographic studies could be made of comet Kohoutek.

Scientists looked forward to the flow of information they could expect from spectrographs and other instruments mounted in orbiting satellites, in Mariner 10, and in Skylab, the manned orbiting observatory. In addition, ground-based astronomers all over the world made observations of the comet.

Comets are members of the solar system. Most of them move around the sun in elliptical (oval-shaped) orbits, as planets do. But the ellipses of comets' orbits are extremely long and narrow. Encke's comet has the shortest known orbit. In 3½ years it swings around the sun, races out almost to the orbit of Jupiter, and returns, drawn by the sun's gravity. Halley's comet follows a similar, but much longer, course. It takes about 75 years to make its full trip, which carries it far beyond Neptune's orbit, over 3,000,000,000 (billion) miles from the sun. Some comets travel far out of the solar system. They take thousands of years to return. The observed path of comet Kohoutek shows that it is one of these far-ranging comets.

A planet like the earth is mainly solid material. But the only solid part of a comet is its rather small center, or nucleus. Scientists believe that the nucleus is mostly frozen water and frozen gases, with some dust mixed in. The nucleus of an average comet is perhaps 1 mile in diameter. Early studies of comet Kohoutek seemed to point to its having a huge nucleus, perhaps 10 to 15 miles in diameter.

The sun's warmth causes the outer layers of a comet's nucleus to evaporate, and thus frees the gases and dust. The gases spread out into a cloud called the coma, which forms the head of the comet. Within this cloudy head, the bright, starlike nucleus may be visible. As the comet comes nearer the sun, more frozen material evaporates. The vast cloud of gas and dust, up to 100,000 miles in diameter, runs into electrically charged particles from the sun (the solar wind). The particles cause the gases of the comet to glow. This glow, and the sunlight reflected by the dust, enable us to see the comet.

Sunlight and the solar wind press gently on the gas and dust in the coma. Some of the material is pushed into a long streamer, or tail, that may be up to 100,000,000 miles

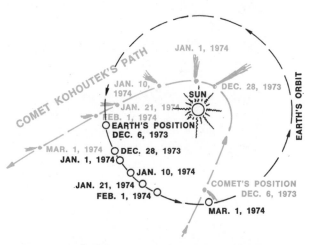

Orbits of earth (black line) and comet Kohoutek (blue line) are shown. Position of earth and of comet on a given date can be found by putting one finger on a black date, and another finger on same date in blue. Measuring between such pairs of dates, can you find when earth and the comet were closest?
Answer: January 10–21

long. The tail always points away from the sun. As the comet moves farther from the sun the tail shortens, then disappears, and the glowing coma grows dimmer.

Many astronomers think that comets originated at the time the solar system was formed. If so, comet Kohoutek may give us clues about the kinds of materials that made up the solar system at its beginning. On the earth the heat and pressure of earthquakes and volcanoes have changed these materials. It had been thought that the Apollo astronauts might find rocks of the original, unchanged type on the moon, but they did not. Now it is hoped that observations of comet Kohoutek, which has spent nearly all its time in the icy depths of space far from the solar system, may tell us how that system was formed.

COMET KOHOUTEK AT A GLANCE

Discovered: by Luboš Kohoutek on March 7, 1973.
Greatest observed speed: 250,000 miles per hour.
Closest approach to sun: 13,000,000 miles, on December 29, 1973.
Closest approach to earth: 75,000,000 miles, on January 15, 1974.
Diameter of nucleus: 10 to 15 miles.

San Francisco Bay area, before and after the energy crisis dimmed the lights.

THE ENERGY CRISIS

Recently you have been hearing a lot about the energy crisis. In fact, it is probably making quite a difference in your life. Because of the energy crisis, your house is very likely cooler this winter than it was last winter. The crisis may be preventing your family from using the car as much as they once did. And your parents probably remind you, even more than they used to, not to waste electricity—to turn out the lights when you leave a room or turn off the television set when you're not watching it. Can you think of other ways in which the energy crisis is affecting your life?

Energy is what we use to do work. Anything you do uses up energy. Some of the energy you use comes from your own body and is supplied by the food you eat. The energy crisis has nothing to do with this form of energy, with body energy. It has to do with the fuels we burn to produce heat. The heat from these fuels does many kinds of work for

us. The energy crisis has been brought about by a shortage of heat-producing fuels.

The major heat-producing fuels are oil, natural gas, and coal. Oil is made into many products, including home heating oil and gasoline for the family car. Natural gas makes the little blue flames that probably cook the food in your house. Or perhaps your mother cooks on an electric range; electricity is a major form of energy. Oil, natural gas, and coal do the very important work of running the big generators that furnish us with electricity. Together these three fuels account for about 95 percent of the energy produced today in the United States. Oil, natural gas, and coal provide more energy today than man has ever had at his service before.

▶ THE ARAB OIL BOYCOTT

Why, then, do we have an energy crisis? The immediate cause of the crisis is the cutoff of oil shipments from the Middle East—a cutoff that began late in 1973. The Arab lands of the Middle East have the world's largest reserves of petroleum, or crude oil. They are an important source of oil for many nations. In October, 1973, the Arabs fought a war with Israel. As a result of this war, the Arabs began to withhold oil from the United States and other nations friendly to Israel. An energy fuel, oil, became a political weapon.

Actually, the United States gets only a relatively small part of its oil from the Arab lands of the Middle East. Most oil products in the United States are refined from petroleum that comes from wells in the United States. The Arab boycott did produce some shortages, although energy might have been in short supply even without the boycott.

Oil is particularly important in the winter because it is used for heating. And, of course, oil is vital at any time because it is made into gasoline and other motor vehicle fuels. Thus, when the oil boycott began, the United States and other countries passed laws designed to conserve oil and prevent hardship.

▶ THE LARGER ENERGY PROBLEM

Although the Arab boycott is the immediate cause of the energy crisis, there have long been signs that an energy shortage was coming. In fact, you may have noticed shortages even before the Arab boycott began. Perhaps your family took a trip last summer. Your father drove into a gas station but could not buy gasoline, because, he was told, there was a gasoline shortage. Or perhaps, if you live in a big city, you remember brownouts. On very hot days almost all the air conditioners were turned on, and this created a huge demand for electrical energy. A brownout occurred because the electric company could not meet this huge demand and had to reduce the voltage—or force of the electricity —it produced. As a result, lamps dimmed very slightly and your television set may have taken a little longer than usual to warm up.

Brownouts and gasoline shortages reflect an energy problem that goes far beyond the Arab boycott. The problem is nothing less than how to prevent the world from running out of energy. People are demanding more and more energy all the time.

Because of this larger problem, some energy experts see the Arab boycott as having a good side. They believe that the boycott is focusing attention on the real energy crisis— the rapid increase in the consumption of energy all over the world. These experts hope that the boycott will help curb the ever-rising demand for energy. They hope it will convince people of the importance of conserving energy. Experts also hope that the energy crisis will speed up the vital effort to find new sources of energy.

▶ THE DEMAND FOR ENERGY

Why has the demand for energy been growing so fast? One good reason is that people like energy. Energy makes life easier. Energy fuels do work for us, so that we don't have to do the work ourselves.

Today the United States—the world's greatest consumer of energy—uses about 17 times as much power as it did 100 years ago. Of course the United States has a lot more people today than it did then—more than 5 times as many. But the average American of today uses far more energy than the American of a century ago.

Think of some of the ways energy has made life easier than it was 100 years ago. To keep your house warm or to provide cooking fuel then, someone in the family would probably have gone out to chop wood. Wood was the major source of energy in the United States a century ago. Today, few people have to chop wood. We heat our houses and cook by means of energy fuels delivered to our homes.

A hundred years ago people could not call on electricity to do work for them. There

Sign of the times.

were no electrical appliances to help with the housework—no washing machines or vacuum cleaners or electric mixers and blenders. There were no refrigerators to preserve food and no air conditioners to keep houses cool. Think how much easier life has become because of these electrical appliances. Today we have means of transportation and communication that were unheard-of a century ago—automobiles and airplanes, radio and television. We have vast industries that turn out all kinds of goods to make life easier for us. All this progress and change has required energy—enormous amounts of it.

Today the United States alone consumes about a third of all the energy consumed every year in the world. And the American demand for energy continues to rise. Experts estimate that if the demand for energy keeps expanding at its present rate, the United States will use twice as much energy in the year 2000 as it uses today. Part of this increase will be caused by a continuing increase in population. But energy use has been increasing even faster than population. From 1960 to 1970, for example, the number of cars in the United States increased twice as fast as the number of people. This greatly increased the consumption of the energy fuel gasoline.

▶ THE RICH AND THE POOR

As fast as energy consumption is increasing in the United States, it is increasing at an even faster rate for the world as a whole. Experts estimate that the world's yearly consumption of energy in the year 2000 will be three times what it is today. Furthermore, the world will consume about as much energy from 1970 to 2000 as it did from the time of man's first appearance on earth to 1970.

One of the sad facts about this vast increase in the world's energy consumption is that it will probably bring little benefit to most of the world's people. The greatest increase in energy consumption will occur in the countries that are already consuming the most power—that is, the richest ones. In poorer countries energy production has tended to rise only slightly faster than population.

How much energy would it take to bring these poor nations up to the current standard of living of the United States? Experts have estimated that if this were to be accomplished by the year 2000, world energy consumption would be 100 times what it is today!

▶ FOSSIL FUELS—THE MAIN SOURCE OF ENERGY

Oil, natural gas, and coal—the major sources of energy today—are called fossil fuels. The word "fossil" comes from a Latin word meaning "dug up." Fossil fuels are dug out of the earth.

In addition to being used as primary sources of energy, fossil fuels are converted into another very important source of energy—electricity. About 25 percent of the energy consumed in the United States is in the form of electricity. Some of this electrical energy is produced by waterpower—that is, by electrical power plants in which generators are turned by water running over a falls or through or around a dam. A small amount of electricity is produced in nuclear power plants, where energy is obtained by breaking apart atoms of matter. Most electricity is produced in plants using fossil fuels.

Today oil and natural gas account for about three fourths of the total energy produced in the United States. Oil comes from underground wells that are often near deposits of natural gas.

In addition to underground oil wells, the western United States has an abundance of oil shale. This is slate-like rock containing a thick fluid from which oil products can be refined. Western Canada has large deposits of tar sands, which are varieties of sandstone containing thick, tarry oil. Shale oil and sand oil are still expensive to extract, but may eventually supplement underground oil.

Coal, once the main source of energy in the United States, today accounts for about 20 percent of the energy consumed. Natural gas and oil have proved in many instances to be more convenient to use than coal. Another disadvantage of coal is that it tends to be a "dirty" fuel—it pollutes the air. There are ways to reduce air pollution from coal, but they are still fairly expensive.

Despite its disadvantages, coal does have one very great advantage today over natural gas and oil—there is a lot more of it. United

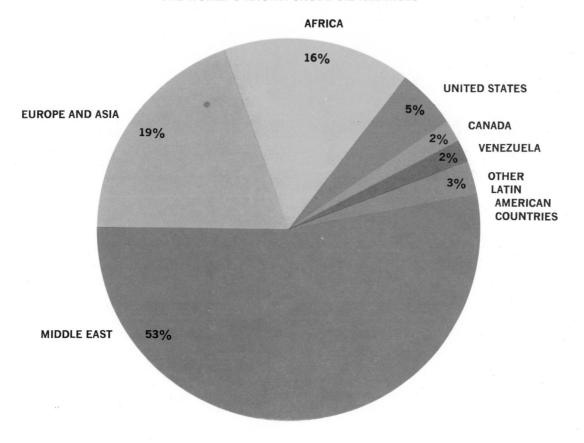

THE WORLD'S KNOWN CRUDE OIL RESERVES

AFRICA
16%

UNITED STATES
5%

CANADA
2%

VENEZUELA
2%

OTHER
LATIN
AMERICAN
COUNTRIES
3%

EUROPE AND ASIA
19%

MIDDLE EAST 53%

The Middle East has more than half the world's known petroleum reserves.

States and world reserves of coal far exceed those of oil and natural gas combined. Because it is so plentiful, coal may very well become the world's leading source of energy once again. It is hoped, too, that a cheap way will be found to convert coal to clean-burning liquid and gaseous forms.

▶ ENERGY AND THE ENVIRONMENT

Speaking of the effort needed to "clean up" coal leads us to a more general subject that you may have been wondering about. Many people are wondering what effect the energy crisis will have on the effort to reduce pollution and clean up the environment. Often the desire for energy comes into conflict with the desire to preserve the environment.

One recent example of such a conflict concerned whether an oil pipeline should be built across Alaska. This conflict dates from 1968, when large reserves of oil were discovered in

northern Alaska. Oil companies wanted to build an 800-mile pipeline to transport the oil to southern Alaska. From there, it could be shipped to the west coast of the United States. Conservationists opposed the pipeline. They were afraid that it might break, and spill oil over a vast area. They felt that the pipeline threatened the ecology of the region.

In 1973, Congress passed and President Nixon signed a bill authorizing the construction of the pipeline. Perhaps the Alaskan pipeline would have been built eventually anyway. But the energy crisis certainly speeded up this project, which still worries many conservationists.

Here we have an instance, then, of how the energy crisis may work against the environmental movement. On the other hand, there would seem to be important ways in which the crisis will tend to reduce pollution. One major effect of the energy crisis will be to promote

In this geothermal plant, underground steam runs electrical generators.

the conservation of energy. People will try to use less energy, and therefore will create less pollution. For example, they will tend to drive small cars, which use less gasoline and produce less pollution than current models.

▶ NEW ENERGY FOR THE FUTURE

Energy experts agree that sooner or later new forms of energy will have to replace fossil fuels. It has been estimated that by the year 2000 the world will probably have used up close to half of its fossil fuel reserves. New reserves may be discovered. But even so, new sources of energy will undoubtedly have to be developed.

One likely alternative to fossil fuels is nuclear energy. Today nuclear power plants are already producing electric power in the United States and other nations. Today's nuclear plants are fission plants, in which energy is obtained by breaking apart heavy atoms. This energy in turn is used to create steam, which operates electrical generators.

Although electricity is already being produced by fission, many scientists consider fission less promising than another process for obtaining nuclear energy. This process is called fusion, because it involves fusing, or combining, light atoms, such as atoms of

hydrogen. The fusion process is the source of energy in the hydrogen bomb. Controlling fusion reactions in nuclear power plants is far more difficult than building a bomb, and at the moment is in only the experimental stage. Despite this, fusion promises to have some big advantages over fission, the biggest being that it doesn't produce radioactive wastes.

In addition to nuclear energy, a number of other forms of energy have been suggested as alternatives to fossil fuels in the future. Some people think that the rays of the sun can be harnessed to provide energy for man on a large scale. This is known as solar energy. Geothermal energy, or energy from the heat inside the earth, is another possible source of power for the future. This would involve tapping the heat of underground rock formations to obtain energy.

All of this remains in the future, of course —and fairly far in the future at that. In the coming years and decades, fossil fuels will continue to furnish the great bulk of the world's energy. Actually, the energy crisis has only just begun. No one is very sure at this point how the world's energy problems will be resolved. One point does seem fairly certain, however: It will be a long time before any of us takes energy for granted again.

CANADA'S ENERGY CRISIS

Next to the United States, Canada consumes more energy per person than any other nation in the world. Canadians have lately been trying to use less energy. Canada finds itself in the strange position of being short of oil. What makes this position strange is the fact that Canada still produces more oil each year than it uses.

How can there be an oil shortage in a country that produces more oil than it needs? The main reason for this odd situation is that Canada exports most of its crude oil to the more heavily industrialized United States, its neighbor to the south. The greatest bulk of Canada's petroleum comes from wells in the western provinces. Most of this petroleum then goes by pipeline to the United States. No large oil pipeline now exists to carry oil to the portion of Canada that lies east of the Ottawa Valley. Eastern Canada imports its oil from abroad. About one third of Canada's imported oil comes from the Middle East.

Unlike the United States, Canada has not suffered a direct boycott of oil shipments from Arab lands. However, in addition to boycotting particular countries for political reasons, the Arabs have reduced their oil production in general. The entire world trade in oil has therefore been disrupted. This situation has contributed to Canada's energy problems.

Late in 1973 the Canadian Government announced a new program in response to the energy crisis. The new program is aimed at making Canada self-sufficient in oil and oil products. A large oil pipeline will be built to carry oil from the western provinces to the eastern provinces; this will end eastern Canada's reliance on imported oil. Canada's National Energy Board will oversee the construction of the pipeline. The new pipeline may mean that in the future western Canada's biggest oil customer will be eastern Canada—not the United States.

In addition to building the new pipeline, the Canadian Government will also set up a national petroleum corporation to explore for natural gas and oil and to conduct other research and development projects in the energy field. An important part of the work of this new government corporation will be to explore western Canada's extensive deposits of oil-bearing tar sands. The corporation will also try to develop new techniques for extracting oil cheaply from these tar sands.

MAP OF CANADA'S FOSSIL FUEL RESOURCES

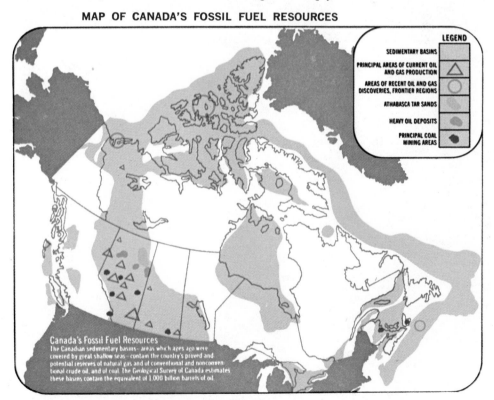

LEGEND

SEDIMENTARY BASINS

PRINCIPAL AREAS OF CURRENT OIL AND GAS PRODUCTION △

AREAS OF RECENT OIL AND GAS DISCOVERIES, FRONTIER REGIONS ○

ATHABASCA TAR SANDS

HEAVY OIL DEPOSITS

PRINCIPAL COAL MINING AREAS

Canada's Fossil Fuel Resources
The Canadian sedimentary basins - areas which ages ago were covered by great shallow seas - contain the country's proved and potential reserves of natural gas and of conventional and nonconventional crude oil, and of coal. The Geological Survey of Canada estimates these basins contain the equivalent of 1,000 billion barrels of oil.

ANIMAL WORLD

ANIMALS
IN THE NEWS

Jack McCarthy (*right*), a New York City policeman, gets a grateful pawshake from a German
shepherd he rescued from the ice on Indian Lake,
in Crotona Park. Lieut. Caesar Sanservero (*far
right*) rescues Mini-Beast, a very scared cat, from
a ledge as New York City firemen lead people
from a burning building to safety.

Francis, a white "whale in waiting," swam lazily about in her pool at the New
York Aquarium at Coney Island as officials kept a close watch over her. A
white whale's pregnancy lasts 14 months, but no one was sure how long
Francis had been pregnant and when her calf was due.

Weird-O is a chicken that grew and grew until it reached turkey size: 22 pounds. The bird is a hybrid developed by 17-year-old Grant Sullens of Calaveras County, California, shown with his oversized chicken. Weird-O resulted form cross-breeding White Leghorns with other breeds. Weird-O's offspring have been registered as the breed of "White Sullies."

There's an elephant (as well as a lion cub) in the parlor of the Hammond family in Gillette, New Jersey. She's the new family pet, 900-pound Mignon, seen with Jennifer Hammond.

A rare Spanish imperial eagle, taken by bird-nappers from a preserve in Spain, was found in Hayward, California, in October, 1973. Clifford Lindquist, a San Francisco bird specialist, planned to take the eagle back to Spain.

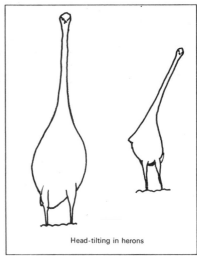

Head-tilting in herons

Why does the great blue heron tilt its neck as it stands in the water? Two Canadian zoologists decided that the heron tilts its neck to avoid the glare of the sun on the water. Thus the bird improves its chances of seeing and catching fish. John R. Krebs and Brian Partridge published their study in *Nature*, April, 1973.

Would you like to see an albino wallaby? There is one—the only one known in captivity in the United States—in the Cleveland Zoo.

Patty Cake likes to be independent (*left*), but she also needs her mother.

PATTY CAKE, THE BABY GORILLA

On September 3, 1973, Patty Cake celebrated her first birthday. Patty Cake is the famous baby gorilla born in New York City's Central Park Zoo. (It is very rare for gorillas to be born in captivity.)

From the instant Lulu, Patty Cake's mother, gave birth to the little gorilla, it was obvious to everyone that Lulu was unusually fond of her daughter. In fact, she would not put the little gorilla down. As spectators crowded around the cage, Lulu rolled over on her back, cuddled the baby on her massive chest, and kissed her.

Then one day Kongo, Patty Cake's huge father, was allowed into the cage. He, too, showed his love for Patty Cake. But Lulu and Kongo are gorillas, and gorillas often have little notion of their own great strength. On March 20, 1973, Patty Cake reached out through the bars to her father, who was in the next cage. Lulu jealously tried to grab Patty Cake away from Kongo, and Patty Cake's delicate arm was broken.

Patty Cake was rushed from her home in the Central Park Zoo to the animal hospital at the Bronx Zoo, where good medical care was provided day and night. Lulu was devastated. Kongo sat against the bars of his cage and sulked.

Young Patty Cake recovered quickly. But she still stayed on at the Bronx Zoo. Soon word got back to the Central Park Zoo that the little gorilla was being cuddled by human beings. In fact, "overcuddled" was the charge publicly made by the angry Central Park Zoo officials. They pointed out that when Patty Cake had been with her mother, she had been in a more natural environment. Lulu had been teaching Patty Cake all the things she had to learn in order to grow up to be a well-adjusted adult gorilla. Then the final blow fell on the Central Park Zoo. The Bronx Zoo wanted to keep Patty Cake.

The dispute between the two zoos raged on until the Parks Department called in a noted authority on primates. After much study, thought, and consultation, he decided that Patty Cake should be returned to Lulu at the Central Park Zoo.

The reunion of Patty Cake and Lulu was heartwarming. At first Patty Cake was puzzled when she saw her huge mother again. But Lulu let the little gorilla become accustomed to her once more. Finally, she grasped Patty Cake in her brawny arm and swung up to a platform in the cage with her and sat there. Soon Patty Cake began to relax. Patty Cake had come home.

In a traffic jam at Jungle Habitat, the animals always have the right-of-way.

DRIVE-THROUGH ZOOS

What do you do when a lion casually leaps onto the hood of your car? Or when an ostrich leans over, stares at you with his huge eyes, and pecks inquisitively at your windshield? Answer: you keep calm and enjoy the closest possible view of a wild animal.

The new, drive-through zoos, where the animals roam free and the people are caged in their cars, have long been known in Africa. There, people drive hundreds of miles to find the animals, which are thinly scattered over broad ranges. Visitors to African animal parks endure days of jolting travel over the veld, suffocating heat and humidity, and the presence of some creatures with which they want no contact—insects that bite, sting, or carry disease.

The new animal parks outside Africa, on the other hand, have large numbers of animals so concentrated that in a day you can see 1,500 of them, yet they have room to move around freely and do not look or act imprisoned, as animals often do in traditional zoos with small cages and heavy iron bars.

Typical of the new drive-through parks is Jungle Habitat in West Milford, New Jersey. This 1,000-acre animal preserve in the rolling Ramapo hills has about 1,500 wild birds and other animals in a setting of natural trees and shrubs. Near the park is the Nairobi Airport, a small, private airport that handles many exotic passengers, such as peacocks and zebras. Zebras become nervous and upset when confined for a long trip, so while other animals from the animal park board trucks for the trip south to escape the cold winter, the zebras fly down in style.

▶ PEACEFUL COEXISTENCE

If all the animals were loose together within one surrounding wall or moat, the predators would soon kill off the nonpredatory, grass-eating animals. And some animals would get into other kinds of trouble. To prevent this, Jungle Habitat has special compounds, one for each of five groups of animals. Outside these compounds the other animals wander at will. The special com-

Elephants at Kings Dominion are not in the least bothered by cars.

pounds are called Tigers' Lair, Bear Country, Simba Station (for lions), Baboon Hill, and Elephant Camp.

Elephants and baboons are not predators, but are confined for other reasons. Elephants strip the bark from trees and kill them, so elephant movement must be restricted. Baboons are both mischievous and quite clever, which is why they are segregated. For example, it was found that a high fence would not keep the baboons in, so the fence was electrified to give any escaping baboon a slight shock and thus check his movements. The baboons soon realized that an electrical hum went along with the shock. Not hearing any hum at the gate to their compound, they assumed it was not going to shock them— and they were right. The next morning, after having climbed the gate to their compound, they were scattered all over the area.

Although baboons live on fruit, berries, insects, and leaves, a large one will occasionally kill a small antelope for food. Baboons are also very curious and investigative, so car windows are never opened on Baboon Hill.

The five compounds are scattered along two trails, Lion Safari and Tiger Safari. These are roadways, paved with asphalt and some-

times three lanes wide, but the animals still block traffic. Outside the predator and "problem animal" compounds are the peaceful animals, including rhinoceros, camels, bison, water buffalo, deer of many kinds, and ostriches. They wander along the roads, knowing they have the right-of-way, and often a park ranger has to shoo them away so traffic does not stop entirely. There was a camel that loved to stand in the road and lick the windows of cars. It would not move off until it saw the rangers' zebra-striped Jeep approaching. As soon as the rangers left, the camel would return. The camel finally had to be exiled, because 4,000 cars a day were going through the park.

Animals that might never have met in the wild have become fast friends at Jungle Habitat. There is an ostrich that always follows a Bactrian camel. And there are a sable antelope and a zebu that have become inseparable.

▶ JUNGLE JUNCTION

All of the new animal parks have sections where you may leave your vehicle and walk. Here you may look at newborn, infant, and "teenage" animals, and enjoy shows, rides,

103

Fences surround compounds at Jungle Habitat.

restaurants, and shops that carry everything from plastic souvenirs to true African art. At Jungle Habitat this area is called Jungle Junction. Scattered in a woodsy setting are a variety of attractions that can keep a family interested and busy for 2 or 3 hours. The animal nursery usually has 20 to 40 very young animals—the only animals in the park that are kept in small cages. In a semicircle of glass-fronted cells may be seen lion cubs and the young of raccoons, black panthers, and a dozen other exotic species—including a 60-

A clever dolphin performs at Jungle Junction.

pound baby python. Inside the nursery are incubators and other aids for the newborn. The nursery attendant can usually be seen holding a tiny tiger or baboon in her arms while she feeds it from a bottle. The youngest animals are fed five times each day.

In the Affection Section, young people (and many of their elders) can pet and feed young goats, llamas, deer, and even a young giraffe—and several huge Galápagos tortoises.

The *boma* is a special compound for young lions not mature enough to join the 40 adults in the big Simba Station. Until they form a pride of their own, you may look down from a walkway at the cubs with their mothers. There are several of these habitats, for various kinds of young animals, including caribou, moose, emu, and East African crowned cranes.

Rides may be taken on elephants and camels, and for the youngest set there are rides in tiny cars on tracks, with imitation alligators and tigers leaping from the bush along the way.

There is also a tent with a giant air-cushion floor, where children may jump and jump until tired.

Shows at Jungle Junction include a lively and clever performance by dolphins; African dancing led by a genuine witch doctor who eats fire to prove his magic power; and Looney Tunes shows in which real people impersonate cartoon characters such as Bugs Bunny, Porky Pig, and Speedy Gonzales.

At the entrance to Jungle Junction is a little zoo composed of the pets of visitors. Most are dogs, and each is tied to his own tree in the shady woods and is given water by rangerettes, as the young women who run the area are called.

▶MONORAIL PARKS

Most of the animal parks that are springing up across North America and in other parts of the world are like Jungle Habitat in that you drive through them in an automobile. (If you arrive at the park by motorcycle, bicycle, or convertible, or on foot, you must go through in a park bus or rented car.) But some of the new parks have monorail trains in which they transport visitors over or past the animals.

Spectators in monorail cars watch a herd of African hartebeests.

The San Diego Zoo has long been one of the best modern zoological parks in the United States. It is so large that the only way to see most of it in a reasonable time is to take a guided bus tour through it. This forward-looking municipal zoo has established an 1,800-acre preserve, the San Pasquale Wild Animal Park. Visitors there take a 1-hour trip on an electric monorail. Authorities at San Pasquale say that the animals act more naturally because their habitat is not disturbed by cars; but they admit that seldom is there eye-to-eye confrontation with a wild animal, as often happens in an automobile drive-through park.

At Busch Gardens, a huge entertainment complex in Tampa, Florida, one of the most interesting sections is the 186-acre Wild Animal Kingdom. A new sky ride, 1 mile long, was built in 1972 to give visitors an overhead view of the hundreds of wild animals.

▶ LION COUNTRY SAFARIS

The idea of moving an African wild-animal preserve to North America, along with the concept of freeing the animals while caging the humans, was developed in a 640-acre stretch of the Florida Everglades in 1967, at a spot 17 miles west of West Palm Beach. It was called Lion Country Safari.

In 1970 a Lion Country Safari opened on 485 acres of the Irvine Ranch, near Disneyland, in California. Two more went into operation in 1972—one in the Dallas–Fort Worth area of Texas, and another south of Atlanta, Georgia. A Lion Country Safari opened on 120 acres north of Richmond, Virginia, early in 1974, as the first part of the huge Kings Dominion family leisure center. Another opened as part of another great entertainment complex, Kings Island, near Cincinnati, Ohio. One more was under construction near St. Louis, Missouri.

A lion and a lioness pose for a family portrait at Lion Country Safari.

Warner Brothers, the operator of Jungle Habitat, is developing a Florida park and has announced that it will open 10 drive-through parks in the next several years. It is apparent that before long there will be some kind of large wild-animal park near most major cities in North America and Europe, and Asia. Africa already has vast animal preserves.

▶ **THE ANIMALS LOVE IT**

When the new type of wild-animal park first opened, many curators of traditional zoos said that wild-animal parks were a step backward. Commercial zookeepers, they speculated, would not take proper care of the animals. There would be little or no breeding of the animals, and animals on the list of endangered species would be further endangered by being taken to the parks.

However, the current figures seem to prove otherwise. There are about 180 noncommercial zoos in the United States. So far there are only about a dozen large commercial animal parks in operation. But it looks as if the commercial parks can beat the zoos at reproduction. The reason is the huge commercial success of the commercial parks. When millions of people spend millions of dollars to visit the animals, the operators can afford to have a large number of each species in the park, and to take excellent care of them.

Charles E. Clift, zoological director of Jungle Habitat, was formerly a zoo curator. When his colleagues at noncommercial zoos ask him why he has gone to work for a commercial animal park, he replies, "Because *only* the commercial zoos can do what now *must* be done—give the animals plenty of room, get them in large numbers, and give them special 'breeding diets' so they'll be prolific. We have animals breeding now that never before bred in captivity—the difference is mainly in the expensive diet that we can afford to feed them. Freedom such as we give the animals gives them different personalities. There's no pacing back and forth, or other 'cage behavior.' There is random grouping of animals, which is not permitted in zoos, and this makes for more prolific breeding and stronger offspring. We've had mountain sheep, elk, wapiti, and lions born here. The Siberian tiger is on the endangered-species list, and we've had four of them born here."

At Lion Country Safari parks, zoologists are participating in an international effort to save the Asiatic lion, of which only about 150 individuals remain alive, nearly all in a wildlife sanctuary in India. At all the Lion Country Safaris, zoologists report "population explosions" among many species, including those on the endangered list. One specialist wrote: "Lion Country Safari is the greatest thing to happen to endangered species of African wildlife since Noah's Ark."

▶ SAFETY

Showing wild animals in animated cartoons as cute, lovable, and harmless is quite charming in the movie theater, but it has had an unfortunate influence as well. It has helped people to forget that it is natural for predatory animals to be dangerous—from a human's point of view—at times. At a boat basin in the Okefenokee Swamp near Waycross, Georgia, the local alligators had to be driven away because visitors on the way home from Disney World had no sense of the danger they presented.

In one of the wild-animal parks a war hero wanted to have his picture taken with his arm around a lion's neck. When a friend with a camera was ready, the veteran drove close to a lion and reached his arm over the lion's back. The lion, apparently feeling threatened, grasped the man's shoulder in his mouth and started pulling him out of the car. Friends in the car held the man by his legs, tugging against the lion's strength. Before the lion could be stopped, he had injured the man severely.

In all the drive-through parks there are strict rules that car windows must not be opened when driving among the animals. The temptation is often strong to open the window in order to take pictures, but the temptation must be resisted. Instead, clean the car windows thoroughly before going to the park. When you take a picture through the glass,

This is the youngest inhabitant of Bear Country.

These antelope are at peace in Busch Gardens.

It seems just like home to this splendid cheetah as he perches on a palm tree.

hold the camera close to the glass to avoid reflections. Do not let the camera touch any part of the car if the motor is running, or the vibration will blur the picture. The animal should be close for good pictures—preferably within 5 to 20 feet.

Rangers in the predator compounds generally have two kinds of guns—one loaded with tranquilizers and the other with bullets—so that they only kill an animal when it is necessary to save a human.

▶ APPEAL OF THE JUNGLE ANIMAL PARKS

The parks are generally far enough from urban areas to be clear of smog and other kinds of pollution. They are generally in natural woods or other settings enjoyed by man and animals alike. They can be as educational as the visitor wishes, since he can spend from dawn to dusk observing the animals, or a single animal if he likes. Zoologists on the staffs of the parks are generally eager to talk with anyone who has more than a passing interest in the animals.

The recreational aspect includes both seeing the animals and visiting the shows and rides near the commercial center of the park. In most of the parks, the shows and rides are included with the price of general admission, so that nothing costs extra except food, drink, and souvenirs or art objects.

The greatest appeal, however, is in the face-to-face confrontation with the animals themselves. It is strange and wonderful, and still a new sensation for most people, to be so close to a really wild animal and not be in danger.

Keepers of traditional zoos have complained that the animals do not act naturally in a drive-through park, because automobiles are not part of their natural habitat. That is true, of course, but most of the animals seem to get used to cars fairly readily, and pay little attention to them.

What gives the visitor a special thrill is meeting an animal that takes an interest in him or his car—the camel that slobbers on the windshield, the bear that chews on the door handle, the rhinoceros that stand in the road and stares at a car as if trying to figure it out. This is almost touching minds, almost understanding.

For humans are animals, too, and humans delight in seeing actions or facial expressions in animals that reflect those of people. For example, the camel's supercilious expression, and his chewing from side to side delight us because they look so much like the habits of some people we know. When a grizzly bear takes a full-arm swipe at another bear, it reminds us of a husky football player doing the same thing. The huge elephant who nods his head wisely from side to side is bound to make us think of someone we know. And his trunk, cleverly searching for peanuts, seems directed by an almost human intelligence. Spending a day with these many kinds of animals can help us to see ourselves as we are.

ROBERT SCOTT MILNE
Society of American Travel Writers

Stately giraffes find their Florida habitat much like their native Africa.

LOOKING OUT FOR SPRING

The groundhog is a small, furry animal with stumpy legs, tiny ears, and a squirrel-like face. In fact, the groundhog (or woodchuck) belongs to the same animal family as the squirrel and the chipmunk. Groundhogs are found in Canada and the United States. According to a long-held American tradition, the groundhog unofficially announces the arrival of spring. It is believed that on February 2, which is known as Groundhog Day, the animal awakens from his winter sleep and comes out of his underground den. If the day is sunny and the groundhog sees his shadow, he becomes frightened and pops back into his den. This is taken as a sign that 6 more weeks of winter are still to come. But if it is a cloudy day, the groundhog will not see his shadow and will remain outdoors—an indication that spring is on its way. But that is just one of the many tales about the origin of Groundhog Day. Here is an Indian legend about how the groundhog became the herald of spring.

There was a time, long ago, when the buffalo wandered in great numbers, and the Indians were the only people living in the land. At that time there were many large bears. They roamed freely through the woods during the warm months, when the forests were green and lush and there was plenty to eat. But then came the cold season. The leaves fell from the trees, the grass turned brown, and the fruit and berries were gone. Then the bears grew lean and hungry. They shivered in the cold and huddled together in their caves for warmth.

It happened that the Great Spirit saw all of this and He took pity on the bears. He decided to tell them how they could survive the bleak winter months.

"Listen to me," the Great Spirit said. "If you want to live through the winter months, you must do as I say. Eat as much as you can during the warm season until you grow very fat. When winter comes and snow blankets the ground, you will go into a deep sleep. This sleep will last until the snow melts and the forests are green again."

The bears listened attentively. But when the Great Spirit had finished speaking, one of them asked: "But how will we get food?"

The Great Spirit replied, "If you eat as much as you can, you will be able to store enough fat to keep you alive until the warm season returns."

So the bears followed the good advice of the Great Spirit. They went out into the forests and feasted day in and day out through the summer and the autumn. They ate everything in sight. They

The bears frolicked in the forest and ate everything in sight.

nibbled at the grass, gobbled up berries and roots, and devoured the corn in the fields. Some went down to the streams and rivers and used their giant paws to scoop up fish, which they downed with a single gulp. Sad to say, they even ate some of the smaller animals in the woods.

By the time the leaves began to fall and the wind began to blow more fiercely, the bears were very fat indeed. In fact, they were so gorged with food that some of them could barely walk. They lumbered about at a slow gait, growling at one another and getting more and more surly and drowsy. They looked about for cozy, dry caves in which to spend the long winter months when they would be fast asleep.

But just when they were getting ready to settle down, one bear

The groundhog looked around and knew that spring had come.

popped up with a question. "Who is going to tell us when it is time to come out again?" he asked.

The bears puzzled about that one for some time. If they woke up too early they would still have cold weather to face. They would be so weak from their long fast that other animals might try to attack them. Finally they came up with a solution. They would assign one bear the task of being their lookout. He would be the first to go out to see if warm weather had arrived.

The bear chosen was the biggest and fattest of them all. He wasn't very happy about the job, but he accepted it. Years went by, and each spring it was the same. The big, fat lookout bear would awake one morning, yawn, stretch out his paws, and then stagger out to sniff the air and see if it was spring. Sometimes he would get up too early, and a chill winter wind would send him scurrying back to the cozy warmth of his cave.

After a while the big bear really hated his job. But there seemed to be no way to get out of it. So each year he went through the same ritual. He rubbed the sleep from his eyes and stumbled out into the cold light of day to see if spring had arrived. Then, one morning in the month we call February, something happened to change all that.

That morning the big bear was half asleep, when suddenly he felt a strange sensation. It felt as if something were curling up to his great hulk of a body. Was he dreaming? The big bear opened one eye slowly. And what did he see? Why, it was a furry little groundhog nestling up to him.

Being very hungry, the bear thought immediately: "Something to eat!" With a quick swipe of his paw, he grabbed the poor, frightened groundhog and brought it up to his large, sharp-toothed mouth. But just as he was about to pop the groundhog down his gullet, the little animal spoke up in a meek voice.

"Oh, please don't eat me," the groundhog pleaded. "I only came in here to escape the cold. And besides, there's not enough of me to fill that great stomach of yours. If you spare me I will do any favor you ask."

The bear roared with laughter. Then he began to think about what the groundhog had said. In a flash it came to him: Why not have the groundhog go out and do his job for him? Let the groundhog find out if spring had come.

"If you go out and see about the weather," the big bear said with a growl, "then I won't make a meal of you. After all, you really spoke the truth. You're too scrawny to satisfy my appetite."

The groundhog was only too happy to accept this offer. It was certainly better than ending up in the big bear's belly. So out he went, sniffing around and testing the air. A few minutes later he came back. "I took a good look around," he told the bear, "and sure enough, spring is on its way. Please, Bear, may I go now?"

"Not so fast," roared the bear, grabbing the groundhog by the neck. The old bear knew a good thing when he saw it. "I just thought of another job for you. I feel like taking one last little nap. So while I doze off, you go around to all the caves and wake up my fellow bears. And mind you, don't miss a single one or you'll end up being my first breakfast."

Naturally the trembling groundhog obeyed. He went from cave to cave, poking the bears, and telling them that spring had come. Some of them just snarled and tried to go back to sleep. Gradually, though, the little groundhog was able to wake them all up.

But that's not the end of our story. When the bears were fully awake, they glanced around for their lookout bear. "Where is he?" they asked. The groundhog told them what had happened. All the bears were angry with their lazy companion. They rousted him out of his den and chased him away in disgrace. In his place, the groundhog was appointed to be the new lookout for spring. From that time on, he and all his children and grandchildren were to be the ones to announce that warm weather had arrived.

And that, according to our Indian legend, is how the groundhog became the one to tell us that spring is on its way.

Wide-eyed children feel and examine the objects in the Touch and See Room.

One youngster dons a wolf pelt and meets another wolf head on.

THE TOUCH AND SEE ROOM

A group of wide-eyed children enter a room. One young girl is fascinated by a stuffed squirrel. She pets and hugs the furry mammal. The huge teeth of a rhinoceros are examined by a boy's small hands. Another child puts on an animal skin and tries to scare his friends. All this and more happens in the Touch and See Room at the James Ford Bell Museum of Natural History in Minneapolis, Minnesota.

This unusual and exciting room contains animal exhibits that are meant to be touched, explored, and enjoyed. The room itself, 100 feet long and 40 feet wide, is fully carpeted, and is illuminated by 120 lights. Scattered about the room are tables displaying animal bones, horns, and antlers. They come from many different animals—including elephants, horses, cows, lions, dogs, sheep, turkeys, deer, and rhinoceros. Animal skins and a huge polar bear rug lie on the floor. A youngster can peer down this polar bear's throat without being afraid of the large white fangs.

The walls are filled with different animal heads, all mounted low enough for children to touch. On one of the walls hangs a stuffed Cape buffalo head from Africa. If a child thinks it looks lonely so far from home, he might go over and stroke it, being careful of the sharp horns. Perhaps the gentle-looking deer is more to another's liking, and she might want to feel its velvety nose.

One corner of the room has been made into a "shadow area." The visitor is encouraged to pick out a pair of antlers or horns, place them on his or her head, and walk over to this area. As he stands in front of a light, his shadow falls on the wall. Suddenly he seems to have been transformed into an elk, a deer, or a bison.

Drawers filled with "feelies" provide still more surprises. Children reach inside a drawer without looking. They feel an object and try to guess what they are holding. Perhaps it will be a bone, a feather, or a small stuffed animal.

The museum officials feel that an effective way for a young person to become more familiar with the world of animals is by active participation. "Do Not Touch" and "Keep Off" signs are taboo in the Touch and See Room. Children are encouraged to touch, stroke, pick up, put on, or hug the specimens. Examining an animal's fur or comparing the size and weight of bones of different animals helps children to learn through discovering things for themselves. Youngsters may even put on an animal pelt and make believe that they are that animal.

The museum guides, who know a lot about the displays, encourage the young people to discover new things by themselves. For instance, one might see a pair of antlers lying on a table. There is no label to tell from what animal the antlers came. But by looking around the room, a curious youngster will find a mounted, stuffed head with the same antlers. By comparing the antlers, the child will be able to identify the owner.

The horns are sharp and the nose is soft.

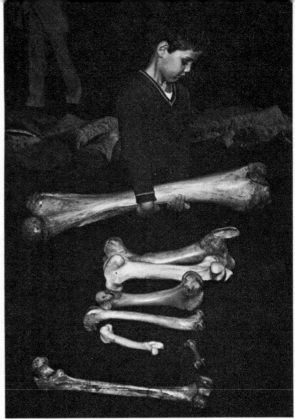

Some leg bones are longer than others.

"My, what big teeth you have!"

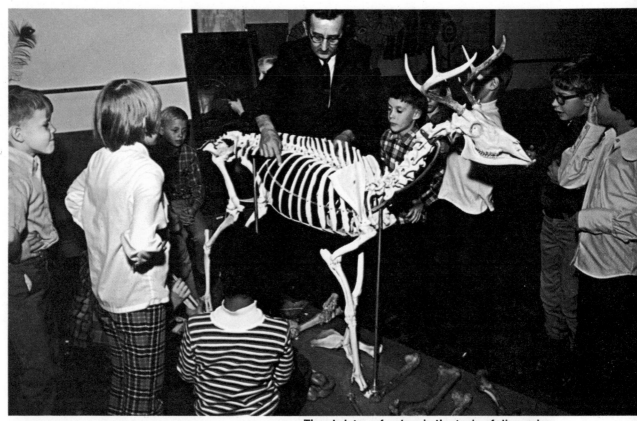

The skeleton of a deer is the topic of discussion.

Shadow, shadow on the wall . . .

It's fun to be a deer for a while.

Once you are adopted by a skunk, every inch of your house is his home.

RAISING A SKUNK

He flares his tail and stamps his feet: Thump! Thump! Thump! He wants to play. You slap the floor three times with your hand. The game is on.

He skitters under the bed. You bend down to look for him. Suddenly, there he is—behind you on the far side. Fooled you! Under the bed he goes again. You dangle a string over the edge. He rushes out, seizes it in his teeth, and braces for a tug-of-war. You let go. He tumbles over, and drops the string. You pick it up and drag it across the floor. He scurries wildly after it.

After 15 or 20 minutes of this he has usually had enough. He is ready to be picked up. Soon, snuggled in your lap, he will go contentedly to sleep. A round of play, a short nap, and when he wakes up, a tasty supper. Not a bad life for a little skunk.

Affectionate, playful—it is easy to see why the skunk is becoming more and more popular as a pet. He can also be strikingly beautiful, with his gleaming black fur and snowy stripes. Wherever you take him, he is an attraction. And if he is used to gentle handling from strangers, anyone can hold him and he will not mind being petted.

Sociability is not what you might expect from skunks if you have known them in the wild. Generally speaking, the wild skunk is a hermit even among his own kind. You almost never see a wild skunk with another skunk, except a baby with his mother and littermates and later a pair of adults during the mating season. The rest of the time, each skunk would rather go his own way, alone.

Not many animals challenge his right-of-way. When a small skunk comes nosing along, hunting for insects, even the mighty grizzly bear retreats. Only the great horned owl, striking noiselessly from above, sometimes dares to prey on skunks.

The skunk's well-known defense is an eye-stinging, evil-smelling fluid that he can shoot for 10 feet or more from two scent glands hidden under his tail. Some skunks are quicker on the trigger than others. (Wild or tame, animals have individual personalities.) But as a rule, a skunk never uses his unique weapon unless absolutely necessary. He gives fair warning by stamping his front feet and fanning his tail into an angry plume. Usually, a would-be attacker takes the hint and backs off. So does the skunk. He doesn't want trouble. He just wants to be left alone.

The skunk is not born with this love of solitude. Just as natural is his great capacity for affection. The striped skunk, which is the type most often sold as pet, is friendly and inquisitive when he is a baby. (The small spotted skunk of the South and West does not seem to have this quality to the same degree.) It is only as he grows older that he learns from his mother and from experience to be independent and cautious. But if you get him in June, when he is 5 or 6 weeks old, he will not have learned to be a lone skunk. At this age, it is just as easy for him to become an affectionate, outgoing pet.

This is the age, too, for having a veterinarian remove the scent glands. (A pet skunk will probably never try to use them, but you don't want to run any risk.) Generally the operation is performed before the skunk is sold.

Your skunk should be bought from a good breeder or pet shop. In most states, it is illegal to capture a wild skunk because of rabies, a terrible disease fatal to humans and many other animals. Rabies is caught from the bite of an animal that has the disease; skunks, not used to running from danger, are especially liable to get bitten.

Skunks that have been raised by a breeder are safe, of course. In some states, however, the law does not recognize this fact. It is important to check local and state laws before buying a skunk. Then have your new pet vaccinated for rabies and get a certificate to prove it.

He should also be inoculated for both dog and cat distemper. But otherwise, he will probably not need many trips to the veterinarian. Most house skunks enjoy rugged good health and may live to be from 8 to 10 years old.

Training a pet skunk often means finding a middle ground between the ways of the wild and the ways of domesticity. The skunk is said to be the most easily tamed of American wild animals. He has no instinctive fear of humans, and he is a very mild-tempered and peaceful animal indeed.

Still, a skunk *is* a wild animal. Dogs and cats have been bred for centuries to produce

A skunk has the soul of a master detective.

A pet skunk, no matter how well fed, searches instinctively for food.

the qualities that help them to get along in human society. Not so the skunk. He can be trained, but only if you respect his own nature.

Certainly no skunk, or any wild pet, should ever be physically struck, not even lightly. Instinctively he associates being struck with hostility and danger. He feels that he must defend himself. No longer having his scent glands, he may run and hide—or he may bite. And he will hold a grudge for a long time, perhaps for life.

Mischief (and a skunk is capable of plenty) can best be handled by making loud noises. A sharp "No!" or a whack on the floor with a rolled-up newspaper will make it plain to him that you don't like what he is doing.

Where food is concerned, you will have to take a firm stand. In the wild, food is a skunk's main interest in life. He spends most of his waking hours in a constant search for

it. (Though his eyesight is poor, his hearing and sense of smell are keen.) His passion for grubs, caterpillars, and beetles makes him the farmer's friend. In addition, he likes nuts and berries and sometimes a mouse. And if a garbage can has been left open—well, why not?

Food is no less important to a pet skunk. He will gobble down his bowl of cat food and table scraps, mixed with vitamins, and still beg for an extra tidbit. But life indoors doesn't require huge quantities of food. He can easily become too fat, especially in the fall when instinct tells him to store up for the winter. At such times, instinct simply has to be denied for his own good—no matter how much he protests.

Luckily, many human rules come naturally to a skunk. House-training him to use newspaper or a cat pan is easy. In the woods, it is natural for a skunk to have his special place for use as a bathroom. It is just as

A little affection is the ideal conclusion to a busy day in a skunk's life.

natural in the house. Special places for eating and sleeping are likewise easy for a skunk to accept.

A skunk is a clean, tidy animal. He likes his world in order, with everything in its place. The only problem is to make sure that humans and skunk agree very early on what the proper places should be.

He may choose a corner of the living room as his bathroom, for instance, or want to use a wastebasket as a den. It is better to sidestep such problems. Shut him out of the living room for a few weeks. Set the wastebasket on a carton. Then provide other places for him to use. After a while, he will start to use them.

In some ways, of course, your skunk will live according to his instincts, almost as if he were in the woods. For example, even a skunk living indoors will follow the seasons. In fall he will be hungry all the time. In winter he will want to sleep, although skunks don't have a true hibernation. He will always wake up for mealtime! In spring he will be restless and active. And in summer he will feel playful and mischievous.

On the other hand, a skunk will make friends quickly with the cats and dogs in the house, something he would never do in the wild. He won't mind an occasional bath or a ride in the car. He can be taught to walk on a leash. And even though he is nocturnal by nature, he can be trained to stay awake in the daytime and to sleep at night.

Train your skunk with gentleness. The first thing he should learn is that human hands are good for three things: to pick him up, to pet him, and to give him food. Train him with patience. Pay attention to what he is showing you about skunk nature before you try to force him to conform to human nature. In return, he will reward you with affection, trust, and plenty of fun.

CONSTANCE TABER COLBY
Author, *A Skunk in the House*

LIVING THROUGH WINTER

The second northern mission of the Kingdom of Tropicalia had returned to the capital city on the Congo River, and its leader presented his report.

"O Tropical Majesty, my men and I have visited the northern continent concerning which the first mission reported its findings two and a half years ago. Tropical Majesty, it is not as has been reported. We returned to the same place, following the star charts, and there were no smiling grasslands, no green-leaved forests, no rich brown soil, no singing birds or hopping animals.

"Instead there was painful cold, and the ground was covered with a soft, white material that turned to liquid in our hands. The liquid looked like water, but naturally we dared not drink it. There were no leaves on the trees, merely dead brown branches; there were no birds, no animals, no grass, no soil. Tropical Majesty, it is a dead land."

The King listened carefully, then rose in the awful grandeur of his ostrich-plume headdress and lion-skin tunic. Holding up his spear, he said, "Listen to my proclamation. Since both expeditions were led by honest men who tell the truth, I must believe both. The northern continent is sometimes warm and beautiful and as alive as is our own gracious land; and it is sometimes cold and dreadful and dead. Since a land cannot be both, but must be either one or the other, I declare the north to be bewitched, and no citizen of Tropicalia may ever visit it again."

And no citizen of Tropicalia ever did.

Of course, the story about Tropicalia is made up. It never happened. Yet there is a true point here. The northern lands vary from warmth and life to cold and death. The trees shed their leaves as the cold approaches, and the ground comes to be covered with snow. To those who have never seen such a thing happening, it must be frightening indeed. They might even think it the result of an evil and deadly magic.

And dangerous it is. If the winter lasted forever, as it does in Antarctica, no living thing could endure—and Antarctica is, indeed, largely a lifeless continent. And although the winter in the temperate zones is only temporary, 3 to 6 months of frigid cold and

Arctic terns on their amazing flight.

of dead vegetation is still dreadful. How do living things withstand the coming of cold and the dwindling of vegetation, and last through it all to the return of warmth and food?

Many animals do so by adopting a cyclic behavior that matches the cycle of the seasons: they live one way in the warmth of summer and quite another way in the cold of winter.

▶ **COLD-BLOODED ANIMALS**

It may surprise you to learn that it is particularly important for cold-blooded animals —that is, for all animals but birds and mammals—to adapt to the cold. The inner temperature of cold-blooded animals is usually very close to that of their outer environment. This means that in winter their inner tem-

A frog avoids freezing by staying at the bottom of his own pond.

perature begins to drop toward the freezing point. If the temperature drops below freezing, ice crystals form within the cells of their bodies, and these animals die.

One way of avoiding death by freezing is to lose water as the cold approaches—to dry out a bit. What water is left is bound to the complicated molecules of the tissues. Such "bound water" doesn't freeze as easily, and doesn't form ordinary ice crystals when it does freeze.

In some species of small animals, such as insects, the adults may only live through the warm weather. They leave behind eggs or larvae, however, which can partially dry out; what water is left in them is bound. Insect eggs, cocoons, and even small caterpillars can freeze during the winter; but when the warmth of the spring sun melts the ice, it melts them, too. All the living reactions in these bits of life speed up. The eggs hatch, the cocoons open, the larvae begin to feed.

There are cold-blooded animals that are too large and complex to be able to go through the freezing and thawing process. Exposure to actual freezing conditions would kill them. This group includes some fish, frogs, turtles, and snakes. Fortunately for them it is the surface of the ground, and the top water layer of lakes, ponds, and rivers, that lose heat and freeze first. The deeper layers are covered with snow or ice, which are insulators. What warmth lies underneath is lost only slowly. This means that all through the winter the water and mud underneath the ice, and the soil underneath the snow, remain at temperatures above freezing. Many of these cold-blooded animals go into the depths, burrowing under rocks or into mud. There they remain until the cold months of winter pass.

Why don't they starve while they're waiting for winter to be over?

They don't because the fires of life burn

low. In general, all the reactions that go on in living tissue become slower as the temperature drops. With the approach of really cold weather, however, cold-blooded animals enter a period in which the rate of their bodily reactions (the metabolic rate) drops particularly low. It may become only a small fraction of what it normally is. The animal may breathe only once in 5 minutes; its heart may beat only once in 30 seconds. At this slow rate, a supply of food that might ordinarily last it a day will last last it 2 months, so it doesn't have to eat. The animal can live on its own fat and not use up that supply until winter is past.

Animals in which life is reduced to a slow crawl in this way are said to hibernate (from a Latin word meaning "winter"). It is a way of waiting out the winter, of passing into a sort of suspended animation until the world is good again.

It is not only the cold of winter that can make it necessary for a cold-blooded animal to suspend activity. In some areas, the heat of summer causes lakes and rivers to dwindle during periods of drought. Water creatures that live in such areas must be able to survive these periods. The most extreme example of this can be seen in various kinds of lungfish.

As the water begins to diminish, lungfish burrow into the bottom mud, leaving a channel that reaches to the surface. In the burrow they coil up, and their metabolic rate goes down. All the water may dry up, and the mud around the lungfish may harden into clay. The lungfish, with a very occasional gulp of air, can remain alive. It is undergoing a process called estivation (from a Latin word meaning "summer"). When the rains finally come, and water enters the burrow and begins to soften the mud, the low flame of life begins to flicker upward in the lungfish once more. When the water is plentiful, the lungfish wriggles out of its burrow, gets rid of all the wastes it has accumulated during estivation, and becomes a swimming, feeding creature as before.

▶ WARM–BLOODED ANIMALS

What about the warm-blooded animals— the birds and mammals?

They don't have to fear the freezing of their bodies, since they have ways of regulating their body temperature, of keeping it at some constant level (98.6 degrees Fahrenheit in human beings) whatever the outside temperature may be

Even in the coldest winter weather, at temperatures of 40 or 50 degrees below zero, warm-blooded animals can remain warm. To do so, they must not lose body warmth too quickly to the frigid outside world. They are insulated by nature with thick coats of fur— or efficient layers of feathers—and with thick layers of fat under the skin.

In order to keep the temperature within the body high, the metabolic rate of the animals must remain high, since body heat arises from rapid chemical reactions. This means that a bird or mammal makes a continual search for food; and during the winter, getting food can be a problem.

Winter food gathering is not a problem for mammals and birds that live on seafood. There is no real winter in the ocean. Salt water may get a little colder in the winter, and ice may form on its surface in polar latitudes; but even so, the water beneath always stays above the freezing point. Ocean life is adapted to this condition and flourishes throughout the coldest winter. Seals, walruses, and polar bears can easily live through winter on the Arctic ice floes, and penguins eat well on the shores of Antarctica.

It is also possible for mammals to survive the winter by living on forms of vegetation that are to be found beneath the snow. Reindeer and musk-oxen can survive on a form of lichen popularly known as "reindeer moss," which is reached by scraping the snow away from the rocks on which it grows.

Some mammals, however, cut down on their food requirements by sleeping through the winter, as cold-blooded animals do. As the days of autumn decrease in length, they eat a great deal (while they still can) and grow fat. Some animals, such as chipmunks and hamsters, also store nuts and grain in their burrows.

As the mammals grow fat, they also slow down and grow sleepy. Finally they retire to their burrows, or into caves where the temperature does not sink too low, and sleep away the cold weather.

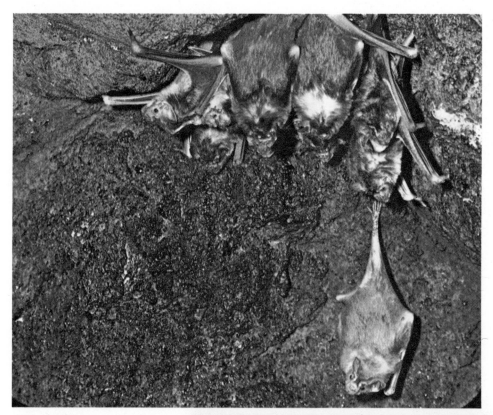

Some bats travel to escape winter; others (*above*) cluster, upside down, in their home caves.

A squirrel (*right*) is careful to store away some nuts in his home for a winter snack.

A polar bear (*left*) is quite happy spending the winter on a familiar ice floe.

This is sometimes spoken of as hibernation, and most people think of the bear, for instance, as hibernating. Actually, most mammals merely sleep and do not truly hibernate. For one thing, their body temperatures drop by only a few degrees, so they are still actively metabolizing. They are conserving some energy by remaining quiet, but these sleepy mammals must rely a great deal on all the fat they have built up in their bodies, or on their supplies of nuts and grain. Animals that have stored away such supplies wake up every week or so to do a little eating. A bear may wake up at any time during the winter and prowl about for a while.

By the time the spring comes, these animals are still alive—but they are skinny and very hungry.

Some small mammals really hibernate, however. The smaller the mammal, the more difficult it is for it to last through the cold weather. The heat of a small mammal's body is nearer the surface and more easily lost. And so, for its weight, the small mammal must eat considerably more food than a large animal if it is to keep up its temperature.

Some mammals, therefore, such as woodchucks, hedgehogs, and dormice give up the fight. As the cold weather approaches, not only do they eat and grow fat, but their body temperature starts dropping. This places them on the road to true hibernation.

They enter their burrows, and little by little they become almost cold-blooded, as their temperatures drop toward the freezing point. Their heartbeat slows to as little as three beats per minute and their metabolic rate is as small as one-thirtieth of what it normally would be. Some hibernating mammals remain in this situation for over 6 months at a time—and survive.

▶ MIGRATION

Of course, not all land animals are trapped by winter. If they can move easily and rapidly, they can follow the good weather. If they live in areas where there are summer droughts, they can migrate to other, moister areas where grass still grows.

The animals that can move most quickly and freely are those who have wings and can fly. They can migrate far and efficiently and can survive the winter simply by leaving it. Animals that migrate include some insects, some bats (which are flying mammals), and, most important of all, many birds. Birds do not need to hibernate. If they can't find food during the winter, they just fly to some other place, where food is plentiful.

Some birds migrate long distances to avoid the winter. Birds that spend the summer in New England may spend the winter in Florida. Birds that summer in Wyoming may winter in Texas. Hummingbirds from the United States may store enough fat in their tiny bodies to carry them on their very long flight to escape winter, a flight that takes them to the more tropical climate of Mexico.

The most amazing migratory feat of all is that of the Arctic tern, a gull-like, fish-eating bird that breeds and spends the summer in the northernmost parts of North America. There is no problem of food, then. The ocean teems with it.

As the summer passes, the days begin to shorten. Once the young birds are full-grown, all the terns take off and fly southward for 11,000 miles to Antarctic waters, where they go through another summer of long days and ample fish. Then, when it is the turn of the Antarctic to enter the period of shortening days, the terns fly back to the Arctic again, where they lay eggs and produce a new generation of young birds.

Because of their amazing migration, the Arctic terns see more daylight and experience less night than any other species of living things on earth.

▶ A GREAT MYSTERY

Scientists do not understand all the details of the ways in which animals survive the winter. They do not know exactly what makes a hibernating animal choose the time and place of its hibernation. They do not know exactly what sparks the body to begin its slowdown at the beginning of winter or what causes the arousal at the end of winter. Hormones are involved, and the spark may be caused, in part, by changes in temperature and humidity. It is likely that the most important signal the animal receives is the change in the length of the day, since that is a more fixed rhythm than anything else.

This is a portrait of the world's greatest traveler, the Arctic tern.

Nor does science know how hibernation habits developed over the ages of evolution. Fossils give hints of how animals changed and developed with time, at least as far as their physical structure is concerned, but they cannot indicate much about animal behavior. Scientists do not know if any of the dinosaurs hibernated, for instance, or when hibernation first developed.

The migration of winged animals is even more mysterious. A particular species of birds will head southward at a particular time of year. Then it will fly back at a particular time along a particular route to the same area that it started from—often to precisely the same acre, and often on the very same day every single year.

Scientists are not certain about how birds manage to be such accurate navigators and time tellers. Some theories involve the positions of the sun and stars or the nature of the earth's magnetic field, but no one is sure. Whatever it is that helps birds navigate, it must be quite instinctive. Even young birds who have never migrated before know how to do it.

The only thing that is certain is that the snows of winter do not defeat life. The frost may force a retreat; but when the winter is over and the sun shines warm again, vegetation returns, and with the return of vegetation the animals return, too. They have survived in one way or another, and they have come back.

ISAAC ASIMOV
Scientist and Author

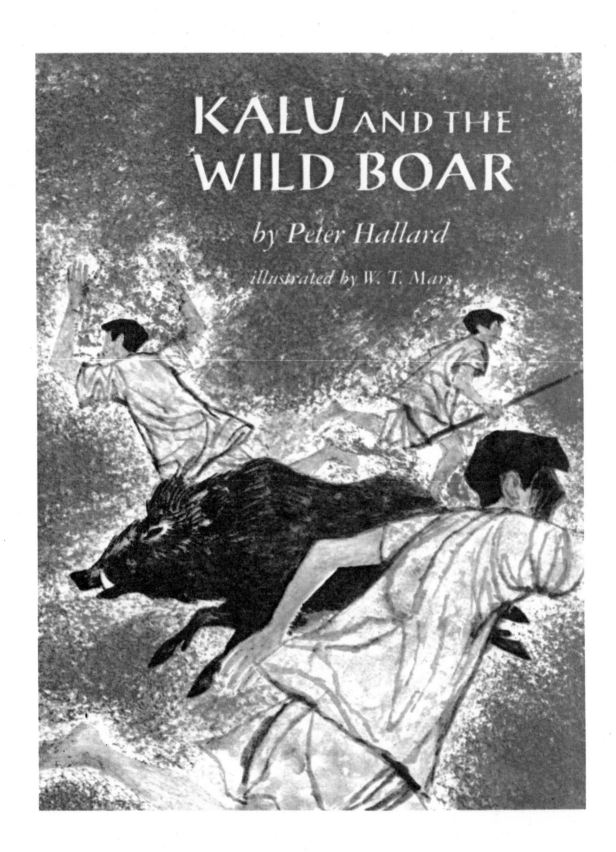

KALU AND THE WILD BOAR

by Peter Hallard

illustrated by W. T. Mars

BATTLE AT DAWN

As the gray light on the eastern hills brightened, Kalu's fears increased. The thieves who had been busy in the field throughout the night would leave before the sun rose, and Kalu's father, Kunwar Lal, was guarding the gap in the thorn hedge through which they would have to make their retreat. Kunwar Lal was not the man to let them get away unpunished.

Throughout the night thirteen-year-old Kalu had been perched on a flimsy bamboo platform some six feet above the ground. Like his father he was armed with a metal tin and a rusty iron spike. By banging on the rusty tin, he and his father had hoped to frighten away the family of wild pigs that had been coming to their field for the past week, eating and trampling down the growing crop.

No matter how they banged their gongs, the four-legged thieves had not been scared away. Nor could Kalu do more than make them grunt when he fired sun-baked balls of clay at the pigs with his sling. For the first few hours of the night there had been a moon, and it was possible to see the pigs wandering about, eating the grain and trampling lanes in the growing crop.

Kalu's father had brought along a spear, and if he had thought he had a chance, he would certainly have tried to kill the leader of the wild pigs, for their devastation of his crop threatened to ruin him. It was the thought of his father tackling the boar that made the boy shiver with fear. The people of the Indian village of Chandwari had already named the boar *Burra Dhantwallah* (the big-tusked one), and it was a name he well deserved.

Once during the night the boar had come quite close to the platform on which Kalu crouched, and he had seen the tusks glinting in the moonlight. They were long and curved upward from the lower jaw—terrible weapons in a fight.

As the light grew brighter, the boar began to grunt, and at once all the pigs moved toward him. Seconds later Burra Dhantwallah came in sight. He walked into an open space where the grain had all been eaten and the stalks trodden flat. It provided a clear area in which the family could gather together, and was less than thirty feet from the platform on which young Kalu crouched.

Looking up the field toward his father, Kalu saw two arms making a motion. His father was calling on him to use his sling. Dry-lipped and frightened though he was, Kalu grabbed several of the sun-baked clay balls. They were about an inch in diameter, and at such a short range they could hurt.

"I'll aim for his head," Kalu muttered. "If I could blind him in one eye, then he might not come here again."

As the rest of the wild pigs began to merge with their leader, Kalu knelt, took careful aim, and sent a shot singing through the cool morning air. There was an angry grunt almost at once. Kalu had not managed to hit Burra Dhantwallah in a vital spot, but he had struck him just below the left eye.

At the grunt the rest of the pigs quickened their pace while Kalu hurriedly fired a second shot. Burra Dhantwallah had his mouth partly open, and the hard clay ball went straight into the boar's throat. For a moment Burra Dhantwallah stood as if paralyzed. Then he reared on his short but powerful hind legs. He gave a tearing, coughing grunt, and a moment later he had gotten rid of the clay ball.

Kalu was already firing his third shot, and again his aim was good. This time he struck the boar hard on the ear, bringing another angry grunt of pain. It was as Kalu was about to fire his fourth shot that Burra Dhantwallah realized where the stinging shots were coming from. Kalu's movements made the rickety platform sway a little. The bamboo creaked, and the boar heard the sound.

Kalu never fired his fourth shot. He had to grab at the side of the platform to avoid overbalancing, and in the next few seconds Burra Dhantwallah was charging.

Standing a yard high at the shoulder and a good five feet from snout to the tip of his little tail, the boar weighed several hundred pounds. Nor was there any fat on him. He was all bone, muscle, and sinew. He did not charge the platform, or he would have brought it crashing to the ground at once. Instead, he reared on his hind legs and tried to slash at Kalu with his vicious-looking tusks.

The platform swayed horribly, forcing a scream of terror from Kalu. Thinly across the field came a yell from Kunwar Lal: "Bang your plate, my son, bang your plate!" And Kunwar Lal began to bang his metal plate and shout as loudly as he could.

Burra Dhantwallah's family panicked. They turned up the gentle slope and headed for the hilltop. But their lord and master was made of sterner stuff than any of them. If he had an enemy, he preferred to fight him at once. This gave his family a better chance of getting out of danger.

On his four legs again, he slashed angrily at one of the bamboo supports of Kalu's platform. Kalu wailed again as the platform shivered under the blow.

"Bang your plate, bang your plate!" his father bellowed, and continued banging his plate in an effort to distract the boar. Burra Dhantwallah was not listening. He drew back to get a good look at the platform with the young Indian crouched on top. Then he charged.

His snout was hardened by years of rooting in sun-baked soil, and though it must have given him some pain when he struck one of the platform supports with his snout, it did what he wanted. The bamboo snapped with a brittle cracking sound, and the platform tilted. Burra Dhantwallah charged again, and the platform collapsed just as Kalu leaped clear. He dropped to his knees, took one terrified glance behind him, then ran.

For all his ponderous size the boar was amazingly nimble. He spun around on his back feet, gave an angry grunt, then rushed after the boy. Up the slope Kalu's father was shrieking commands: "This way, Kalu . . . come to me, come to me!" And at the same time he was leaping off his platform, though his only weapon was a six-foot bamboo tipped with a spearhead.

The growing grain was over a yard high, and though it had been trampled badly in places by the feeding pigs, there were other places where it was thick. Kalu seemed to be forcing his way through a jungle, and all the time he could hear the angry grunting of Burra Dhantwallah and the stamping of his small hoofs on the hard ground.

He knew his father was racing toward him, yelling encouragement; but he also had a sick feeling that before he would cover the fifty yards that now separated them, the boar would catch up with him.

Suddenly he ran out of the tall grain into a space eaten clear of all but low stubble. Now he could hear the snorting of Burra Dhantwallah. Then came a scream from his father: "Turn left . . . turn left . . . leave him to me!"

Kalu turned left, leaping to safety as the boar was almost at his heels. He looked toward his father and stopped dead. Kunwar Lal was not a big man. Years of terribly hard work and poor feeding had kept him small and lean. Now he stood and faced the charging boar who must have weighed five times as much as his human opponent.

In the growing light—for the sun had now tipped the hills—Kalu saw his father draw back his right arm. He saw the spear held steady for a moment; then the yellow bamboo shaft hurled through the air—and missed!

an excerpt from *Kalu and the Wild Boar*
by PETER HALLARD

The old days of the circus live on at the Circus World Museum.

A CHILD'S PARIS

Paris, the capital of France and one of the oldest and most beautiful cities in Europe, is a fascinating place to visit. It is a treat for adults and for young people alike. Some of the city's famous attractions will appeal to everyone, regardless of age. But there are some places and things in Paris that are especially fascinating to young people—to young people who have visited Paris or hope to visit it one day. This tour is designed for young people.

The best way to start learning about any big city is to see it. And there is no better way to see a city than from the highest point possible. If you wanted to see what New York was like, you would probably go to the top of the Empire State Building or one of the towers of the new World Trade Center. If you wanted to see San Francisco, you might well go to the top of Coit Tower. When you come to Paris, the very best place from which to see the whole city spread out before you is the top of the most famous landmark in Paris, the Eiffel Tower.

▶ FROM THE EIFFEL TOWER

It would be possible for you to walk up the long flights of stairs that go to the second and third terraces of the Eiffel Tower. However, you would probably enjoy your visit to the tower a little more if you took the elevator, which is faster and less tiring than the stairs. You can't go to the very top of the tower, because it houses a television transmitting station. People from France and from all over the world have been viewing Paris from the top of the Eiffel Tower since it was opened for the Paris Exposition of 1889. The tower is made entirely of iron and is 984 feet tall. It was the highest man-made structure in the world when it was opened. It's still a very tall tower, even by modern standards.

There isn't a better view of Paris than that from the Eiffel Tower. You can see most of the great city spread out at your feet. You will see some of the city's famous churches. The great medieval cathedral of Notre Dame is there on its island in the Seine River. An unusual and enormous white church, the Sacré Coeur (the Church of the Sacred Heart), crowns the hill of Montmartre. It was built to celebrate the liberation of France from foreign invaders at the conclusion of the Franco-Prussian War in 1871. On another rise you can see the dome of the Panthéon, where many great Frenchmen are buried.

You will notice immediately that Paris is not a city of many tall buildings like New York. You will see a few skyscrapers—but not too many—in the center of the city. The true lovers of Paris would rather not see any at all, for Paris has been called the most beautiful city in the world. They feel that too many modern buildings will ruin the beauty of the city.

As you look out over the city you will spot a golden dome nearby. It is the dome of the Invalides, the place where the great French emperor Napoleon I is buried. It also houses the Army Museum. You would enjoy visiting the Army Museum even if you don't know a lot about French history. It has weapons and brilliantly embroidered battle flags and standards from the many wars the French have fought over the centuries. You will undoubtedly find some things there connected with the Marquis de Lafayette, the French officer who helped the 13 American colonies win their independence from England.

While you're still at the Eiffel Tower, you can see another fascinating place that is practically a neighbor of the tower. Look across the Seine. The modern building on the other bank of the river is the Palais de Chaillot. One wing of the Palais de Chaillot houses one of the largest theaters in Paris. It is the home of the Théâtre National Populaire (the French call it the TNP), one of France's finest repertory theaters.

The other wing of the Palais de Chaillot houses two truly fascinating museums that you would certainly enjoy visiting—the Naval Museum and the Musée de l'Homme (a museum of the history of mankind). The Palais de Chaillot would be the best place to start your tour of Paris.

The Naval Museum is often filled with children because it is a wonderful place to learn the history of ships in a most interesting way. The museum has models of ships

The modern Palais de Chaillot is really a complex of interesting buildings.

from all ages and all countries. Among the most fascinating models are those of galleys from the time of Louis XIV. The galleys were rowed by teams of convicts condemned to this mercilessly hard work—sometimes for life— for a variety of offenses. You can see in these models the rows of benches where the convicts sat and rowed under the watchful eyes of their guards. In contrast to the grim way in which they were powered, the appearance of the galleys, as you will see, was splendid. Their prows and sterns were elaborately decorated. The Naval Museum also has many interesting paintings of French harbors and of naval battles. There is a collection of navigation instruments from many centuries. They are often beautifully designed and decorated. It is very exciting to follow the development of ships from the majestic galleons with their forests of masts and billowing cloudlike sails to the great transoceanic liners of today.

The other museum in the Palais de Chaillot, the Musée de l'Homme, may seem a little be-wildering to you at first. It really does attempt to trace the entire history of the human race in all its aspects—culture, clothing, housing, tools, and many other things. Once you have gotten used to the idea of how enormous the subject is—and how large the museum itself is—you will see how well organized and easy to follow the exhibits are. You will pass exhibits that deal with each of the earth's continents, starting with Africa and ending with America. The museum is, in fact, an around-the-world voyage of discovery that takes only an hour or two to complete.

▶ANIMALS AND GARDENS

If you are a little exhausted by your trip around the world in the Musée de l'Homme, you may feel like relaxing a bit outdoors. Don't leave the Palais de Chaillot without walking awhile on the huge terrace that lies between the two wings of the building. You will find that from this spot you have a wonderful view of the Eiffel Tower—where you started your tour—and of the formal gardens nearby. However, you will find that the terrace of the Palais de Chaillot also has one of the finest views of the rest of the city. If you feel like looking at odd and curious fish, the Aquarium is nearby. Although it is small, it has a fascinating and beautiful collection.

If you want to see living things of all kinds —both plants and animals—a visit to the Jardin des Plantes ("the plant garden") would be fun. Despite what its name suggests, the Jardin des Plantes has fish and animals as well as plants for you to see. There is an interesting assortment of animals—American bison, or buffalo, reptiles from all over the world, colorful fish, and a unique form of donkey. It is a long-haired donkey once very common in France. Now there are only 50 of them left. In the days when many kinds of hauling and farm work were done by mules, these donkeys were bred with horses to produce a crossbreed—the sturdy little mule.

And, as you would expect, there is indeed a fascinating collection of plants in the Jardin des Plantes. There is even a cedar tree that was brought to France from Lebanon as a tiny plant inside someone's hat. There are huge greenhouses with exhibits of rare and exotic tropical plants.

And in case you haven't seen enough in the Jardin des Plantes, there are galleries with exhibits in the fields of mineralogy, geology, zoology—something for everyone. Just remember to check the visiting hours of the Jardin des Plantes and of the other places you plan to visit in Paris, too. All of the museums and other monuments in Paris are closed on either Monday or Tuesday. Some places are closed both days.

There are two other places in Paris to see animals: the Jardin d'Acclimatation in the famous park called the Bois de Boulogne, and the zoo in the park at Vincennes. Both of these places are on the outskirts of the city, but they are quite easy to reach. The Jardin d'Acclimatation is as famous for its playgrounds and rides as it is for its animals. It would be a good place for you to spend a day sometime.

One of the most fascinating things at the Jardin d'Acclimatation is called La Prévention Routière. It is both fun and instructive, for it is a kind of game in which you learn all of the rules of driving—of driving a car or a bicycle. You ride along a maze of tracks. There are traffic lights, crosswalks, and a real *gardien de la paix* (a French traffic policeman) in full uniform—including white gloves —who regulates the flow of traffic and makes sure that the young drivers are obeying the traffic rules. If you feel you don't want to work quite so hard at having fun, take a ride on the miniature red train that runs through the Bois de Boulogne. In addition to the zoo and the rides in the Jardin d'Acclimatation, the Bois de Boulogne also has bridle paths for horseback riding and two lakes for boating.

The biggest and most impressive place to see animals in Paris is the zoo in the Forest of Vincennes, just to the southeast of the city. The zoo is located near an interesting castle that was once a residence of the kings of France. In the zoo at Vincennes the animals appear to be almost free. They roam in wide fields separated from visitors by a few fences and by wide ditches. The zoo officials are especially proud of their okapis (odd relatives of the giraffe) from Africa. Vincennes had the first okapis in Europe.

All aboard—for a tour of the Bois de Boulogne.

In Paris you can sail boats (*above*) in the Jardin du Luxembourg or watch a Punch-and-Judy show (*below*), called *le guignol* in French.

The two other parks you would enjoy visiting are very much in the midst of things —the Jardin du Luxembourg and the Jardin des Tuileries. Both parks have playgrounds, flower gardens, and delightful walks, and are oases in the midst of a busy city. The Jardin du Luxembourg has exceptionally beautiful formal gardens. It also has a Punch-and-Judy show that you will enjoy.

Under the trees of the Champs-Élysées, near the Tuileries, there are many interesting things to see. In fact, there is another Punch-and-Judy show. There is also a place where stamp collectors meet to discuss and trade stamps. Another interesting place to visit, just off the Champs-Élysées, is the Palais de la Découverte, a museum with displays on all the latest scientific discoveries. There is also an interesting planetarium connected with the museum.

▶ **UNDERGROUND**

When you have gotten a little tired of the things that you can do above ground in Paris, why not try underground Paris? When you say "underground" in Paris, you don't necessarily mean the city's famous subway, the Métro. Paris has a unique system of sewers under the city. They are clean, well cared for, and not in the least unpleasant. You can actually take an underground tour of the city.

If you want to see the mysterious underground city, go to the Place de la Concorde. The entrance to the sewer system is there. You will be taken in a boat through the strange light of the underground canals. The canals have the same names as the streets under which they run. You will begin to feel a little like Alice when she walked into the strange, reverse world in *Through the Looking Glass*.

▶A TRIP ON THE RIVER

The odd thing about Paris is that the more you see of it the more you want to see of it and know about it. There is another way of seeing a panorama of the city. Why not get a horizontal view of the city as well as the vertical one you had from the Eiffel Tower? The way to do that is to take a boat trip on the Seine, the lovely river that flows through the heart of the city.

A boat tour of Paris takes about an hour and a half and allows you to see the famous buildings and monuments on both banks of the river. The most pleasant time to take the trip is on a summer evening. Then the famous places along the river are illuminated and stand out beautifully against the dark sky.

Your trip will probably start at the Alma Bridge. You will then sail on and pass under the Alexander III Bridge, the most elaborate of all the numerous bridges of Paris. Then, on the Right Bank—which is on your left, for we are sailing upstream—you will see the Assemblé Nationale (the lower house of the French Parliament). On the opposite bank is the widest square in Paris, the Place de la Concorde. The center of the Place de la Concorde is marked by an ancient Egyptian obelisk brought from Luxor. It was in the Place de la Concorde that the guillotine was erected for executions during the French Revolution. Thousands of people died there, including Louis XVI, the king of France, and his wife, Marie Antoinette. The boat then passes the Tuileries gardens and the Louvre. The Louvre, which is now one of the world's great art museums, was once a residence of the kings of France. Louis XIV moved the court to the outskirts of the city, to Versailles,

where he built another, even grander palace. When you visit the Louvre be sure you look at the really wonderful collection of Egyptian art. The enormous statues of Egyptian gods and sacred animals in the Egyptian collection were brought back by Napoleon from his military campaigns in the Middle East.

Not long after you pass the Louvre you will see the first of the two islands in the Seine that formed the original center of the city. They are the Île de la Cité and the Île Saint-Louis.

You will see the Île de la Cité first. Two of the most famous religious buildings in France are on this island: the Cathedral of Notre Dame and the Sainte Chapelle. Notre Dame, which is one of the oldest Gothic cathedrals of Europe, has seen a staggering number of historic events. Henry VI of England was crowned in Notre Dame, and the heir to the throne of France (who became Francis II) was married there to the ill-fated Mary Stuart (Mary Queen of Scots). And these are just a few of the things that have happened at Notre Dame. Recently a daring young man was arrested for stringing a tightrope between the cathedral's famous towers and walking on it from one tower to the other. He was arrested because this kind of stunt is illegal. However, he was given the Prix de la Vocation, an award given by Parisians to people who have an irresistible urge to do risky and unusual things and carry them through.

The Sainte Chapelle, which is world-famous for its exceptionally beautiful stained-glass windows, was founded by a French king, Louis IX, who was declared a saint.

The Île de la Cité is shaped more or less like a ship. If you have a chance to look at the coat of arms of the city of Paris, you will notice that it includes a ship in full sail (representing the island) and the Latin motto *Fluctuat Nec Mergitur* ("it is tossed about by the waves, but doesn't sink"). At the "prow" of the Île de la Cité stands a statue of King Henry IV on horseback. He was the monarch who tried to reconcile the French Catholics and Protestants during the nation's religious wars. He also originated the idea that every Frenchman should have a chicken to eat every Sunday. Henry's belief in religious toleration and his views on the rights of

Notre Dame at its most beautiful is seen from a tour boat on the Seine.

Frenchmen to eat chicken made him one of the country's most popular monarchs.

On the other end of the Île de la Cité there is an impressive monument to the 200,000 Frenchmen who were killed during the German occupation of France in World War II.

The second island your boat will pass in the Seine is the Île Saint-Louis. Until the 17th century, it had a much less elegant name, *Île aux Vaches* ("cow island"). It was called that because cows were once put out to pasture there. In all of Paris, the Île Saint-Louis is one of the most beautiful places to live. Some of the oldest houses in the city are to be found there. You will notice as you pass the island that most of the ancient buildings on the island look very clean. Both the monuments and the private houses of the Île Saint-Louis have been cleaned and restored over the last 10 years. If you want to see the Île Saint-Louis really clean, however, you'd better come to Paris soon. Nothing remains clean for long in a modern city.

Your boat will probably now make a turn and start downstream, passing between the Right Bank and the islands. After you pass Notre Dame you will see, below it on the Île de la Cité, the Conciergerie, an old prison. During the French Revolution various members of the royal family, including Marie Antoinette, were imprisoned there. If you visit the building you will be shown their dark cells.

As you continue down the river, you will pass under the Pont d'Iéna (named for Napoleon's victory at Jena, in Germany). It connects the Champ de Mars (where the Eiffel Tower stands) with the gardens of the Palais de Chaillot on the Right Bank. You are on familiar ground again. By the way, the Champ de Mars ("the field of Mars") is called that because long before the Eiffel Tower was built, soldiers used to drill on the field, which was a vast parade ground. It is named for Mars, the Roman god of war.

Your boat will probably continue a bit farther downstream. It will pass the round modern building of the Maison de la Radio et Télévision (the headquarters of the French radio and television systems) and make a last turn around a small island. Under the Grenelle Bridge you will see a statue that will look very familiar indeed to people from the United States. It is a smaller replica of the

142

The Place des Vosges is at the heart of the old district of Le Marais.

Statue of Liberty which stands in New York harbor. The original statue was a gift of the French people to the United States.

▶ AN OLD QUARTER

Now that we've finished our boat trip, there are a few more places you would probably enjoy seeing. Although Paris is a large city, there are, within walking distance, monuments of at least five centuries of French history. It would be interesting to take a last tour through one of the oldest parts of the city. It is an area on the Right Bank that was one of the most elegant districts in the city in the 17th and 18th centuries, when Paris was a small city surrounded by fields. The quarter was called Le Marais ("the marsh") because the whole area, lying below the level of the Seine, had once been a vast marsh. The houses on the main square of Le Marais were all built over 300 years ago. And there are many other beautiful old houses throughout the district. Over the centuries the rich inhabitants of Le Marais gradually moved away, abandoning their houses. The houses were taken over by working people, especially artisans of various kinds. After many years of decay, however, the beautiful buildings of Le Marais are finally being restored and are illuminated at night.

But wait! Don't go yet. The best place to say good-bye to Paris is the Place de la Bastille. It is not far from Le Marais. The old fortress called the Bastille used to stand on this site. On July 14, 1789, the Bastille, which had been used as a political prison, was stormed by revolutionaries. This event marked the beginning of the French Revolution. The fortress, which had become the symbol of political oppression, was torn down in the same year, and the 14th of July became the French national holiday, Bastille Day. Look around the Place de la Bastille. If you come here on Bastille Day any year you will see this square filled with dancers, and see fireworks bursting in the sky above the column that stands in the middle of the square. Atop the column is a figure called the Génie de la Bastille, representing the winged spirit of liberty about to take flight. I think this spot, where modern France was born, would be the very best place to finish your tour of Paris.

JEAN LAMBERT
Smith College

Mounties in dress uniforms pose with their trained German shepherds.

ROYAL CANADIAN MOUNTED POLICE

On July 4, 1973, Queen Elizabeth II of England (who is also Queen of Canada) led Canadians in a ceremony marking the 100th anniversary of the Royal Canadian Mounted Police, one of the world's most famous law enforcement groups. In the course of the anniversary year of 1973, many people remembered the exciting history of the Canadian Mounties and discussed their future role in Canadian life.

"The Mounties always get their man." That's the reputation of Canada's Royal Canadian Mounted Police. People the world over are familiar with the legendary square-jawed, scarlet-coated policeman. In film and story, aided only by his faithful horse, trusty dog team, or frail canoe, he doggedly braves

hunger, cold, dangerous odds, and all the terrors of the northern bush in successful pursuit of wrongdoers.

It's an appealing picture—but a misleading one. Although the RCMP, as Canadians often call the organization, can boast many colorful heroes, some of its proudest exploits have been, and are, team efforts carried out by men in drab uniforms. There have been manhunts, it is true, but other achievements have been in the establishment of peace and order, in exploration, and in counterespionage.

▶THE FOUNDING OF THE FORCE

The RCMP's story begins in 1873. At that time, Canada had no official force to uphold its claim to the lands lying between the Red

River and the Rocky Mountains. Canada also lacked an organization to enforce Canadian law and keep the restless Plains Indians of Canada under control. The 3,000,000–square-mile area, called the Northwest Territories, was an almost trackless wilderness. It differed from the United States territories to the south where settlers with families were staking out farms. The only settlements in the Northwest Territories of Canada were scattered trading posts, and its only inhabitants were Indians, trappers, and traders. All three groups—Indians, trappers, and traders—were a law unto themselves and roamed free.

Military experts advised the formation of an armed police force of mounted men (men on horseback) which would "have the advantage of military discipline." Accordingly, the Northwest Mounted Police (or NWMP), as it was originally called, was founded by order of the Canadian Parliament on May 23, 1873. Recruitment of over 300 men began in September. Cultured aristocrats; rough lumberjacks; teachers and poorly educated farm boys; office workers and drifters—every sort of man enlisted. Whatever their race or background, they were united by a spirit of high adventure.

▶ THE LONG MARCH

Throughout the following winter, the recruits drilled. On July 8, 1874, 275 men set out from Fort Dufferin in Manitoba. Behind them lay months of stiff training under comfortless conditions. Many of the original recruits had deserted. In fact, 31 recruits deserted on the eve of the departure for the Northwest when Lieutenant Colonel George French, Commissioner of the Force, warned that hard times were only beginning.

The first goal of the expedition was to find Fort Whoop-Up, as the headquarters of traders who were illegally selling whiskey to the Indians was called. The exact location of the fort, some 800 miles distant, was unknown. Competent guides and accurate maps were unavailable. Yet the little force set out with spirits high despite their belief that hostile Indians and bands of lawless desperadoes would try to stop them.

In fact, the worst enemies of the new Mounties were heat, cold, hunger, thirst, and sickness. Often the country they traveled through could provide neither game nor fresh water. Burdened with heavy military equipment and machinery and with cumbersome oxcarts, the column moved slowly. As summer wore on, men and horses sickened. By

The proud Northwest Mounted Police in the uniform they wore about 1875.

The handsome, official guidon of the RCMP.

September, night temperatures were falling below freezing. The ragged uniforms of the men were inadequate. The desolate country-side gave little shelter. As a crowning blow, when the Police reached the supposed site of Fort Whoop-Up, they could find no trace of it.

Leaving most of his men to rest, Lieutenant Colonel French led a wagon train to Fort Benton, Montana, to obtain information and supplies. On his return to his troops in Canada, French ordered three divisions under Assistant Commissioner Macleod to continue the search for Whoop-Up while the remainder of the force established posts at Fort Edmonton, Fort Ellice, and Swan River.

When the Whoop-Up whiskey traders learned of Macleod's approach, they packed their liquor and fled. Other traders were tracked down and fined. By December, the end of the whiskey trade was in sight, and the Assistant Commissioner could concentrate on cultivating good relations with the Indians.

▶ THE INDIANS

James Macleod, an able, tough soldier, treated the Indians with dignity and honor, promising them justice and fair dealing under the law. His greatest achievement was to win the confidence of Crowfoot, the distinguished chief of the formerly hostile Blackfoot Confederacy. Four years later Crowfoot expressed his gratitude:

If the Police had not come to the country, where would we all be now? Bad men and whiskey were killing us so fast that very few of us would have been left today. The Police have protected us as the feathers of the bird protect it from the frosts of winter.

Indeed, the Plains Indians did need help badly. Their traditional way of life, which depended on the buffalo for food, clothing, and shelter, was becoming impossible. By 1874 the buffalo herds were fast disappearing, and the Indians faced starvation. To make matters worse, tribes like the Sioux and the Cree, pushed westward by the advancing white civilization, had crowded into Black-foot, Assiniboin, and Ojibway territory. On their heels came the white man, annexing Indian hunting grounds, destroying game, and introducing strange customs and diseases. In 1869–70 alone, almost one third of all the Plains Indians in the United States and Canada died of smallpox.

From the time of their arrival on the prairie, the Mounties worked to help the Indians to adjust to the changing conditions of their lives. In recognition of the redcoats' courage and fair dealing, the Indian chiefs pledged their loyalty. Without that protection, the small outposts of Police could easily have been wiped out.

Sitting Bull was the most famous chief to swear allegiance. After Sioux warriors wiped out four divisions of the United States Cavalry in the Battle of the Little Big Horn, Sitting Bull led some 5,600 of his people to refuge in Canada. For 4 years NWMP Inspector James Walsh enjoyed his reputation as "Sitting Bull's Boss." At the end of that time, the Sioux made peace with the United States authorities and returned across the border.

▶ THE CHANGING WEST

Ten years after the NWMP trekked west, the white population of the Northwest Territories had jumped from a few hundred people to 35,000. This increase was made possible by the building of a Canadian transcontinental railroad. The NWMP was enlarged to help it handle a growth in police duties; increased crime; labor problems on the railroad; and the government's decision to put the Indians onto reservations and keep them there.

The Indians found reservation life dull and confining. Their cousins the métis (who were of mixed Indian and white blood) feared that their own rights and traditional way of life were threatened by the population growth. After asking vainly for government help and sympathy, the two groups—the Indians and the métis—joined together in March, 1885, in the North West Rebellion. Militia troops were rushed by train from the east, and the NWMP fought alongside them on several occasions. On May 11 the rebels were defeated in the Battle of Batoche. Three days later the métis leader, Louis Riel, surrendered to the Mounted Police.

After the rebellion, the NWMP set up a system of patrols, riding out regularly in all weathers to visit farms, villages, towns, and Indian reservations. With few exceptions, the Canadian West remained peaceful and law-abiding.

THE KLONDIKE GOLD RUSH

In July, 1897, news reached the outside world that gold had been discovered at the junction of the Yukon and Klondike rivers, and the Klondike gold rush began. Thousands of fortune seekers swarmed north to crowd the mountain passes from Alaska to the Yukon. As winter advanced, they floundered in snow 12 feet deep, and froze in temperatures of –60 degrees Fahrenheit. Many of the gold prospectors became half-crazed with hardship and frustration. Food and other supplies ran short, and prices skyrocketed.

Given these conditions, lawlessness prevailed in the Alaskan town of Skagway, but across the border in Canada the men of the NWMP maintained order. Established in the Yukon from 1895, they acted now as policemen, magistrates, postmen, customs and immigration officers, tax collectors, mining claims recorders, welfare officers, and civic leaders. Superintendent Sam Steele encouraged the improvements that in 2 years transformed Dawson City from a dirty huddle of

tents into a safe and comfortable modern community.

By September, 1899, the gold rush was over, and the reputation of the Mounted Police stood at a new high. In 1904, in recognition of the services performed by the Mounties, King Edward VII commanded a change of the Mounties' official name to Royal Northwest Mounted Police.

NORTHERN SERVICE

The Yukon gold rush had focused Canada's attention on its northern territories. In 1903 the NWMP was asked to move into the Arctic, explore it, and establish Canadian law and sovereignty there. The following years saw police patrols pushing their way thousands of miles through the Barren Lands by dog team and canoe, often encountering severe hardships. Since the 1920's the North has been opened up by ships, planes, radio, and the snowmobile. Northern service is no

Modern Mounties use snowmobiles in the Arctic.

longer as lonely or hazardous as it once was. Yet there is still plenty of work for the Mounted Police in the North. One of their chief jobs is to help white settlers and Eskimo residents get along together.

The Canadian Arctic was the scene of one of the most heroic achievements in the history of the Mounties. Anxious to demonstrate its rights in the Arctic during World War II, the Canadian Government, in 1940, sent the Mounties' patrol ship *St. Roch* out with orders to attempt a voyage through the Northwest Passage from west to east. Roald

A Mountie transmits fingerprints by videotape.

Amundsen had completed the reverse journey in 1906, but the voyage of the *St. Roch* was the first eastward voyage ever completed. The 9,745-mile journey of the *St. Roch* from Vancouver, British Columbia, began on June 21, 1940. The journey ended at Halifax, Nova Scotia, on October 11, 1942. Along the route chosen, ice conditions allowed only 2 months' traveling time. Amazingly, another voyage, in 1944 by a more northerly route, took the *St. Roch* a little under 3 months.

In 1950 the *St. Roch* sailed from Vancouver to Halifax by way of the Panama Canal, thus becoming the first ship to circumnavigate the North American continent.

▶ **THE FORCE TODAY**

In 1920 a second name change—to Royal Canadian Mounted Police—marked an extension of the Force's authority over the entire Dominion of Canada. No longer a frontier police, the RCMP prides itself on being a modern law enforcement, security, and counterintelligence organization, which co-operates with police forces the world over through bodies like Interpol.

In law enforcement, the RCMP maintains federal law throughout Canada. The Mounties act as provincial police in all provinces but Ontario and Quebec. In the Yukon Territory and the Northwest Territories, they are the only police force.

In security and counterintelligence the RCMP works, often under cover, to control espionage and subversive activity. Its record of success in the field goes back to the 1930's.

The RCMP Criminal Investigation Branch employs every kind of modern scientific crime detection apparatus. In addition, it maintains records of crimes, criminals, missing persons, wanted persons, firearms, handwriting, fingerprints, footprints, and tire prints. The Fingerprint Section, founded in 1910, is one of the world's oldest fingerprint filing systems.

Its own radio communications network enables the RCMP to flash information in minutes from Whitehorse in the Yukon to St. John's, Newfoundland, and on to police contacts around the world. The ships and aircraft of Canada's Marine Services and Air Services are particularly dependent on the RCMP communications network. These services

Canadian children learn about the RCMP from an expert—a real Mountie.

provide transportation to isolated localities, patrol areas inaccessible by land, assist in rescue operations and searches for lost persons, combat smuggling, and report on migrating birds and on other wildlife.

What has happened to the faithful sled dogs and horses of the Mounties? Although no longer relied on for transportation, horses and dogs still have their places. The RCMP continues to breed its characteristic handsome dark horses to take part in ceremonies and the famous musical ride. It also breeds German shepherd dogs for tracking and guard duty. Recently, Labrador retrievers have proved valuable in uncovering illegal drugs.

"Review Order" (as the famous dress uniform of the Mounties is called)—the scarlet tunic, blue breeches, felt hat, boots, spurs, gauntlets, lanyard, and full Sam Browne side-

arm equipment—has gone the way of the horse. Today it is used only for ceremonies. The everyday uniform of the RCMP now consists of brown jacket, blue trousers, black oxfords, and a visored service cap.

Since 1873, *Maintiens le Droit*—Maintain the Right—has been the motto of the Mounted Police. Over the years, its members have proudly carried out this command. Whatever their role—mounted redcoat, buffalo-coated customs official, pilot, ship's captain, motorcycle policeman, lab technician, or stubble-cheeked undercover agent —they have responded to the challenge of serving their country in an ever-changing force with proud traditions and a noble history.

M. A. MacDonald
Author, *The Royal Canadian Mounted Police*

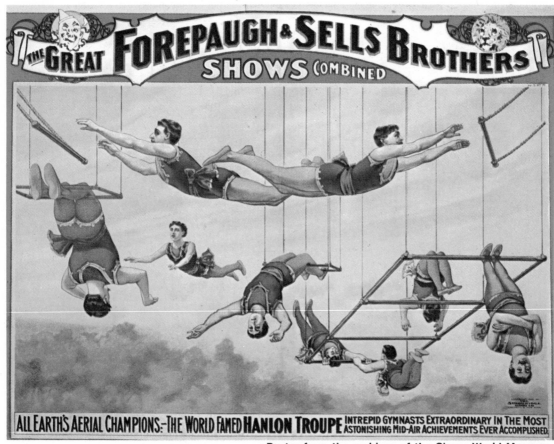

CIRCUS WORLD MUSEUM

"La-a-dies and gentlemen and children of all ages! Step right up and see the Greatest Show on Earth. Thrill to the sound of the big brass band. Watch animal trainers tame fierce lions. See dancing bears and daring aerial acts and the world's funniest clowns."

If these words remind you of the special excitement of a circus, you'll enjoy a visit to an unusual museum whose purpose is to collect, display, and preserve everything connected with the history of the circus.

The Circus World Museum is in Baraboo, Wisconsin, where more than 20 percent of the circuses of the United States began. The museum is the realization of the dream of John Kelley, a lifelong friend and the personal lawyer of the famous circus family the Ringlings. Kelley feared that over the years the outdoor circus would become a thing of the past, and that eventually the unique excitement of the old-time circus days would be forgotten. With the help of a handful of friends, Kelley awakened the interest of civic groups and of the State Historical Society. Famous circus owners from all over the world donated equipment and mementos, and on July 1, 1959, the Circus World Museum was officially opened to the public.

The museum, owned and operated by the State Historical Society of Wisconsin, covers about 25 acres of land that was once the headquarters of the Ringling Brothers circus.

The excitement of another era is re-created on the museum's grounds.

From 9 A.M. to 5:30 P.M., from the middle of May to the middle of September, thousands of visitors come to the museum to relive the excitement of the world of the circus.

Six display buildings, plus the 1,200-seat Moeller Hippodrome, offer endless delights for the circus lover. One of the buildings, the Circus Parade Pavillion, houses more than 75 circus wagons, the largest collection of its kind in the world. The ornately decorated vehicles, some of which are 100 years old, have been restored to look just as they did when their appearance on thousands of Main Streets heralded the annual arrival of the circus.

On a specially built railroad track stands a train that once belonged to the Ringling Bros. and Barnum & Bailey Circus. Crowds gather each morning to watch as circus equipment of a generation or two ago is loaded onto the train with the help of a team of Percheron horses.

Goat carts, pony carts, and a glittering carousel provide happy hours of fun for youngsters. Familiar tunes pour from the old-fashioned steam calliope *America,* and the delicious aroma of fresh popcorn fills the air.

One of the museum's most highly prized possessions is an elaborate miniature circus, perfect in every detail, with over 3,000 moving parts. Inside an old-time big top, tiny animated lion tamers, acrobats, animals, and clowns perform spectacular acts.

Providing exciting entertainment is not the museum's only purpose. For students of circus history the Circus World Museum offers a complete research service and a school. The Circus Library and Archives Building houses a vast collection of old posters, photographs, and programs, which

Circus wagons from the museum's unique collection: *Pawnee Bill* (*above*).

Twin Lion, an English wagon of a century ago.

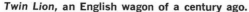

are loaned to museums and art centers around the world for special displays.

Every summer a 27-car circus train packed with some of the museum's most valuable possessions makes the 125-mile journey from its permanent home in Baraboo to Milwaukee, the state's largest city. Thousands of people line the route and wave as the train passes by. On the Fourth of July tens of thousands more jam the downtown streets of the city to see a real circus parade complete with animals, clowns, and gaily painted wagons drawn by teams of plumed horses. Elephants, camels, and zebras form part of the procession; lions, bears, and tigers peer at the crowds from behind the bars of their wheeled cages. All of the performers, led by a resplendent ringmaster, wear beautiful, traditional costumes. Acrobats turn cartwheels, clowns joke with the spectators, and trumpets blare. For one glorious day the city's streets come alive with all the excitement of a real old-fashioned circus.

The ornately decorated *Star Tab.*

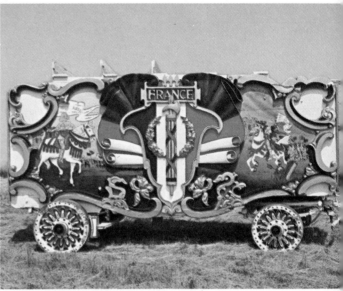

An old-fashioned French bandwagon.

Columbia, the museum's first bandwagon.

alberobello come venezia

salviamola
Iᴬ MOSTRA
di pittori veneti contemporanei
dal 5 al 20 agosto 1973

The *trulli* of Alberobello are seen in the foreground of this panorama.

THE HOUSES OF ALBEROBELLO

The people of Alberobello—a truly unusual town in southern Italy—have a problem. It is a problem they share with the people of every other town or city that has become a popular place for tourists to visit. For people come from all over Europe—and many other parts of the world—to see this little town. And the residents of Alberobello must go about their normal daily routines and raise their families. But they must also make sure that the unique things about Alberobello, the things the visitors come to see, are maintained.

Alberobello (its name means "beautiful tree" in English) has about 10,000 inhabitants. It is located in the Apulia region of southern Italy, 40 miles south of the Adriatic seaport of Bari. Although it is frequently very hot in summer, the climate is dry, the air pure, and the nights cool. There are other towns in Italy—and in other countries—that have all of these characteristics. But Alberobello has something special. It has its own special houses, called *trulli,* and they are unlike anything else in the world.

To begin with, the *trulli* of Alberobello get their odd name from the *trullo,* the cone-shaped, stone roof which is the most unique part of their design. The *trullo* gives each house a gnomish, fairy-tale look. As one contemporary travel writer has suggested, Alberobello might well be the dwelling place of Snow White and the Seven Dwarfs.

In August, 1973, an exhibition of work by Venetian artists was held in Alberobello. It was the first of a number of cultural exchanges planned between the great Adriatic city of Venice in the north and little Alberobello in the south. The two unique places had decided to unite in a common cause. Both cities, according to posters that could be seen on the walls and in the shopwindows of Alberobello, are in great danger. "Alberobello is like Venice," the posters read. "Let's save it."

Save it from what? Venice, we know, has two enemies—the sea, and industry, which pollutes the surrounding area. Each year, Venice sinks farther into the waters of the Adriatic. Alberobello, built on rocky terrain in the agricultural south, is beyond the direct reach of both industry and the Adriatic Sea. But it has other, equally threatening problems.

Alberobello's problem is double. The people of the town must maintain the already existing *trulli,* for it is the *trulli* that make Alberobello unique. But in order to keep the *trulli* and the ancient look of the town, the people must obey very severe building restrictions. The building restrictions that protect the *trulli* hold back the natural growth of the community. The strange thing is that a good many of Alberobello's modern problems are not new at all. Building restrictions were first imposed on the people of the city in the 15th century.

▶ **THE HISTORY OF THE *TRULLI***

The story of how the *trulli* came to be built is as interesting as the pointed houses themselves. It begins in 1481. In those days Alberobello was part of an area called the county (or countship) of Conversano. When the feudal ruler of Conversano, Giuliantonio Acquaviva, died in the successful defense of Otranto against the Turks, his land and all his feudal privileges were passed on to his son, Andrea Matteo. The whole transaction was recorded in a document dated May 15, 1481. It is in this document that Alberobello is mentioned for the first time. The full name of the town was then Silva Alberobelli ("forest of beautiful trees").

Andrea Matteo, the new count, had simple houses built in Alberobello. They were originally built of wood from the oak forests of the area. In fact, the "beautiful trees" for which the town was named were these very oak trees. The result was a village of round, wooden huts with pointed, thatched roofs. In shape, the tiny houses probably looked a good deal like the stone *trulli* you can see today in Alberobello. But the fact that the first houses of Alberobello were built of wood and had round thatched roofs suggests—some historians think—a relationship or connection between the houses of Alberobello and certain ancient African and Oriental buildings. Perhaps, the experts say, the *trulli* were built according to a design that some traveler or seafarer had found in a far corner of Asia or Africa.

According to documents, however, the first stone house with a *trullo* was built in Alberobello in 1550. This is an astonishing fact when you remember the pictures you have seen of the huge, elaborate palaces that were being built in Rome and Florence and throughout Italy at the same time as the almost primitive little *trulli.* Yet there is no doubt, as odd as it seems, that the first classic stone *trullo* in Alberobello dates from the 16th century.

The ruler of Alberobello and the surrounding country at the time the first stone *trulli* were built was Giovanni Antonio Acquaviva. He was one of the sternest of all the counts of Conversano. One of his many decrees concerned the building of houses. All houses in Alberobello were to be built, the decree said, according to one model. Each house, although independent of the houses on either side, was to touch them in front, so as to form a continuous wall along the street. Each house was to be made of native stone that had been cut into blocks and stacked "dry" (that is, no mortar or cement was to be used). This method of construction was to be followed so that the local authorities could easily tear down the house of any citizen who did not pay his debts or was disobedient to the orders of the counts.

The Count's ruling that all the houses of Alberobello look the same was followed for over 250 years. During those long years the *trulli* style of building spread throughout the nearby Valley of Itria. Even today the valley is dotted with *trulli.* Nowhere, however, is there as impressive a collection of the little houses as on the two hillsides of Alberobello.

In 1797 the 300-year rule of Alberobello by its feudal lords, the counts of Conversano, came to an end. The town came directly under the authority of the kingdom of Naples. The people of Alberobello lost no time in using their new independence. On August 1, 1797, the foundation stones were laid for the Casa D'Amore (named for the D'Amore family, who were to live in it). The Casa

A street of classic *trulli* on one of the hillsides of Alberobello. It is this look that the town government and the government of Italy are trying to preserve. In the house at the left you can see clearly the traditional dry-stone construction of the walls and of the *trullo*.

The Trullo Sovrano is a unique house in a town of unique houses.

D'Amore was built with mortar and cement and it was not built in the *trulli* style. In fact it looked—and looks, for it's still standing—much like any other house in southern Italy. Today tourists visiting Alberobello rarely notice the Casa D'Amore. But in its day, when it stood alone—not 150 yards from the palace of the counts of Conversano—it was the symbol of the town's new freedom from the stern rule of the counts. On the facade of the Casa D'Amore is a plaque whose inscription—now quite dim because of many coats of white-wash—reads *Ex auctoritate regia—Hoc erectum AD 1797* ("by royal authority this building was erected in 1797").

Poor Alberobello! Its freedom to build as it pleased lasted little more than 100 years. By a decree of the Italian government on June 20, 1909, the two *trulli*-covered hillsides of the town—as well as the Casa D'Amore—were declared national monuments. The law decreed that the existing buildings could not

A traditional house in a quiet corner of town.

be altered. And it became illegal in the historic district to construct any new buildings that were not traditional *trulli,* built as they had been built for 400 years.

And that was not all. Further strict laws dealing with zoning and the preservation of the *trulli* were passed between 1912 and 1930. Even today, the Italian government keeps a close watch on any structure built in Alberobello.

Despite all of the building codes, the people of Alberobello—like most Italians—are very independent. The most famous of all the *trulli,* and the one mentioned most often in the guide books, is essentially illegal in its design. Called the Trullo Sovrano, it has two stories instead of the traditional one and looks enormous by comparison with its small, story-book neighbors.

▶ BUILDING *TRULLI*

The classic *trullo* building is essentially a one-family house of two to four rooms, including a kitchen, with a tiny garden in back, and a well to collect rainwater. Its exterior design has not changed in four centuries. By law, the method of construction is unchanged too. The floors are of stone. The outside walls of the houses, although 2 or 3 feet thick, are not higher than 6 feet. They are still built of native stone, cut into blocks. More modern building materials, such as brick or cement blocks, are not allowed. The rooms are each from 12 to 15 feet square. (The rooms must be square in order to accommodate the round *trullo,* which is, at the same time, the ceiling and the roof of each room.)

The *trullo* is raised, without using scaffolding, by the skilled *casedaro,* or house builder. The builder lays precisely cut stone blocks around the top of the room walls, spiraling them gradually inward toward the peak, thus gradually transforming the square into a circle. When the *trullo* is completed, each room of the house is higher than it is wide, measuring from 18 to 21 feet from floor to peak. The outside of the *trullo* is then flagged with stone roofing shingles, its peak is crowned with an ornamental device of sculpted stone, and it is sometimes decorated with crosses or other traditional symbols painted in white.

▶TOURISTS

In the past 10 years, the *trulli* have become very fashionable. Alberobello has become a tourist center. The charm of the *trulli;* the hot, dry climate of the region; and the beaches on the Adriatic, only a half hour's drive away, have led a new generation of prosperous Italians to build summer houses in Alberobello. Many of the newcomers would like to build in the *trulli* style. However, only the wealthiest of them can afford to. The *maestri,* the master builders skilled in the art of building *trulli,* are a vanishing breed.

The disappearance of the *maestri* is of even greater importance because of the great need of keeping the remaining old *trulli* in good repair. And the cost of this kind of skilled maintenance, even when it is available, is beyond the means of many of the people who live in the *trulli.* Often the inhabitants of the *trulli* are poor—but very proud—farmers, who leave Alberobello early each morning to work their few acres in the surrounding countryside.

There is still another sense in which Alberobello needs to be saved. It needs to be protected from tourism, even though tourists bring the townspeople much-needed business and money. Even the tourists themselves see the problem. For the streets of this beautiful, small city throng with visitors. Shops offering garish souvenirs spring up on unexpected corners. The traffic is thick. It all has a carnival atmosphere that is alien to the true spirit of the place, which is closed, sober, and austere. A dozen years ago, people spoke of Alberobello as one of the "undiscovered" beauties of southern Italy. All of that is changing. This is the reason why the people of Alberobello—like the people of Venice—know that they must work hard to save their very rare and special homes.

RICHARD TEDESCHI
University of Massachusetts (Amherst)

A banner announces Alberobello's exhibit of work by modern Venetian painters.

A MONSTER IN LOCH NESS?

Once upon a time—in the 6th century, to be exact—Saint Columba, with some fellow monks, was roaming over the hills and vales of the Scottish Highlands. (They were there to convert the people to Christianity.) Suddenly a strange thing happened: They saw a giant animal rear out of the waters of a nearby lake and lunge toward the shore. Apparently the great sea monster became frightened when he heard the monks scream because he wasted no time retreating into the murky waters.

This story may or may not be just a legend; but since that time there have been countless stories of huge sea monsters' being seen in many of Scotland's picturesque lakes. Most of these sightings have occurred in Loch Ness, a beautiful stretch of water in northern Scotland. In fact, it is the very same loch, or lake, where Saint Columba spotted his famous monster.

Loch Ness, with its surrounding country-side, lends itself quite well to stories of mysterious goblins, monsters, and the like—particularly on cloudy, misty days or in the eerie shadows of early evening. The loch is about 24 miles long and 1 mile wide, and its dark waters reach a depth of 750 feet. Grassy banks framed by green wooded hills form an impressive and appropriate backdrop. The ruins of Castle Urquhart, a medieval fortress, are situated on a bluff overlooking the loch. Just the right atmosphere for a ghost or two —or maybe even a monster.

This region of Scotland was isolated until a road was built alongside the loch in the early 1930's. The construction of the road involved felling trees and dynamiting rock. The blasting of rock and the avalanches down the hillsides are thought to have disturbed the sleeping Loch Ness monster. Soon after the road was completed, there were reports that Nessie, as the creature is affectionately called, had come to the surface many times and had been spotted by villagers and visitors alike. Several people told of having seen "two black shiny lumps 5 feet long protruding 2 feet out of the water." Others described "a giraffe-like neck and absurdly small head, out of all proportion to the dark gray body; skin like an elephant; two very short forelegs or flippers clearly seen." Now, when you think

Three mysterious humps rise from the dark waters of Loch Ness.

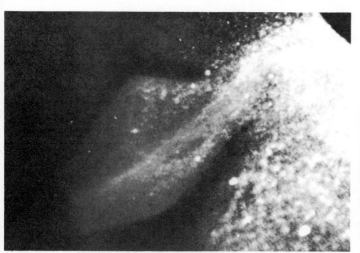
Underwater photograph of the monster's "flipper."

An avid monster fan holds a model of Nessie.

of it, that's not exactly a description of your simple, everyday sea urchin.

These remarkable monster sightings were reported in newspapers throughout the world. Since that time, thousands of people have claimed to have seen "something" in the loch. In 1934 the only satisfactory photograph of Nessie was taken. It shows the long neck and small head of an unknown creature thrust up out of the water. There's no telling what's at the other end of that long neck!

Most scientists and many doubting Thomases, in spite of the photograph, believe that there isn't now, never was, and never will be a monster in Loch Ness. They attribute the numerous sightings to very busy imaginations. But that hasn't discouraged the avid "monster devotees." A large number of nonscientists—and a few scientists for that matter—believe that Loch Ness contains a breeding colony of large, unknown acquatic animals. They think that huge saltwater creatures may have been trapped in Scotland's lakes when the inland waters were cut off from the sea at the end of the last ice age.

Almost every year, full-scale monster investigations are held during the summer months. Curious people come from far and wide to set up their own spotting stations. And there they stay, binoculars and cameras in hand, waiting for just a glimpse of Nessie. Some determined Nessie fans have even launched mini-submarines to see if they can

rout the elusive sea creature from its mysterious, watery hiding place into the open.

In 1972, investigators from the Academy of Applied Science, in Boston, gathered together their most modern scientific equipment and traveled to Loch Ness. From the shore they kept nightly watch on the waters of the loch, and sure enough, their persistence paid off. The sonar gear suddenly indicated that something large was lurking nearby in the water. Whatever it was disappeared from the sonar screen, only to reappear a few minutes later, and then vanish again. A series of color and black-and-white underwater pictures verified that there definitely was "something unusual" swimming about.

All of the evidence gathered by the scientific team was examined by experts, who concluded that the sonar had picked up not one but *two* Nessies. The creatures appeared to be at least 20 to 30 feet long, with several humps, fins, and long tails.

And that's where we stand today. The mystery hasn't been solved; the plot has only thickened. Most people like a good mystery, and the Highlands of Scotland seem to have provided one: Do we have a Loch Ness myth or a Loch Ness monster? Is Nessie the product of a legend dating back to the 6th century and overactive imaginations? Or is there really a sea monster lurking in the waters of Loch Ness, waiting for the right moment to make a grand entrance upon the world scene?

Mount Carmel overlooks the harbor of Haifa, Israel's chief port.

ISRAEL: PAST AND PRESENT

Israel celebrated its 25th anniversary as a nation in 1973. Its first 25 years had been years of achievement and fulfillment. At last, after centuries of living in other countries and suffering persecution, the Jewish people had their own homeland. Isaiah's prophecy had come true:

"And they shall build houses, and inhabit them; and they shall plant vineyards, and eat the fruit of them. They shall not build, and another inhabit; they shall not plant, and another eat . . . ."

But the first 25 years were also a time of war and conflict. And the conflict goes on. The Arab states have never recognized Israel, and there have been four major wars between the Arabs and the Jews since Israel's declaration of statehood. The latest war broke out with stunning suddenness on October 6, 1973.

Israel came into being on May 14, 1948. On that day leaders of the Jewish people in Palestine met in the city of Tel Aviv, and David Ben-Gurion, who was to become Israel's first prime minister, read the proclamation of the nation's independence.

Between World War I and World War II, Palestine had been a British mandate. During those years there had been outbreaks of hostilities between Arab and Jewish nationalists. At the end of World War II the British asked the United Nations to help solve the problem. In November, 1947, the United Nations recommended that Palestine be partitioned into an Arab state and a Jewish state, and that Jerusalem be established as an international city under United Nations control. But the United Nations recommendation was never carried out.

The British had set May 15, 1948, as the date by which they would have their forces out of Palestine. Hours before the deadline Israel declared itself a state. And hours after that, Palestinian Arabs, joined by the armies of neighboring Arab states, attacked. Before it was a day old the state of Israel was fighting a full-scale war.

The Israelis drove back the Arabs and in 1949 signed armistice agreements with them. The agreements left Jordan in possession of the west bank of the Jordan River, and the city of Jerusalem divided between Israel and Jordan.

A severe problem, and one that has not yet been solved, came out of the war. During the fighting, thousands of Palestinian Arabs left their homes. They have been living in refugee camps, many of them on the west bank of the Jordan River and in the Gaza Strip, ever since.

The Arab position is that these refugees should be allowed to go back to live in Israel. Israel's position is that settling the refugees must be part of a broad peace plan, and that has not yet been reached.

The next large-scale fighting took place in 1956. In that year Egypt nationalized the Suez Canal and refused to let Israel use it. Israel, joined by Britain and France, invaded Egypt and occupied the Sinai Peninsula. However, the United Nations stepped in and ordered the occupying nations to leave. A United Nations peacekeeping force moved into the Sinai.

War broke out again in 1967. In May, 1967, Egypt moved troops to Israel's southern border and closed the Gulf of Aqaba, so that Israel had no water route to the East. In June, Israeli troops struck so swiftly and with such strength that in 6 days they defeated the forces of Egypt, along with those of Jordan and Syria.

At the end of the Six-Day War the Gulf of Aqaba was open once more, and Israel controlled Egypt's Sinai Peninsula, the Gaza Strip, Syria's Golan Heights, and the west bank of the Jordan River. The west bank included the part of Jerusalem that had been controlled by Jordan. In this part of Jerusalem is the holiest site of Judaism—the Western Wall, or Wailing Wall.

Israel continued to occupy the territories over which it had gained control in 1967. Many of the 1,000,000 Arabs who live in these lands became part of Israel's work force. The United Nations Security Council asked Israel to withdraw from the occupied territories, but it was Israel's position that it would not withdraw unless the Arab states entered into direct peace negotiations.

Peace negotiations did not take place. Six years after the Six-Day War a fourth war— known as both the October War and the Yom Kippur War—broke out. Hostilities began on Yom Kippur, October 6, 1973. As religious Jews were praying on this holiest of days,

On a clear day the city of Jerusalem seems bathed in a golden light.

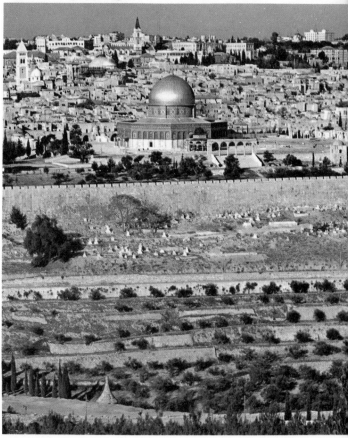

Clusters of modern housing units have been built in the Negev.

Arab forces attacked on two fronts at once. Egyptian forces crossed the Suez Canal to the Israeli-occupied Sinai Peninsula, and Syrian forces attacked the Israeli-occupied Golan Heights in the north. Other Arab states, including Jordan, entered the war, and the loss of life on both sides was high in the fighting that followed.

On October 22 a cease-fire approved by the United Nations Security Council went into effect. A United Nations peacekeeping force moved into the area. On November 11, Egypt and Israel signed a formal cease-fire agreement. Following the signing, the two nations exchanged prisoners of war.

Until there is a firm peace between Israel and its Arab neighbors, Israel stays armed and ready to defend itself. But the costs of defense are high. A large part of Israel's budget goes to pay these costs, and Israelis share the burden through the taxes they pay. Young Jewish men and women know that as soon as they are 18 they must serve a term in the armed forces, and afterward remain in the reserves.

But the emphasis for Israelis is less on burdens and costs than on accomplishments and rewards. When Israel became a state its leaders were faced with two enormous tasks: to make a home for hundreds of thousands of homeless Jewish people and to build a nation.

One of the laws of the state of Israel is the Law of the Return, which gives every Jew everywhere the right to enter Israel as an immigrant. David Ben-Gurion has called this "ingathering of the exiles"—many of them victims of Nazism—a major objective of Israel. Since 1948, more than 1,250,000 Jews from eastern and central Europe, from such Arab countries as Yemen and Iraq, from North Africa, and from western Europe and the Americas have immigrated to Israel. Their languages and backgrounds have been different, but their needs have been the same: a place to live, schools for their children, and work to do.

There has been a huge program of building towns and villages, of setting up social and educational services, of creating jobs in agriculture and industry, and of training people to do them.

Israel has managed to do more than open its gates to the exiles. It has been able to absorb them. Today Israel is home to 3,000,000 people. The population has more than tripled since independence.

The business of building a prosperous nation has gone forward at the same time. The land has been improved, and the number of crops has increased. Large-scale irrigation projects have turned acres of the barren Negev into fruitful farmland. Israel grows most of the food it needs, raises cotton for its textile industry, and exports citrus fruit and cut flowers. Most farming communities are run as collectives (*kibbutzim*) or as co-operatives (*moshavim*).

Israel has also emerged as an industrial

nation. Its most important industrial export is polished diamonds. Its other industries include food processing, oil refining, and the manufacture of textiles and clothing, chemicals, electrical equipment, and aircraft.

In May, 1973, there was a huge military parade through the streets of Jerusalem, followed by fireworks and dancing, to celebrate the nation's first 25 years.

But even with all the emphasis on the past 25 years, no one in Israel ever forgets that 25 years is a very short time indeed in a land whose recorded history goes back 4,000 years. The modern Jews are the descendants of the Old Testament Hebrews. Most of the Jews were driven from Palestine by the Romans in the 1st and 2nd centuries A.D. and were scattered throughout the world.

The people in the new nation of Israel are conscious of their long history in this ancient land, and of the places associated with that history. The Biblical names—Jerusalem, Jericho, Beersheba—are all names on the map of modern Israel.

Millions of people share a feeling of closeness to this land. It is an area of deep meaning for Christians and Muslims, as well as for Jews. The town of Bethlehem, where Jesus was born, is sacred to Christians. Hebron, with its Tomb of Abraham, is a site revered by Muslims.

But the one place for which members of all three religions have a special feeling is Jerusalem. It is the holiest place of Judaism and Christianity, and the third holiest of Islam, after Mecca and Medina.

The Psalmist sang of it centuries ago, and in the Middle East of today his words still have meaning: "Pray for the peace of Jerusalem."

A soccer game is part of the school day for youngsters in Eilat.

. . . there was neither hammer nor axe nor any tool of iron heard in the house, while it was in building. . . . So Solomon built the house, and finished it.

I Kings 6:7, 14

The temple Solomon built in Jerusalem was destroyed, but it was later rebuilt on the same spot. The Western Wall, once called the Wailing Wall, is the last remnant of the rebuilt temple. This wall is Judaism's most revered site.

And he said, Take now thy son, thine only son Isaac, whom thou lovest, and get thee into the land of Moriah; and offer him there for a burnt offering . . . .

Genesis 22:2

A gold-domed mosque, the Dome of the Rock, has been built over the huge rock that is believed to be the one on which Abraham prepared to sacrifice his son Isaac. It is also believed that the prophet Mohammed ascended to heaven from the same rock. For Muslims the site is the holiest in Jerusalem.

And he bearing his cross went forth into a place called the place of a skull, which is called in the Hebrew Golgotha: where they crucified him . . . .

John 19:17–18

The Via Dolorosa, or Way of Sorrows, is a winding street in the old part of Jerusalem. Jesus is said to have taken this path to Golgotha, or Calvary, the place of his Crucifixion. Today the Church of the Holy Sepulcher stands on the traditional site of the Crucifixion. For Christians the Via Dolorosa and Church of the Holy Sepulcher are places of deep religious meaning. Each year on Good Friday a procession reverently retraces Jesus' journey to Calvary.

Our feet shall stand within thy gates, O Jerusalem.

Psalm 122:2

Jerusalem, like other ancient cities, had a wall around it. The only way people could enter and leave the city was through one of the gates in the wall. Walls built in the 16th century still surround the Old City of Jerusalem, and people still enter and leave the Old City through gates in these walls. The Damascus Gate, pictured here, is in the northern wall.

. . . Jesus was born in Bethlehem of Judea in the days of Herod the king . . . .
Matthew 2:1

The Church of the Nativity in the town of Bethlehem marks the birthplace of Jesus.

And Jesus went about all Galilee, teaching in their synagogues, and preaching the gospel of the kingdom . . . .

Matthew 4:23

Much of Jesus' ministry took place in the region around the Sea of Galilee, which in modern Israel is called Lake Kinneret. A Franciscan convent, the Mount of Beatitudes, stands on its shores.

. . . the name of the city is Beer-sheba unto this day.

Genesis 26:33

And so it is. Beersheba, where the Old Testament patriarch Abraham lived, is the leading city of the Negev and the scene of a lively Arab market.

DOLLHOUSES OF THE PAST

Last Christmas I got . . . a new doll house, with real glass windows, a mantelpiece and doors that will open and shut. It has shades and curtains to the windows, a clock on the mantel, and furniture. Afterwards my sister gave me a pug dog, a grey cat and a stove and a coal scuttle, and a . . . doll named "Dina" to take care of the house. They are the right size for the house and make it look real.

From a young girl's letter written in 1891
to the magazine *The Doll's Dressmaker*

The dollhouse has been a popular children's toy for centuries. There is evidence that the children of ancient Egypt, Greece, and Rome may have played with some form of miniature houses. Archeologists have discovered scale models of houses, shops, and gardens in the tombs of ancient Egyptian

The Van Cortlandt House

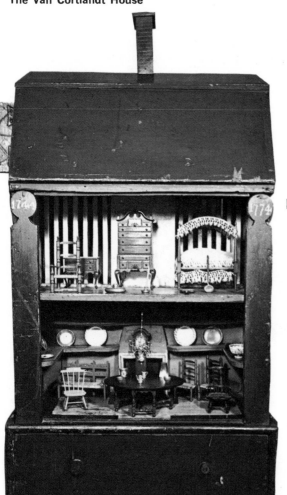

nobles. Although these models were placed in the tombs for religious reasons, they may also have been used as toys. If so, the dollhouse dates back over 4,000 years. However, the first dollhouse definitely known to have been used as a toy was made in Bavaria in the 1500's.

In the United States, many antique dollhouses were boxlike cabinets, with windows and doors but with no architectural design. Some, however, were constructed to resemble actual buildings. They had realistic exteriors in the front, and removable backs so that the children could play with the furniture and dolls. (In some dollhouses, each room had a separate front on hinges that could be swung open like a door.) There are replicas of mansions, country houses, and city brownstones. There are also farms, southern plantation manor houses, and New England homes with turrets and spires.

▶ THE VAN CORTLANDT HOUSE

The earliest known American dollhouse is the Van Cortlandt House, which dates from 1744. Originally made for a Boston family, it eventually passed into the hands of the Van Cortlandts of New York. It is still preserved in the old Van Cortlandt Mansion. This dollhouse is a simple affair in appearance, standing up in boxlike fashion. It is over 4 feet in height and has four rooms. The base of the house is a drawer that may have been used for storing other toys.

The house has a Colonial-style roof, dull red in color, with a chimney, and an attic window that swings out. The original furnishings were lost over the years, but they have

The Brett House

been replaced with replicas of period pieces. For example, in the upstairs bedroom there is a canopied bed, typical of the 18th century, a night table with candleholder and candle, a chest of drawers, and a chair. The dining room has the original mantelpiece and crockery shelves. There are a chandelier, dining table, and several chairs.

▶THE BRETT HOUSE

A notable historic American dollhouse is the Brett House, named after its builder, the Reverend Dr. Philip M. Brett. He built the house in his spare time over a 2-year period (1838–40).

It is a realistic model, with each detail painstakingly crafted by the maker. It is a two-story house, with a pitched roof, a shuttered attic window, and a garden enclosed by a brick wall. The front of the house can be removed to display the beautifully furnished rooms. A lovely drawing room is comfortably furnished in early Victorian style. On the music stand is an open music book, in which the actual notes can be read. Nearby is a little harp. Over the mantelpiece is a tiny portrait of Dr. Brett.

Among the furnishings in the other rooms is a hutch (kitchen storage cabinet), complete with tiny silver goblets, coffeepot, punch bowl, and French wine server. A bookstand comes complete with postage stamp–size editions of the Bible, books of poetry, and a number of the classics. There is a tiny engraving of Rutgers College over the library mantelpiece. (Dr. Brett's grandfather was president of the college from 1825 to 1840.) There is even a pretty garden surrounding the house.

▶THE WARREN HOUSE

When it comes to elaborate furnishings, few dollhouses can match the Warren House, built in 1852 for the four daughters of Mrs. J. Mason Warren. Mrs. Warren supervised every detail of the house, which was constructed by a Salem, Massachusetts, cabinetmaker. The house has eight rooms, each with its own glass window. No detail was spared in decorating the three-story building, which is 6 feet high.

Every piece of linen—from table napkins to sheets and pillowcases—is monogrammed with the letter "W." The library contains tall

The Warren House

oak bookcases, and has silk wall hangings at both sides of the fireplace. Chairs and sofa are upholstered in velvet. At one time there was even a replica of a chess table with chessmen no bigger than grains of rice.

The dining room contains one particularly notable piece of furniture: a mahogany drop-leaf table. It is said to have been taken from a British ship captured by an American privateer during the War of 1812. The table was part of a collection of toys in the baggage of a British family en route to India.

▶A CIVIL WAR HOUSE

A particularly fine example of a Civil War dollhouse is in the possession of the Delaware Historical Society. Philadelphia craftsmen built the house for an 1864 fair held in that city to raise money to aid wounded and disabled Union soldiers. The three-story house stands 5½ feet in height. A brass nameplate

on the front door makes known that this is the residence of the famous Union General Ulysses S. Grant. For additional patriotic effect, the house number is 1776.

The front part of the house has six handsomely furnished and decorated rooms flanking a central hallway. Three additional rooms are found in the rear of the house. The exterior walls are divided into separate sections that swing out on their hinges to reveal each of the rooms. A most unusual room is the art gallery, complete with little paintings contributed by noted Philadelphia artists of the time. There is also a reproduction of a painting by a 17th-century Italian master.

The house was valued at $1,000 at the time of its display—a sum equal to more than 10 times that amount in today's money. Each item of furniture, drapery, carpeting, and the various accessories was exquisitely fashioned by hand. A trio of marble cutters worked 3

A Civil War House

The Uihlein House

days to produce the house's marble fireplaces. Although the house was very expensive for that time, it was not bought merely for display. The house was sold to a Union Army officer who presented it to his daughter.

▶THE UIHLEIN HOUSE

A beautiful example of a late Victorian dollhouse is the Uihlein House. It was originally given by a Mr. and Mrs. Fred Vogel to their 7-year-old daughter as a Christmas present. There is no doubt about when the house was built. A stained-glass window over the front door tells us the year, 1893.

The house is on a small stand and has four main rooms and several smaller ones. Over the years, the house was passed from one generation of children to another. It continued to be used as a toy until the 1930's. Doll-residents of the house represent the actual family members, including a set of

twins. The furnishings are mainly Victorian, but newer pieces were added in later years.

▶PRESIDENTS' DOLLHOUSES

Throughout the years many of the children of United States presidents have played with specially made dollhouses. One, still preserved, was given to Fanny Hayes, the daughter of President Rutherford B. Hayes, when she was 10 years old. It is an imposing three-story mansion, with a realistic front that includes balconied windows, a tall steeple-like turret, and a decorative roof with four chimneys. The back is open to reveal an assortment of rooms surrounding a spacious hall with a stairway.

Unfortunately, a unique dollhouse of another president's child has been lost. This one belonged to President Grover Cleveland's daughter Marion. It was a miniature reproduction of the White House.

173

In a *puja* ceremony, offerings are placed at the feet of a sacred statue.

JAINISM—2,500 YEARS OLD

"He who looketh on the creatures of the earth, big and small, as his own self, comprehendeth this immense world." If we think about these words and what they can mean, we can understand something of the spirit of the Jain religion and the importance of its teachings in our modern world.

These words are attributed to a man named Mahavira, who has been called the founder of Jainism. Mahavira lived in the 6th century B.C. and was a contemporary of the Buddha. The spiritual message of his life and teachings remains so important today that a special year-long commemoration of his death and his passage, as Jains believe, into eternal glory (which they call *parinirvana*) has been planned in India. These celebrations will begin on November 13, 1974.

What is Jainism, and why should we learn about it? It is little known outside India, its homeland. Even in India, Jains are today one of the smallest of religious groups. In the vast population of India, the Jains number only about 2,600,000 people. The majority of the Jains live in the Indian states of Gujarat and Rajasthan. Yet Mahavira's life and teaching are rich in meaning, not just for India but for the whole family of nations.

Jainism, with its strong command of non-violence, has influenced such modern leaders as Mahatma Gandhi and, through him, Martin Luther King. Its followers claim that Jainism is the oldest religion in the world. In one sense, Mahavira can be called the founder of Jainism, because his followers organized his preaching into a system of beliefs (like the Buddha and Jesus, he left no personal writings). But Jains think of him as only the last of 24 supreme saints, or Tirthankaras, whose line stretches back into the earliest history of the human race.

The word "Tirthankara" itself means "ford

maker," one who makes a place to cross a stream. Jains gave their 24 supreme saints this title because they believe that the Tirthankaras had crossed beyond the flowing stream of earthly existence and had reached the ultimate state of nirvana. Jains believe that the Tirthankaras, from the height of their wisdom, taught others the way to follow them. The term "Jain" itself comes from the word *jina,* meaning "one who has conquered," and the title *mahavira* means "great hero."

▶ EARLY BELIEFS

The claim of Jainism to such ancient origins is not difficult to understand if we take a look at what is known of religious life in ancient India. Jainism, along with Buddhism and Yoga, comes out of the tradition of wandering holy men. These men lived in caves and forests, depending on alms (money given to them as charity), and gathering simple plants for their food. They kept their physical needs at an absolute minimum so that they could free themselves from worldly cares and attain a pure vision of spiritual truth.

This ancient spiritual life of wandering holy men is part of a tradition called the *sramanic,* or ascetical, tradition. Although no one knows exactly how ancient this tradition is, it is certainly very old. Figures of people in the cross-legged "lotus position" of holy men in religious meditation have been discovered by archeologists in the ancient ruins of Mohenjo-Daro. Located in what is now Pakistan, this is the site of one city of the Indus Valley culture. This civilization extended over into northwestern India and dates back to at least 2800 B.C.

Jains do not teach belief in one great god or supreme being, as some Hindus do. Its *sramanas,* or holy men, did believe in spirits that had various good or evil powers. But none of these gods was an all-powerful supreme being. The power for divine goodness, they believed, rested only in man himself. Man is born a prisoner, the holy men thought, and the chains that bind him are a circle of cause and effect (karma) that is produced by and produces his own self-centered actions. By striving to overcome self, man can increase his power of goodness until it is finally so strong that he breaks these chains to attain perfect freedom. Obviously, such a goal is too difficult to achieve in a single lifetime. Hence this tradition logically teaches that everyone must go on being reborn for additional lifetimes until he attains perfect goodness, which is called nirvana.

▶ MAHAVIRA AND HIS FOLLOWERS

Mahavira was born into a princely family at Kundagrama, near the ancient city of Vaisali in the northern Indian state of Bihar. He was born at the end of the 6th century B.C. He married and had a daughter; but after his parents died he received his older brother's permission, as was the custom, to leave his family to become a wandering holy man. After 12 years as a holy man, Jains believe, he reached perfect spiritual enlightenment as a *kevalin,* "one who knows the unity of all things." Because he believed that what he had learned was not only for wandering holy men but for all of mankind, Mahavira spent the last 30 years of his life preaching and teaching. His followers included not only monks (called either *sramanas* or *sadhus*) and nuns (*sadhvis*), but laymen (*sravakas*) and laywomen (*sravikas*), who worked and had families.

For Mahavira really believed that "humanity is one." The depth of this vision is expressed in the term "ahimsa." Literally this means "non-killing." The word also means, to Jains, the "state of one who loves."

▶ JAIN BELIEF

The Jains believe that ultimate truth is perfect love. Destiny, they say, is to reach this state. In Jainism, ethics, based on human nature, is raised to the level of a science. To the Jains, the world is a closed system in which spirit (*jiva*) and everything else, which is non-spirit (*ajiva*), are continuously in motion and reacting on each other. Only when a soul is perfectly free from *ajiva* can it rise to the top of the world, where it will remain forever.

All beings, the Jains believe, have the same destiny, that of becoming perfect light: humanity is only the highest stage of the many stages in this journey.

But what is most important for Jains is the belief that just as every living thing—even the lowest forms of life—has the same ultimate destiny, so nothing "just happens." Selfish actions by one person hinder the development of other beings. Jains believe that since every creature has a right to life, any interference with that right is a form of killing. In Jain teaching, violence can breed only more violence. Those who are abused or oppressed, Jains believe, not only will fail to develop fully and contribute to society, but will also react against others to protect their rights. So ahimsa really extends to include such other ideals of Jainism as not lying (*satya*), not stealing (*acarya*), and not being attached to possessions (*aparigraha*).

Jain monks and nuns observe these precepts, or great vows, in their strictest forms. Monks of the Digambara ("sky-clad") sect wear no clothes and own nothing at all except a whisk of peacock feathers. This whisk, a sign of regard for all life, is used, before they sit down anywhere, to brush away any insects they might otherwise crush.

Svetambara ("white-clad") Jains believe that clothing is acceptable. Their monks and nuns wear simple white clothes, often made of "khaddar," as the handloomed cotton spun in India's cottage industries is called. Except for a change of clothing, strict Svetambara Jains own nothing else but their insect whisks, which are made of cotton fibers.

In the effort to live the vow of *aparigraha* to the fullest, monks and nuns do not own or even handle money. In all their needs they are cared for by pious Jain lay people, who give them shelter and food. In the early days of Jainism, the ideal of being a homeless wanderer was enforced so strictly that monks and nuns stayed in one place only during the monsoon, or rainy season. This exception was made to avoid stepping on the many small insects and other creatures that come out in great numbers during the monsoon.

In the course of time some monks and nuns did begin to live permanently in monasteries attached to temples. It became obvious to the 15th-century monk Lonka Sa that this custom of living in monasteries was causing too much interest in security and possessions. To combat this, he ordered his followers to live only in simple houses built for them by lay people. Members of this group are called Sthanakavasis ("staying in a place").

Whether or not they "stay in a place," Jain monks and nuns never travel very far, as they are permitted no form of transportation except walking. They also wear the *mukhavastrika,* a small white cloth that covers the mouth and protects them from breathing in and killing small insects.

Devout Jain lay people strive to follow ahimsa as closely as possible. To overcome possessiveness, some make a vow to acquire and spend only a certain amount of money within a given period. Other important duties are helping the poor, relieving fear and anxiety, instructing the ignorant, giving medicine to the sick, and showing hospitality to guests and strangers. Jains are strict vegetarians and do not drink alcoholic beverages,

An ancient Jain cave temple is cut into a rocky hillside in south India.

which they believe may harm their judgment, or smoke, because it might injure their health. Friendliness to all is the very heart of Jain religion, for every being is regarded as one's own self. A Jain's morning prayer, in which he forgives all who may have hurt him and expresses sorrow for any hurt he may have inflicted on others, is the central act of his life.

In Jainism there is a close community spirit. Holy men and lay people are well known to each other. Monks and nuns do not close themselves off behind monastic walls. They share their ideas and meditations with everyone who is interested.

A small, newer sect of Jains called Terepanthi does not have monks or nuns, but follows gurus (spiritual teachers). Terepanthis do not give to charity; instead they are working to create a new social order, in which no one will be proud because he has given to others and no one will feel bemeaned or inferior because he has had to receive.

Jains regard wastefulness as immoral. The goods they possess are meant to be put to the best possible use. A large number of Jains are prosperous businessmen. In the spirit of sharing with others, they have formed many philanthropic organizations. One of the most important of these is the Sahu Jaina Trust, which provides funds for research and for scholarships for poor Jains, helps pay for the printing of religious literature, maintains temples and hospitals, and makes contributions for restoring art treasures. It also promotes vegetarianism, nonviolence, and the preservation of animal life.

Jainism has a rich heritage of art in the temples built to honor its saints. Some spiritual leaders, following the reformer Lonka Sa, have pointed out that the worship of the Tirthankaras is not mentioned in the holy scriptures. They also reason that as these perfect beings are now in nirvana, beyond the action of cause and effect, they cannot hear prayers or grant favors. Such ideas, however, have little influence among most Jains. Offerings of flowers, coconuts, rice, and coins to statues of the Tirthankaras are made to honor them in the hope of obtaining blessings. These *puja* ceremonies, conducted by priests (who are not monks), are often very beautiful.

Jains gather in a beautiful temple in Bombay.

▶ THE ANNIVERSARY YEAR

The celebrations planned for the 2,500th anniversary of Mahavira are, in the true spirit of Jainism, directed largely toward improving social conditions. Among other things, the sum of 500,000 rupees is being allocated for the building of roads, schools, and hospitals in Mahavira's "home state" of Bihar. Sixteen libraries and children's centers for the rural poor are also to be built.

Jainism is also working for world peace. In the quest to realize, throughout the world, its vision of a society based on human spiritual capacity and ruled by nonviolence, Muni Sushil Kumar founded the Conference of World Religions. This group has scheduled a meeting for November, 1974, as part of the celebrations of Mahavira's anniversary.

With its teaching that all things are related to one another and that love is the supreme reality, this ancient religion has great meaning for people today.

BARBARA T. BLAIR
Kent Fellow
Danforth Foundation

FUN TO READ

An illustration from *The Funny Little Woman*, winner of the 1973 Caldecott Medal.

EXCITING NEW BOOKS

An especially exciting picture book has reached the bookshelves. It is called *Anansi the Spider: A Tale from the Ashanti*. It was adapted and illustrated by Gerald McDermott. Anansi is a favorite folk hero of the Ashanti people, who live in the modern African nation of Ghana. The stories about Anansi, in one form or another, have been carried by black people wherever they have settled. And now Anansi's truly amazing adventures are being read by people everywhere. In this tale, we learn of the adventures that befall Anansi and we hear how his six brave sons—and no one's sons ever had stranger names—come to their famous father's rescue again and again. The story is illustrated in the bright and beautiful colors of African fabrics and paintings.

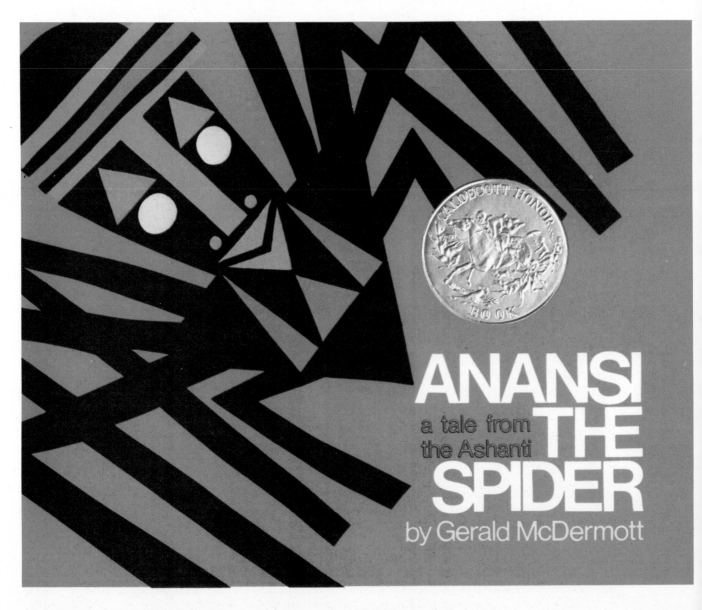

Piper Paw is the name of the bold young cat glowering at you from the cover of *No Kiss for Mother,* a very funny new book written and illustrated by Tomi Ungerer. Piper has problems with his terribly sweet mother, Mrs. Velvet Paw. Piper does not like being kissed, for one thing; and for another, he likes being naughty. It comes to him naturally. But most of all, Piper does not want Mrs. Velvet Paw to kiss him quite so much. You'll see how he solves his problem if you read the book.

The moment you see it, you will understand why Blair Lent won the Caldecott Medal in 1973 for his picture book *The Funny Little Woman*. You can tell just by looking at the cover that the illustrations are going to be exciting and funny—and very Japanese. But look inside, too, because this Japanese folktale, retold by Arlene Mosel, is wonderful reading. You have probably never heard about the mysterious and very hungry creatures called *oni* who live underground and who just adore the dumplings whipped up for them by the funny little woman. But you'll learn all about the *oni* and their amazing appetites when you read this book. And you'll learn about something else, too—the Japanese sense of humor. Japanese folktales are often filled with laughter. The adventures of the little woman are very funny and the illustrations are as lovely as the nicest Japanese prints.

The Funny Little Woman

RETOLD BY
Arlene Mosel

PICTURES BY
Blair Lent

The John Newbery Medal, the highest award for a book for young people, was won in 1973 by Jean Craighead George for her book *Julie of the Wolves*. This is a serious and exciting novel about the adventures of an Eskimo girl named Julie who is 13 and determined to escape the problems she is having among her people. She goes off into the vast Arctic tundra and is saved from death by a pack of wolves with whom she lives. You will not be bored for a second by this book. It lets you enter a world completely different from the one you live in. In a fascinating way, it helps you understand the problems of another human being. And you will be amazed to find that many of Julie's problems are like those we all face. The fine illustrations by John Schoenherr capture the mysterious world of the Arctic tundra. Everyone will enjoy *Julie of the Wolves*.

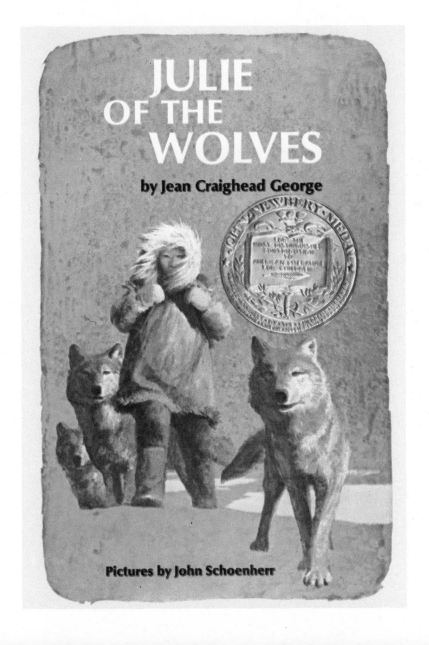

JULIE OF THE WOLVES

by Jean Craighead George

Pictures by John Schoenherr

It is quite likely that you have never known a witch or her mother or her cat. It is even more likely that you have never known a goblin. There is no guarantee that you will be interested in actually meeting any of these characters once you have read about them in *Dorrie and the Goblin,* written and illustrated by Patricia Coombs. But you will enjoy every minute of their adventures. For Dorrie is, indeed, a witch, and has a mother, and a cat named Gink. She also has, she discovers, a goblin for whom she is responsible. And that's where the trouble—and the fun—start.

DORRIE
and the Goblin

Patricia Coombs

The new edition of *Snow-White and the Seven Dwarfs* is probably one of the most beautiful books you will ever see. The text—which is translated from the original German of the Brothers Grimm by a famous poet, Randall Jarrell—is wonderful. But you will remember the illustrations for a very long time. They were done by Nancy Ekholm Burkert. In lovely, delicate color they capture the very spirit of the tale—they capture the look of the past, of secrets locked in splendid tapestries and in precious old manuscripts. And it all comes alive for us to enjoy now.

Snow-White and the Seven Dwarfs

A TALE FROM THE BROTHERS GRIMM TRANSLATED BY
RANDALL JARRELL · PICTURES BY NANCY EKHOLM BURKERT

I DON'T UNDERSTAND

I don't understand why people hurt each other. I don't understand why people who love one another . . .

I just don't understand it.

Every year when the circus came to the Garden I would pick out a night and then I'd go up to see him. I'd sit high up and look down at the three rings until I picked him out. Then I'd lean forward and watch him do his act. He did a clown act on the low wire. He was good and he was graceful. I remember one year they gave him the center ring. The whole arena hushed (he worked higher up then) and he pretended he had lost his balance and that he was falling and the people gasped—but he never fell. The act was a really good one, and at the end of it he got a lot of applause. He used the clown suit then, it's true, but the act was different. He was a high-wire artist. Now he had come lower, nearer to the ground, and as he did, year after year, I could see (and I was growing older, mind you, I was 18 now) that he was becoming nothing but an old and tired clown.

He was working hard for laughs.

So this year, after the show was over, I went downstairs and showed the pass that he always sent me when the circus came to the Garden. The guards let me go to the dressing room where he was taking off his clown suit.

"Hello, Eddie," he said.

· "Hello."

"You catch the act?"

"Uh-huh."

He was wiping his face, and with each wipe the clown colors came off. I could see him as he really was—a man close to fifty who was beginning to look tired and weary about it all, especially around the eyes.

"How did it go, Eddie?"

"All right."

He stopped his wiping and looked at me.

"Just all right?"

I nodded because I always found it hard to lie to him. He shrugged his shoulders slightly and went on wiping off his makeup.

"How's your mother?"

"Okay."

"Still teaching school?"

"Yes."

"And you?"

"I just finished."

He smiled at me, almost proudly, and then he went over to the small sink and turned on the water and washed his face and hands briskly.

"Going on to college?"

"Yes."

"Going to study anything in particular?"

He was combing his jet black hair, and I could see that it was beginning to thin out. His face that had always been so strong and handsome was slack and lined.

"I think I want to be a lawyer."

He turned from the mirror, the comb in his hand held high and his eyes lit up with that old flash and sparkle. For an instant his face was young and glowing again.

"Say, that's good to hear, Eddie. Good to hear."

"I'll take a crack at it."

He came away from the mirror briskly and now stood close to me. Something inside me began to ache—terribly.

"You'll do more than take a crack at it. You'll make a success of it. You will, Eddie."

"Maybe," I said.

His hand came down and hit the small, old table for emphasis.

"No maybes at all. You'll do it. You'll go out and do it, Eddie. I know you will. I know it in every bone in my body. That's how sure I know it."

Then we were silent for a while.

And all the time the ache was in me. All the time that I watched him get into his street clothes. He was still a neat and nice dresser and he was the kind of a man that you looked at twice when you walked with him.

No, that's not so. Not so at all anymore. Maybe when I was younger and I walked with him that happened. But it didn't happen when we walked across the street, across Eighth Avenue and into a diner and sat down together.

"What do you feel like eating, Eddie?"

"I'll take a roast beef sandwich."

"And drink?"

"Milk."

"No coffee? You're old enough."

"Just milk."

He smiled as he ordered coffee for himself and I thought there was a bitterness in his smile when he said, "Your mother brings you up right, Eddie."

"I just don't care for coffee. That's all."

"You don't care because she made you not care. Isn't that it?" And now the voice was bitter.

"Maybe she had good reason to make me that way," I said.

He flushed as if I had hit him and then looked away from me. And I wanted to reach over and put my hand on his and say, I didn't mean it. The words just came out. But I just sat there and did nothing.

He drank down his coffee and then said, "So she still teaches."

"History."

"Uh-huh." Then he said, "Do you mind if I order another coffee?"

"Why should I?" I said.

"How does she look?"

The waitress brought the second cup and put it down on the table. He let it rest there while his eyes sought my face for the answer.

"I think she's beautiful," I said. I thought I heard him sigh.

"Her hair?"

"Sort of blonde."

"Like it always was?"

"Yes."

"She will always be a beautiful woman," he said. The second cup of coffee still rested on the table, untouched.

"She still loves you," I said.

His hands trembled and his blue eyes stared at me.

"She said to tell you to come home."

And now I was lying. But the ache in me was getting too overpowering.

"You're getting to be a big fellow," he said. "You're even taller and huskier than I am. Do you play football?"

"I was on the team."

"Yes. You're big and strong."

And suddenly I could bear it no longer. "Come on home, Dad. For God's sake, come home."

He turned his face away from me and I knew how much he loved her and how much he loved me.

"Why does this go on? Why did it ever happen? Year after year. Why did you break up?"

Still he wouldn't speak.

"It can't be the awful act you do." And now he turned to me. "It is awful—really terrible. I'm telling you it is. They'll be throwing it out altogether soon. You know it yourself."

And suddenly he hit me hard in the face.

"Shut up," he shouted. "Shut up. I don't want to hear any more. Get out of my life. Stay out of it."

I put my hand to my lips and there was blood on the hand, and for a moment I felt the ache leave me and a rage come in. Then he slowly sat down on the chair and his voice almost broke.

"I can't go back any more, Eddie. Don't you see? Don't you, son?"

I left him sitting there and went out into the night street. And all the time I kept saying to myself, I don't understand why people who love each other hurt each other so.

I don't understand.

a short story by JAY BENNETT

189

BIRTHDAY

We wake as the snow
Lowers its slow
Gift to her daughter—
You choose hoops of gold
The inward ear
In time to be explored.

Mother of tradition
Physician
Of symmetry, I am firm as any foe
Off your elbow.
The needle clean-black
Centers on the pencil mark.

Blood surprises
My fingers
Wrist. Peroxide foams
Through new holes
Like kisses.
You blow clockwise.

We sing a light round—
Candles on the angel food
Thirteen falling hot and cold.

MARY JANE MENUEZ

POETRY

DESIGNS

Do you know where you've
Been today? Hard to tell,
You say. And I agree.

Take last year's leaf and
Hold it close.
It's not a map, but a tree
On its way to
Something else.
Just like you. Just like me.

If we could follow the course
We took, we'd find everything
We knew.
Together we'd meet, and out
Of it all we'd find new things
To do.
We might not see it at first,
But looking around we'd know,
We've never been here before
But it's where we wanted to go.

ROSAMOND DAUER

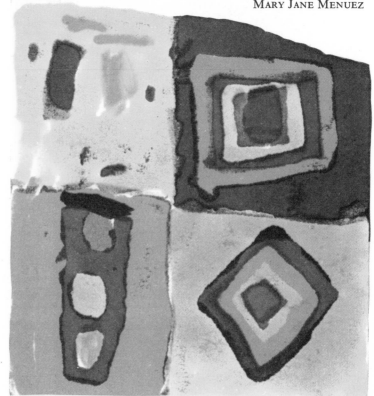

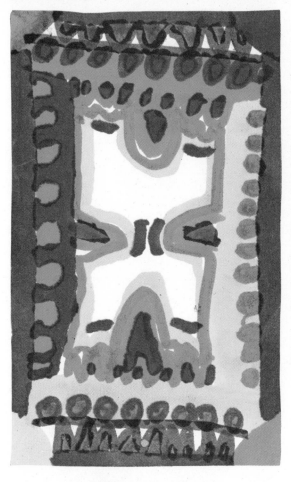

CHRISTINE'S DREAM

I saw within a flower bed
a yellow rose with spots of red.
"Ridiculous" I said aloud
and quick looked up at a purple cloud.

I ran beneath a candy tree
as tears and laughter captured me.
I chased an orange rabbit hopping
to an ice cream brook with whipped cream
    topping.

I met a dog on a silver log
playing jacks with a giggling frog.
I ran and ran over chocolate hills
singing with birds with golden bills.

Tired, I stopped to rest and think
on the cushioned grass that was tinted pink.
"Christine—wake up you've got to get
    dressed,
it's the first day of school—
    you must look your best!

MILDRED B. CAVALLO

WHAT IS PINK?

What is pink? A rose is pink
By the fountain's brink.
What is red? A poppy's red
In its barley bed.
What is blue? The sky is blue
Where the clouds float through.
What is white? A swan is white
Sailing in the light.
What is yellow? Pears are yellow,
Rich and ripe and mellow.
What is green? The grass is green,
With small flowers between.
What is violet? Clouds are violet
In the summer twilight.
What is orange? Why, an orange,
Just an orange!

A RIDDLE

There is one that has a head without an eye,
   And there's one that has an eye without a
    head.
You may find the answer if you try;
   And when all is said,
  Half the answer hangs upon a thread.

poems by CHRISTINA ROSSETTI (1830–1894)

It's Raining Said John Twaining

Translated and Illustrated by

N. M. Bodecker

Three little Guinea pigs
went to see the King.
One brought a rose;
one brought a ring;
one brought a turnip
to give to the King.

Two went back home
neither fatter
nor thinner.
One sat on the Queen's lap
and ate the King's dinner.

The circle is formed: The mysterious Ghost Dance is about to begin.

THE GHOST DANCERS

THE SUN DIES

On January 1, 1889, the Sun died. There was a great eclipse. As the noon sky grew darker and darker over Nevada, the Paiute Indians went wild with fear. They wailed and shouted and fired guns at the sky to drive away the dark demon.

Through the walls of his tule wickiup, Wovoka could hear their cries. He could see the light on the red rocks sicken and grow dull. The Sun was the Indians' high god, second only to the Great Spirit. Wovoka knew he should be out there, fighting off the monster who was eating the Sun, for he had more power than any of the others. Wasn't he after all their shaman, their holy man?

He struggled to rise, but he could not move. His head was hotter than a stone in a fire. The fever burned his very bones, and his body shook like a tule reed in the wind.

Slowly the sounds began to fade. There was nothing now but a black swirling mist. Perhaps he, too, was dying along with the Sun, for he could no longer feel the pain in his limbs—or feel his body at all! His spirit broke free and floated up like a dry leaf in a whirlwind.

When the mist cleared, he gazed with wonder on a fair land. All around stretched the green prairie, and for as far as he could see,

194

herds of buffalo were grazing. Indians came, greeting him by name—men he had last seen on their deathbeds. Now they were young and strong. They told him there was no sickness here, no old age, no death—only hunting and feasting. They took him to see the Great Spirit. The Great Spirit told Wovoka that he had a great mission on earth. Wovoka must take a message back to his people. He must tell them how to live so they too could one day reach these lovely prairies, which were Heaven, for the world was going to end.

THE MESSIAH COMES

The eclipse passed: Once again the dark monster had been driven off and the Sun reborn. Recovering from his fever, Wovoka too was reborn. He had become the Messiah, the spiritual leader of the Indians.

It was not the Messiah's first appearance among the Indians. On both American continents, prophets had arisen among the Indians from time to time. In 1870 another Mason Valley Paiute, Tavibo, had spoken with spirits and brought back teachings and rituals similar to those of Wovoka. Growing up in the same village, Wovoka had listened to Tavibo's preachings and watched the sacred dance of the Paiutes.

After his parents' death, Wovoka was raised by a family of devoutly religious white ranchers, the Wilsons. They named him Jack Wilson, taught him English, and instructed him in the Christian religion. He also learned from Mormon settlers whom he met. Thus Wovoka was well prepared to be a prophet of a religion that combined Christian ideas with Indian rituals. The Heaven he visited looked much like the Heaven the missionaries described, except that it was populated only by red men and contained Indian delights.

To prove that he was the divine messenger, the Great Spirit had given Wovoka power over the elements. When summer came, drought struck Nevada and famine threatened. The people came to Wovoka for help. He told them, "On the morning of the third day, you will have all the water you want."

Rejoicing, they spread the word that the drought would end. Storms broke over Walker Valley, and within three days the Walker River was overflowing its banks.

After that amazing event, the local Paiutes were not the only converts. From all over the Rockies the Indians came to hear the new gospel and learn the Ghost Dance ritual that the Great Spirit had taught Wovoka.

In order to be saved, Wovoka told the Indians, they must sing the Ghost Songs and do the Ghost Dance. If he danced the sacred dance for a long time, a lucky dancer might even be allowed to visit Heaven before the end of the world, as Wovoka had done.

A photograph of Wovoka, the Indian Messiah.

Wovoka also told the Indians that they must live according to a strict code of conduct. They must harm no one, red or white. They must tell no lies. They must love everyone as a brother. And, Wovoka said, they must put away their guns and never fight or kill again. It was even bad, he said, to think violent thoughts.

THE GOSPEL SPREADS

In the summer of 1889, rumors of the new gospel began reaching the Sioux of the Great Plains. By the end of the year, the Sioux had gathered in council and had chosen delegates to travel west and investigate these stories.

The Teton Sioux (or Dakota) included a number of tribes allied in a loose confederation. After their defeat in a war with the white men in 1866–67, about 16,000 of them had been confined in the Great Sioux Reservation in South Dakota, west of the Missouri River. In 1889 they were forced to sign the last of several treaties that were chipping away their land. This time, their territory was cut in half and they were pushed onto five smaller reservations. Some were in the north and some in the south, with a wide belt of white man's land between. White Indian agents were assigned to administer the reservations for the government in Washington.

During the 1880's the weather—drought and severe winters—

and the white man's increasing efforts to seize land and to force new ways on the Indians had combined in a very destructive way. The morale and the whole way of life of the Sioux had begun to break down. The famous Sun Dance, the great Sioux religious festival, was outlawed. The buffalo had disappeared, and with it the buffalo hunt that had been the climax of the Sioux year. Now the Indian hunter was forced to learn to be a farmer almost overnight.

Since the farms would not support families at first, rations were doled out by the federal Indian agents. Indian children were put in boarding schools to learn the white man's ways. Fiercely family-minded, the Sioux often tried to keep their children away from the school people. When this failed, they watched with heavy hearts as their children went to white schools. They knew that if they tried to resist, the agent had a powerful weapon: Indians who did not co-operate did not get rations.

But Indians who did co-operate were not necessarily rewarded. Those who helped move supplies in wagons through the frontier West did well. Farmers were not so lucky. In the drought years of the later 1880's, they watched their crops dry up and blow away. They saw grain destroyed by hailstorms or grasshoppers. Cattle raising, an occupation the Sioux liked better than farming, flourished at first. Yet here, too, nature seemed to join in a conspiracy against the Sioux. The terrible winter of 1886–87 struck with Arctic fury, killing up to 75 percent of the Sioux cattle herds.

By 1889, it seemed clear to the Sioux that nothing they did worked. They had tried fighting, negotiating, co-operating, farming; still they went hungry and their lands dwindled. At this point, they sent their delegates to Wovoka to see if he could help.

The delegates went on their mission to Wovoka without being sure he had the power to help them. They returned in March, 1890, as ardent disciples.

But the Sioux saw Wovoka's vision in the light of their own bitter experience and twisted the message a little. Wovoka was a man of peace. He preached that the Great Spirit would restore the land to his children. The Indians did not need to do anything but dance and love everyone, according to Wovoka. A Cheyenne disciple even interpreted the message to include the revolutionary idea that white men and red men would become "all one people." However, in the Sioux mind Wovoka became a fiery prophet of vengeance who promised brutal destruction for the white enemy. The Sioux developed the Ghost Shirt idea, which was not part of Wovoka's teaching. This shirt, painted with sacred designs, was supposed to make its wearer invulnerable. Bullets fired against it, it was said, would drop to the ground harmlessly.

That spring Wovoka's apostles Short Bull, Kicking Bear, and Good Thunder called their people together and began teaching them the new Ghost Dance. The dancing frightened the Indian agents. What had gotten into these people? They were dancing like lunatics when they should be planting crops. Short Bull got a stern lecture, Good Thunder spent time in jail, and Kicking Bear went off to visit friends in Wyoming.

The United States Congress chose this moment to cut the Sioux food rations again. (The Indians were costing the Federal government a lot of money.) In desperation the Sioux planted large crops. As the grain sprang up thickly under heavy rains, their hopes rose, only to be cruelly dashed by the scorching drought of July. In the little gardens, beans and squash blackened under the merciless sun. The fall harvests promised no relief.

By August, the shape of the disaster was plain. The Sioux began to call the famine they were heading into "the starving time." They saw little hope of any human help, but they began to listen in greater and greater numbers to Wovoka and his disciples.

THE DANCING BEGINS

In the starving time, the Ghost Dance spread across South Dakota like a prairie fire in a high wind. The dancing epidemic began in August in the south at Pine Ridge Reservation. During September it swept east to Rosebud Reservation and north to the Cheyenne River. By October it reached Standing Rock Reservation, the home of Sitting Bull, the great Sioux chief and medicine man. Sitting Bull was a strong defender of the old ways. Because of this attitude, the whites considered him the most dangerous trouble-maker on the reservation.

When Sitting Bull wanted to go south to the place where the Ghost Dance was to be performed, the Indian agent in charge of his reservation refused to let him travel. Sitting Bull therefore invited Kicking Bear, Wovoka's follower, to visit him at the Standing Rock Reservation. Kicking Bear convinced Sitting Bull to become a follower of the new religion.

Deserting their dreary farms, the Sioux who followed Wovoka's religion began to come to the camps where the Ghost Dance was performed. The Ghost Dance camps were arranged in a special way. In the center of a large circular area, surrounded by tipis, stood the prayer tree, a sapling crowned with colored cloth streamers. After a dawn purification rite (a sweat bath—a kind of sauna) the dancers' faces were painted with crosses, circles, and crescents (representing stars, sun, and moon, respectively). Then the dancers put on their Ghost Shirts, which were painted with the same symbols as the face and with sacred birds and animals as well. The dancers wore no weapons, no metal, no objects that came from the white man.

The dancers—men, women, and children—sat in large concentric circles around the prayer tree and their leader, who prayed that they might all be carried to the spirit land. Then they stood, holding hands, singing Ghost Songs. As they sang, the people

The great chief Sitting Bull, in full regalia.

began shuffling slowly to the left, bending their knees, bobbing up and down as they stepped. As the tempo of the songs speeded up, the dancers spun faster and faster in their rings, dipping and weaving. People began wailing, twitching, leaping high in the air. Some dropped to the ground. While their bodies lay rigid, their souls visited the spirit land. On their return they told marvelous tales to envying friends who had not yet gone into a trance. The dance sometimes went on for 4 or 5 days at a time.

By November the Sioux were doing almost nothing but dance and share their visions with one another. To the white man, the religious frenzy meant just one thing: war dance, plans for an armed uprising. Madness had overtaken the Sioux, Washington decided, and the Army was needed to protect white settlers.

THE ARMY IS MOBILIZED

Troops began moving on November 20. Later, orders went out to arrest the Ghost Dance leaders, particularly Sitting Bull. On December 15, 1890, 43 Indian policemen surrounded the chief's cabin at dawn. Bull Head, the leader, went in and told Sitting Bull he was under arrest. Sitting Bull dressed and went with them quietly enough. But outside the cabin, hearing his people raise a great cry of sorrow, he pulled back from his captors. The people cursed and threatened. Then one of them, Catch the Bear, fired at Bull Head. As he was falling fatally wounded, Bull Head whirled and shot Sitting Bull through the chest. At the same moment another policeman, Red Tomahawk, shot the old chief in the head. A great leader was dead.

Some of Sitting Bull's people fled west to join Chief Big Foot, who had also joined the Ghost Dancers. Big Foot's name was high on the list of trouble-makers. An order went out for his arrest.

Chief Big Foot had begun leading his band, swelled by refugees, south to Pine Ridge, where they were to join forces with Chief Red Cloud, now the most powerful Sioux chieftain. The Army wanted to prevent this at all costs. By the time they caught up with him on December 28, Big Foot was critically ill with pneumonia. When Major Samuel Whitside told him he must take his people to the Wounded Knee camp of the United States Cavalry at Pine Ridge, Big Foot replied calmly that he was going that way anyhow.

The most delicate problem still remained: disarming the Indians. No attempt was made that day, nor that evening when they made camp at Wounded Knee Creek. During the night additional troops set up artillery on Cemetery Hill overlooking the camp.

The next morning the cavalry commander, Colonel James Forsyth, called the braves together and told them they must give up their Winchester rifles. The Indians said they had none. The colonel sent a messenger to Big Foot: "Tell your men to give up their guns." Big Foot replied that the guns had already been seized and burned. Actually he had told his braves to hide their weapons.

Suspecting this, the colonel ordered the camp searched. Soldiers dug guns from under blankets and wrested them from behind protesting Indian women. All the while Yellow Bird, a medicine man, danced the Ghost Dance and muttered spells.

Still suspicious, the colonel lined his troops up four ranks deep and ordered a body search of the Indians. The soldiers pushed Indians down the line one by one, pulling blankets from their shoulders, hunting for weapons.

At this point Black Coyote began stalking about holding his rifle over his head, yelling that he'd paid a lot for it and would not give it up unless paid. The soldiers seized him from behind, spun him around, and tried to wrench the gun away. In the struggle the gun went off. At the same moment, Yellow Bird tossed a handful of dust in the air. Instantly everyone began firing at once.

When it was over, there were 153 known dead among the Indians, and the Army had lost 39. Among the Indian dead were 44 women and 18 children. How many died later of wounds or froze in the blizzard that followed will never be known. Over half of Big Foot's band perished in the Wounded Knee Massacre.

When spring failed to bring the expected end of the world, Wovoka changed the date. He said it would happen "some time." Among some western tribes, Ghost Dancing gradually faded out; among others, it took new forms. But for the Teton Sioux, the world did indeed end. With Wounded Knee, the last military engagement of the 19th century Indian wars, the world they had known was gone forever.

a historical adventure by ELISABETH MARGO

WHEN THE PRESIDENT WAS IMPEACHED

"The President, Vice President and all civil Officers of the United States, shall be removed from Office on Impeachment for, and Conviction of, Treason, Bribery, or other high Crimes and Misdemeanors."

THE UNITED STATES CONSTITUTION,
ARTICLE II, SECTION 4

It was one of the most dramatic moments in the nation's history. The Senate chamber was filled with members of both houses of the Congress. Spectators packed the galleries and overflowed into the corridors. It was Thursday, March 5, 1868, and the first impeachment trial of a president of the United States was about to begin. Andrew Johnson, the 17th president of the United States, had been charged by the House of Representatives with "high crimes and misdemeanors."

The events that led to the impeachment of President Johnson had begun almost at the very moment he took the oath of office on April 15, 1865. A few hours earlier, Abraham Lincoln had died from an assassin's bullet, and Johnson, Lincoln's vice-president, succeeded him.

When Johnson became president, the members of the Radical wing of the Republican Party were overjoyed. The Radical Republicans favored extreme political measures in Reconstruction—the postwar program for re-establishing the Union. They believed Johnson would follow their hard line against the South. But it soon became evident that Johnson had a mind of his own. In spite of his hatred of the Southern "slavocracy," Johnson was committed to following Lincoln's generous policy of forgiving the former Confederate states and bringing them back into the Union without acts of vengeance. During the summer months of 1865, Johnson fashioned a lenient presidential plan for Reconstruction. The Radicals were furious. When the new congressional session began, they rejected the plan. A Senate-House committee, dominated by Radicals, was appointed to prepare a congressional Reconstruction plan.

And so the battle lines were drawn. Presidential authority was pitted against congressional power. The big test came when Congress proposed the Fourteenth Amendment to the Constitution, which provided that no state could pass laws that would violate the basic civil rights and liberties of any person. The amendment was partly intended as an answer to the Black Codes, laws enacted by Southern states to curb the freedom of emancipated black slaves.

President Johnson is handed the summons to his impeachment trial.

The Radicals insisted that the Southern states ratify the Four-teenth Amendment before they could be readmitted to the Union. But Southerners felt the amendment was an effort to humiliate them. Of the former Confederate states, only Tennessee voted to ratify the amendment. The other 10 rejected it, and it was temporarily defeated. (It was eventually ratified in 1868.)

The rejection of the Fourteenth Amendment by the South led to a hardening of Northern opinion, and to support for the harsher measures called for by the Radical Republicans. In the congressional elections of 1866, the people were given a choice between supporting the President's soft line or the Radicals' hard line.

Public opinion favored the Radicals, and they won a stunning victory in the November elections. Both houses of Congress were dominated by the Radicals. The Radicals drew up their own Reconstruction plan. Under it the former Confederate states were divided into five military districts, each commanded by an army general. It was a tough, vengeful policy designed to build Republican power.

Having gained control of the Congress, the Radicals now moved against the last obstacle between them and total control of the government—the presidency. To weaken the president's ability to govern, two acts were passed. The Tenure of Office Act prevented the president from removing government officials, including members of his own Cabinet, without the consent of the Senate. The Army Appropriations Act (also known as the Command of the Army Act) provided that the president could only issue orders to the Army through the commanding general.

Johnson was convinced that both acts were unconstitutional, and he hoped to have an opportunity to test them in the courts. A main purpose of the Tenure of Office Act was to protect Secretary of War Stanton, an arch-foe of Johnson and a staunch Radical supporter. As secretary of war, Stanton was essential to the Radical plan for military Reconstruction in the South.

On February 21, 1868, Johnson dismissed Stanton and replaced him with an army officer. The Senate refused to confirm the new appointment, and the President's effort to put the issue before the courts failed. The situation had finally come to a head. Congress was up in arms; the public was aroused. Talk of impeachment began to spread in the halls of Congress.

An impeachment resolution was introduced in the House of Representatives. On February 24, 1868, the House voted overwhelmingly to impeach (or indict) President Johnson for "high crimes and misdemeanors."

A House committee promptly drew up 11 articles of impeachment and presented them to the Senate. Eight of the articles dealt with Johnson's alleged violation of the Tenure of Office Act and his removal of Stanton as secretary of war. Article 9 accused him of directly issuing orders to an army officer, thereby violating the Command of the Army Act. Article 10 charged him with having made speeches attacking and ridiculing Congress in order to undermine its "rightful authority." Article 11 was a summary of all the charges rolled into one.

On March 5, with appropriate fanfare and publicity, the preliminaries began in the Senate. The trial proper did not begin until March 13—appropriately, a Friday. In the meantime, on March 7, President Johnson had been served with a formal summons. The President received it calmly, remarking only that he would "attend to the matter."

One thousand tickets were printed for each day's session. Since the trial was the "hottest" show of its day, tickets were at a premium. As the trial progressed, it became obvious that legality and justice were not major concerns of the Radicals. While evidence favorable to the President was often excluded from the record, his accusers were allowed to make every possible charge against him. Many senators openly stated that they believed the President was guilty even before the evidence had been presented.

Congressman Benjamin Butler of Massachusetts was the chief

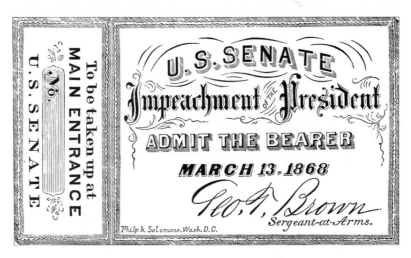

spokesman for the prosecution. Butler lashed out viciously at Johnson as he tried to prove that the President had committed criminal acts. Butler hammered home his points with fiery rhetoric but with little concrete evidence.

By contrast, the President's lawyers challenged the prosecution with reasoned legal arguments. They stuck strictly to points of law as they picked apart the 11 articles of impeachment. The President's dismissal of Stanton, they stated, was designed to test the legality of the Tenure of Office Act, not to violate it. By dismissing Stanton, Johnson had hoped to force the matter into the courts, where he believed the law would be declared unconstitutional. The defense tried to show that the charges against the President were neither serious—certainly not "high crimes and misdemeanors"— nor legally valid. The prosecution continued its emotional attack, determined to oust Johnson from office by any means, fair or foul.

As the trial progressed into May, President Johnson continued to perform his duties. Johnson had wanted to testify on his own behalf, but his attorneys had cautioned him against it—knowing that he could easily lose his temper. And so, at no time did Johnson appear at his own trial. Instead he contented himself with holding private talks with newsmen in which he defended his actions.

Finally the testimony and the cross-examinations were completed. The time had come for the Senate to render its verdict. The Senate then had 54 members, representing 27 states. (Ten Southern states were not represented in the Senate.) If the two-thirds majority necessary for conviction was to be obtained, 36 senators would have to vote guilty. Twelve of the senators were Democrats or pro-Johnson Republicans who would definitely vote for acquittal. That left 42 solid Republicans, and the Radicals were certain they had the votes to convict. But in a series of private meetings, the Radicals found to their dismay that six Republican senators did not feel that there was enough evidence to convict the President. A seventh, Edmund G. Ross of Kansas, was undecided.

From the moment they made known their views, the seven

senators—and particularly Senator Ross—became the target of every form of pressure the Radicals could bring to bear. They were hounded, spied upon, and branded traitors. The threats and abuse continued until just before the vote was taken.

Saturday, May 16, dawned bright and clear. At noon Chief Justice Salmon P. Chase arrived and took his seat. The Senate hall and the galleries were choked with congressmen, spectators, and newsmen. When all of the senators were present, the Chief Justice brought the proceedings to order. The first vote was to be on Article 11, thought to have the widest Radical support. As the voting began the tension in the hall became unbearable. Not a sound was heard. "Every fan was folded, not a foot moved, not a rustle of a garment, not a whisper was heard," one senator later recalled.

The roll was called alphabetically. First to answer was Henry B. Anthony of Rhode Island. In a clear voice he called out, "Guilty!" One by one the names of the other senators were called.

By the time the roll call came to Senator Ross, 24 guilty and 14 not guilty votes had been tallied. Four more votes of not guilty were expected. Here was the moment everyone had been waiting for. How would Ross vote? The fate of the President rested on his shoulders. The Chief Justice put the question to the senator from Kansas. "Mr. Senator Ross, how say you? Is the respondent Andrew Johnson guilty or not guilty as charged in this Article?"

Ross's first attempt to speak was so low it could not be heard by everyone. Many senators cupped their ears and asked him to repeat his vote. This time the answer came loud and clear: "Not guilty!" A muffled groan came from the Radicals and their supporters. They had lost. When the final vote was in, the President had been acquitted of the charges in Article 11 by a vote of 35 to 19—one short of the two thirds needed for conviction.

Votes on the remaining articles of impeachment were taken on May 26. The votes on Articles 2 and 3 were 35 to 19, with Ross's vote once more turning the tide. The Radicals admitted defeat. The Senate adjourned as a court of impeachment. The trial was over. President Johnson had been acquitted.

And what of the seven Republicans who had voted for acquittal? Not one of them was ever re-elected to the Senate. All were cast into political obscurity because of their stand. They were burned in effigy, denounced by the press, shunned by friends.

Andrew Johnson completed the remaining months of his term in office and returned to Tennessee. In 1874 he had the satisfaction of being re-elected to the very body that had nearly driven him from the White House—the United States Senate. The following year Johnson died of a stroke.

In 1926 the United States Supreme Court declared that the Tenure of Office Act—the basis of Johnson's impeachment—was unconstitutional.

WOMEN OF THE WEST

The women of the West roped cattle and panned for gold; hunted buffalo and taught school; cleaned and cooked and robbed banks; learned to handle plows and politics. The women who traveled across the western United States in the years after the Civil War did everything—including things no women anywhere had done before.

They traveled long distances in covered wagons, in stage-coaches, on trains, on horseback, and on foot. They were house-keepers and actresses, outlaws and missionaries, wives and widows, saloonkeepers and cowgirls. Most of them were white, some were black, and while some traveled alone, most came with their families. They came into a land of danger—a land where war raged between settlers and Indians, sodbusters and cattlemen, outlaws and lawmen.

All the women faced hardships—disease, poverty, drought, fire, loneliness. Some found rewards—land, independence, success; some found failure; some found death.

On the wide, sweeping prairies and the high, soaring mountains some of these women found freedom. The women of the western territories and states were the first women anywhere in the world to have the right to vote, to have legal freedom and legal rights. For the first time in the United States equality between men and women became a possibility.

"A Woman's Life Is so Hard"

In the year 1818 a black woman living on a plantation in Virginia held her newborn baby and wept. She cried because she knew that this baby would be taken from her as had all her others. As soon as her children grew old enough to work in the fields they were sold. Just as the farmer sold his horses and cows, so he sold his healthy young slave children. The mother knew that once her children were sold they would be sent far away and she never would see them again.

In that same year a white woman in Massachusetts wept over her new baby. She cried because her eighth child was a girl. "Oh dear," she moaned, "I am sorry it is a girl. A woman's life is so hard." Hannah Stone was a farmer's wife and she knew all about the hard life women led. She cooked for her children, her husband, and the hired men on the farm. In addition, she cleaned and scrubbed, milked the cows, churned the butter, preserved food for the winter, made soap and candles and clothes for all the family. And she, like all women, black and white, was expected to have as many children as possible.

This old engraving shows the way in which many people saw the pioneer family; father and son are heroic figures in the foreground while in the background mother washes the clothes. While the males wear comfortable working clothes the woman wears long bulky skirts and a sunbonnet.

The black woman and the white woman wept for their children in a country ruled by white men. All the people in high positions in the United States were white men—senators and members of the House of Representatives, governors, soldiers, lawyers, and doctors. Almost all the people who went to college were white men. Most of the jobs, money, power belonged to white men.

The men who wrote the Declaration of Independence said: "We hold these truths to be self-evident, that all men are created equal . . ." They did not mean "all men." The black men who had been brought from Africa were not to be free in this new nation. Most black people, men and women, were slaves who could not travel nor vote nor go to school. They belonged to the man who owned them as if they were animals, and he could beat his slaves or starve them or take their children away as he pleased.

The Indians who lived here long years before white men came from Europe were not to be free to roam the forests and the prairies, nor were they to be citizens of these United States. Instead, they were to be hunted and killed and their lands were to be stolen from them.

No woman in the United States—white or black or Indian—was free. No woman could vote or be president or a member of Congress. A woman could be arrested, tried, and jailed; but the policeman who arrested her was a man; the judge and members of the jury who tried her were men. A woman could not even give evidence in court.

A married woman had few rights at all. If she was hurt in an accident she could not sue in court, but her husband could sue for the amount that the loss of her labor had cost him. Everything that she had belonged to her husband and he could sell whatever he wanted to. If she went out to work and earned a little money, it too belonged to her husband. If she built up a business, it belonged to her husband. She had no protection against her husband if he was cruel to her. By law he was allowed to beat her and the children, and even if he were a drunkard and spent all the family money on liquor there was nothing she could do. It was almost impossible for a woman to get a divorce.

Hannah Stone's baby was named Lucy. When she grew up she became determined that life should not be as hard for all women as it had been for her mother. The first thing Lucy wanted was more education, but men thought too much schooling was not good for women. Only one college in the entire country—Oberlin in Ohio—admitted black people and women. For nine years Lucy taught school and saved her money, until she had the seventy-five dollars she needed to go to Oberlin. But even there she found that women students were treated differently from men. Unlike men, women were not allowed to debate or to read their own essays at graduation. Instead a teacher read the women's essays for them.

Women had asked for their rights. Before the Declaration of Independence was written Abigail Adams wrote to her husband John: ". . . in the new code of laws which I suppose it will be necessary for you to make I desire you would remember the ladies and be more generous and favorable to them than your ancestors. Do not put such unlimited power in the hands of the husbands. Remember all men would be tyrants if they could. If particular care and attention is not paid to the ladies, we are determined to foment a rebellion, and will not hold ourselves bound by any laws in which we have no voice or representation."

John Adams, who later became the second president of the United States, did not take Abigail seriously. He wrote to her: "As to your extraordinary code of laws, I cannot but laugh."

Men laughed at women's demands for freedom for a long time. While men laughed, women wept.

The Declaration of Independence spoke only of men. "Life, liberty, and the pursuit of happiness" were not for women. The signers of that declaration did not think that women were as intelligent or as capable as men. Almost 150 years passed before the women of the United States were given the vote. All during the nineteenth century women struggled to gain the freedoms that white men had already won.

Work! Work! Work!

Women who had to work for money to support themselves or their families did not have many jobs open to them. They could not become doctors or lawyers or scientists. Teaching or taking care of children, doing housework or sewing were jobs for women.

Many worked as housemaids, doing all the cleaning, sweeping, and mopping of a house. Since there were no washing machines or vacuum cleaners everything had to be done by hand. Human labor was cheap, so women who had money hired other women to do their housework and cooking and to take care of their children. Women even worked as wet nurses. Babies were breast-fed, and if a woman did not have enough milk or did not want to feed her baby herself she hired another woman who had recently given birth to breast-feed her baby. Other women made money by sewing, for this was a time when men, women, and children wore elaborate clothing. Women's skirts were full and came to the ground, men's shirts were decorated with frills, and children were dressed as if they were small adults. All these clothes were sewn by hand. Thomas Hood wrote a poem about the poor women who earned a living by sewing:

> Work—work—work!
> Till the brain begins to swim,
> Work—work—work!
> Till the eyes are heavy and dim!
> Seam and gusset and band,
> Band and gusset and seam,
> Till over the buttons I fall asleep,
> And sew them on in my dreams!

Men talked about how helpless and frail women were and about how much they needed protection; but men did not make laws to protect women. There were no laws to say how long a woman should work each day nor how old she should be when she started work. In the cotton mills of Massachusetts girls only ten years old worked fourteen hours a day. The girls lived in company-owned boarding houses, six in a room, two girls in each bed. After they paid for their board, many girls had only two dollars a week left for themselves.

If the life of white women was hard, that of black women was harder. Sojourner Truth fought all her life for the rights of black women. Once at a convention she listened to a man talk about how women needed the care and protection of men. That was too much for Sojourner Truth, who had been a slave, had worked in the

Sojourner Truth was born a slave and named Isabella. When she became free she chose a name for herself just as many black people do today. Sojourner never learned to read or write but she spoke eloquently at many meetings called to discuss women's rights and rights for black people. That was her life's work. "I am sitting among you to watch; and every once and a while I will come out and tell you what time of night it is."

fields as a slave, been beaten as a slave. As a free black woman she had been treated with contempt by white men. She said:

That man over there says that women need to be helped into carriages, and lifted over ditches, and have the best place everywhere. Nobody helps me into carriages, or over mud puddles, or gives me any best place! And ain't I a woman? Look at me! Look at me! Look at my arm! I have ploughed and planted, and gathered into barns, and no man could head me! And ain't I a woman? I could work as much and eat as much as a man—when I could get it—and bear the lash as well! And ain't I a woman? I have borne thirteen children, and seen them most all sold off to slavery, and when I cried out with my mother's grief, none but Jesus heard me! And ain't I a woman?

In the United States before the Civil War most black women had no rights at all. They belonged to their masters and so did their husbands and children. A slave woman might marry but that marriage had no legal standing. She or her husband or children could be sold and sent far away. She worked long hours in the field or in the kitchen, and if she did not work hard enough the overseer whipped her. He put chains on her legs or a heavy iron collar around her neck if she tried to run away. Her master was pleased when she had babies because they brought him money.

In the years before the Civil War those who wanted rights for women and those who wanted to end slavery worked together.

Sojourner Truth said: "Well children, where there is so much racket there must be something out of kilter. I think that twixt the Negroes of the South and the women of the North, all talking about rights, the white men will be in a pretty fix soon."

Women held meetings and signed petitions. In 1848 hundreds of women met at Seneca Falls in New York and demanded the vote, the right to own property, and divorce laws that would recognize the rights of women and children—all the rights that men already had. That same year New York State passed a Married Women's Property Act, the first in the country to allow women to inherit property and keep it for themselves.

During the Civil War black people gained their freedom and white women had experiences they had never had before. Many worked as nurses to help the wounded soldiers. Others maintained farms and businesses while their husbands and sons were away fighting. And still other women collected thousands of signatures for petitions asking for the end of slavery.

When the war was over Congress passed the Fourteenth Amendment giving the vote to black men but not to any women, black or white.

Many women were disappointed. They hoped that black leaders would not support the Fourteenth Amendment unless women were included. Frederick Douglass felt that black men needed the vote even more than women did. He explained that although white women did not have the vote they were not attacked and killed as black people were. The ex-slave who had fought so long to make all his people free had always fought for women's rights but, he said: "When women, because they are women, are dragged from their homes and hung upon lamp posts, when their children are torn from their arms and their brains dashed upon the pavement . . . then will they have an urgency to obtain the ballot."

Sojourner Truth felt differently: "There is a great stir about colored men getting their rights, but not a word about the colored women; and if colored men get their rights and not colored women theirs, you see the colored men will be masters over the women, and it will be just as bad as it was before. So I am keeping the thing going while things are stirring."

Many white women agreed with Sojourner Truth. Feeling betrayed, they quarreled with their old allies, the antislavery leaders. Women all over the United States continued to fight for their rights—for better education, for jobs, for the right to own property, for divorce, for the vote. Many of their victories were first won in the western territories and states, where women had to be strong and independent to survive, and where life was new and different, where both men and women were more willing to try new ways of doing things than in the more settled East.

an excerpt from *Women of the West*
by DOROTHY LEVENSON

CAPTAIN WHITE BEAR

On a storm-swept day during World War I, a Canadian cargo ship was wallowing in the rough seas of the North Atlantic. High waves smashed at the vessel, which was carrying war supplies to England. The wind was so fierce that the sailors were nearly blown from the decks. On the bridge, the captain valiantly tried to steer his ship through the gale. The captain was a man in his sixties, with white hair and moustache. His eyes were fixed, and his ruddy, weather-beaten face was set as he gave orders to the helmsman.

Suddenly one of the ship's other officers appeared. "Captain, the waves have smashed most of the lifeboats," the officer reported, "and the others are being torn loose from the ship. We're starting to list badly."

Captain Joseph Bernier, the ship's master and a veteran Arctic explorer, looked grim as he received the report. "Then there's nothing to do but keep a steady course and hope some ship has picked up our distress signal," he said, without a trace of emotion.

For several harrowing hours the supply ship rolled and pitched in the churning sea, battered from side to side by the merciless waves. Finally the vessel began to sink. But just as Captain Bernier prepared to give the order to abandon ship, a rescue vessel appeared on the horizon. Moments later it pulled alongside the sinking freighter. Captain Bernier calmly remained at his post on the bridge until every one of his crewmen had been safely taken off. Only when the last seaman was over the side did the captain leave his doomed ship and board the rescue vessel.

For Captain Joseph Bernier, the experience of that day was only one of many narrow escapes from disaster during his long career as an explorer and ship's captain. Born on January 1, 1852, in the French-Canadian province of Quebec, Joseph Elzéar Bernier came from a family of seamen. Both his father and grandfather were ship's captains. Joseph Bernier was to outdo both of them in his accomplishments. His Arctic explorations resulted in the claiming of vast territories for Canada. Rear Admiral Richard E. Byrd of the United States, the first man to fly over the North and South Poles, called Bernier "the dean of Arctic explorers." Bernier made nine trips to the Arctic regions, crossed the Atlantic 251 times, and made several voyages around the world. Before his death in 1934 he had logged over 500,000 miles as the master of more than 100 ships.

Early in his childhood, the future French-Canadian hero developed a love for the sea. Even before he was old enough to go to school, young Bernier was taken on several sea voyages by his

The SS *Arctic* was photographed in 1910, during Bernier's third voyage.

father. At school his favorite subject was geography. He would spend hours studying maps and pictures of faraway lands. Then he would daydream about going to sea in his own ship and visiting exotic places—perhaps even some that had not yet been explored.

When he was 12, young Bernier helped his father build a sailing ship. Later, he went to sea on this vessel as a ship's boy. During the next few years he served as an apprentice seaman, doing all of the different jobs that have to be performed on a ship. Bernier had a keen mind, and he learned very quickly. He performed his duties well and quickly won a series of promotions. By the time he was 17, Bernier was such a good seaman that he was made the captain of his own ship. For the rest of his life he proudly boasted that he had been the youngest sea captain in the world.

The youthful captain's career nearly ended on his first voyage, when the sailing vessel he commanded ran into a fierce storm. The strong wind snapped two of the ship's masts, and Bernier was trapped under a pile of fallen rigging and splintered sections of the wooden mast. As he struggled to free himself, a huge wave washed over the deck and nearly swept him overboard. But one of his sailors rushed to his assistance. Grabbing hold of the young captain, the seaman cut away the tangled ropes and freed him.

As the years went by, Bernier began to develop an interest in the Arctic region. He looked at the map of Canada and saw vast unclaimed lands in the northern seas. Most people felt these Arctic islands were too cold and barren to be of any use. But Bernier thought otherwise. There was only one way to find out about these lands, and that was to sail there himself. But first he read every book and carefully studied every map and navigators' chart of the Arctic he could find.

After learning as much as he could, he tried to persuade Canadians to sponsor voyages to the north. He gave lectures in many cities, explaining how important it was for Canada to explore the Arctic region and take over all of the unclaimed lands. Some people laughed at his idea. The waters of the Arctic were dangerous, and the lands there seemed useless. But Bernier told them that the islands might have valuable minerals and other resources. Since the 1600's, explorers had searched for a Northwest Passage around North America through which men could sail from Europe to Asia and back again. Bernier believed he could find it. He summed up his feelings in this impassioned plea:

France, England, the United States and Norway are currently racing each other in the discovery of the North. Why allow ourselves to be outdone? I can try to find, and even succeed in finding, the Northwest Passage as well as anybody. In the near future the North will become a strategic asset for Canada. Why wait for other nations to plant their flags there? Canada must officially take possession of the islands of the [Arctic] Archipelago . . . .

Years of frustration followed, while Bernier tried to persuade the Canadian Government to outfit a ship and allow him to explore and claim the Arctic islands. But his patience and persistence were finally rewarded. In the early 1900's the Canadian Parliament gave him $200,000 to purchase a three-masted German sailing ship called the *Gauss*. Bernier renamed the sturdy wooden craft the *Arctic*. In 1906 he embarked from Quebec on the first of his Arctic explorations.

Bernier sailed into the frigid waters of the north, going as far as Melville Island—halfway to the Pacific Ocean. Along the way he landed on a number of islands. Each time he went ashore he took formal possession of the territory by raising a Canadian flag and depositing documents under a cairn—a pile of stones used as a landmark. Then he would gather the native Eskimos and read a proclamation telling them that they were now subject to Canadian law. Bernier also collected license fees from whalers and fishermen in the area to further establish Canadian authority.

During the voyage Bernier had to steer his ship around large icebergs. He had to be careful not to collide with these treacherous mountains of ice. Finally, when winter came, the ice became so thick that the ship could no longer move. There were no ice-breakers in those days, and once the sea froze, a ship was locked in for the winter. Bernier spent the winter at Pond Inlet and sent a report overland by dogsled to the Canadian Government, stating that he had taken possession of all the islands in the region.

His first voyage had been so successful that Bernier was ordered out again the following year. The explorer left Quebec in July of 1908. The city was then celebrating the 300th anniversary of its founding, and as the *Arctic* sailed out of the harbor, it received a royal salute from the guns of a British naval squadron. On this trip Bernier headed straight for Melville Island, in the western part of the Arctic region. The waters were free of ice at this time, and Bernier reported that he could have sailed all the way to the Pacific "if our instructions had included the making of the Northwest Passage."

But his orders were to explore the region and report on weather and navigation conditions. He accordingly put in at Winter Harbor, in the southern part of Melville Island. When winter came and the sea froze over, Bernier sent out parties to explore Banks and Victoria islands. Guided by Eskimos, he and his men traveled by dogsled. Bernier made friends with the Eskimo people wherever he went. He gave presents of supplies and tools to the adults and candy to the Eskimo children. The Eskimos nicknamed the husky captain with the white hair and moustache "Captain White Bear."

Exploring the cold northern islands was not easy. The men had to wear heavy coats and fur hats to protect them from the freezing weather. Icy winds whipped at their faces. At night, as they attempted to sleep, large polar bears would wander into their camp and try to get at their food supplies. Bernier and his Eskimo guides often had to fight them off. The following summer, just before returning home, Bernier formally claimed the Arctic islands on behalf of Canada. On July 9, 1909, he unveiled a small monument at Parry's Rock on Melville Island. On it was the following statement:

This memorial is erected today to commemorate the taking possession for the Dominion of Canada of the whole Arctic Archipelago lying to the north of America . . . C. G. S. Arctic, July 1, 1909. J. E. Bernier, Commander.

Bernier returned to Quebec in the autumn of 1909. But the following year he went out on a third Arctic voyage. This time he meant to complete the Northwest Passage to the Pacific. But the severe Arctic weather was against him. First he went to Melville Island and tried to get through by way of M'Clure Strait. However, his ship was stopped by a solid wall of ice. Next he tried Prince of Wales Strait, between Banks and Victoria islands, but again the ice was too thick. Finally he turned back and spent the winter at

Bernier (*center*) on the bridge of his ship during the 1910 expedition.

Baffin Island, where he conducted explorations and collected license fees from whalers.

The intrepid sea captain later made trading voyages to the northern islands. During World War I, he commanded cargo ships bringing supplies to Great Britain. After the war, Bernier resumed his Arctic explorations. Not even old age could stop him, for as Bernier once remarked: "Once you get the Arctic fever . . . you cannot escape it." His last trip to the Arctic was made in the 1920's, when he was 75 years old. Bernier's death in 1934 brought to an end the exploits of this brave Canadian explorer.

But he left his countrymen an important legacy. As a result of his explorations, 500,000 square miles of new territory—about one seventh of Canada's total land area—was added to his native land. Today these islands supply Canadians with fish, furs, and other valuable products. Coal has been discovered on the western islands, and mineral experts are searching for oil. The lives of all Canadians have been enriched by the vision and courage of Joseph Elzéar Bernier—"Captain White Bear."

YOUTH IN THE NEWS

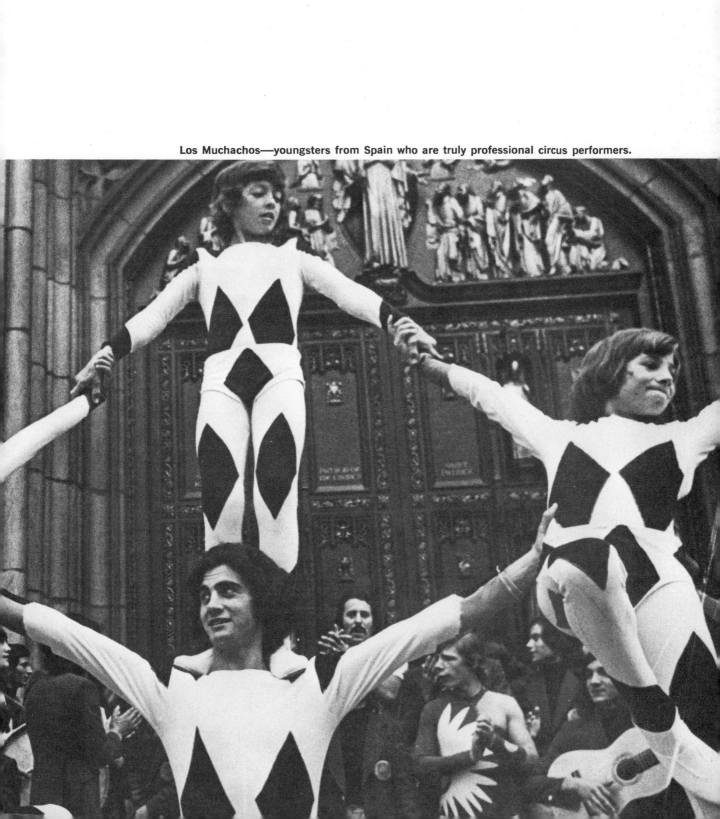

Los Muchachos—youngsters from Spain who are truly professional circus performers.

YOUNG HEADLINERS

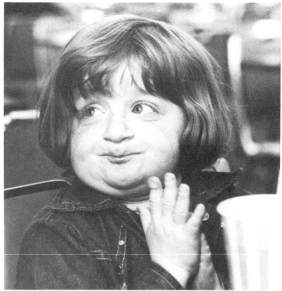

Mason Reese is a red-haired, freckled 7-year-old who started a successful television career by eating his way through a number of commercials. At first viewers didn't believe, and then they couldn't forget, that special face and deep voice. Off camera, Mason attends a Montessori school in New York.

Lovely Lori Matsukawa, a 17-year-old from Hawaii, is 1974 Miss Teenage America.

Los Muchachos, a Spanish circus troupe made up of boys aged 8 to 19, appeared in North America for the first time in 1973, making a 4-month, 24-city tour. The 100-member troupe is from Ciudad de los Muchachos ("city of boys"), Spain.

A new child star, 10-year-old Tatum O'Neal, made her film debut in *Paper Moon*. She starred with her real-life father, Ryan O'Neal. Tatum played the part of Addie Pray, a cigarette-smoking orphan traveling through the Midwest with a Bible salesman in the 1930's. Critics praised her, and audiences loved her.

John Malachowsky, 13, of West Babylon, New York, builds model rockets as a hobby. When the price of the enamel he uses rose from 15 to 19 cents (a 27 percent increase), John felt the strain on his allowance. He wrote to the Price Commission. As a result, the Justice Department filed suit against the manufacturers, and in March, 1973, they agreed to reduce the price of the enamel.

Felda Looper, an 18-year-old Oklahoman, made Congressional history in May, 1973, when she became the first girl page in the House of Representatives. She is shown with Speaker of the House Carl Albert.

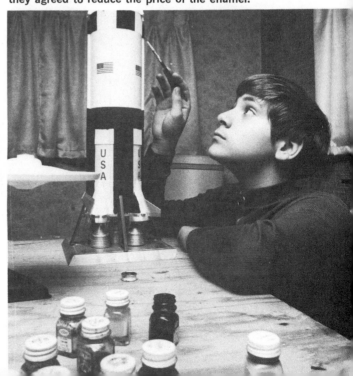

Jane Blanksteen, a 17-year-old New Yorker, has written a Russian cookbook, translating and testing recipes for such dishes as *kulebyaka* and chicken Kiev. The cookbook was a term project for Jane's Russian course at Phillips Exeter Academy in New Hampshire.

From high school right into the major leagues—that's the story of David Clyde, 18, a left-handed pitcher from Houston, Texas. Baseball's number one draft choice, Clyde received a big bonus when he signed with the Texas Rangers in June, 1973.

A new Pavlova won first prize in the International Ballet Competition in Moscow in 1973 and went on to her U.S. debut with the Bolshoi Ballet. She is Nadya Pavlova, 17—no relation to the great Anna Pavlova, who died in 1931.

Arvind Narain Srivastava, a 16-year-old high school senior from Fort Collins, Colorado, won the $10,000 scholarship in the 32nd annual Westinghouse Science Talent Search. In his science project, the Indian-born student examined the possibility that the universe is finite, rather than infinite.

In 1973, Stephen J. Erickson, 21, became the new mayor of Gardner, Massachusetts. He campaigned while he was in his last semester at the University of Massachusetts in Amherst.

Olga Korbut on the uneven parallel bars.

OLGA KORBUT, A RUSSIAN PIXIE

At the 1972 Olympics in Munich, West Germany, 17-year-old Olga Korbut captured the hearts of millions of sports fans with her dazzling display of gymnastic skill. The petite Russian star won three gold medals as she performed with the grace and agility of a prima ballerina.

Some seven months later her American fans had a chance to see her in person. Olga and the rest of the six-woman Soviet gymnastic team arrived in the United States in March, 1973, for an eight-city, coast-to-coast tour. The leader of the group, 20-year-old Ludmilla Turischeva, is considered by some to be the world's best female gymnast. However, it was the 4-foot–10-inch, 85-pound Miss Korbut whom the American audiences took to their hearts.

When the troupe arrived in California,

Olga was greeted by a cheering throng of enthusiasts wearing "Olga Korbut Fan Club" T-shirts. In New York City, a record-breaking crowd of 19,694 people filled Madison Square Garden. It was the largest audience turnout for a gymnastic event held in the Western Hemisphere.

At the Garden, Olga performed high swings and twists on the uneven parallel bars; leaps and flips on the narrow, 4-inch balance beam; and ballet-like floor exercises. Although she slipped and fell at the beginning of her routine, she was up a few seconds later, encouraged by members of the audience waving banners that read "Shake it up, Olga!"

The pixieish gymnast's scene-stealer is her electrifying backflip (backward somersault). When she succeeds at it, it is truly an amazing feat. She is the only woman ever to have performed a backflip on the balance beam in competition.

Olga's performance on the uneven parallel bars is also spectacular. But there are occasional mishaps. In Munich, frustrated with herself for slipping on the bars, she broke into tears. The judges, however, rated her good enough for a silver medal in the event. That disappointment did not prevent her from triumphantly returning home with three golds: in the balance beam, the floor exercises, and the team event.

Her gymnastic abilities are a result of years of training, strenuous daily workouts, rigid discipline, and strict diet. However, during her United States tour, she was allowed enough time to sample some American pleasures—television; that old American favorite, the hot dog; and eggs drenched in catsup.

Olga has come a long way from Grodno, her small hometown in the Soviet Union. At the youthful age of 17, she has been permitted the luxury of her own apartment in order to be near her personal coach, Renald Knysh.

Although she enjoys the excitement of travel and seeing new places, she says that she misses her parents when she is away from home. She says that she has no steady boyfriends. But she certainly has plenty of admirers—both male and female. While in the United States she remarked, "I expected a warm welcome. But not this warm."

The brothers Jackson, with Michael (*center*), during a Jackson Five concert.

THE SOUND OF MICHAEL JACKSON

The Jackson Five is not your ordinary "family next door." Far from it. They've hit the music scene so hard, they've practically taken possession of the best-selling–record charts. Each single record and each album—as long as it's by the Jackson Five—is almost sure to be a hit.

Fifteen-year-old Michael Jackson is the lead-voice of the Jackson Five, and he is also the youngest member of the super-brother group. He's joined by brothers Marlon, the group's dancer; Jermaine, the bass guitarist, who sang lead before Michael; guitarist Tito; and Jackie. And, occasionally, when youngest brother Randy plays the bongos, the group takes on another dimension and becomes the Jackson Five plus one.

Michael was born on August 29, 1958, in Gary, Indiana, and began singing with the group when he was 4 years old. In 1967 the Jackson Five was discovered by actress-singer Diana Ross. She was so impressed with the group that she took them to Motown, the recording company in Detroit, Michigan. Their first album, *Diana Ross Presents the Jackson Five,* was a smash hit, earning the group their first gold record.

Motown saw the star potential in young Michael Jackson. In addition to his singing with the group, they encouraged him to strike out on his own. He appeared on the Academy Awards show in 1973, singing one of the nominated songs, and went on to record albums as a soloist. *Got to Be There, Ben,* and *Music and Me* established Michael Jackson as one of the music industry's youngest sensations.

In addition to singing with an expressiveness unusual for his years, Michael has displayed remarkable talents as a mimic, drummer, and pianist. (Because of his versatility, he has been compared to Sammy Davis, Jr.) He is also good at card tricks; and he enjoys drawing so much that he plans to study art in college. His great amibition, however, is to be an actor.

When Michael isn't making music, he enjoys listening to it. Despite his "shouting" style as a singer, Michael says his personal taste runs to "classical music and soft, listening music. I sit and listen to soft stuff like Johnny Mathis. I like Ray Charles. And most of the time, I listen to the Three Dog Night."

Michael lives with his parents in a trophy-filled house in Los Angeles. The walls of the house are covered with gold and platinum records, each one signifying a best-selling record. Of course, with Michael now recording on his own, as well as with the Jackson Five, there's a question as to whether or not there's enough wall space to handle the awards.

Richard Thomas stars as John-Boy, and Kami Cotler plays his youngest sister, Elizabeth, on the top-rated television show, "The Waltons."

RICHARD THOMAS: AN ACTOR'S LIFE

All those overnight acting sensations you've read about—well, forget them. They exist only in the movies or perhaps in a work of fiction. An actor's life is not an easy one. There are ups and downs, flops and hits, successes and failures. An actor learns to live with these uncertainties. He studies hard and works hard, and sometimes—just sometimes—fame and fortune strike. But it takes a lot of work, determination, and a total belief in oneself to achieve success as an actor.

Acting means rising early in the morning, pounding the pavements in search of a job,

waiting with 300 other aspirants to audition for the only role available in a play, and hearing over and over again that familiar old theater cliché, "Don't call us, we'll call you." But if fortune strikes and an actor does get a part, there's more work in store. An actor may spend all day on a motion-picture set waiting to say one line, or devote months to a play rehearsal only to have the show close on opening night. There are lots of lines to memorize; and perhaps in his spare time, he may also attend singing, dancing, and acting classes. But ask any actor if he would trade it all for the security of a nine-to-five job in an office, and chances are you will hear a resounding "No!" As far as an actor is concerned, his life is indeed a happy one, and worth every agonizing moment.

Take Richard Thomas, for example. (It's Richard Thomas who plays John-Boy Walton on the popular television series "The Waltons.") His rise to stardom is an exception to the usual rule. He never went to acting school, but he did the next best thing: Richard was born into the acting profession—on June 13, 1951. His parents are ballet dancers and now run the New York School of Ballet.

As a child, young Richard traveled extensively with his parents, watching them perform all over the world. He literally spent his youth backstage. Actually, it was the very early part of his youth, because Richard moved from the wings to center stage in 1957 (at the ripe age of 6) singing "You Gotta Have Heart" in a summer stock production of *Damn Yankees*.

A year after this "triumph," he had his first taste of professional competition, Broadway style. He auditioned for a role in *Sunrise at Campobello* and was chosen for the part of young John Roosevelt.

A few years later, Richard joined Geraldine Page, Ben Gazzara, and Jane Fonda in the Actors' Studio's all-star revival of Eugene O'Neill's *Strange Interlude*. Soon after came work in *Everything in the Garden, The Playroom,* and the Shakespeare festival's *Richard III* in Stratford, Connecticut. That's quite a list of credits for someone who had just barely passed the age of 15.

In 1969, Richard "retired" from the legitimate stage and made his movie debut playing Paul Newman's racing-car enthusiast stepson in *Winning*. Other films that followed were the critically acclaimed *Last Summer, The Todd Killings, Red Sky at Morning,* and *You'll Like My Mother*.

When you've conquered the movie and stage mediums, what's left for a successful actor? Obviously television is the next step. Richard wasted no time heading in that direction. Some years back, he made his television debut in the Hallmark Hall of Fame Christmas special "The Christmas Tree." After that he played a variety of roles on the daytime soap operas, but that was all preliminary work. Now that he had proved himself as an actor, it was on to prime time and guest star appearances. Richard played a Portuguese boy on "Medical Center," an insane kidnaper on "Bracken's World," and a criminal on "The FBI." There were also appearances on "Marcus Welby, M.D." and "Night Gallery."

None of these television roles, however, has won him the acclaim he received for the 1971 Christmas special, "The Homecoming, A Christmas Story" in which he costarred with Patricia Neal. When it was decided that "The Homecoming" would be made into a series, Richard was signed to recreate his role of John-Boy Walton. The name of the show was changed to "The Waltons" and the rest is television history. "The Waltons" went on to become the runaway hit of the 1972–73 TV season. When award time rolled around, in May, 1973, the Academy of Television Arts and Sciences honored the show with six Emmys. Richard Thomas won the Emmy for the best actor in a dramatic series.

▶A PRIVATE LIFE

It's hard to believe, but with all that work, the actor really has a private life outside of the studio. At the end of a day's shooting in Burbank, Richard returns to his house in Hollywood where he raises dogs—championship toy Brussels griffons and King Charles spaniels. He also finds time to play the dulcimer (a medieval stringed instrument) and study Spanish, French, and Chinese. (He attended Columbia University in New York before moving to California, and majored in Chinese studies.) Richard collects works of art and at the moment is very much interested in writing poetry.

But all of these outside interests have to take a back seat to his chosen profession. Richard Thomas, dog breeder, poet, and linguist, is still Richard Thomas, actor. And at the moment acting is what his life is all about. More movies are in the works, a return to the stage is imminent, and "The Waltons" may go on indefinitely. With all of this going for him, it appears that Richard Thomas is living the life that fulfills the dreams of every aspiring actor.

Mexico's Heritage, Oscar Amaro, age 14

Spirit of Mexico, Tina Francisca, age 10

Ceremonial Procession, Cynthia Norton, age 11

228

YOUNG ARTISTS

Schoolchildren, from kindergarten age through high school age, participated in the 1973 Youth Art Exhibit. Paintings, drawings, and graphics were selected from among hundreds of works done by students in the United States, Mexico, and Japan. The theme of the exhibit was "Exchanging Cultures Through Art."

The exhibit was sponsored by United States and Mexican cultural organizations. The young finalists were selected by a panel of judges from the two countries and Japan. The exhibit opened in August in Torreón, Mexico, and went on display in the California Museum of Science and Industry, in Los Angeles, a month later. Then, after being shown in various U.S. cities, it was sent on an international tour.

These pictures illustrate some of the art of students from U.S. schools.

The Nightingale, Katherine Shintaku, age 8

Pedro and the Piñata, Nancy Lee, age 11

229

Cherry Blossom, Janet Collins, age 14

The Happy Prince, Lauri Williams, age 14

Hanging the Piñata, Tami Castro, age 18

230

Song of the Swallows, Becky Krause, age 6

Indian God, Jessica Baugh, age 14

On the Way to Sunday Mass, Susan Gonzales, age 18

U.S. Scouts take part in the anti-litter drive on April 28, 1973.

BOY SCOUTS OF AMERICA

In 1973 the Boy Scouts of America entered the last half of its 8-year expansion plan, BOYPOWER '76. The organization is trying to encourage at least one third of all American boys of ages 8 through 17 to join. It is hoped that membership will increase to over 6,500,000 by 1976, the 200th anniversary of the founding of the United States.

The fastest growing program of the organization continued to be Exploring, designed for and run by young adults of 15 through 20 years of age. Through a wide variety of activities, Exploring prepares young adults for their future roles in society. Different career possibilities are stressed. The Explorer presidents' congress was held in April in Washington, D.C. Nearly 2,400 members and representatives of local Explorer posts elected national officers.

Operation REACH was successfully continued during the year. Initiated in 1971, the program stresses a new approach to drug-abuse prevention, and has been a source of encouragement and information for young people. By urging them to "reach" for positive goals instead of drugs, the program has helped young people decide for themselves

against drug experimentation. In 1973, President Richard Nixon presented the Boy Scouts of America with an award for exceptional initiative in developing this program.

As part of Project SOAR (*S*ave *O*ur *A*merican *R*esources), nearly 1,000,000 Scouts and their leaders joined other organizations on April 28, in an anti-litter drive. About 1,000,000 tons of rubbish were collected, and the material that could be recycled was sent to reclamation centers.

The 1973 National Scout Jamboree, which was held in two different states, had a large turnout. Some 45,000 boys attended the jamboree in Moraine State Park in Pennsylvania, and 25,000 boys attended the jamboree in Farragut State Park in Idaho. The theme of the jamboree was "Growing Together."

The improved Scouting program, which was launched in September, 1972, was set forth in a revised *Scout Handbook*. The new program offers more leadership training; greater Scout involvement in planning and decision making; and increased emphasis on environment and conservation.

ALDEN G. BARBER
Chief Scout Executive, Boy Scouts of America

Canadian Scouts on a canoe trip in northern Ontario.

BOY SCOUTS OF CANADA

There have been changes in society since Scouting began more than 60 years ago. Boy Scouts of Canada, through its new programs, projects, and printed materials, recognizes these changes. The organization is making every effort to move in a positive way to fulfill its responsibility to today's youth.

SCOUTING 77, the long-range plan of the Boy Scouts of Canada, places its emphasis on growth in six main areas: membership, finance, program, communications and relationships, manpower, and management.

In 1973 the organization made strides in meeting most of the objectives it had set for itself. Scouting's programs were taken to youth in the inner city, and in high-rise apartments, and were expanded to rural settings. Expanded service was also taken to Eskimo and Indian boys in the north and to special groups, such as the handicapped.

The TREES FOR CANADA project was a major conservation effort. Members planted more than 1,000,000 trees as part of the nationwide interest in reforestation and ecology. TREES FOR CANADA will become an annual event. Anti-litter days and clean-up and paper collection drives were held in many centers across the country in a continuing effort to keep Canada clean.

BEAVERS, an experimental program, involves a young group—boys aged 5 to 7½. The program grew at a controlled rate during 1973 to a membership of 12,000.

OPERATION AMIGO is a 4-year program to help pay the salaries and travel expenses of two full-time professional workers. Boys in Bolivia, Colombia, Ecuador, Peru, and Venezuela benefit from this program.

The Chief Scout's Award was introduced in 1973. This award is presented to boys of Scout age who have reached a certain level of accomplishment and participation in leadership skills, in voluntary service to the community, and in outdoor skills.

Hundreds of members took part in national and international events during the year. These included Boy Scouts of America Jamborees; Swedish International Camp; New Brunswick Operation Adventure; Handicapped Camporee at Camp Borden; and the first Northwest Territories Jamboree.

SID YOUNG
Executive Director, Communications Service
Boy Scouts of Canada

The new look in uniforms for the Camp Fire Girls.

CAMP FIRE GIRLS

In the most significant Camp Fire program change in a decade, brand-new program materials were released to Camp Fire members and leaders throughout the United States in 1973. Self-awareness, decision-making and planning, and the elimination of sex-stereotyping are emphasized as much in the new materials as crafts and games are.

The new materials will be used by more than 400,000 girls and leaders in the two youngest Camp Fire groups. *Adventure,* for Camp Fire Adventurers (ages 9 through 11), replaces the traditional *Book of the Camp Fire Girls.* The old book had been a mainstay of the Camp Fire program since it was first published in 1913. *It's All About Me, Here I Am,* and *I Can Do Lots of Things* are the first distinctive materials for Camp Fire Blue Birds (ages 6 through 8). The two older groups, Camp Fire Discovery Club members (ages 12 through 13) and Camp Fire Horizon Club members (age 14 through high school age), had received new program materials in 1971. (The Horizon Club is open to both girls and boys.)

The activities in all Camp Fire program books are designed to answer different needs and to give members a choice in achieving their goals. The emphasis is on helping youngsters learn attitudes and skills that will help them not only while they are growing up, but also when they are adults.

The Camp Fire Blue Bird and Adventurer program books can be used in a variety of settings, whether urban, suburban, or rural. They encourage girls to develop creativity, initiative, and perseverance. Activities are designed to help girls develop strong self-identity based on competence, sensitivity, awareness, and respect for others. They also encourage an interest in one's personal background and heritage, and in those of others.

LESLIE VERTER
Camp Fire Girls, Inc.

BOYS' CLUBS OF AMERICA

In 1973 the Boys' Clubs of America achieved their goal of "1,000 Boys' Clubs for 1,000,000 Boys"—a full 3 years ahead of schedule. They then went on to launch a development program to preserve and enrich the quality of their services to these clubs and members.

Through this program, called DESIGN FOR THE SEVENTIES, Boys' Clubs hope to expand and develop their services to meet their growing enrollment; strengthen their national image; and enhance the quality of life for all Boys' Clubs members.

Work has already begun on several parts of the program. Many clubs have projects to help slow readers or those who cannot read at all to develop adequate reading ability. Other clubs are encouraging unskilled members to develop manual skills that will help them find employment in the future. Some clubs offer scholarships, and also college counseling for members who do not have any help at home in making decisions about higher education. Some clubs have set up nutrition and cooking classes in an effort to improve the quality of the food their members eat. These and many other services will be expanded and increased as work on DESIGN FOR THE SEVENTIES goes on.

At the 67th annual Boys' Clubs conference, held in May, National Director William R. Bricker reviewed these plans with an enthusiastic audience of 1,200 professional workers from Boys' Clubs. He explained that to accomplish these goals, it will be necessary for the Boys' Clubs of America to double their present national budget during the 1970's.

Gilbert Baez, from the R. W. Brown Boys' Club of Philadelphia, Pennsylvania, was chosen Boy of the Year. During the many interviews and public appearances made by 17-year-old Gil since he received the award in April in Washington, D.C., he proved himself to be an excellent representative of Boys' Clubs.

E. J. STAPLETON
Boys' Clubs of America

Some Boys' Clubs have set up nutrition and cooking classes.

Fun and games at the 1973 Boy Scout jamboree.

"The world is so full of a number of things . . ."

ROBERT LOUIS STEVENSON

A Canadian Brownie inspects a butterfly.

A Girl Scout cooks out during the "Wyoming Trek."

4-H members learn about growing corn.

FFA students at work on a modern farm.

The "Mulligan Stew" cast teaches 4-H members about nutrition.

4-H CLUBS

With the 1973 theme "4-H Gets It All Together," 5,500,000 4-H'ers did just that—they got it all together in the nation's largest co-educational youth organization.

One of the fastest-growing programs was the Expanded Food and Nutrition Education Program (EFNEP). Through this ambitious project, many young people have learned that it's fun and easy to choose a balanced diet no matter where they live. They have learned about food selection through games such as nutrition bingo; by producing their own nutrition skits and puppet shows; through visits to farms and food processing plants; by growing vegetables in small gardens; and by preparing foods in such ways that few nutrients are lost.

Over 1,000,000 4-H members in 16 states enrolled in a special nutrition education television series. The six-part program, called "Mulligan Stew," teaches 9-to-12-year-olds about well-balanced diets through the songs and adventures of a cast of five lively youngsters. The young people who enrolled in the series were able to follow along with programed-learning comic books and with participation in special experiments and activities.

During 1973, young people took part in many 4-H projects to improve their communities. 4-H'ers are studying inadequate housing, environmental ecology, adult-youth conflicts, and career exploration. They have also set up solid-waste recycling centers, renovated and cared for historical sites, and built or renovated community centers and recreation areas.

Since many of today's members come from urban and suburban areas, many 4-H programs are geared to city living. Urban 4-H'ers are involved in creative writing, news reporting, photography, public speaking, animal science projects, and textile science. Even some of the established 4-H horticulture projects have taken on a new, urban look: 4-H'ers with a green thumb are making corsages, terrariums, and dish gardens.

The 4-H organization in Canada celebrated its 60th anniversary in 1973. In honor of the occasion, Canada's 78,000 4-H members took part in many special activities and projects. The highlight of the year's celebration was a national conference attended by delegates from across Canada.

E. DEAN VAUGHAN
Director, 4-H Programs

FUTURE FARMERS OF AMERICA

Food shortages and a year of record agricultural sales in the United States and to other countries gave new importance to agriculture in 1973. This meant new opportunities for students of vocational agriculture who are members of the Future Farmers of America (FFA). The organization, founded in 1928, is made up of young people who are preparing for careers on the nation's farms and in the hundreds of agricultural businesses that assist farmers.

The new importance of agriculture was reflected in increased membership. In 1973, membership in the FFA rose by over 15,000 members to 447,577 students in 49 states (all but Alaska), Puerto Rico, and the U.S. Virgin Islands.

At the same time that FFA membership was rising, students were being offered many new opportunities to participate in award and recognition programs. These challenge them to be better leaders and better agriculturalists. In 1973 the National FFA Foundation provided incentive awards for more than 70,000 FFA members. The awards, which are presented at local, state, regional, and national levels, recognize student activities in several areas. These include leadership, citizenship, and career preparation. Awards are also presented in chapter-sponsored safety and community improvement programs.

A record 15,500 FFA members, vocational agriculture instructors, and guests attended the 46th National FFA Convention in Kansas City, Missouri, in October. Traditionally the convention is managed by six student officers who have spent the preceding year traveling throughout the nation as representatives of the FFA organization. The 3-day convention included business sessions, agricultural contests, and recognition of hundreds of members for their achievements.

The FFA Public Speaking Contest winner in 1973 was Neil Bowman, 18, of Yuma, Arizona. The highest awards—Star Farmer and Star Agribusinessman of America—were presented to William A. Sparrow, 22-year-old crop and livestock farmer of Unadilla, Georgia, and, in a tie, to two agribusinessmen, Jack Rose, 21, of Elko, Nevada, and Steven Redgate, 21, of Waynoka, Oklahoma. The top chapter in the community improvement program Building Our American Communities was the FFA chapter of Bloomer, Wisconsin.

A. DANIEL REUWEE
Director of Information
Future Farmers of America

FFA members view greenhouse plants during a horticulture class.

Girl Scouts organized and participated in CISUM, a 2-week music workshop.

GIRL SCOUTS OF THE U.S.A.

In 1973 the Girl Scouts of the United States of America increased its efforts to bring the benefits of Scouting into the lives of more young girls. The age limit was lowered to permit 6-year-olds to become Brownie Girl Scouts. A campaign was also undertaken to recruit more adult troop leaders and assistant leaders. Many thousands more girls could be served if more adults would volunteer to form and lead new troops.

Many special events took place during the year. "Wider opportunities," for example, are events that take 14-through-17-year-old girls geographically beyond their own troops or councils. One such event took place in July in Nashville, Tennessee. There, girls worked with adult volunteers to organize a highly successful music workshop, called CISUM ("music" spelled backward). This program was attended by 150 Girl Scouts from nearly all the 50 states, and six Girl Guides from foreign countries. CISUM received the full support of Nashville's music and recording industry. For 2 weeks recording artists, technicians, musicians, arrangers, and songwriters led workshop sessions on everything from classical music to rock and country and western.

During the summer, more than 7,000 girls took part in international, national, and council-operated events. The nationally sponsored events included the "Wyoming Trek." Nearly 5,000 girls journeyed to a 15,000-acre wilderness area in Wyoming. They spent 2 weeks camping, hiking, backpacking, and horseback riding, and going on archeological digs and geological explorations.

Other Girl Scouts attended conferences and worked on projects to learn such things as folk arts, river running, theater, and wilderness survival. Boy Scouts were included in a wilderness backpacking trip in Alaska, and in a mountaineering adventure in the Wallowa Mountains area of Whitman National Forest in the Pacific Northwest.

Through their ECO – ACTION program, the Girl Scouts continued their work to improve the environment. In April they joined forces with other youth groups on Keep America Beautiful Day. The several million member youth task force rolled up its sleeves to clean up highways, urban areas, and seashores. The task force also planted more than 7,000,000 trees and shrubs.

RICHARD G. KNOX
Girl Scouts of the U.S.A.

Canadian Girl Guides on an outdoor adventure.

GIRL GUIDES OF CANADA

Girl Guides are members of a worldwide group—the World Association of Girl Guides and Girl Scouts. When Robert Baden-Powell organized the Boy Scouts in 1908, he received many requests from girls asking if they could become Scouts, too. His sister Agnes Baden-Powell formed an organization for girls, known as Girl Guides. The first Girl Guides were those in Britain. Soon the idea spread to other countries. The first Guide Company in Canada was organized in 1910 in St. Catharines, then a small town tucked away among the orchards and vineyards of Ontario's Niagara Peninsula.

Today the Guiding family in Canada has close to 300,000 members. The family includes Brownies (aged 7 to 10), Guides (10 to 14), and Rangers (14 to 18).

Guiding is a program designed to challenge and train girls and to create a love for the healthy outdoor life. The program develops an appreciation of the beauty and wonder of nature, and emphasizes the importance of conservation. Guiding also promotes individual growth—in initiative, self-reliance, resourcefulness, and self-discipline.

Because of their membership in a world organization, Girl Guides of Canada have the opportunity to participate in international camps and special events in all parts of the world. Members are enriched by meeting girls from other countries and cultures. For the Canadians, who were the hostesses, one of the most important international events of recent years was the 21st World Conference of Girl Guides and Girl Scouts, held in Toronto in June, 1972.

Current programs range from ecology through the crafts, arts, and sciences. The established live-in camp still offers its challenge to the Brownie and the young Guide, but in a country as vast and varied as Canada, the call of the wild and the open road attract hundreds of Guides and Rangers. Interprovincial events featured canoe trips, backpacking expeditions, and bicycle trips.

In 1973 an experimental program called An Adventure in Discovery was introduced for Guides across Canada. The experiment, which was to run from September, 1973, until April, 1974, was based on the existing Guide program, but encouraged girls and leaders to use their own initiative more.

RUTH WARBURTON
Executive Director
Girl Guides of Canada

JUNIOR ACHIEVEMENT

For more than 50 years Junior Achievement (JA) has been giving high school girls and boys practical experience in how to run a business. Learning by doing is the basic philosophy of this unique international business-education and training program. With the help of adult advisers from the world of business and industry, teenagers organize and manage their own small companies for a 30-week period that begins in September and ends in May of each school year.

Today Junior Achievement is at work in over 1,000 communities across the United States. It also has an extensive program in Canada, and in nine other countries. In 1973 about 170,000 Junior Achievers were actively involved in running over 7,000 mini-corporations in the United States. JA business activities ran the gamut from manufacturing leather goods and running a bank to pro-

Cartoon illustrates JA anti-crime project.

ducing television and radio shows and organizing a burglary-protection program.

JA members take charge of their company's day-to-day operations, sell stock, advertise and promote their product or service, and issue a year-end company report. JA receives financial support from over 90,000 contributors. These include many of the largest corporations in the United States, as well as smaller business firms and individual business and professional people. Thousands of other business executives contribute time, energy, and know-how, serving as advisers to the JA companies. Many educators encourage the program as a practical means of teaching young people about economics and the business world. Some school systems actually give course credit or activity credit for participation in JA.

For thousands of its members JA has been a stepping-stone to executive positions in business and industry. One JA alumnus, who is now the vice-president of a bank, recently recalled what the program had meant for him: "When I was in junior high school, I was floundering. I didn't know what I wanted to do—except play basketball. But then I joined JA. It decidedly directed my interest toward business. I went to college, graduating in business, and JA was my first contact."

How does JA operate? Each JA company is staffed by 20 to 25 student Achievers. They meet every week for about 2 hours in one of the 700 JA business centers across the land. They decide what sort of business they will set up and then plan company policy. The students are the entire staff of the company—the board of directors, the work force, and the sales and promotion staffs.

To finance their company, the Achievers sell stock at $1 a share. In 1973 there were close to 700,000 JA stockholders throughout the United States. Once they have the necessary capital, the Achievers begin regular business operations. Production lines are set up, and steps are taken to provide for distributing the product. While this is going on, the advertising staff gets to work on a promotional campaign. Finally, when production is in full gear, the sales staff takes over. Most JA products are sold through door-to-door sales or at trade fairs.

CHICAGO'S NEW LOOK

JA business firms are as varied as their locales. In Chicago, for instance, an enterprising team of Achievers set up their own teen modeling agency, which they called Chicago's New Look. The company was sponsored by a professional modeling school and one of the city's major department stores. Company members screened some 250 teenage girls—all recent graduates of modeling schools. Sixteen girls, including a set of twins, were selected to be company models.

The 13 Achievers who ran the company prepared a portfolio, with photos and blurbs, on each of their models. New Look's public relations staff then went into action, making the rounds of fashion showrooms, photo studios, and advertising agencies. Potential customers were shown the girls' portfolios and encouraged to give them modeling assignments. Each girl was paid by the hour, and the JA company took a small agent's fee.

New Look's young president, Gregory Snow, reported at the end of the project that running the modeling agency had been "the most fantastic experience of my life."

PROJECT IDENTIFICATION

Two New Jersey JA companies found a way to make crime pay—but not for the criminal. They formed an organization to combat burglary, America's number one crime. The company was called Project Identification, and the anti-crime weapon used was a simple electric engraver.

For a modest fee, company workers engraved the customer's driver's license number on television sets, electric typewriters, radios, cameras, stereo systems, bicycles, and other items of value that are most often the targets of thieves. After the items were engraved, the customer received stickers for doors and windows. The red and yellow sticker carries this warning to potential burglars: "All items of value on these premises have been marked for ready identification by law enforcement agencies."

Most thieves steal household items and resell them. They tend to shy away from any valuables that are easily identifiable. Project Identification was designed to discourage burglars by making the risk too great.

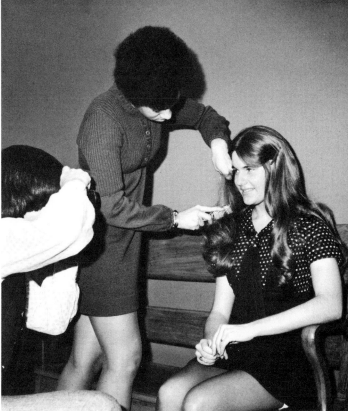

Hair stylist gives a last-minute touch-up to model from Chicago's New Look agency.

Sticker given out by Project Identification.

WARNING!
ALL ITEMS OF
VALUE
ON THESE
PREMISES
HAVE BEEN MARKED
FOR READY
IDENTIFICATION
BY
LAW ENFORCEMENT
AGENCIES

FIRST NATIONAL SALES COMPANY

A "super sales" outfit was started by a group of Achievers in Jackson, Michigan. The company was made up of second-year JA members who were aiming at careers in sales. The company made no products of its own. Instead, its members sold the products of its sponsoring organization, as well as products made by other JA companies.

The products were sold on a commission basis. The principal goal was to provide teenagers with practical experience in direct sales methods. The firm was called the First National Sales Company, in recognition of the fact that it was the country's first company engaged exclusively in sales.

CINCY

Another interesting JA project was the work of 18 Cincinnati, Ohio, teenagers. They decided to go into the publishing business and put out a general interest magazine geared to high school students. Without any previous knowledge of the publishing field, the Achievers put out a magazine called *Cincy*, which was sold at high school bookstores.

Company members did every bit of the work themselves—from writing articles and designing page layouts to printing and marketing the publication. *Cincy* carried articles on sports and entertainment figures, and other popular teenage celebrities. There were interviews with rock groups and disc jockeys, and reviews of current motion pictures. The JA company was sponsored by a local publishing firm, and *Cincy* proved to be a very successful magazine.

BANKING

The ever-growing field of banking has attracted the attention of a number of Achievers. Encouraged by the nation's banking community, JA now operates more than 200 banks in the United States. JA banks handle checking and savings accounts, and perform such services as cashing payroll checks and renting safe-deposit boxes. Some also sell money orders, travelers checks, and savings bonds.

In Memphis, Tennessee, there were four JA banks housed in the JA business center. One of them, the First Associates Holding

Company, branched out into other areas. Like many regular banks, it was also a holding company operating other business firms. The Memphis JA holding company managed both a supply and a sales company in addition to performing its banking functions.

A JOB EDUCATION PROGRAM

In recent years JA has also been involved in an important community service program aimed at helping teenagers from disadvantaged families learn useful business skills. The program is called Job Education and is held each summer in a number of JA areas throughout the nation. Job Education offers summer employment to high school students

Teller conducts transaction in a JA bank.

Students receive training in Job Ed program.

between the ages of 14 and 18. Most of these students had been tagged as potential high school dropouts and were considered unemployable because they lacked the necessary job skills.

But with the co-operation of nearly 100 business firms, jobs were provided for nearly 2,000 disadvantaged youths. The program involves working 15 to 20 hours weekly over an 8-week period. Like the members of regular JA companies, the participants in this program are paid for producing some product or providing a service.

The youths get more than just technical knowledge out of the program. According to one of Job Ed's advisers, "They're learning what it means to get to work on time and to do their best on the job." In addition to working at their part-time jobs, the students also attend business-education sessions. These deal with career planning and opportunities, general business practices, and other related subjects.

JA's varied activities have helped thousands of young people to learn about the day-to-day functioning and organization of different types of businesses. JA also builds self-confidence among its members. Achievers get an idea of the rewards and responsibilities of individual enterprise. In addition, teenagers are able to test career interests in the real-life laboratory of an actual business.

245

FUN TO MAKE AND DO

Yarn-o-rama: Fourth grade children made this delightful picture with bright-colored yarns.

STAMP COLLECTING

The hobby of stamp collecting continued its worldwide growth in 1973. A survey—the first of its kind—made by the United States Postal Service gave an indication of the popularity of stamp collecting. The survey showed that as many as 16,000,000 people collect the stamps of the United States.

▶ **NEW UNITED STATES STAMPS**

Among the most unusual stamps issued by the United States Postal Service in 1973 was a series honoring the people of the Postal Service themselves. There were ten 8-cent stamps showing postal workers at their jobs. On the back of each stamp was a short description of the job pictured.

During the year memorial stamps were issued for two U.S. Presidents—Harry S. Truman and Lyndon B. Johnson. Each of the two commemoratives was an 8-cent jumbo portrait stamp.

The United States Postal Service also issued four stamps in its American Arts series. The 8-cent semi-jumbo stamps paid tribute to composer George Gershwin, poet Robinson Jeffers, painter Henry O. Tanner, and writer Willa Cather.

In 1976 the United States will celebrate the Bicentennial of the American Revolution. In 1973 a series of four stamps was issued to portray features of the period leading up to the Revolution. The 1973 series was called "Rise of the Spirit of Independence."

The first of the four 8-cent stamps shows men printing a pamphlet. Many of the ideas of the American Revolution appeared in pamphlet form. The second stamp pictures a man nailing up a broadside, or handbill, in a public place. A broadside was one way of spreading ideas to a large group. The third stamp shows a colonial postrider on the Post Road between New York and Boston. The letters and newspapers postriders carried were an important means of spreading ideas. The last stamp shows a drummer calling men to take up arms against the British.

The Boston Tea Party, one of the famous incidents that led to the American Revolution, was commemorated with a block of four 8-cent stamps issued on July 4, 1973. Each of the stamps shows a complete scene, and the four together make up the larger scene of Boston Harbor on the night of the tea dumping.

UNITED STATES STAMPS OF 1973

Boston Tea Party

Rural America

Rise of the Spirit of Independence

LOVE stamp

A TOPICAL COLLECTION OF WALT DISNEY STAMPS

Peg Pete

Gyro Gearloose

Pluto

Minnie Mouse

Walt Disney,
creator of the
cartoon characters.

Donald Duck

Uncle Scrooge

Mickey Mouse

Goofy

Huey, Dewey, and Louie

Australia's Metric Conversion Series

Among other new issues of the year was a "LOVE" stamp. The red, blue, and green stamp uses the famous design of pop artist Robert Indiana. An Angus cattle stamp honors rural America. A postal card celebrates the 100th anniversary of the first U.S. postal card (which for many years cost a penny). The price of the new "penny" postal card is 6 cents.

NEW WORLD ISSUES

A number of topics of the day served as inspiration for stamps issued by other countries in 1973. Australia's planned conversion from the imperial system of weights and measures to the metric system is the theme of an unusual series. The four 7-cent stamps use cartoons to announce the changes ahead.

Three commemoratives were brought out in honor of one of the most romantic and famous Canadian institutions—the Royal Canadian Mounted Police. The 8-cent, 10-cent, and 15-cent stamps celebrate the 100th anniversary of the force's founding. Canada also issued a pair of stamps—8 and 15 cents in value—in anticipation of the Olympic Games to be held in Montreal in 1976.

The year's favorite romantic theme was the wedding of Britain's Princess Anne to Captain Mark Phillips. Britain and many other Commonwealth countries issued stamps in honor of the event.

Israel marked its 25th anniversary as a nation with the issue of a special souvenir sheet. The sheet reproduces Israel's Declaration of Independence. At the bottom of the sheet is a rectangular stamp reproducing the signatures at the bottom of the Declaration.

Many countries issued stamps in honor of the 100th anniversary of the World Meteorological Organization, a specialized agency of the United Nations. The agency began long before the existence of the United Nations.

Britain saw itself as a key piece in the Common Market jigsaw puzzle. The design of three stamps, issued as Britain joined the Common Market in 1973, shows a puzzle with the British piece falling into place.

A TOPICAL STAMP COLLECTION

For many collectors the real interest of the hobby is in collecting stamps related to a theme. A collection built around a theme is called a topical collection. The Walt Disney stamps of San Marino suggest the fun of building a topical collection around cartoon characters—Mickey Mouse, Donald Duck, Pluto, and the rest.

CHARLESS HAHN
Stamp Editor, *Chicago Sun-Times*

A BASEBALL CARD COLLECTION

There was a time not too many years ago when most American boys, and even some girls, had an unsightly, square bulge in their back pockets. Their mothers often complained about it. The bulge was a valuable collection of baseball cards, which were well thumbed and often slightly soiled. Most of them had originally come from packs of bubble gum. Collections were rounded out by trading with other young people, or by winning cards from other collectors in various games. The cards had pictures of famous major league baseball players on the front, and batting averages and other statistics on the back. They usually smelled of bubble gum. Baseball card collecting first became popular in the 1880's. Today some young people collect basketball, football, soccer, and hockey cards as well. However, baseball cards remain the most popular collecting items.

Although young people still collect baseball cards, the hobby has gotten a bit more complicated in recent years. Some of the older cards—cards with Babe Ruth and other baseball greats on them—are really quite valuable. But you can still collect current baseball cards in the good old-fashioned way. Even if you don't like bubble gum, I'm sure you have a younger brother or sister or a friend who does! Not only are the cards good looking, they are a wonderful way of keeping track of baseball history.

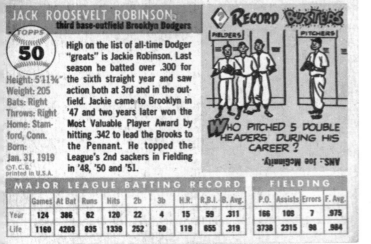

The back (below) of the Jackie Robinson card gives a typical rundown of a player's career.

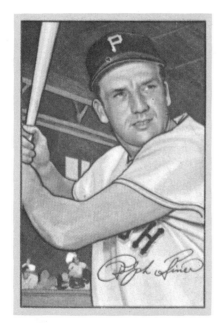

VIRDON

McGINNITY, NEWARK

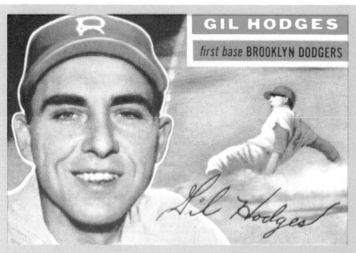

GIL HODGES

first base BROOKLYN DODGERS

Gil Hodges

DON NEWCOMBE

pitcher BROOKLYN DODGERS

Don Newcombe

WILMER MIZELL

pitcher ST. LOUIS CARDINALS

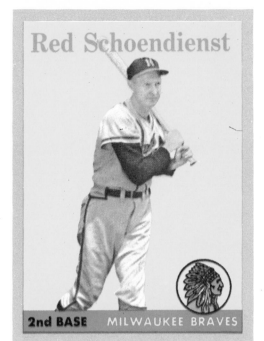

Red Schoendienst

2nd BASE MILWAUKEE BRAVES

CHARLEY NEAL

2nd base BROOKLYN DODGERS

MARTY MARION

PHIL RIZZUTO

shortstop NEW YORK YANKEES

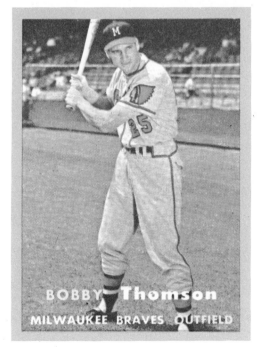

BOBBY Thomson

MILWAUKEE BRAVES OUTFIELD

BOBBY SHANTZ

NEW YORK YANKEES PITCHER

Students learn about organic gardening by going right into the fields.

MAKING AN ORGANIC GARDEN

It is possible to take an outdoor space the size of your living room and turn it into a garden that will provide you with vegetables every day of the summer. Making an organic garden can be one of the most rewarding hobbies you have ever undertaken.

An organic garden differs from other gardens in two basic ways. The soil of an organic garden is enriched for planting with natural fertilizer from a compost heap, instead of commercial fertilizers made with chemicals. When vegetables grown in organic soil come up, they are freed of pests by the use of natural substances and the removal of pests by hand.

Vegetables that you grow yourself in organically enriched soil taste better and are better for you than the ones available in most grocery stores. Your homegrown, organic vegetables will be rich in natural vitamins and minerals. They will be free of residues of pesticides and herbicides that are used widely in commercial agriculture. And when you eat fresh vegetables from your own garden, you won't have to worry about the effects of the chemical additives and preservatives that are present in most canned or frozen food you buy.

Besides improving your health, your organic garden is a way of helping to improve the environment in which we live. You will be strengthening the balance of nature rather than altering it. Organic gardening is not an expensive hobby. In fact, with organic gardening you will have many opportunities to recycle materials that would otherwise be wasted.

Organic gardening is a year-round, all-weather hobby. Tending the garden with chores like sowing seeds, watering, and weeding will keep you busy during the fair, warm days of the year. At almost any other time you can work on plans and on a soil building program.

▶ BASIC PLANNING

It's fun to use the winter and rainy weather for planning your organic garden. You will need to find a sunny spot for your garden, about 10 or 12 feet square. If your own yard is not suitable, ask a neighbor if he is willing to let you use some of his land in return for some of your produce. If you live in an apartment in a city or a large town, you can sometimes obtain permission to use vacant lots for organic-gardening projects.

Classes and groups in schools all over the United States, Canada, and other countries are turning some playground space into organic gardens. Through these gardens, students are learning about agriculture, botany, nutrition, and ecology. Books, filmstrips, and other learning materials are available to guide you, your classmates, and your teachers in your work.

Here are some steps you should take in starting your garden.

(1) Start a notebook for the plans you make and the information you gather. Include a diary section for daily entries once the growing season begins.

(2) Make a list of the vegetables you like best and begin to collect information about them. There are basic things you should find out about the vegetables you plan to grow. How much space do they need? How long do they take to mature? Which varieties are best-suited to the area in which you live? You can order your seeds through a catalog, or you can buy packets at a hardware store or garden center.

(3) Find out what the usual planting and harvesting dates are for your region and learn about any gardening problems common in your location. Most gardeners are delighted to find someone else interested in their hobby. Talk to people who have gardens near your home. They will probably be glad to tell you which crops have been the most successful for them.

(4) Write to your nearest state, county, or provincial information office for further in-formation about climate and soil conditions in your specific area. They can tell you how to take a soil sample from your garden and where it should be sent. Since much governmental material recommends chemical fertilizers, make sure you ask what natural, organic substances may be used if your soil shows any deficiencies.

(5) Spend time locating sources of organic materials such as leaves, manure, old hay, sawdust, and seaweed. Telephone, write, or visit people who may be able to supply you with these and other items. You may need to add rock fertilizers to your soil. Dolomitic limestone, greensand (glauconite), and rock phosphate are natural products that slowly release important nutrients for plant growth. Find out where you can obtain these substances.

(6) Different kinds of plants grown side by side seem to protect one another. These combinations are called companion plantings. Nasturtiums, marigolds, and members of the onion family, such as garlic and chives, are frequently used as companion plants. Plan to include some of these in your garden.

(7) Plan to make your garden a haven for helpful birds. Swallows, wrens, martins, and bluebirds have tremendous appetites for bugs. Which of these are likely to spend a summer with you? Look in your *New Book of Knowledge* for plans for building a birdhouse. Then spend part of a winter weekend building one from pieces of scrap lumber. Be on the lookout for a large shallow container, dishpan size, that you could use for a birdbath.

(8) Encourage your town or city to conserve organic materials. Service organizations and municipal departments in many communities have combined efforts in order to recycle organic wastes on a large scale. Not only can sanitation costs be lowered, but resulting compost is made available to home gardeners. Find out whether you can obtain clean sludge from a sewage treatment plant in your community for use as an element in your compost pile. It could be a valuable addition.

▶ SOIL BUILDING THE ORGANIC WAY

To grow healthy plants you must start by making healthy soil. The methods used by

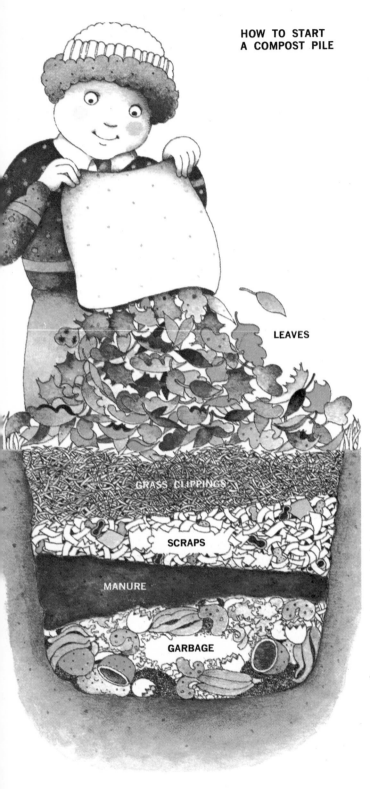

**HOW TO START
A COMPOST PILE**

LEAVES

GRASS CLIPPINGS

SCRAPS

MANURE

GARBAGE

organic gardeners to enrich the soil follow the example of nature.

In undisturbed areas of meadow and forest, soil building is a continuous natural process. Leaves, grasses, and other remains from plants and animals fall to the ground and decay. This decaying organic material, called humus, nourishes the plants and the animals that eat them. Many home gardeners choose to make their own soil-enriching fertilizer of organic matter found around their own houses or grounds. It is called compost and is made in a compost pile or heap.

Organic materials added to the soil in your garden provide many different kinds of food necessary for plant growth. These nutrients are released slowly, as required by the plants. Organic matter in the soil can absorb large amounts of water, serving to protect your plants from becoming waterlogged during heavy rains, and from drying out during periods of drought. It also supplies food for earthworms and other soil organisms that keep the soil healthy. A rich soil will produce plants that are strong enough to resist many diseases and pests, and that will bear abundant and full-flavored crops.

Whenever the ground is bare, you can work on a soil building program. Late fall and very early spring are the best times to build a compost heap. At these times of year, there will be time for organic materials to decompose, and you will not be so busy with other work in your garden.

Choose a spot at the back corner of your garden plot and mark off an area about 3 feet square. Some gardeners dig out a pit, 1 or 2 feet deep, saving the soil to cover their layers. Others simply begin their heap at ground level, surrounding it with a sturdy fence to discourage dogs and other animals from digging into it.

Either way, start collecting all kinds of organic materials for your compost heap. You will be pleased to find that you can re-cycle a large amount of waste from your own home. The kitchen is the best place to start your search. Save wilted outer leaves from salad greens; crushed eggshells; and apple cores. Vegetable peels, stale bread crumbs, and leftover bits of cereal are excellent. The liquid used for soaking pots and pans after cooking can be added for moisture. Avoid greasy meat scraps, however, as these may attract pests to your pile.

Remind other members of the family to save materials that would otherwise be thrown away. Sweepings and the lint from a home dryer as well as dust from the vacuum cleaner can go into the compost heap. Small amounts of paper and cloth are all right too. Add hair clippings from haircuts. Collect sawdust from your workbench area. Save ashes from the fireplace.

Extend your search for compost materials by exploring your neighborhood. Arrange to pick up leaves and grass clippings when your neighbors do their yard work. Offer to clean out fireplaces in return for keeping the ashes. A riding stable, pet shop, or animal hospital would be a good place to obtain manure mixed with old hay or straw. A hardware store, carpenter's shop, or lumberyard may have sawdust you could take away. Gardening the organic way not only builds soil, but it cuts down on waste through the recycling of resources.

Add your materials in layers, shredding large pieces of organic material and covering each layer with soil. Normal rainfall should keep the pile moist. Every few weeks, take a pitchfork and turn over the contents of the heap. Notice what is happening to the layers. Which scraps decompose quickly? Which need more time? Has your heap attracted many earthworms? Put your hand on one of the inside layers and compare the heat of the inside and outside of the pile.

In a real compost heap, the decomposition of organic matter produces heat. Enough heat should be created in the heap to destroy weed seeds and plant diseases that may have been carried with the materials added to the pile. The process of decay should be fairly rapid and complete. If you construct your compost heap properly, it should not give off an unpleasant odor.

▶ STARTING THE GARDEN

After you have planned your garden and made your compost heap, the real fun begins —working in your garden. When spring planting season comes, test a handful of soil from your garden. If it is moist and crumbly but not dripping wet, you will know that it is time at last to take out your spade or garden fork and your rake. A pair of cotton work gloves may prevent blisters during your first few sessions.

Your first job is to turn over the soil. Dig down the depth of the shovel blade or of the prongs of the garden fork and turn over large chunks of soil. You may occasionally hit roots and stones. Dig them out. Decide on a spot outside the garden for collecting any stones larger than an orange.

Once the soil is turned, break up the clumps with a fork or the back of a rake. Spread well-decayed compost from your compost heap over the garden, and mix it into the soil. Rake back and forth until the surface of the soil is smoothed out.

Preparing the soil in this way will probably be the hardest part of your work all season, especially if there has never been a garden in the spot you have picked. Do a little at a time over a period of days. Pause to enjoy the warmth of the sun, the clean, fresh smell of the soil, and the sounds of the birds.

You can save a lot of effort by arranging for someone to prepare your soil with a rotary tiller. Spread your compost and rock fertilizers over the garden so that they can be worked into the soil as the machine moves along. The tiller will probably have to be wheeled over the garden several times, with the tines set for greater depth on each pass.

Plant your seeds on the advisable dates for your area. Follow the detailed planting instructions printed on the seed packets. Mark your rows with small labeled stakes. Write down in your gardening diary what you have planted and the date.

Watch your garden carefully. In 3 to 5 days—certainly before the week is out—you will find that your first seeds have germinated. It is a wonderful day when you can write in your diary, "The corn is up!"

As the growing season progresses, you will be taking care of your plants in many ways. Thin your plants as directed on the packets, using lettuce and radish seedlings for salads. Be ready to put up a fence for peas, poles for beans, and stakes for tomatoes. A fence around the garden may be necessary for keeping animals out. If there is no rain for a long time, water your garden thoroughly in the evening once a week.

WEEDS AND PESTS

Every garden has weeds and pests. Powerful herbicides and pesticides have been developed for killing unwanted plants and insects. Unfortunately such poisons also destroy or harm helpful organisms, and they are even dangerous to the skin and eyes of the people using them. You can control weeds and insects in your garden with other methods.

Why not eat the weeds? Dandelions, purslane, sour grass, and lamb's-quarters (all common weeds) are edible either raw in salads or cooked as a green vegetable. Ask a more experienced gardener to help you identify these and other weeds, or refer to a guide.

Other weeds should be pulled, but wait for second leaves to appear. The first pair, or seed leaves, of some crops is difficult to distinguish from that of weeds. With a sharp trowel, follow and remove the underground

This garden has been mulched between the rows.

stems of deep-rooted weeds to prevent new runners from surfacing. Leave the weeds to dry in the sun so that they won't take root again, and then add them to your compost pile.

Smothering is another good way to control weeds. Cover the soil among your plants with a thick layer of old hay, straw, or sawdust. To be effective, the covering, or mulch, should be several inches deep. Mulch not only keeps down the weeds, but it holds moisture in, helps to maintain a steady soil temperature, and provides organic matter for earthworms to pull down into the soil.

Look over your garden every day for any signs of insect damage. Without resorting to poisonous sprays, you can control harmful insects and hungry larvae. Your garden will be small enough so that you can simply remove undesirable larvae by hand. Check under the leaves and in the soil around the plants until you find the culprits that have been eating your vegetables. Slugs go into hiding during the daytime, so get out into your garden early for them, especially in humid weather.

Use ingenuity, not poisons, in your garden. A dusting of ashes or of ground limestone will discourage many kinds of beetles. A tin can, top and bottom removed, can be pushed into the soil around a cabbage plant to turn away cutworms. An onion, several cloves of garlic, and a piece of hot pepper, blended together with two or three cups of water and strained, makes a safe yet effective repellent that you can apply with a clean paintbrush or a simple sprayer.

Learn to recognize and appreciate the helpful creatures that come to your garden. Ladybugs and praying mantises are so significant in the control of some garden pests that organic gardeners buy them in quantity through the mail. Is there a toad in your garden, helping you, even when you're not there, by eating insects? Which birds stop off during migration and which have stayed to nest nearby for the summer?

HARVEST TIME

Enjoy your harvest. From the first tender radish thinnings to the last head of cabbage picked after frost, your vegetables are sure to be the best you've ever tasted. You'll be delighted with the sweetness of corn that is cooked within minutes of being picked. You'll be amazed at the number of beans you get from just a few seeds.

At the end of the season, bed down your garden for the winter. Pull all remaining stalks and add them to the compost heap, which you can add to throughout the year. Turn over the soil lightly and cover the whole patch with a good layer of compost, hay, or leaves. A few evergreen boughs will keep your topping from blowing away.

Looking back on your gardening work, you will gain satisfaction from knowing that you have not disturbed the patterns of nature through the use of poisons. And you can feel pleased that you have made a small part of our planet a little bit more fertile and fruitful than it was when you began.

Every gardener makes mistakes, and every gardener finds out that some crops are more successful than others. But the memories of juicy red tomatoes and crisp carrots, and of crunchy lettuce and tender peas will probably make you want to start another garden year as soon as you have finished your first one.

JUDY ADAMS HINDS
Maplevale Organic Farm

The end of a good season—a rich fall harvest.

GLOSSARY

Companion planting: A method of arranging different plants in the garden to take advantage of their natural way of protecting each other. Examples: basil with tomatoes; beans with summer savory; tomatoes and asparagus; beans and potatoes.

Compost: A balanced plant fertilizer made from plant and animal residues, rich soil, and naturally occurring minerals. Compost is produced in a carefully layered pile where bacteria and other decay organisms can reproduce rapidly. These organisms change organic substances and minerals into readily available plant nutrients.

Humus: A highly complex, dark, organic substance found in undisturbed soils. Humus holds plant nutrients and water.

Mulch: A soil covering, usually of organic materials such as straw, sawdust, woodchips, and grass clippings. It keeps down weeds, retains soil moisture, and supplies nutrients as it decays.

Nutrients: The substances required for plant growth. The most important elements needed are carbon, hydrogen, oxygen, phosphorus, nitrogen, potassium, sulfur, calcium, iron, magnesium, and manganese. In addition to these, plants need very small amounts of boron, copper, and zinc, often referred to as trace elements. Well-made compost contains all these nutrients.

Organic: Any substance of plant or animal origin. The word "organic" is used to describe methods and materials that are not destructive to biological systems.

Soil test: A way of measuring the nutrients in your soil. Soils are classed on a scale ranging from acid (pH 1–6) through near neutral or circumneutral (pH 6–8) to alkaline (pH 8 plus). Most vegetables do best in a soil that is only slightly acid. Add ground dolomitic limestone if your soil is too acid, or peat moss if it is too alkaline.

MAKE A DÉCOUPAGE BOX

Have you ever painted a picture, made a dress, done any embroidery, worked in clay, or made a collage? If you have, you have probably experienced the feeling that comes from knowing that the object you have created is different from anything that has ever been made before.

Because handmade articles are unique, they have a value that something manufactured can never have. Particularly these days, when so many of the things we need and use in our daily lives are mass-produced, handmade items seem very special. And for this reason, too, the gifts that we make ourselves are extra pleasing to the people who receive them.

Crafts have become so popular among people of all ages that finding materials for projects is no longer a problem. Many craft shops have opened up all over the country, and large department stores now have special sections where they sell nothing but craft supplies. Even if you live far away from shopping centers, there are mail-order houses from which you can order craft materials.

Although Sandy, who is 12, had never done découpage, she decided that she would like to learn the craft in order to make Christmas presents for her family and friends. She wanted to make a card box for her grandmother, a purse for her mother, and a "treasure" box for her brother.

Her first project was something for herself—a pencil box for her desk. Since she is very fond of birds, she wanted to decorate her box with pictures of them. Then the finished box would reflect her own interest, in addition to being something that she had made herself from start to finish.

Découpage is a very old craft that was revived a few years ago and has been steadily growing in popularity. Basically, découpage is the craft of cutting out pictures, gluing them onto a box, plaque, or other object, and then applying many layers of varnish (sanding between coats until the surface is completely smooth). Some découpeurs (people who do découpage) will apply 30 or more coats of varnish, which can make a project very time-consuming. However, there are now fast-drying découpage finishes that require only about 10 coats, so that the time spent can be greatly reduced.

No matter what craft you are going to take up, it is important to follow three steps in order to complete your project successfully: (1) plan your project carefully; (2) be sure that you have all the instructions you need; (3) assemble all of your materials and tools before you begin.

After Sandy had decided to make a découpage box, she thought about what size and shape she wanted it to be, what color, and what kind of pictures she would decorate it with. Since there have been a number of books and magazine articles on découpage, she did not have difficulty in finding découpage instructions. She carefully read some of these, and decided to use a quick-drying, fast-building finish (directions for using the varnish were on the can). At a nearby craft shop, she was able to buy the following items: a wooden box, bird prints, a small jar of acrylic paint, varnish, fine steel wool, sandpaper, a pair of tiny hinges, and a bottle of découpage glue (white craft glue can also be used). She already had a pair of small sharp scissors, brushes for applying the varnish, and some attractive striped wrapping paper for lining the inside of the box.

1. Paint the box.

2. Cut out the pictures.

3. Arrange the pictures on the box.

4. Apply glue and paste down the pictures.

5. Pat down edges with a sponge.

6. Varnish the box.

The first step in decorating the box was to paint it. It happened that the box Sandy had bought was already sanded, but of course if there had been any rough spots it would have been necessary for her to sand these off before painting. She applied two coats of yellow acrylic paint, and let the box dry thoroughly.

Cutting the bird prints was not easy. In découpage, all of the background paper is cut away, so that only the subject you are going to paste remains. Sandy's bird prints were intricate, and she had to cut very carefully. She found it best to first cut away the part of the picture she didn't need; then she carefully cut around the outside of the smaller picture.

After all the birds were cut out, Sandy arranged them on the box. She placed some on the cover of the box, and some on the four sides. When she had arranged them in the way that she thought looked best, she put découpage glue on the backs of the cutouts and glued them on the box, wiping off excess glue with a damp cloth and patting the edges down with a sponge. It is important that all the edges are glued down securely.

The next day, when the glue was thoroughly dry, Sandy started to varnish her box. She applied eight coats of fast-drying finish. She let the first coat dry for an hour before she applied the next one, and lengthened the drying time between coats as the finish built up. After eight coats, she let the box dry for 24 hours, then lightly sanded it with the fine steel wool. After three more coats were put on, her box was smooth and shiny. She dried it an additional 24 hours, then sanded it for the last time with fine, wet sandpaper.

7. Sand lightly with fine steel wool.

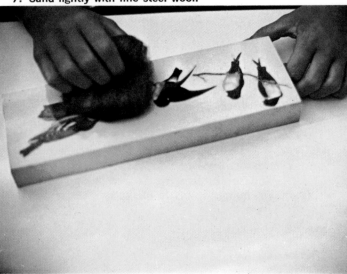

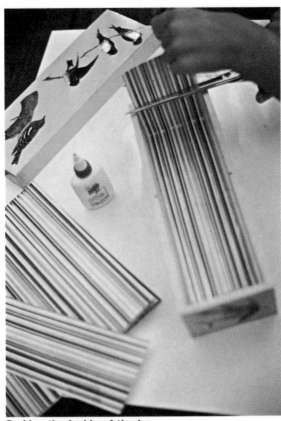

Now there were only two steps remaining to finish her box. Sandy cut some of the striped gift-wrap paper to fit the inside of the box and glued it into place. She brushed this with one coat of découpage finish. When she had nailed the tiny hinges into place, her box was complete and ready to hold her pencils, pens, and crayons.

Sybil C. Harp
Editor, *Creative Crafts* Magazine

8. Line the inside of the box.

9. Nail the hinges into place.

The finished découpage box.

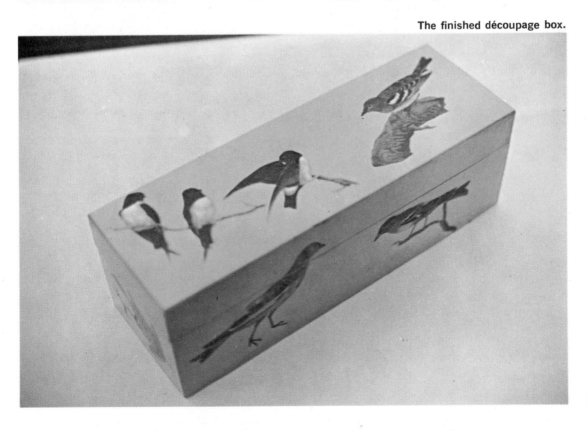

WIRE SCULPTURE

Wire is one of the most commonly used materials in today's world. Coat hangers, paper clips, springs, nails, and safety pins are all made of wire. Telephones, radios, automobiles, bicycles, toasters, and even mouse traps contain many wire parts. Florists, watchmakers, builders, and television repairmen all work with wire. And since there are so many different kinds of wire, people are finding new ways to use them.

Wire is used not only in industry and manufacturing, but in art, too. For example, wire is a favorite material of sculptors who make constructions and mobiles. Jewelry makers like to work with wire, and many create beautiful and valuable pieces from costly gold and silver wire.

The best thing about working with wire is that anyone can do it. All sorts of things can be made from wire that is very inexpensive or costs nothing at all. Because so many things are made of wire, it's easy to find bits of it for almost every kind of project. Coat hangers, for instance, are made of tough, sturdy wire that's just right

1. Select several pieces of wire of equal length, one for each link of your bracelet.

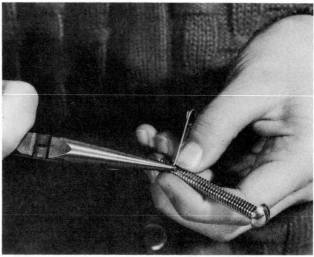

2. With a pair of pliers, wind the ends of each wire around a bolt.

3. Pull each end downward to form loop.

4. Tighten and even out circles.

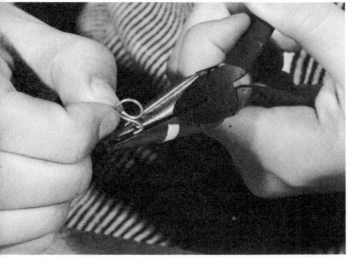

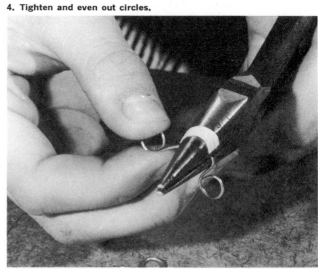

for mobiles. Discarded telephone wire can be hammered into beautiful jewelry. Scraps of wire netting or chicken wire can be twisted into exciting animal forms. Tools are no problem either, as many lovely objects can be made with the simplest tools or no tools at all.

Many other materials can be used along with wire to make your projects more interesting. Old corks or styrofoam both make excellent bases for your sculpture to stand on. Beads, feathers, and silver foil can all be used to make your constructions more exciting.

The most important thing to remember before you start a project is to make sure you choose the best material. Soft florist's wire is excellent for jewelry or for binding heavy shapes. Choose heavier wire if you're making a mobile or a figure. Start with a simple project and go on to more difficult ones.

The illustrations on these pages will show you how you can make a simple, attractive link bracelet.

JOHN LIDSTONE
Professor of Education
City University of New York
Author, *Building with Wire*

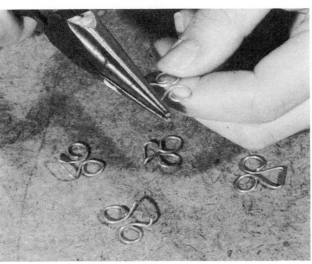

5. Twist each loop upward.

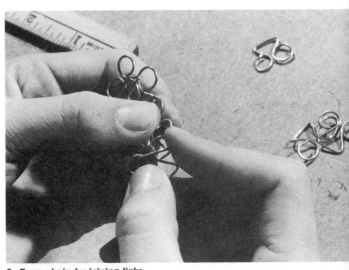

6. Form chain by joining links.

7. Add a simple copper wire hook as a fastener.

8. This is how your finished bracelet will look.

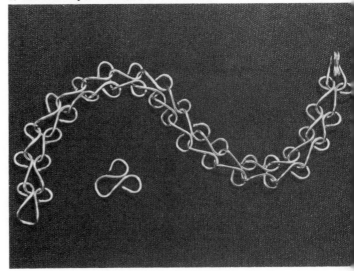

RAINY DAY ACTIVITIES

RIDDLE ME THIS!

What well-known animal drives a car? *A road hog.*

What odd number is even without the *s*? *Seven.*

Why did the bandit take glue with him? *To stick people up.*

Why does a hen lay eggs? *Because they would break if she dropped them.*

Why is a nobleman like a book? *Because they both have titles.*

What flies when it's on and floats when it's off? *A feather.*

Why is the number 9 like a peacock? *Because without its tail it's nothing.*

What did the balloon say to the pin? *Hello, buster.*

What does a peanut say when it sneezes? *Cashew.*

What do you lose when you stand up? *Your lap.*

What two things can't you ever eat for breakfast? *Lunch and dinner.*

MISSING NUMBERS

by G. B. Willis

A number has been hidden in each sentence below. The numbers have been spelled out (one, two, three) and may often be found by combining more than one word in the sentence. Now find all the numbers from one to ten!

1. Both reels broke when the great fish struck.
2. John and I cut wood with his new axe.
3. The sun will set when day is done.
4. Ants even have gardeners in their underground homes!
5. When I reached the cliff I veered away.
6. Joey loves to sit and watch the freight trains go by.
7. This holiday is the happiest of our lives.
8. My older brother has run in every race today.
9. The doctor insists I X-ray my finger.
10. When I opened the gate no one was there.

ANSWERS:

1. three; 2. two; 3. one; 4. seven; 5. five; 6. eight; 7. four; 8. nine; 9. six; 10. ten.

266

HIDDEN PICTURE

by Cindy Doerr

It's Mother's Day and this boy and
girl have some surprises for Mom.
They've also hidden some things. Can
you find the hidden objects? They are:
a safety pin; a bobby pin; a brush;
a pair of scissors; eyeglasses;
a comb; a lipstick; a purse;
a glove; a book; and a ring;

MOM

FINGERPRINT PICTURES

Simply press your fingertip on an ink pad and then onto paper. Draw a few lines and you will have a "fingerprint picture."

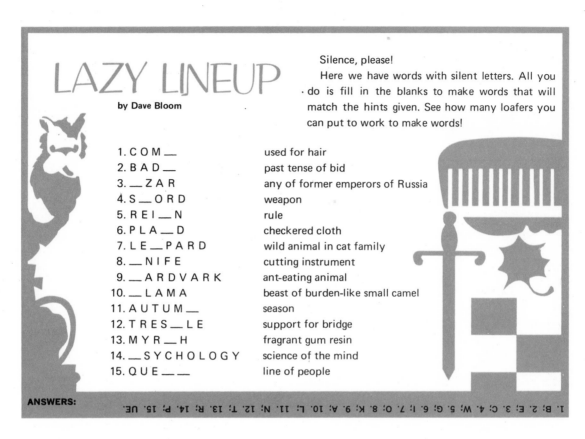

LAZY LINEUP
by Dave Bloom

Silence, please!
Here we have words with silent letters. All you
do is fill in the blanks to make words that will
match the hints given. See how many loafers you
can put to work to make words!

1. C O M __   used for hair
2. B A D __   past tense of bid
3. __ Z A R   any of former emperors of Russia
4. S __ O R D   weapon
5. R E I __ N   rule
6. P L A __ D   checkered cloth
7. L E __ P A R D   wild animal in cat family
8. __ N I F E   cutting instrument
9. __ A R D V A R K ant-eating animal
10. __ L A M A   beast of burden-like small camel
11. A U T U M __   season
12. T R E S __ L E   support for bridge
13. M Y R __ H   fragrant gum resin
14. __ S Y C H O L O G Y science of the mind
15. Q U E __ __   line of people

ANSWERS: 1. B; 2. E; 3. C; 4. W; 5. G; 6. I; 7. O; 8. K; 9. A; 10. L; 11. N; 12. T; 13. R; 14. P; 15. UE.

THE WONDER
OF WORDS

Almost everyone at one time or another has worn BLUE JEANS. You probably have at least one pair and maybe two or three. For many years BLUE JEANS have been a very popular item of wearing apparel.

The material used in making BLUE JEANS dates back hundreds of years. A long time ago, many European cities specialized in the manufacture of a special type of cloth. The city of Janua (now called Genoa) produced a heavy twill type of cotton. The fabric was called *jene* or *jean* for the city from which it came. In 1495, King Henry VIII bought 262 bolts of it for use in the royal household.

Eventually, *jean* became a popular fabric for trousers. People began referring to the trousers as *jeans* because of the name of the material. At that time the trousers were made from undyed *jean* material. Then someone had the idea to dye the material dark blue. The trousers became an instant success and were quite popular with workmen and outdoors men. However, it was America's youngsters who finally made a household word of BLUE JEANS.

WHO COLLECTS WHAT?

by Charlotte Dowdall

Almost everyone has a collection of some kind. You probably do, too. For example, boys like to collect models of cars or airplanes; and girls, dolls or stuffed animals. Many people collect things in their occupations or hobbies. In the list below are the names of some kinds of collectors. Can you match them with what they collect?

_____ 1. Rock hound
_____ 2. Folk singer
_____ 3. Numismatist
_____ 4. Ham radio operator
_____ 5. Cook
_____ 6. Lexicographer
_____ 7. Philatelist
_____ 8. Antique collector
_____ 9. Railroad buff
_____ 10. Book lover

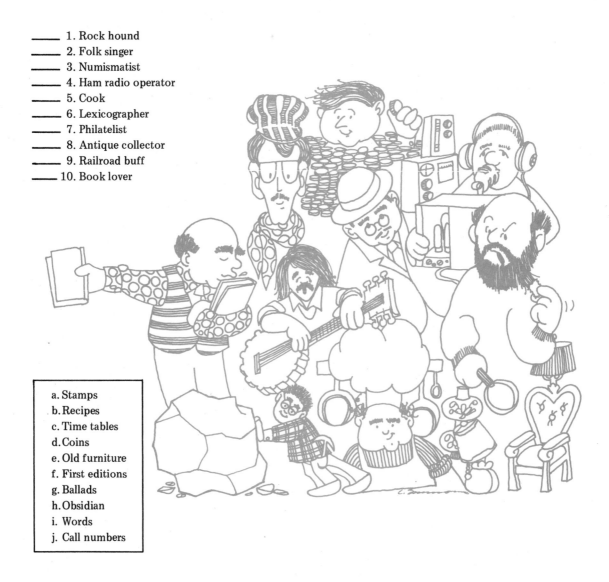

a. Stamps
b. Recipes
c. Time tables
d. Coins
e. Old furniture
f. First editions
g. Ballads
h. Obsidian
i. Words
j. Call numbers

ANSWERS: 1. h; 2. g; 3. d; 4. j; 5. b; 6. i; 7. a; 8. e; 9. c; 10. f.

IN-STATE HUNT

by Mildred Grenier

All of the following states contain the word "IN." See if you can place the correct letters in the blank spaces to complete the puzzle.

1. I N _ _ _ _ _
2. _ _ _ _ I N _
3. _ _ _ I N _ _ _
4. _ _ _ _ I N _ _
5. _ _ _ _ _ _ _ I N
6. _ I N _ _ _ _ _ _
7. _ _ _ _ I N _ _ _ _
8. _ _ _ _ _ _ _ _ I N _ _
9. _ _ _ _ _ _ _ _ _ _ I N _
10. _ _ _ _ _ _ _ _ _ _ I N _

ANSWERS:

1. Indiana; 2. Wyoming; 3. Illinois; 4. Virginia; 5. Wisconsin; 6. Minnesota; 7. Washington; 8. West Virginia; 9. North Carolina; 10. South Carolina.

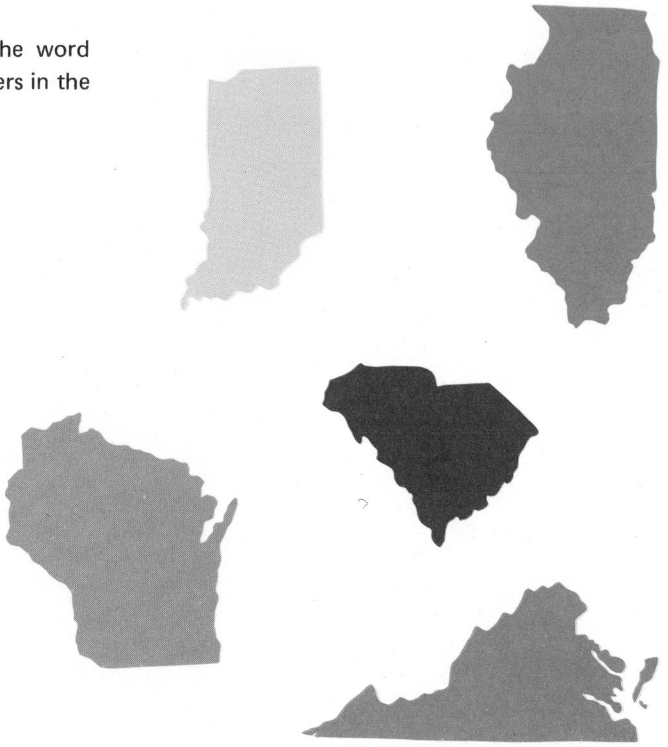

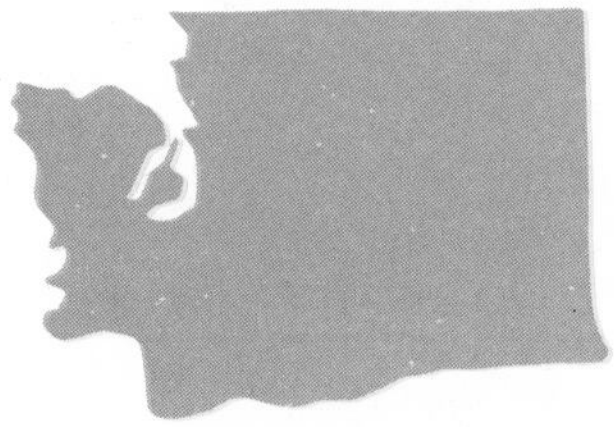

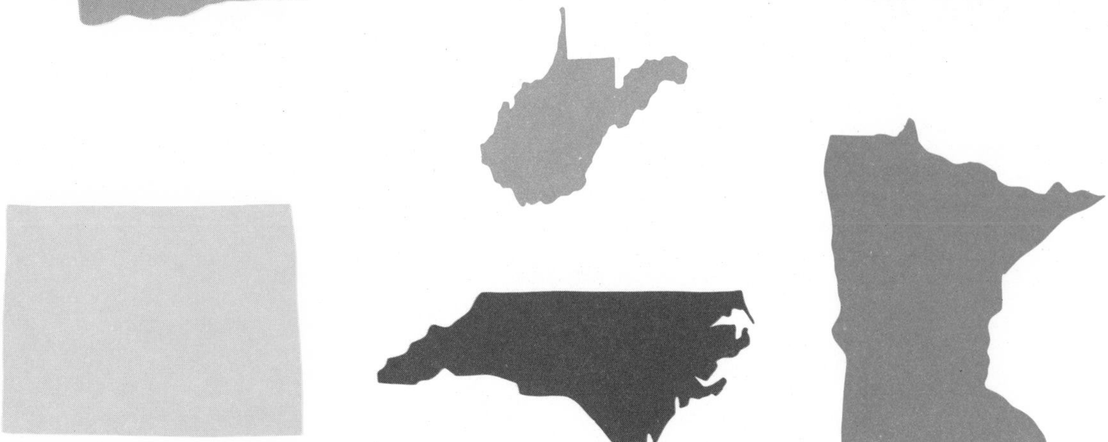

COIN COLLECTING

Coin collecting caught on in 1973 as it never had before, and the values of coins climbed to record high levels.

There was no important change in the United States coin series. But as the year wore on and the price of raw copper steadily climbed, it became clear that soon the content of the cent would have to be changed. Otherwise, the value of the copper in a cent would be more than the coin's face value. There was a similar situation in 1965 at the time that silver was dropped from United States coins.

As silver has become more precious, collector enthusiasm for this metal has grown. Demand for silver collectibles continued in 1973. Interest in 1-ounce silver bars, which had been a collecting novelty just a short time earlier, blossomed. A large assortment of bars was introduced, providing desirable pieces for small investors who wanted to set aside some silver.

Liberty head $20 gold piece.

The value of Liberty head $20 gold pieces in dates that are easily obtainable doubled during the year. And the price of gold bullion (uncoined gold) jumped from about $60 an ounce to more than $100 an ounce. United States citizens are not permitted to own gold bullion, but there is no restriction on their owning pre-1934 gold coins, like the United States $20 gold piece.

The interest in Morgan silver dollars (silver dollars coined between 1878 and 1904, and in 1921) pushed values in the series sharply higher. The 1892 issue from San Francisco advanced from the $3,000 level to $9,500 if uncirculated. A similar, 1883 issue rose from $130 to $350, and the 1893 went from $7,500 to $15,000.

A sprinkling of other record prices set during the year included: 1870-CC $20 gold piece, $24,000; 1927-D $20 gold piece, $60,000; 1794 silver dollar, the first year of issue, $7,500; one of the first half dollars struck at the New Orleans Mint in 1838, $41,000.

American colonial coins won top billing during the year. A nearly perfect specimen of the 1652 Massachusetts Willow Tree shilling sold for $32,000. One of the two known specimens of one of the first coins struck by the United States Mint changed hands during the year for an undisclosed high figure. The coin is a 1792 disme (dime) said to have been struck from melted down table silver of George and Martha Washington.

Greater popularity and higher prices were also in evidence for world coins. In one auction a rare Carl XV Norwegian specie daler of 1871 went for $12,000. In the same sale two Japanese pieces, a gold oban and a silver yen, were not far behind at $11,000 each.

1-ounce silver bars.

▶ SOARING COIN VALUES

Coin collecting drew a lot of investment interest during the year. As people became more concerned about the shrinking dollar, many of them became more aware of coins as a way of protecting their savings. The values of coins have been rising every year. Many coins sold in 1973 for record prices.

NEW COIN ISSUES

Several new coin issues were launched during the year, including first-ever issues of Barbados, Mauritania, the United Arab Emirates, and the British Virgin Islands. The designs of the British Virgin Islands coinage were devoted to the exotic birds of the islands, and were executed by Gilroy Roberts. Widely acclaimed for his finely detailed bird sculptures, Roberts is also the designer of the Kennedy half dollar.

France announced that its silver 10-franc coin is being discontinued. A non-silver substitute and a new silver 20-franc piece are to be introduced in 1974. Israel issued a complete set of trade coins and special commemoratives to mark its 25th anniversary as a nation.

In Canada the 100th anniversary of the Royal Canadian Mounted Police was marked by the issue of a special silver dollar and regular issue quarter commemoratives. Canada also introduced the first four issues in a planned 28-piece set of $5 and $10 silver coins. They are to commemorate the 1976 Olympic Games in Montreal.

BICENTENNIAL ISSUES

Efforts to introduce a $25 gold coin for the American Revolution Bicentennial in 1976 failed. However, six other commemorative coins were approved for the Bicentennial. The cupronickel-clad copper quarter, half dollar, and dollar, to be produced for circulation in 1976, will bear appropriate designs. In addition, three special silver commemoratives intended for sale to collectors will be issued.

Committees of Correspondence medal.

The Committees of Correspondence medal, the second official Bicentennial commemorative medal, was released on July 4, 1973, as part of a stamp-medal combination. The bronze, undated medal was offered in an envelope stamped with four Boston Tea Party stamps and postmarked in Boston. The medal recalls the work of Samuel Adams and Patrick Henry in the early 1770's in organizing the Committees of Correspondence. These letter-writing committees helped unite and arouse the colonies with a communications linkage. The commemorative medal became available later in the year in sterling silver and in bronze, dated 1973.

OTHER NUMISMATIC ITEMS

One minor coin change took place during the year. The dies employed in minting the cent were reworked—for the second time in 4 years—to sharpen the coin's design. The most noticeable difference can be seen on the reverse of the coin. At the right cornerstone of the Lincoln Memorial, the initials of designer Frank Gasparro—FG—are enlarged.

During the year, Congress authorized the issuance of a medal honoring professional

Roberto Clemente medal.

baseball star Roberto Clemente. The medal is an addition to the United States Mint's national medal series. Clemente, the Pittsburgh Pirates outfielder, was killed in an airplane crash on New Year's Eve, 1972. He was taking off from Puerto Rico to fly to Nicaragua in behalf of earthquake victims there.

Congress also passed the Hobby Protection Act, which is of particular importance to beginning numismatists (collectors of coins and medals). The Act protects collectors from imitations by making it unlawful for anyone to manufacture or sell copies of coins or medals that are not "plainly and permanently marked 'copy.' "

CLIFFORD MISHLER
Coins Magazine and *Numismatic News*

WORLD OF SPORTS

In a blur of action, Cincinnati Bengals quarterback Ken Anderson gets ready to pass.

AUTO RACING

WORLD DRIVING FORMULA 1 CHAMPIONSHIPS

Grand Prix	Driver
Argentina	Emerson Fittipaldi, Brazil
Brazil	Emerson Fittipaldi
South Africa	Jackie Stewart, Scotland
Spain	Emerson Fittipaldi
Belgium	Jackie Stewart
Monaco	Jackie Stewart
Sweden	Denis Hulme, New Zealand
France	Ronnie Peterson, Sweden
Great Britain	Peter Revson, U.S.
Netherlands	Jackie Stewart
Germany	Jackie Stewart
Austria	Ronnie Peterson
Italy	Ronnie Peterson
Canada	Peter Revson
United States	Ronnie Peterson

World Driving Champion: Jackie Stewart

OTHER CHAMPIONSHIPS

NASCAR Grand National Champion:
David Pearson, United States

SCCA Canadian-American Challenge Cup:
Mark Donohue, United States

USAC Champion: Roger McCluskey, United States

Indianapolis 500: Gordon Johncock, United States

Jackie Stewart of Scotland, 1973 World Driving Champion, takes a break during a race.

Jackie Stewart streaks across the finish line to win the Monaco Grand Prix.

A New York Met is out at the plate in World Series game with Oakland A's.

BASEBALL

In 1973, major league baseball remained constant in at least one respect: the powerful Oakland Athletics captured the World Series for the second year in a row. It was the first such repeater since the New York Yankees won the Series in 1961 and 1962.

Hank Aaron of the Atlanta Braves overshadowed all team efforts in 1973 with a spectacular bid to surpass Babe Ruth's career total of 714 home runs, a record that had been considered unbreakable. When the season ended, the 39-year-old Aaron was just

one home run short of Ruth's record. But there was no question that Aaron would reach his goal early in the 1974 season.

The other startling development of the year was the surge of the New York Mets to the National League pennant. In last place in the Eastern Division in August, the Mets capped a spectacular drive by winning the division title in the final game of regular season play. Then they defeated the heavily favored Western Division leaders, the Cincinnati Reds, in a five-game playoff for the

1973 WORLD SERIES RESULTS

		R	H	E	Winning/Losing Pitcher
1	Oakland	2	4	0	Holtzman
	New York	1	7	2	Matlack
2	New York	10	15	1	McGraw
	Oakland	7	13	5	Fingers
3	Oakland	3	10	1	Lindblad
	New York	2	10	2	Parker
4	New York	6	13	1	Matlack
	Oakland	1	5	1	Holtzman
5	New York	2	7	1	Koosman
	Oakland	0	3	1	Blue
6	Oakland	3	7	0	Hunter
	New York	1	6	2	Seaver
7	Oakland	5	9	1	Holtzman
	New York	2	8	1	Matlack

Reggie Jackson of the world champion Oakland Athletics. Jackson, who excelled both in the field and at the plate, was voted the American League's Most Valuable Player in 1973.

National League championship. In the World Series the Mets battled the Oakland Athletics to the seventh and deciding game before succumbing.

The Athletics had three 20-game winners on their pitching staff (Jim "Catfish" Hunter, Ken Holtzman, and Vida Blue) and the American League's leading home run hitter, Reggie Jackson. They reached the World Series by defeating the Baltimore Orioles in the five-game league championship series. The A's achieved their goal despite internal dissension in the team. After having led the club to three division and two World Series triumphs during his 3-year tenure, the A's manager, Dick Williams, resigned after the World Series.

The two top pitchers were the 1973 Cy Young Award winners, Tom Seaver of the New York Mets and Jim Palmer of the Baltimore Orioles. Palmer's 22–9 won-lost record was a vital factor in restoring the Orioles to leadership in the American League East after a lapse of one year. Palmer's earned run average was 2.40. Seaver had a 2.08 earned run average, and a 19–10 won-lost record. The most sensational pitching in either league was produced by Nolan Ryan of the California Angels, who struck out a record 383 batters. This was one more than the record set by Sandy Koufax of the Los Angeles Dodgers in 1965.

Pete Rose of the Cincinnati Reds was the batting champion in the National League with a .338 average. His counterpart in the American League was Rod Carew of the Minnesota Twins, with .350. Reggie Jackson's home run total for the season was 32, and Willie Stargell of the Pittsburgh Pirates was the National League leader with 44 home runs.

FINAL MAJOR LEAGUE STANDINGS

AMERICAN LEAGUE

Eastern Division

	W	L	Pct.	GB
Baltimore	97	65	.599	—
Boston	89	73	.549	8
Detroit	85	77	.525	12
New York	80	82	.494	17
Milwaukee	74	88	.457	23
Cleveland	71	91	.438	26

Western Division

	W	L	Pct.	GB
* Oakland	94	68	.580	—
Kansas City	88	74	.543	6
Minnesota	81	81	.500	13
California	79	83	.488	15
Chicago	77	85	.475	17
Texas	57	105	.352	37

* pennant winners

NATIONAL LEAGUE

Eastern Division

	W	L	Pct.	GB
* New York	82	79	.509	—
St. Louis	81	81	.500	1½
Pittsburgh	80	82	.494	2½
Montreal	79	83	.488	3½
Chicago	77	84	.478	5
Philadelphia	71	91	.438	11½

Western Division

	W	L	Pct.	GB
Cincinnati	99	63	.611	—
Los Angeles	95	66	.590	3½
San Francisco	88	74	.543	11
Houston	82	80	.506	17
Atlanta	76	85	.472	22½
San Diego	60	102	.370	39

MAJOR LEAGUE LEADERS

BATTING
(425 or more at bats)

AMERICAN LEAGUE

	G	AB	H	Pct.
Carew, Minnesota	149	580	203	.350
Scott, Milwaukee	158	604	185	.306
Davis, Baltimore	137	552	169	.306
Murcer, New York	160	616	187	.304
May, Milwaukee	156	624	189	.303
Munson, New York	147	519	156	.301
Otis, Kansas City	148	583	175	.300
Holt, Minnesota	132	441	131	.297
Yastrzemski, Boston	152	540	160	.296
Jackson, Oakland	151	539	158	.293

NATIONAL LEAGUE

	G	AB	H	Pct.
Rose, Cincinnati	160	680	230	.338
Cedeno, Houston	139	525	168	.320
Maddox, San Francisco	144	587	187	.319
Pérez, Cincinnati	151	564	177	.314
Watson, Houston	158	573	179	.312
Simmons, St. Louis	161	619	192	.310
Cardenal, Chicago	145	522	158	.303
Singleton, Montreal	162	559	169	.302
Matthews, San Francisco	148	540	162	.300
Garr, Atlanta	148	668	200	.299

PITCHING

	W	L	ERA
Hiller, Detroit, AL	10	5	1.51
Rogers, Montreal, NL	10	5	1.54
Fingers, Oakland, AL	7	8	1.92
Reynolds, Baltimore, AL	7	5	1.95
Seaver, New York, NL	19	10	2.08
Acosta, Chicago, AL	11	6	2.23
Borbon, Cincinnati, NL	11	4	2.24
Palmer, Baltimore, AL	22	9	2.40
Sutton, Los Angeles, NL	18	10	2.42
Blyleven, Minnesota, AL	20	17	2.44

HOME RUNS

	HR
Stargell, Pittsburgh, NL	44
Johnson, Atlanta, NL	43
Evans, Atlanta, NL	41
Aaron, Atlanta, NL	40
Bonds, San Francisco, NL	39
Jackson, Oakland, AL	32
Burroughs, Texas, AL	30
Robinson, California, AL	30
Bando, Oakland, AL	29
Luzinski, Philadelphia, NL	29
McCovey, San Francisco, NL	29

LITTLE LEAGUE BASEBALL

The Little League baseball team from Tainan, Taiwan, captured the Little League World Series for the third straight season—and for the fourth time in 5 years. Objections to the victory were voiced.

The first objection had been raised before the championship tournament started in Williamsport, Pennsylvania. And the objection had nothing to do with the now almost traditional victories of the team from Tainan. It all had to do with efforts by girls to become part of the traditionally all-boy Little League competition.

In Ypsilanti, Michigan, local officials had voted to permit 12-year-old Carolyn King to play on the local Little League team. In response to this action, national Little League officials revoked the franchise of the Ypsilanti team, citing a rule that made girls ineligible to play in Little League competition. In another instance, the city council of Mill Valley, California, refused to allow the use of Mill Valley's public ball park for local Little League games in 1974 unless girls are permitted to play. The action followed a protest by 10-year-old Jenny Fuller, who had wanted to play and had been refused.

The real issue at Williamsport in 1973,

Huang Ching-huy of Taiwan, pitching star of the Little League World Series.

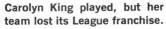
Carolyn King played, but her team lost its League franchise.

A close play at first base, as Far East (Taiwan) battles West (Tucson, Arizona) in the Little League World Series.

however, was the regularity with which the amazing team from Tainan, Taiwan, had won the Little League series. In 1973 the Tainan team simply overpowered the opposition. They won three no-hit games. In the game with the Bitburg (Germany) Air Force Base team, they won 18–0; in their game with the Tampa, Florida, team, they won 27–0; and in the game against the Tucson, Arizona, team, the Tainan team won 12–0. Huang Ching-huy pitched a perfect game against Bitburg and another no-hitter against Tucson as well. Kuo Wen-li pitched the no-hitter against Tampa.

The Williamsport tournament is the last stage of competition involving Little League teams based in 31 countries. The United States alone has 2,500,000 Little Leaguers.

The volunteer coaches and officials at Williamsport were disturbed by Taiwan's overwhelming victories and consistent success. Questions were raised of possible violations of Little League rules concerning player eligibility, district size, and practice time. But the explanation of Taiwan's amazing record may be quite simple: In Taiwan's semi-tropical climate, baseball is played all year. No other sport rivals it in popularity.

The Knicks and the Lakers battle it out in the final game of the NBA playoffs.

BASKETBALL

The New York Knicks regained their winning touch and captured the National Basketball Association (NBA) title. In the other professional league, the American Basketball Association (ABA), the Indiana Pacers were champions for the third time in four seasons. While the pros attract most of the attention, the continuing success of the University of California at Los Angeles is one of the most remarkable phenomena in basketball.

The UCLA Bruins, coached by John Wooden, won their seventh straight National Collegiate Athletic Association (NCAA) championship, their ninth in the last 10 years. In the process they extended their winning streak to 75 consecutive contests, 30 during the 1972–73 season.

Regardless of the turnover in players, UCLA simply runs over the opposition. During the last two seasons, Bill Walton, the 6-foot–11-inch center, has been the team's spearhead. He led the squad to a 25–0 record during the regular campaign, and through the NCAA championship tournament, which culminated in an 87–66 victory over Memphis State. To add to the frustration of the Bruins' opponents, Walton has another year to play.

In the NBA, the Boston Celtics dominated the season play and reached the playoffs. Their record, 68–14 for an .829 percentage, was by far the best in the circuit, and gave them an 11-game bulge over the Knicks in the Atlantic Division. But when the Boston and New York clubs met for the Eastern title, the Knicks were the surprising victors, four games to three. The Celtics, behind three games to one, recovered to tie the series, but were eliminated in the decisive seventh game, 94–78.

The Knicks went on to stun the defending champions, the Los Angeles Lakers, in the battle for the NBA title. The Lakers captured the opening game, but the Knicks swept the next four, reversing the pattern followed by

FINAL NBA STANDINGS

EASTERN CONFERENCE

Atlantic Division

	W	L	Pct.
Boston	68	14	.829
New York	57	25	.695
Buffalo	21	61	.256
Philadelphia	9	73	.110

Central Division

	W	L	Pct.
Baltimore	52	30	.634
Atlanta	46	36	.561
Houston	33	49	.402
Cleveland	32	50	.390

WESTERN CONFERENCE

Midwest Division

	W	L	Pct.
Milwaukee	60	22	.732
Chicago	51	31	.622
Detroit	40	42	.488
K.C.–Omaha	36	46	.439

Pacific Division

	W	L	Pct.
Los Angeles	60	22	.732
Golden State	47	35	.573
Phoenix	38	44	.463
Seattle	26	56	.317
Portland	21	61	.256

NBA Championship: New York

FINAL ABA STANDINGS

East Division

	W	L	Pct.
Carolina	57	27	.679
Kentucky	56	28	.667
Virginia	42	42	.500
New York	30	54	.357
Memphis	24	60	.286

West Division

	W	L	Pct.
Utah	55	29	.655
Indiana	51	33	.607
Denver	47	37	.560
San Diego	30	54	.357
Dallas	28	56	.333

ABA Championship: Indiana

Virginia Tech players hoist NIT victory cup.

COLLEGE BASKETBALL

Conference	Winner
Atlantic Coast	North Carolina State
Big Eight	Kansas State
Big Ten	Indiana
Ivy League	Pennsylvania
Mid-American	Miami
Missouri Valley	Memphis State
Pacific Eight	UCLA
Southeastern	Kentucky
Southern	Furman
Southwest	Texas Tech
West Coast Athletic	San Francisco
Western Athletic	Arizona State
Yankee	Massachusetts

NCAA: UCLA

National Invitation Tournament: Virginia Tech

the same teams in 1972. Willis Reed was chosen the most valuable player in the five-game series. He had able cooperation from his teammates Dave DeBusschere, Walt Frazier, Earl Monroe, and Bill Bradley. Defense was their strong point.

On the strength of Boston's spectacular regular season performance, Tom Heinsohn of the Celtics was voted coach of the year. However, New York Knicks coach Red Holzman had the final chuckle.

Indiana finished second to Utah in the West Division standings in the ABA. But the Pacers survived the preliminary seven-game series for the title. George McGinnis, a 6-foot–8-inch second-year forward, was the most valuable player for Indiana.

BOWLING

BOXING

WORLD BOXING CHAMPIONS

Division	Champion
Heavyweight	George Foreman, U.S.
Light Heavyweight	Bob Foster, U.S.
Middleweight	Carlos Monzon, Argentina
Jr. Middleweight	Koichi Wajima, Japan
Welterweight	Jose Napoles, Mexico
Jr. Welterweight (disputed)	Bruno Arcari, Italy Antonio Cervantes, Colombia
Lightweight (disputed)	Rodolfo Gonzalez, U.S. Roberto Duran, Panama
Jr. Lightweight (disputed)	Ricardo Arredondo, Mexico Ben Villaflor, Philippines
Featherweight (disputed)	Eder Jofre, Brazil Ernesto Marcel, Panama
Bantamweight (disputed)	Rafael Herrera, Mexico Arnold Taylor, South Africa
Flyweight (disputed)	Betulio Gonzales, Venezuela Chartchai Chionoi, Thailand

He's down! It took less than 5 minutes for George Foreman to win the heavyweight title from Joe Frazier in 1973. Frazier went down six times before the bout was stopped in the second round.

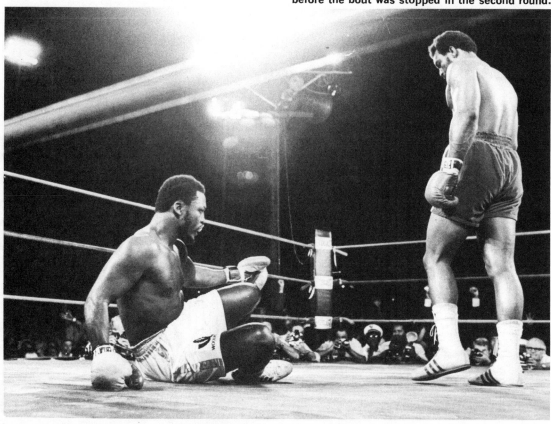

At the International Kennel Club show, held in Chicago, best-in-show honors went to Champion Purston Pinmoney Pedlar, a 5-year-old Westie.

DOG SHOWS

At New York's Westminster Kennel Club show the winner was 2-year-old Champion Acadia Command Performance.

WESTMINSTER KENNEL CLUB

Hound	Ch. Khayam's Apollo, Afghan
Nonsporting	Ch. Acadia Command Performance, standard poodle
Sporting	Ch. Sagamore Toccoa, cocker spaniel
Terrier	Ch. Littleway Haranwal Barrister, wirehaired fox terrier
Toy	Ch. Joanne-Chen's Maya Dancer, Maltese
Working	Ch. Regency's Nite Life, brindle boxer
Best in Show	Ch. Acadia Command Performance

INTERNATIONAL KENNEL CLUB

Hound	Ch. Kemper Dachs Waldemar, long-haired dachshund
Nonsporting	Ch. Liontamer Kudos, chow chow
Sporting	Ch. El Taro's Scotch Flag, English springer spaniel
Terrier	Ch. Purston Pinmoney Pedlar, West Highland white
Toy	Ch. Continuation of Gleno, Yorkshire terrier
Working	Ch. Artula Cristofer V. Gurlin, standard schnauzer
Best in Show	Ch. Purston Pinmoney Pedlar

Viking quarterback Fran Tarkenton (with ball) fades back to pass in playoff game with Cowboys.

FOOTBALL

The Miami Dolphins, winners of the 1973 Super Bowl, continued to dominate the American Conference of the National Football League (NFL). Their 12 wins and 2 losses put them at the top of the Eastern Division.

The other division champions in the American Conference were the Cincinnati Bengals (10–4) in the Central Division and the Oakland Raiders (9–4–1) in the Western Division. Pittsburgh gained the fourth, or "wildcard," spot in the playoffs. Miami defeated Cincinnati and Oakland in the playoffs and won the American Conference title.

In the National Conference, the Los Angeles Rams gained the Western Division title with a three-game margin over Atlanta. After a mediocre showing in 1972, the Minnesota Vikings roared to a first-place finish in the Central Division in 1973. The Dallas Cowboys earned the top spot in the Eastern Division, while the Washington Redskins filled the wild-card berth. In postseason contests, Minnesota emerged triumphant in both playoff games and became the National Conference champion.

Pro football's star performer of 1973 was O. J. Simpson of the Buffalo Bills. The spectacular running back gained 2,003 yards rushing during the 14-game season, breaking the previous single-season record of 1,863 yards established by former Cleveland back Jim Brown in 1963. Simpson, who needed only 61 yards to break the record in the season finale against the New York Jets, rushed for 200 yards on a slippery, snow-covered field.

Among college teams, the University of Alabama, with a 10–0 record, was generally ranked first in the polls. Its opponent in the Sugar Bowl was Notre Dame, another unbeaten team (9–0). Notre Dame upset Alabama 24–23. The Rose Bowl saw Southern California (9–1–1) matched with Ohio State (9–0–1); Ohio won, 42–21.

John Cappelletti, a running back from Penn State, was awarded the Heisman Trophy as the nation's outstanding collegiate player. He led his team to an 11–0 season and an Orange Bowl victory over Louisiana State.

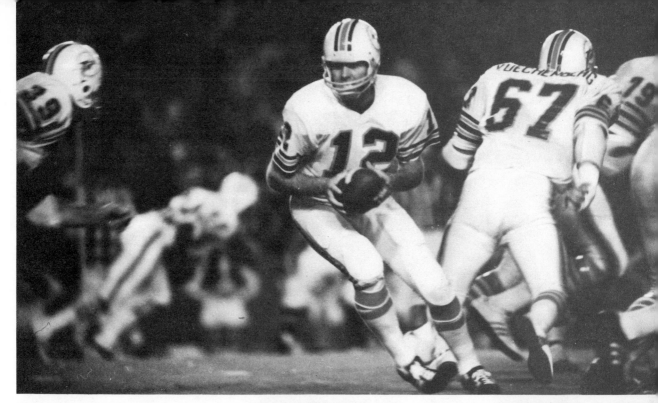

Bob Griese, Miami quarterback, whirls to hand off the ball in playoff game with Oakland. Miami won and went on to Super Bowl contest with the Minnesota Vikings.

Star running back O. J. Simpson of the Buffalo Bills in action. Simpson set a new NFL single-season rushing record by gaining 2,003 yards.

FINAL NFL STANDINGS

AMERICAN CONFERENCE

Eastern Division

	W	L	T	Pct.	PF	PA
Miami	12	2	0	.857	343	150
Buffalo	9	5	0	.643	259	230
New England	5	9	0	.357	258	300
Baltimore	4	10	0	.286	226	341
N.Y. Jets	4	10	0	.286	240	306

Central Division

	W	L	T	Pct.	PF	PA
Cincinnati	10	4	0	.714	286	231
Pittsburgh	10	4	0	.714	347	210
Cleveland	7	5	2	.571	234	255
Houston	1	13	0	.071	199	447

Western Division

	W	L	T	Pct.	PF	PA
Oakland	9	4	1	.679	292	175
Denver	7	5	2	.571	354	296
Kansas City	7	5	2	.571	231	192
San Diego	2	11	1	.179	188	386

Conference Champion: Miami

NATIONAL CONFERENCE

Eastern Division

	W	L	T	Pct.	PF	PA
Dallas	10	4	0	.714	382	203
Washington	10	4	0	.714	325	198
Philadelphia	5	8	1	.393	310	393
St. Louis	4	9	1	.321	286	365
N.Y. Giants	2	11	1	.179	226	362

Central Division

	W	L	T	Pct.	PF	PA
Minnesota	12	2	0	.857	296	168
Detroit	6	7	1	.464	271	247
Green Bay	5	7	2	.429	202	259
Chicago	3	11	0	.214	195	334

Western Division

	W	L	T	Pct.	PF	PA
Los Angeles	12	2	0	.857	388	178
Atlanta	9	5	0	.643	318	224
New Orleans	5	9	0	.357	163	312
San Francisco	5	9	0	.357	262	319

Conference Champion: Minnesota

1974 Super Bowl Winner: Miami

COLLEGE FOOTBALL

Conference	Winner
Atlantic Coast	North Carolina State
Big Eight	Oklahoma
Big Ten	Ohio State; Michigan (tied)
Ivy League	Dartmouth
Mid-American	Miami
Pacific Eight	Southern California
Southeastern	Alabama
Southern	East Carolina
Southwest	Texas
Western Athletic	Arizona State
Yankee	Connecticut

Heisman Trophy: John Cappelletti, Penn State

Pete Johnson (No. 33), a freshman running back from Ohio State, scores one of his three touchdowns in Rose Bowl game against USC. Ohio won, 42–21.

GOLF

The world's four major golf championships were shared among four men. Johnny Miller won the U.S. Open; Tom Weiskopf won the British Open; Tommy Aaron, the Masters tournament; and Jack Nicklaus, the Professional Golfers' Association title. But it was Nicklaus, with his final big push of the year, who reached the goal that had been uppermost in his mind since he became a consistent winner.

Nicklaus' triumph in the PGA tourney, by four strokes, gave him his 14th major crown. He thus surpassed the record of the legendary Bobby Jones. In his bag of titles, Nicklaus has won four Masters, three U.S. Open, three PGA, two British Open, and two U.S. Amateur championships. Since he became a professional in 1962, Nicklaus, at 33, has accumulated $2,000,000 in purses.

Tom Weiskopf's successful year included winning the British Open trophy.

PROFESSIONAL

Individual

Masters	Tommy Aaron, U.S.
U.S. Open	Johnny Miller, U.S.
Canadian Open	Tom Weiskopf, U.S.
British Open	Tom Weiskopf, U.S.
PGA	Jack Nicklaus, U.S.
World Series of Golf	Tom Weiskopf, U.S.
U.S. Women's Open	Susie Maxwell Berning, U.S.
Ladies PGA	Mary Mills, U.S.

Team

World Cup	United States
Ryder Cup	United States

AMATEUR

Individual

U.S. Amateur	Craig Stadler, U.S.
U.S. Women's Amateur	Carol Semple, U.S.
British Amateur	Dick Siderowf, U.S.
Canadian Amateur	George Burns 3d, U.S.

Team

Walker Cup	United States

Weiskopf, like Nicklaus, is a native of Columbus, Ohio. He had the hottest streak on the professional tour, with three victories over a period of 7 weeks leading up to his British Open success. Weiskopf then went on to win the Canadian Open 2 weeks later.

In the women's tournaments, Mrs. Susie Maxwell Berning won her third U.S. Women's Open, at Rochester, New York. Her title was worth $6,000 in prize money. Mary Mills captured the Ladies PGA championship, at Sutton, Massachusetts, and a $5,200 prize.

HOCKEY

Professional hockey has seen a wild bidding for talent between the established National Hockey League (NHL) and its new rival, the World Hockey Association (WHA). More than 40 players have leaped from the old circuit to the new. But on the ice, competition in the NHL followed a traditional pattern.

By the time the last player had been walloped by a foe's hockey stick, the Montreal Canadiens had succeeded the Boston Bruins as possessors of the Stanley Cup, symbolic of the NHL championship. It was an unprecedented 17th triumph for the Canadiens since the trophy became the playoff target in 1893.

However, there was some consolation for the disappointed Boston fans. The New England Whalers won the first WHA Avco World Trophy ever awarded.

The NHL Stanley Cup playoffs closely followed the results of regular-season competition, in which Montreal had led the East Division, and the Chicago Black Hawks the West. They both survived the early playoff rounds and clashed in the Cup final, which the Canadiens captured four games to two. It was an extraordinary triumph for the Montreal captain, Henri Richard. Playing his 18th season, Richard had his name inscribed on the trophy for the 11th time. But the most valuable player in the series was Yvan Cournoyer, Montreal's smallest player (5 feet 7 inches, 165 pounds), called by his teammates "The Roadrunner."

Despite the presence of two outstanding goalies, Montreal's Ken Dryden and Chicago's Tony Esposito, an astonishing total of 56 goals were scored in the six games, almost half of them in the two games won by the Black Hawks, 7–4 and 8–7. The Canadiens' ultimate triumph may have been old hat in the NHL. But their avid fans showed a burst of fresh enthusiasm as 500,000 people turned

Chicago and Montreal battle it out in the finale of Stanley Cup playoffs.

Bobby Hull of the Jets tumbles over Whalers' player in WHA championship series.

out for a welcoming parade through downtown Montreal.

The surprise of the early rounds in the Stanley Cup play was the dethronement of the Boston Bruins by the New York Rangers. The Rangers hadn't won a playoff series from Boston in 33 years.

Post-season competition in the WHA likewise followed the season's pattern. The Whalers and the Winnipeg Jets reached the final series, which the Whalers won by four games to one. New England and Winnipeg had led the East and West divisions, respectively, during the regular season. The Whalers were paced by Tom Webster, and the Jets by their player-coach, Bobby Hull. Hull was the circuit's most valuable player.

FINAL WHA STANDINGS

East Division

	W	L	T	Pts.
New England	46	30	2	94
Cleveland	43	32	3	89
Philadelphia	38	40	0	76
Ottawa	35	39	4	74
Quebec	33	40	5	71
New York	33	43	2	68

West Division

	W	L	T	Pts.
Winnipeg	43	31	4	90
Houston	39	35	4	82
Los Angeles	37	35	6	80
Alberta	38	37	3	79
Minnesota	38	37	3	79
Chicago	26	50	2	54

Avco World Trophy: New England

FINAL NHL STANDINGS

East Division

	W	L	T	Pts.
Montreal	52	10	16	120
Boston	51	22	5	107
N.Y. Rangers	47	23	8	102
Buffalo	37	27	14	88
Detroit	37	29	12	86
Toronto	27	41	10	64
Vancouver	22	47	9	53
N.Y. Islanders	12	60	6	30

West Division

	W	L	T	Pts.
Chicago	42	27	9	93
Philadelphia	37	30	11	85
Minnesota	37	30	11	85
St. Louis	32	34	12	76
Pittsburgh	32	37	9	73
Los Angeles	31	36	11	73
Atlanta	25	38	15	65
California	16	46	16	48

Stanley Cup: Montreal

OUTSTANDING PLAYERS

Ross Trophy (scorer)	Phil Esposito, Boston
Calder Trophy (rookie)	Steve Vickers, N.Y. Rangers
Vezina Trophy (goalie)	Ken Dryden, Montreal
Hart Trophy (most valuable player)	Bobby Clarke, Philadelphia
Lady Byng Trophy (sportsmanship)	Gil Perreault, Buffalo
Norris Trophy (defenseman)	Bobby Orr, Boston
Conn Smythe Trophy (Stanley Cup play)	Yvan Cournoyer, Montreal

Secretariat (*left*) galloping to victory in the Kentucky Derby. He later went on to win the Preakness and the Belmont Stakes, becoming the first Triple Crown winner since Citation in 1948.

HORSE RACING

HARNESS STAKES WINNERS		THOROUGHBRED STAKES WINNERS	
Race	**Horse**	**Race**	**Horse**
Cane Pace	Smog	Belmont Futurity	Wedge Shot
Colonial Trot	Flirth	Belmont Stakes	Secretariat
Dexter Cup Trot	Knightly Way	Brooklyn Handicap	Riva Ridge
Hambletonian	Flirth	Flamingo Stakes	Our Native
International Trot	Delmonica Hanover	Jockey Club Gold Cup	Prove Out
Kentucky Futurity	Arnie Almahurst	Kentucky Derby	Secretariat
Little Brown Jug	Melvin's Woe	Preakness	Secretariat
Messenger Stakes	Valiant Bret	Suburban Handicap	Key to the Mint
Mother Goose Stakes	Windy's Daughter	Travers	Annihilate 'Em
Realization Pace	Keystone Pebble	United Nations Handicap	Tentam
Realization Trot	Spartan Hanover	Wood Memorial	Angle Light
Yonkers Futurity	Tamerlane	Woodward Stakes	Prove Out

ICE SKATING

FIGURE SKATING

United States Championships

Men   Gordon McKellen, Jr.
Women   Janet Lynn
Pairs   Melissa Militano/Mark Militano
Dance   Mary Karen Campbell/Johnny Johns

World Championships

Men   Ondrej Nepela, Czechoslovakia
Women   Karen Magnussen, Canada
Pairs   Irina Rodnina/Alexander Zaitsev, U.S.S.R.
Dance   Ludmila Pakhomova/Alexander
           Gorshkov, U.S.S.R.

SPEED SKATING

World Championships

Men   Goeran Claesson, Sweden
Women   Atje Keulen-Deelstra, Netherlands

SKIING

WORLD CUP CHAMPIONSHIPS

Men   Gustavo Thoeni, Italy
Women   Annemarie Proell, Austria

U.S. ALPINE CHAMPIONSHIPS

Men

Downhill   Bob Cochran, U.S.
Giant Slalom David Currier, U.S.
Slalom   Masayoshi Kashinage, Japan
Combined   David Currier

Women

Downhill   Cindy Nelson, U.S.
Giant Slalom Debi Handley, U.S.
Slalom   Linda Cochran, U.S.
Combined   Susan Corrock, U.S.

NCAA CHAMPIONSHIPS

Downhill   Bob Cochran,
              University of Vermont
Slalom   Peik Christensen,
              University of Denver
Alpine Combined Peik Christensen
Cross-Country Steiner Hybertsen,
              University of Wyoming
Jumping   Vidar Nilsgard,
              University of Colorado
Nordic Combined Pertti Reijula,
              Northern Michigan University
Team   University of Colorado

Atje Keulen-Deelstra, winner of the women's world speed skating championship.

Bob Cochran, winner of the downhill events in the U.S. Alpine and NCAA championships.

Kornelia Ender setting a world record in the 100-meter butterfly.

SWIMMING

Rick DeMont of San Rafael, California, had to return an Olympic gold medal in 1972 when he was disqualified for using forbidden medication to help his asthma. In 1973 he splashed to victory (and a world record of 3:58.18) in the 400-meter freestyle during the world championships held in Yugoslavia.

In the 1,500-meter event, a 15-year-old Australian, Steve Holland, snipped 6 seconds from the world mark as he defeated DeMont and was clocked in 15:31.85.

Other winners in the individual competitions included Gunnar Larsen, Sweden, in the 200-meter medley; Melissa Belote, Virginia, in the 200-meter backstroke; Renate Vogel, East Germany, in the 200-meter breaststroke; Heather Greenwood, California, in the 400-meter freestyle; Ulrika Knape, Sweden, in platform diving; Bruce Robertson, Canada, in the 100-meter butterfly; and Christa Kohler, East Germany, in the 3-meter springboard diving.

Teresa Andersen of Santa Clara, California, became the first world champion in solo synchronized swimming—the art of ballet in the water.

WORLD SWIMMING RECORDS SET IN 1973

Event	Holder	Time
Men		
400-meter freestyle	Rick DeMont, U.S.	3:58.18
800-meter freestyle	Steve Holland, Australia	8:16.27
1,500-meter freestyle	Steve Holland, Australia	15:31.85
100-meter breaststroke	John Hencken, U.S.	1:04.02
200-meter breaststroke	David Wilkie, Britain	2:19.28
200-meter backstroke	Roland Matthes, E. Germany	2:01.87
Women		
100-meter freestyle	Kornelia Ender, E. Germany	0:57.54
400-meter freestyle	Keena Rothhammer, U.S.	4:18.07
800-meter freestyle	Novella Calligaris, Italy	8:52.97
1,500-meter freestyle	Jo Harshbarger, U.S.	16:54.14
100-meter butterfly	Kornelia Ender, E. Germany	1:02.31
200-meter butterfly	Rosemarie Kother, E. Germany	2:13.76
100-meter backstroke	Ulrike Richter, E. Germany	1:04.99
200-meter individual medley	Andrea Hübner, E. Germany	2:20.51
400-meter individual medley	Gudren Wegner, E. Germany	4:57.51

Billie Jean King emerged triumphant from her battle with Bobby Riggs.

TENNIS

Tennis provided the usual competition in historic arenas such as Wimbledon, England, and Forest Hills, New York. But the main attraction in 1973 was the battle between male chauvinism and women's liberation.

In the spring, 55-year-old Bobby Riggs, a tennis champion in the late 1930's, challenged 29-year-old Billie Jean King, five-time Wimbledon winner. Mrs. King ignored the challenge, but it was accepted by Margaret Court, 30, the holder of numerous national and international titles. Riggs trounced Mrs. Court in their match.

Billie Jean King promptly came to the rescue. With $100,000, winner take all, the prize, she carried the banner for Women's Lib to a spectacular, straight-set triumph in the Houston Astrodome in September. With fringe benefits her revenue from the match totaled $200,000.

Among the younger crop of men's tennis players, Jan Kodes of Czechoslovakia captured the Wimbledon championship after many of the prominent performers did not play because of an international dispute. Mrs. King captured the women's crown. Illness forced Mrs. King to withdraw from the U.S. championships at Forest Hills, and Mrs. Court defeated Evonne Goolagong of Australia in the final. Australian John Newcombe was the winner in the men's U.S. Open.

World Championship Tennis, the 6-month professional tour, culminated in a victory for Stan Smith of California. He defeated Arthur Ashe of Richmond, Virginia, in the final match for the $50,000 first prize.

TOURNAMENT TENNIS

	U.S. Open	Wimbledon	Australian Open	French Open
Men's Singles	John Newcombe, Australia	Jan Kodes, Czechoslovakia	John Newcombe, Australia	Ilie Nastase, Rumania
Women's Singles	Margaret Court, Australia	Billie Jean King, U.S.	Margaret Court, Australia	Margaret Court, Australia
Men's Doubles	John Newcombe/ Owen Davidson, Australia	Ilie Nastase, Rumania/ Jimmy Connors, U.S.	John Newcombe/ Malcolm Anderson, Australia	John Newcombe, Australia/ Tom Okker, Netherlands
Women's Doubles	Margaret Court, Australia/ Virginia Wade, Britain	Billie Jean King/ Rosemary Casals, U.S.	Margaret Court, Australia/ Virginia Wade, Britain	Margaret Court, Australia/ Virginia Wade, Britain

Davis Cup Winner: Australia

Faina Melnik threw the discus a record 227 feet 11 inches.

TRACK AND FIELD

WORLD TRACK AND FIELD RECORDS SET IN 1973

Event	Holder	Time or Distance
	Men	
880-yard run	Rick Wohlhuter, U.S.	1:44.6
2-mile run	Brendan Foster, Britain	8:13.8
800-meter run	Marcello Fiasconaro, Italy	1:43.7
1,000-meter run	Danie Malan, South Africa	2:16.0
10,000-meter run	Dave Bedford, Britain	27:30.8
3,000-meter steeplechase	Ben Jipcho, Kenya	8:14.0
110-meter hurdles	Rod Milburn, U.S.	0:13.1
High Jump	Dwight Stones, U.S.	7' 6½"
Shot Put	Al Feuerbach, U.S.	71' 7"
Javelin	Klaus Wolfermann, W. Germany	308' 8"
	Women	
1-mile run	Paola Pigni, Italy	4:29.5
100-meter run	Renate Stecher, E. Germany	0:10.8
200-meter run	Renate Stecher, E. Germany	0:22.1
800-meter run	Svetla Zlateva, Bulgaria	1:57.5
100-meter hurdles	Annelie Ehrhardt, E. Germany	0:12.3
400-meter hurdles	Danuta Piecyk, Poland	0:56.7
Shot Put	Nadezhda Chizhova, U.S.S.R.	70' 4½"
Discus	Faina Melnik, U.S.S.R.	227' 11"
Javelin	Ruth Fuchs, E. Germany	216' 10"

IT RUNS
IN THE FAMILY

Mark Harmon, quarterback for the **UCLA Bruins**, is the son of former football star Tom Harmon. In 1973, Mark received a post-graduate scholarship from the National Football Foundation.

The hockey-playing Howes (Gordie, *center*, and sons Marty, *left*, and Mark, *right*) realized a dream when all three were signed to play on the same team, the Houston Aeros, in 1973.

Jack Nicklaus II, the 11-year-old son of famed golfer Jack Nicklaus, played in his first big golf tournament in 1973—a district championship for boys under 14 in Columbus, Ohio.

Jeanne Evert, at 16, is following in the footsteps of her sister, tennis champ Chris Evert. The girls have the same two-handed backhand and the same coach, their father, Jimmy Evert.

BALLOONING

Would you like to ride in my beautiful balloon?
Would you like to glide in my beautiful balloon?
We could float among the stars together you and I,
    for we can fly!
Up, up and away, my beautiful, my beautiful balloon!
The world's a nicer place in my beautiful balloon. . . .

From the song "Up, Up and Away"

The place to be today is not on the ground, but just slightly above it—or way, way above it. It depends on your means of transportation, and there's quite a variety of celestial transport. We have the ever-popular 747 jet airliners, the manned space vehicles and the orbiting Skylab workshop, not to mention gliders, helicopters, and parachutes. Airborne is definitely the "in" way to travel.

And one of the most "in" sports at the moment fits right into the pattern of flying high. Ballooning has become *the* thing. Not those brightly colored nickel balloons you might buy at your corner store. By ballooning, we mean the real thing—the soaring-above-the-earth kind.

Why ballooning? Has the country wearied of football, baseball, chess, soccer, swimming, and boxing? Or maybe it's part of the "back to nature" phenomenon. Ballooning enthusiasts say that there really is nothing to compare with the experience of floating freely through the air in a mid-morning wind, watching your shadow pass swiftly over meadows, lakes, and pastures. No exhausts from car, train, or bus engines to contend with, no traffic jams or accidents—just good, clear, uncluttered air. Quiet and peaceful.

▶ LESSONS AND COMPETITIONS

Many of the outdoor adventure sports clubs springing up throughout the United States and other countries offer balloon excursions and balloon flying lessons. In the United States, both balloon pilots and the balloon itself must be licensed by the Federal Aviation Agency. Eight hours of instruction are re-

Students at the UCLA campus in California prepare for lift-off.

quired to prepare the student for a flight test. The student must learn everything from how to inflate the balloon to cross-country flying.

Once he's qualified for his license, the balloon enthusiast may want to join one of the many balloon competitions. One of the most exciting international events is held in Mürren, Switzerland. Every year balloonists from all over the world gather at Mürren to make the voyage over the Alps from Switzerland to Italy. The Alps rise in a number of places to over 14,000 feet. This means that the balloons must make the long journey at about 16,000 feet.

Competition is the point of most ballooning events. There are long-distance races, spot-landing matches, cross-country activity, barograph runs, and hare-and-hounds chases.

To win the long-distance race, one must travel farthest and remain aloft for the longest period of time. In both cross-country and spot-landing matches, the pilot must take off and land within a specified time. In the cross-country event the balloonist who goes the farthest is the winner. In spot-landing, the flyer who lands closest to a designated point wins. The barograph race requires the most skill, because the pilot must follow a predetermined, narrow air route.

The hare-and-hounds chase is perhaps the most exciting competition of all. Sports cars (the hounds) follow a balloon (the hare). The first driver to reach the spot where the balloon lands is declared the winner. This race is hard work for the hounds because a balloon goes where the winds take it. The flying altitude can be controlled somewhat, but you can't really steer a balloon accurately. It may come down in a field, a parking lot, a back-yard, or in the middle of a lake.

A championship race in Iowa begins.

▶ HOW DOES A BALLOON WORK?

Part of the fun of ballooning is learning how to make the contraption work. It doesn't come ready for action. A lot of work is needed to get the balloon airborne. The principal gases used to send a balloon aloft are hot air, illuminating gas, hydrogen, and helium. These are lighter-than-air gases.

The modern hot-air balloon is the most popular of the free-flying sports vehicles. It takes about 20 minutes to inflate it fully. The ground crew assembles the gondola (the "basket" in which the passengers ride), lays the balloon (a huge nylon bag) out flat on the ground, and attaches the gondola to it. A ground inflation fan is directed into the mouth of the balloon until it is almost half filled with cold air. Then a double-barreled propane burner is lighted, and the flame is directed into the mouth of the balloon to heat the cold air. As the air in the balloon is heated, the balloon begins to drift upward. The ground crew lets the balloon rise slowly until it has reached the necessary height. The gondola is held on the ground until the pilot has finished his preflight inspection and is ready for takeoff. Then it's up, up, and away. You can fly high over the treetops while the gondola of the balloon is still secured (by a tether, or rope) to the ground. Or you can cut loose completely, and freely float thousands of feet above the earth.

Propane burners regulate the air temperature inside the balloon, enabling the pilot to control the altitude, but nothing else. The hot air captured inside the balloon, which is about 100 degrees hotter than the air outside, is buoyant and rises in the colder air around it, thus creating a skyward lift.

The average balloon flight takes about 2 hours and covers nearly 20 miles. The amount of time the balloon is in flight and the distance it travels depend on how many people are aboard: the more people in the gondola, the less time the balloon can stay aloft.

▶ HOW IT ALL BEGAN

In 1783 the Montgolfier brothers, Joseph and Étienne, sent a duck, a rooster, and a sheep on an 8-minute flight over Versailles, France. The Montgolfiers' balloon was fueled by a foul-smelling gas produced by burning

300

damp straw, old shoes, and decomposed meat. The wide-eyed spectators who witnessed the historic flight stared in disbelief as the balloon ascended. In fact, they chased the flying oddity to its landing place 2 miles away. There they found the wicker cage (the forerunner of the gondola) broken open, and the three animals grazing, unharmed, in a nearby field. This was the beginning of balloon flight. Live passengers had been carried into the air and returned safely to earth for the first time in history.

The first balloon flight in the United States took place at Philadelphia in 1793. A Frenchman, Jean Pierre Blanchard, jumped into his gondola and took off, floating to a height of more than 5,000 feet. A small dog and six bottles of wine kept him company. In 46 minutes the hydrogen-filled balloon traveled 15 miles. It landed, after three attempts, in a field near Woodbury, New Jersey.

In the early 19th century, all Europe went "balloon crazy." Men challenged one another for supremacy in the skies. After several very wet attempts, the English Channel was crossed by a balloon. Soon, the Alps were conquered; and England's most famous balloonist, Charles Green, flew all the way from London to Germany. It took Green 18 hours to complete the 480-mile journey.

Balloons were used during the Civil War in the United States (1861–65), but not for pleasure. The Union Army sent men aloft to conduct aerial reconnaissance of the Confederate Army's movements. Union balloonists flew above the battle lines to observe Confederate troop movements and to direct cannon fire more accurately. This new type of warfare was so successful that the Confederate forces had to expend considerable time and energy in concealing their movements.

Then, for almost 100 years, balloons dropped out of sight. Airplanes came along and captured the interest of fliers. Soon power lines and telephone poles sprang up across the country, making balloon flights hazardous. It was not until the late 1950's that ballooning, the old mode of transportation, was revived. With streamlined balloons and gondolas and the discovery of new types of fuel, ballooning stepped, or flew, into the 1970's as one of man's most exciting sports.

A balloon soars high above the lush green farmland.

Men and horses work together in the dust and excitement of the rodeo.

RODEO TODAY

Rodeo, the only sport that started because of man's pride in his working skills, is growing bigger every year. In 1973 there were over 600 rodeos in the United States and Canada approved by the Rodeo Cowboys Association. The payoff to participating cowboys was in the millions of dollars.

It is surprising to learn that 1973 was a record-breaking year for all kinds of rodeo competition. Ranch work is becoming more and more scientific. The old ranch system, in which a bronc buster broke a string of mature horses by riding them until they stopped bucking, is a thing of the past. Most ranches now raise Quarter Horses (horses bred for short bursts of high speed) and train them as yearlings. Ranchers try not to let their Quarter Horses buck at all. It is the same with working cattle in the open. The old method of roping cattle for branding and other procedures is being replaced by the use of modern corrals and squeeze chutes. In the light of

this, it's amazing that the sport of rodeo has grown—instead of shrinking—since its beginnings on 19th-century ranches.

Shortly after the Civil War, large herds of cattle were driven from the overgrazed Texas plains. They were driven north to railheads—Dodge City, Kansas, was a famous railhead—where they were shipped to eastern markets. Often several trail crews would be in town at the same time. It was only natural that these cowboys should compete in the skills of their trade—riding and roping—when they got together. These informal contests were often held in a clearing, within sight of the town. After weeks on the trail it was a sort of celebration, and many towns made these contests yearly affairs.

▶ HOW A RODEO IS ORGANIZED

A cowboy is a gambler by nature, and much of rodeo is a gamble. Cowboys wouldn't have it any other way.

All the animals used in a rodeo are given numbers, and the animals to be used in each contest are chosen by two judges, who draw the numbers from a hat. This system determines which animal each cowboy has in an event. In the bareback, saddle bronc, and bull-riding events, the two judges give the animal a grade, or mark, of from 1 to 25, based on their evaluation of how hard the animal bucked. And they mark the rider from 1 to 25, basing their scoring on how well they think the rider rode and how well he controlled both the animal and himself. In the timed events—calf roping, steer wrestling, and team roping—the really professional cowboys, who do these things as part of their daily work, can handle bigger and more difficult cattle than some of the other competitors can. Therefore the "luck of the draw" plays an important part in the outcome of the contest—especially for the less experienced competitors.

There are no guarantees or advance financial help of any kind available for people who want to compete in rodeos. Each cowboy pays his own traveling expenses, room and board, and entrance fees. These entrance fees can be as high as $100 for one event. All the entrance fees are added to the purse the individual rodeo puts up. The combined money is split among the winners. At Cheyenne, Wyoming, in 1973, there were 303 calf ropers, who paid $100 apiece to compete. Many of the competitors knew that the only

way they could win would be to outdraw the better ropers—that is, get an easier animal to handle.

HOW TO START COMPETING

Nowadays, fewer rodeo competitors are working cowboys; instead, they are people who have taken up rodeo as a sport. Boys and gïrls can learn about rodeo events in junior rodeos, such as those sponsored by the National Little Britches Rodeo Association. You can begin competing in junior rodeo at 8 and continue through 17. Young people also have high school rodeo competitions. There are both state and national finals on the high school rodeo level. The next step is college rodeo. At the 1973 Intercollegiate Finals, held in Bozeman, Montana, one collegiate champion also led the professional ranks in steer wrestling. As many as 153 colleges from 10 regional divisions compete.

There are also many rodeo schools, where cowboys can get instruction from some of the reigning champions. Most of these schools use very modern aids to help the students improve their performance. Instant replay television tape is used so that a student can see almost immediately after competing what he did that was right or wrong in dealing with an animal. Before these schools

A daring cowboy, age 11, rides a calf with all the skill of an expert.

A lecture on bareback riding is given at a rodeo school in Texas.

started, it was hard for young people to get rodeo experience. Practice animals were scarce for student use. Often the expenses, injuries, and disappointments would discourage a beginner before he really had a chance to learn anything. Rodeo schools have improved this situation greatly and have given many young people a start.

A RODEO STAR

Perhaps the best example of a modern rodeo cowboy is Phil Lyne, a remarkably gifted athlete from a small Texas city called George West. Phil can't remember when he wasn't doing something connected with rodeo. On all levels of rodeo competition there is usually an event called ribbon roping. A contestant on horseback pursues, ropes, and stops a calf. Another contestant rushes in, on foot, and helps hold the calf while the roper jumps off his horse and snatches off a ribbon that has been attached to the base of the calf's tail. He then runs on foot to the point where he started, and his time is noted by the judges. Phil Lyne's mother has a picture of Phil, aged 5, grabbing a ribbon off a small calf's tail; the ribbon is level with little Phil's eyes!

From this early start, Phil dominated Little Britches, high school, and college rodeo and went right on winning in professional rodeo.

He became a professional in 1969 and won $12,638 that year. The remarkable thing was that he was winning in every event. In 1970 he won $18,439, and the very next year he won the highest rodeo award, "All Around Cowboy." This award goes to the man who wins the most money in two or more events. Then in 1972 he set a record: he won his second All Around Cowboy award—and a record-breaking $60,852.

Phil only competed close to home in 1973 and all but quit the sport. He probably couldn't explain this decision even to himself. However, he does love working on his ranch, as well as fishing and hunting, and it probably seemed to him that he'd been on the road ever since high school. The amount of travel involved in winning championships staggers the imagination. Phil went to 126 rodeos in 1972. He flew his own plane to some events, and to others he took commercial flights. He drove his car to other events, with Samanthar, the mare he rides in calf roping, in a trailer behind his car. He spent hundreds of long, weary hours behind the wheel as well as in competition.

THE RODEO CIRCUIT

The rodeo season is now year-round. In January the big indoor rodeos start in

An exciting saddle bronc event at Canada's famous Calgary Stampede.

Denver, Colorado, and in Fort Worth, Houston, and San Antonio in Texas. All spring and summer, rodeos are held from coast to coast in the United States and in Canada. At many rodeos a cowboy can say when he wants to compete. This practice—called "trading out"—makes it possible for him to work two or three rodeos at once.

At the end of the year, for the top cowboys, there's the biggest rodeo of all: the National Finals Rodeo, held in Oklahoma City, Oklahoma, in early December. Only the top 15 money winners for the year in each event are eligible to compete. But what makes the National Finals a truly great rodeo is the quality of the spirited animals—the "bucking stock"—which are selected from all over the United States and Canada.

In the rodeo world, spirited animals are considered stars. They are as well known as many cowboys. It is not uncommon to hear that a proven bucking horse, when sold, brings several thousand dollars.

In a rodeo, a competitor often gets more than one animal in a given event. When every cowboy has competed on his first animal, the "go-round" is over and there is a payoff. Then there is a second go-round, with a new drawing matching animals and competitors, and another payoff. And then whoever has the best score on two animals or the best time—in the timed events—gets an additional payoff. This extra payoff is called the "average." At the National Finals, each of the 10 performances makes up a go-round. The excitement is intense when a championship is at stake. The last three performances of the National Finals are usually sold-out 6 months in advance. During the last performance, when "average" winners are announced and championships decided, the cheering crowd is as excited as a crowd at a deciding World Series baseball game.

▶ THE EVENTS

The most popular event with spectators—and cowboys who ride bucking stock—is the bull riding. It is the most dangerous event of all. Bulls are ridden with a loose rope (a rope tied loosely around the bull), which is pulled up tight, and the slack held in the palm of the cowboy's "riding hand." His other hand is called his "free hand," and he must not touch the bull with it. The cowboy riding a bull must stay astride the animal—which weighs almost a ton and can spin, kick, and buck furiously—for 8 seconds.

When a bull rider leaves the "hurricane deck" (as the bull's back is called)—intentionally or not—he must scramble to safety.

Bull riding—the wildest event in all rodeo.

A bronc does its best to throw its rider.

Pole bending, a fast event for junior and senior girls.

The one man that can help him is the rodeo clown. For years the clown, usually dressed in traditional baggy overalls, has been a real lifesaver. He stays close to the action, and when a cowboy leaves a bull, the clown runs in and draws the bull's attention. Sometimes he grabs a horn or raps the bull on the muzzle. This event is very dangerous, and you may well wonder why cowboys wish to compete in it.

Of course, there is always the unexplainable love of danger, which makes people climb mountains and race cars. But the one thing about bull riding that interests cowboys is that any competitor who is able to stay on half the bulls he draws for the required 8 seconds would most likely be rated in the top 15. There are many really wild bulls that get ridden only once in 60 to 70 tries.

When you think of the danger and uncertainty of rodeo, it is hard to understand why it grows more popular every year. One reason is the spirit of friendship that exists between rodeo competitors. Cowboys are very close to each other, and they'll do all they can to help each other. For instance, the well-known cowboy Larry Mahan might be fighting for the bull-riding title, and his equally well known friend and fellow contender Pete Gay might ask Larry about a certain bull Pete had drawn. Larry would probably tell Pete all he knows. He might tell him the way the particular bull spins, how he acts in the chute, and anything else Larry thinks would help Pete. Because all rodeo cowboys are faced with the "luck of the draw" and the threat of injuries, they really do become friends.

And rodeo competitors can also be completely independent. In no other sport—except perhaps professional golf—can a sportsman be completely "his own boss" in the way that rodeo allows him to be.

Another factor that adds to the growth of rodeo is the ever-increasing interest of spectators in horses. The cowboys in the timed events ride some of the best-trained horses in the world. There is, for instance, an especially interesting event for girls—barrel racing. The girls, on well-trained horses, race against the clock around three barrels arranged in a cloverleaf pattern.

From the time the Grand Entry (the opening procession of competitors) marches into the arena until the last bull turns himself into a wildly gyrating ton of explosive fury, rodeo is an absorbing event. Not only does the crowd see hair-raising danger and excitement, but they also see a bit of what frontier life was like in the United States and Canada not so very long ago.

COLIN LOFTING
Rodeo Cowboys Association

MAJOR RODEO EVENTS

Bareback Riding: One-hand rigging to be used. To qualify, the rider must have his spurs over the break of the shoulders when the horse's front feet touch the ground, on the first jump out of the chute. The horse must be ridden for 8 seconds, and the rider cannot touch the horse with his free hand.

Calf Roping: If the cowboy intends to use two loops, two ropes must be carried. The cowboy must dismount, go down the rope, throw the calf by hand and cross and tie any three of its feet. If the calf is down when the roper reaches it, he must allow it to get up and then throw it. If the roper's hand is on the calf when the calf falls, the calf is considered thrown by hand. The tie must hold for 6 seconds after the roper slackens the rope.

Bull Riding: Riding must be done with one hand and a loose rope, with or without a handhold. The rope must have a bell. The bull is to be ridden for 8 seconds. The rider will be disqualified for being bucked off in less than 8 seconds or for touching the animal with his free hand.

Steer Wrestling: The steer must be caught from on horseback. If the steer gets loose, the dogger (as the steer wrestler is called) may take no more than one step to catch him. The steer will be considered down only when it is lying flat on its side, all four feet and head straight. If the dogger misses the steer, the flagman must ask the dogger if he wishes another jump.

Saddle Bronc Riding: The riding rein and the hand must be on the same side. To qualify, the rider must have his spurs over the break of the shoulders and touching the horse when its front feet hit the ground on the first jump out of the chute. The rider can be disqualified for being bucked off, changing hands on the rein, letting a foot leave the stirrup, or touching the animal, saddle, or rein with his free hand.

An Indian lacrosse game, as portrayed by the 19th-century American artist Seth Eastman. Eastman, who was also an army officer, sketched Indian life while stationed in the West.

LACROSSE:
A NORTH AMERICAN SPORT

The ancient sport of the North American Indians that the white men called lacrosse is gaining new popularity all across Canada and the United States. Though lacrosse is officially Canada's national sport, it took a backseat to hockey for many years. But all that seems to be changing. And the sport is now played more widely in the United States, where it formerly had only limited popularity.

Although Canadians generally play a form of the game called box lacrosse, and United States enthusiasts play the older form known as field lacrosse, the origins of both are the same.

The secret of the exact origin of lacrosse is lost forever in the ancient Indian burial grounds of eastern North America. The first written reference to the game is found in the journals of St. Jean de Brébeuf and was set down in 1636. Brébeuf, a Jesuit missionary to the Indians, was eventually killed by the Iroquois. However, he set down a record of having seen the Hurons play lacrosse in the eastern woodlands of Canada.

The version of lacrosse that the Indians played when the first white men arrived in North America was a field game. The playing area varied from 500 yards to several miles in length. There were few fixed rules. Each tribe or clan set their own rules. The Indian game was midway between a sport and a deadly contest. Players sometimes lost limbs in the course of a game or suffered other equally serious injuries. Although there is no doubt that the Indians played the game as a sport, it also served to teach young warriors about hand-to-hand combat. The Indians called lacrosse "the little brother of war."

▶ THE ANCIENT RULES

Under Indian rules, the ball used in the game was placed in a neutral spot to start the competition. The object of the game, for each team, was to gain possession of the ball and carry it across a specified goal line. Early goal lines were marked by trees, rocks, or poles stuck in the ground. Often these contests involved 600 to 1,000 players and lasted 2 or 3 days before a winning team emerged. Betting was heavy, especially among the women. The score was kept by cutting notches in a tree trunk or stick, or by piling up little pieces of wood to represent points scored. Singing and dancing usually preceded each contest. The original lacrosse sticks were of two types: one was a solid piece of wood with a hollow at the end in which the ball was snared; the other had a rounded loop at one end, which held a net for the ball. Modern lacrosse sticks are more like the second type.

It is estimated that some 48 tribes—ranging from eastern Canada to Florida—played some form of lacrosse. The Indian names for the game and the rules varied from one geographical region to another. For instance the southern Cherokee and Seminole tribes played a type of lacrosse called "stick-ball," and northern tribes played a version of it on ice during the winter. The 13 British colonies first called the Indian game "racquet," and the Ojibway Indians called it *baggattaway*. The Santee Sioux were evidently the only tribe that allowed women to take part in the sport.

The first specific record of a lacrosse game in the official history of North America was scrawled in letters of blood. During the days of Pontiac's Rebellion the Ojibway and Sac Indians put on a display of lacrosse outside the stockade at Fort Michilimackinac, Michigan, on June 4, 1763. Caught up by the excitement of the game, the soldiers of the British garrison came outside the fort to watch, climbing up, undoubtedly, onto the stockade ramparts. The ball—it seemed by accident—sailed over the stockade wall. The Indian players surged into the stockade after it, not forgetting to seize tomahawks and war clubs from under the blankets of their women, who had been watching the game. The final score included 24 British soldiers killed.

The early settlers of North America tended to view the athletic pastimes of the Indians as purely amusements. There appears to have been little serious attention paid to lacrosse until 1834, when some whites from Montreal invited the Caughnawaga Indians to demonstrate the game in Montreal. There were several exhibition games, and interest grew among the whites. In 1844 the first recorded

MODERN RULES

Modern **field lacrosse** is played on a rectangular field 110 yards long and 60 yards wide. The goals, which are 6 feet square and netted, are surrounded by a circle, or "crease," which has a radius of 9 feet. Each team consists of 10 players: a goalkeeper, three defensemen, three midfielders, and three attackmen. A player must run with the ball or pass it. Each team must keep four men in their defensive zone and three in their offensive zone, otherwise the team is counted offside and a penalty is called. The game consists of four 15-minute quarters. During the quarters, each team tries to put the ball into the opponents' goal; if it succeeds, it scores one point.

Present-day **box lacrosse**—called "boxla" for short—is usually played indoors, but can also be played outdoors. Whether it is played indoors or outdoors, the playing space in box lacrosse cannot be less than 160 feet long and 60 feet wide. The playing area is surrounded by a fence to keep the ball in play. Most box lacrosse teams use the playing surfaces of hockey arenas during the spring and summer months. The goals, 4 feet square and netted, are located within a circle, or goal "crease," which has a 9-foot radius. Each team is composed of six players: a goalkeeper, two defensemen, one center, and a right and a left forward. The object of the game is similar to that of field lacrosse: each team tries to put the ball into the opponents' goal. Box lacrosse has three 20-minute periods. It also has a "30-second rule," under which the offensive team must take a shot or lose the ball. Scores in box lacrosse are generally higher than those in field lacrosse, since the playing area is much smaller. Box lacrosse has no offside rules, and the 30-second rule forces the teams to shoot more frequently.

lacrosse game between an Indian team and a white one was played in Canada. In 1856 the Montreal Lacrosse Club was formed, the first organized white lacrosse team.

▶ EARLY TEAMS

The year 1867 marked the turning point in the long history of lacrosse. On July 1, 1867, lacrosse was proclaimed, by an act of Parliament, the national sport of Canada. The year 1867 also saw the writing of the first uniform code of lacrosse rules. The Canadian National Lacrosse Association was also founded in

U.S. players collide in the rough, outdoor game of field lacrosse.

1867. Soon Canada had 80 lacrosse clubs. Many of them were located around Montreal, which was rapidly becoming known as the "cradle of modern lacrosse."

After the winter of 1867, a member of a Montreal lacrosse club started the first lacrosse team in Scotland. Later in the year, W. B. Johnson, of the same Montreal team, introduced lacrosse to England, Ireland, and France. L. L. Mount, another Montrealer, initiated lacross in Australia in 1878.

In the United States the Mohawk Lacrosse Club of Troy, New York, was established in 1867, and was the first American center for lacrosse. Lacrosse, from the very beginning, had to compete with the huge popularity of baseball in the United States. It has never gained the attention there that it has in Canada. This probably accounts for the fact that Canada dominated field lacrosse from the sport's beginnings until the early 1930's. At that point Canadians began to play box lacrosse. United States teams then began to dominate field lacrosse. Interest in field lacrosse in the United States was originally centered around New York City. However, the center of the American sport eventually shifted to the Baltimore area, where it has remained.

Manhattan College in New York City introduced lacrosse into American college sports around 1875. College lacrosse in the United States grew slowly. As recently as 1952 there were only 46 college lacrosse teams in the country. However, from 1952 to 1973, the old Indian game has consistently expanded and is now considered one of the fastest-growing team sports in North America. Between 1952 and 1973 over 110 colleges in the United States added lacrosse to their intercollegiate sports programs. Many of these colleges compete for the Wingate Memorial Trophy, which was established in 1936 and is awarded annually for the United States National Intercollegiate Championship.

▶ **THE GAME TODAY**

Although lacrosse is officially Canada's national game, hockey has usually been of more importance to the general public. Large crowds always turned out for hockey games in Canada, and spacious rinks were built to accommodate them. During the summer months these large arenas were often empty of paying customers. Awareness of this caused concern among Canadian hockey promoters. In 1930 a revolutionary solution to the problem of empty hockey arenas was

A Canadian box lacrosse player drives a ball into the opponents' goal.

proposed, and the ancient sport of lacrosse went indoors. Indoor box lacrosse was born. A professional league was set up and met with instant success. The new enthusiasm for lacrosse swept across Canada, and Canadians found themselves playing indoors with seven men on a side. The seventh man, in this early version of box lacrosse, was called a rover. Rovers remained in box lacrosse until 1952, when the position was dropped.

The United States has never really accepted box lacrosse, although cities near the Canadian border have experimented with it. The acceptance of box lacrosse in Canada was made official when the Canadian Lacrosse Association voted, in September, 1931, to have box lacrosse replace field lacrosse as the official national game. In that year it was also decided that box lacrosse teams—and not, as formerly, field lacrosse teams—should compete annually for the two most prized lacrosse awards in Canada, the Mann Cup and the Minto Cup.

Lacrosse was once an event in the Olympic Games, but has not been since 1932. However, there is still international lacrosse competition among field lacrosse teams from Australia, England, the United States, and Canada. Some of Canada's box lacrosse players become field lacrosse players for these world championships.

The sport of lacrosse—a peculiar hybrid, somewhat resembling both ice hockey and basketball—has recently caught the fancy of the youth of Canada and the United States. Box lacrosse teams for men and boys are springing up at all age levels in Canada. Ontario and British Columbia have the largest number of amateur teams and participants. Quebec, the former "cradle of lacrosse," is again becoming a center for the game. Similarly, field lacrosse is enjoying an increase in popularity throughout the United States, with teams springing up all over the country. Women's lacrosse, first played at Fife, Scotland, in 1890, has also gained popularity, especially in the United States, where many high schools, prep schools, and colleges have women's teams.

The popularity of lacrosse has also changed the technology of the game. The traditional stick made of hickory wood is being replaced by a stick made of synthetic materials. However, the game remains the same exciting sport given to us all so long ago by the Indians of North America.

JAMES G. BISHOP
Member, Canadian Lacrosse Hall of Fame

THE CREATIVE WORLD

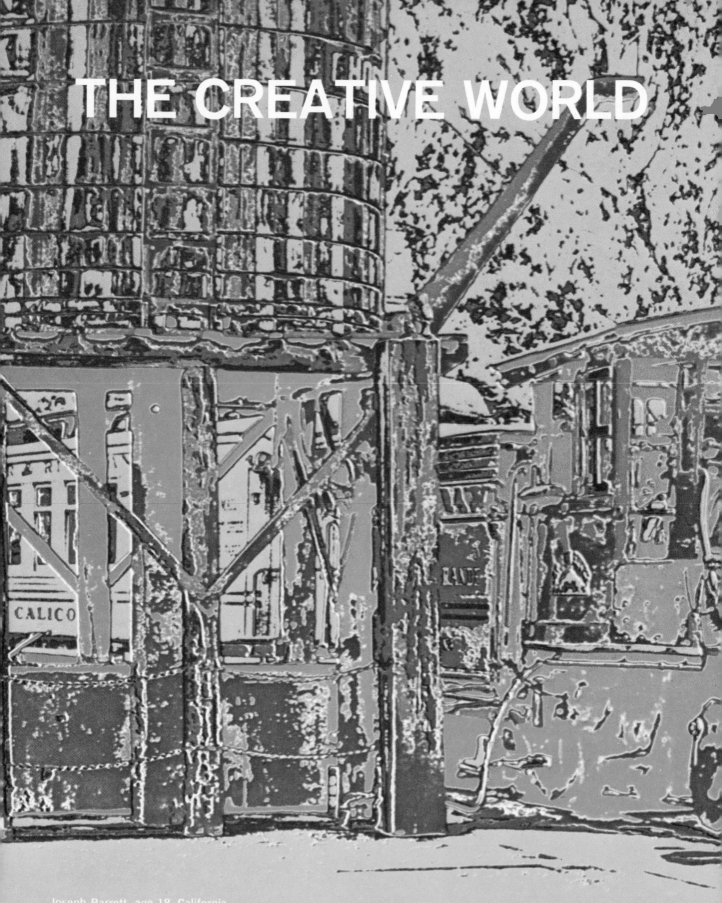

Joseph Barrett, age 18, California.

THE WALTONS

If you don't believe in miracles, just ask the Waltons. Surely you know who the Waltons are. They're the folks who live in the Blue Ridge Mountains of Virginia, and appear on television every Thursday evening. They don't just "appear." "The Waltons" happens to be one of the biggest hits of the 1972–74 television seasons. And that in itself is a miracle.

When the show made its debut in 1972, most critics gave it good marks for sincerity but almost no chance for survival. The competition was just too great. "Flip Wilson" was on one channel, and "The Mod Squad" on another—both very popular programs. In fact, many people in the television industry referred to "The Waltons" as a "throwaway." A throwaway is a TV program that is placed opposite highly successful shows. It isn't expected to attract many viewers, and its run is usually quite short. Many throwaways begin in September and disappear from the tele-

vision screen by January. But to almost everyone's surprise a miracle occurred. "The Waltons" turned out to be a highly successful show.

It wasn't long before this gentle, low-key story of seven children growing up poor during the Great Depression of the 1930's gained on its competition and began to attract viewers by the millions. And along with a large viewing audience came the awards. "The Waltons" won top honors in four categories in the 24th annual poll of television critics conducted for *Fame* magazine. The series was named Best Network Television Program, Best Dramatic Program, and Most Unique New Program. Richard Thomas, the bright young star of the series, was named Most Promising New Male Star. The George Foster Peabody Award was presented to "The Waltons," citing the program as a "sensitive, dramatic interpretation of life during the Depression."

In May, 1973, the Academy of Television Arts and Sciences proved further that "The Waltons" was indeed a smash. The show received six Emmys, including those for best drama series, and best actor (Richard Thomas), best actress (Miss Michael Learned), and best supporting actress (Ellen Corby) in a drama series.

Just what kind of show received these glowing tributes? Is it loaded with violence, action, murder, and mayhem? Quite the contrary. "The Waltons" portrays the struggles and troubles, the tenderness and love of a family living in the Blue Ridge Mountains during the difficult years of the Depression. The episodes recount the homey activities of the close-knit Walton family, their hopes and dreams, and their relationships with one another and with strangers who pass through their small world.

The stories are usually of a gentle sort. In one episode a deaf child is taught to speak. In another a calf that has been a pet is sold, and the Walton children take jobs so they can earn money for the calf's return. A highly rated, 2-hour Easter special centered on the mother, Olivia Walton, who is suddenly stricken with polio. The tender story finds the Walton family facing an overwhelming test of faith and courage. Olivia, fearing that her

The Walton family leaves church after Sunday morning services.

paralysis may be permanent, tries to effect a cure based on faith and force of will. In true Walton fashion, there is a happy ending.

Many of the stories deal with people who are unhappy in one way or another. The faded actress, the lovelorn blacksmith, the unsuccessful writer, and the unforgiving preacher are some of the characters who built new lives for themselves after they came in contact with the Waltons.

▶ A SENSE OF REALNESS

Although the series is filmed on a studio back lot in Burbank, California, there's a definite sense of "realness" to the show. Much attention has been paid to a re-creation of Appalachia during the 1930's. The two-story, white clapboard Walton house sits in the woods just off an unpaved country lane. On the front porch are old wicker rockers, a swing, and hanging baskets of flowers. Just down the road is the old country store, complete with rolltop desk and crank telephone.

If you happen to pop in for a visit at the Walton house, you might find the family sprawled around the living-room Philco radio,

listening to the adventures of Charlie McCarthy. Or some of the children may be off in a corner toiling away at their reading, 'riting, and 'rithmetic. All of this "atmosphere" helps to create realness, the word that most Walton worshipers use to describe the show's appeal.

And the Waltons themselves are probably the most important ingredient in the show. Richard Thomas, highly praised for his performances in the films *Last Summer* and *Red Sky at Morning,* stars as John-Boy Walton, the eldest son of John and Olivia Walton, played by Ralph Waite and Miss Michael Learned. Other members of the Walton family include Will Geer as Grandpa, and Ellen Corby as Grandma. Portraying the other Walton children are Jon Walmsley as Jason, Judy Norton as Mary Ellen, Mary Elizabeth McDonough as Erin, David S. Harper as Jim-Bob, Eric Scott as Ben, and Kami Cotler as Elizabeth.

The Walton children appear to be the reason the series draws three times as many young viewers as its competitors. John-Boy, 17 years old and the central figure of the show, is a sensitive boy who yearns to be a

Elizabeth takes care of the Waltons' pet calf.

writer. Teenage sister Mary Ellen dreams of traveling to far-off places and raises bullfrogs. Young Erin Walton, with her neatly pressed dress and hair ribbons always tied, is the perfect mother's helper. And then there's little Elizabeth—always the one to be watched. There's no telling what she'll do next. You'll not find a dull moment in the Walton household.

▶A BEGINNING

How did this wholesome, bittersweet saga of a Blue Ridge Mountain family happen upon the television scene? Television viewers first met the Waltons in Earl Hamner, Jr.'s "The Homecoming—A Christmas Story," a 2-hour television special presented in December, 1971. The show, based on Hamner's semi-autobiographical novelette *The Homecoming,* related the events of Christmas Eve, 1933, when the author's father was late returning home. The show really had no plot. John-Boy Walton (Hamner as a young man) is sent to look for his father. During the search John-Boy gets mixed up with two old lady bootleggers, a Robin Hood bandit, and the minister of a black church. He never does find his father, but all is not lost. Mr. Walton

returns in the wee hours of the morning, bearing Christmas gifts for one and all.

The show, starring Patricia Neal and Richard Thomas, won great critical acclaim. It was called a "magnificent achievement," a "modern *Christmas Carol,"* and a "Christmas classic . . . one that should be repeated every year."

When a "special" is received with such enthusiastic praise, there's always talk of turning it into a series. "The Homecoming" was no exception. After months of planning, the series became a reality. Richard Thomas, Ellen Corby, and all the younger brothers and sisters in the original "Homecoming" cast were signed to repeat their roles in the "Waltons" series. Author Earl Hamner, Jr., was appointed the executive story editor, and his childhood memories provide the basis for many of the warm, nostalgic stories.

With these ingredients, and then some, the show premiered in September, 1972, and went on to become the most talked about television event of the year. To some people the success of "The Waltons" was a miracle. To most viewers, however, the series was worth every bit of praise it received and was exactly what television needed.

The *Persephone*—with Nick at the helm—comes into the dock at Gibsons.

THE BEACHCOMBERS

On Canada's west coast, where the rugged, snowcapped Coast Mountains reach down to the sea, there's a little town named Gibsons in British Columbia. "The Beachcombers," one of Canada's most popular television shows, is filmed there.

Many people in Gibsons make their living from the great Pacific Ocean. Some of the residents fish for salmon; others work at salvaging giant fir logs that have been cut down in the dense forests of British Columbia and have somehow gotten lost on their way to the sawmill. These logs are about 50 feet long and usually get washed away from log rafts. The logs drift in to shore, where they catch on rocks. The log salvager comes along in his small, powerful boat, ties the ends of the giant logs with steel cable or rope, and tows them off to sell to lumber companies. Since these men "comb" the shore for logs, they're often called "beachcombers."

The actor who plays the log salvager in "The Beachcombers" is Bruno Gerussi, who grew up on the coast of British Columbia. He is one of Canada's best-known actors. Bruno, as most of the people in Gibsons call him, plays the role of Nick Adonidas, a Canadian of Greek descent. Nick's adventures each week are shared in by his young friends Hugh and Margaret Carmody, and by Jesse Jim, a Canadian Indian. There's also a mischievous salvager called Relic. Looking after the entire lot is Molly Carmody, grandmother of young Hugh and Margaret.

A lot of the action in "The Beachcombers" episodes centers on the *Persephone,* Nick's boat. Bruno Gerussi handles the *Persephone* himself in most of the episodes.

All the actors in "The Beachcombers" are from Canada's west coast. Bob Park, who plays Hugh Carmody, lives in Vancouver, British Columbia, where he goes to high school. The work in "The Beachcombers" keeps him out of the schoolroom about half of every school year—as it does Juliet Randall, the young actress who plays Margaret Carmody. They do their schoolwork each night after the day's shooting.

"The Beachcombers" has been a great success. The beauty of the setting, the fine acting, and the exciting adventures of the genuinely likable characters combine to make this series a delightful television experience.

GEORGE GARLOCK
Television Publicity Editor
Canadian Broadcasting Corporation (CBC)

The City Center Young People's Theater encourages children from the audience to come up on stage and act out a solution to the play.

CHILDREN'S THEATER

Children's theater is entertainment for children, usually provided by adults. It can be a puppet show; a performance by a traveling company of professional actors, a magician, or a mime; or even a storytelling hour with a librarian.

Most of the children's theater in the United States is produced by independent acting companies. Some of these groups develop their own original material. Others just retell old, familiar fairy tales and traditional stories. Some groups use highly experienced performers and stage technicians, amateurs as well as professionals. Some children's theater companies travel all over, making stops in many cities and towns. Others have their own theaters, and stay in the same city for years and years. Some com-

panies use young actors in their plays. Most of them employ only adult actors. The best of these groups deserve cheers and thanks for bringing the magic of theater to young people.

The Paper Bag Players are famous all over the world. The adult players of this company make their props and costumes out of nothing but paper bags, cardboard boxes, and other assorted pieces of paper. And, like magic, these bits of paper and boxes become fascinating tools and toys for making delightful plays.

Another favorite is the Little Theatre of the Deaf. This marvelous company has two troupes that tour all over the United States and other countries, taking with them their own special enchantment. One actor tells the story to the audience, while four other actors,

The Paper Bag Players use only paper bags, cardboard, and other bits of paper for their imaginative costumes and scenery.

The Little Theatre of the Deaf performs in "sign mime," their very beautiful language.

who are all deaf, perform the action in a most unusual way. They use "sign mime," a beautiful language all their own. It is a little like mime and a little like dance, and a lot like poetry for the eyes. This very exciting company works closely with its audiences. The children are asked for their ideas and the actors make up pretty stories around these ideas—right on the spot. This is called "improvisational theater," and it is becoming popular with imaginative children's theater companies.

The Proposition Theater for Children, which you may have seen on public television, also uses this technique of creating "instant theater" through improvisation. So does the Academy Theater in Atlanta, Georgia, which takes its plays directly into the schools, and asks the children themselves to make up the endings for the stories.

Several of the more adventurous companies are encouraging children to become more and more involved in using their own imaginations. In that way, they can share in the fun of creating theater themselves. In New York, the City Center Young People's Theater

The Meri Mini-Players are schoolchildren, 6 through 12 years old.

uses talented young adult actors to start off their clever, original stories. For example, in *Poloot-shun!* the actors dramatize how the planet earth has been polluted by mankind. Then they stop the show right in the middle, and have a workshop session with all the children in the audience. The children decide how the show should end. The children come on stage and act out their own answers to how the problem of pollution can be solved.

In the productions of the Meri Mini Players, children not only help the actors, they are the actors. If you have seen them on television, you know that the 40 players are children between the ages of 6 and 12. They are not professionals, but schoolchildren who work in the company for the fun of it.

When we talk about theater for children, we mustn't forget that the actors don't even have to be people. Sometimes they may be puppets. Puppets have fascinated children and grown-ups alike for thousands of years, and puppetry is one of the oldest forms of theater in the world. It is still so popular today that there are more than 20 regional puppetry

guilds throughout the United States and Canada.

There are many different kinds of puppets and puppetry styles. The Bread and Puppet Theater, based in Vermont, uses giant, bigger-than-people puppets. The group often does its shows in the streets so that it can reach more people. Both children and adults can understand and enjoy its plays, which have a strong emphasis on social satire and reform.

The Bil Baird puppeteers have a beautiful theater, a workshop, and a puppet museum in New York City. These skilled puppeteers create puppets that seem to have a life of their own. Top professional writers and musicians compose new, full-length plays every year for these puppets that are almost people. And every year enchanting new puppets are born to act in such thrilling plays as *Davy Jones's Locker,* which has the funniest sea monster you'll ever meet.

As you can tell by now, when adults love children as much as they love the theater, they can make wonderful children's theater. But good theater is not all magic and love. It

The Bil Baird puppets seem to come alive in a scene from *Davy Jones's Locker*.

also takes skill and study. Many high schools, colleges, and special theater schools, and even some communities, are making extra efforts to train people who want to raise the artistic standards of children's theater. Special children's theater programs and workshops are offered.

Some of the schools are not limited to adults, but have opened their doors to young people. Nothing else in the United States is quite like the Children's Theatre Company of the Minneapolis Society of Fine Arts. About 100 students, all under 18 years of age, attend this Minnesota school to learn all about theater, from making sets and costumes to acting.

Some children's theater professionals predict that children will shortly be producing all their own theater, from writing to production. Certainly there are many signs that the theater is going in that direction. And if it should happen soon—Power to the Children!

MARILYN STASIO
Theater Critic
Cue Magazine

Part of the learning is doing at the Children's Theatre Company school in Minneapolis.

Roses can bloom all year in this Cranbury, New Jersey, air structure.

AIR STRUCTURES

One day soon you may see something that will make you think that people from another planet have finally landed on earth. You may see it while driving through the country with your parents or walking on a city street. But in either place, you may be really quite startled to see a kind of building that you have never seen before. It will probably be very big and it may well look like the cocoon of a giant insect—in fact, it may even look as if it were alive! What you will be seeing is a new kind of building designed by an architect who is using a new approach to building and totally new materials. You will be looking at an air-inflated or air-supported structure, and it will probably be made of plastic.

Almost anything could be going on inside the air structure you see. If you are in the country, it may be covering an area where vegetables or flowers are grown all year. If you are in a city or a town, the air structure you see may be used as a warehouse, or a tennis club, or a theater—or almost anything that a conventional building might be used for. And it really might be constructed in almost any shape at all.

People have actually known about air struc-

tures for a long time. Balloons, dirigibles, tires, inflatable life rafts and life vests, parachutes, and even sails on sailboats and sailing ships are truly air structures. Now architects and engineers are creating air-supported or air-inflated "buildings."

▶ BREAKTHROUGH

The United States Pavilion at EXPO'70, held in Osaka, Japan, gave notice that air structures might well be the best solution for the modern world's rapidly changing needs. The largest air structure ever built at that time, the United States Pavilion was new in both appearance and structure. It was 265 feet wide and 465 feet long. The construction cost was $2,600,000. This is much less than an old-fashioned structure of masonry and steel would have cost. The architects who designed the pavilion, and the engineer who supervised its construction, believe that areas of up to one square mile—and perhaps more—can be covered by air structures. And once man has learned to use air-structure techniques to make large buildings, the same methods could be used to control climate within very large areas, covered by an air-

The Antioch air structure hugs its Maryland field as if it grew there.

structure "roof." Air structures could also be used to cover industrial areas to prevent the spread of air pollution.

The pavilion at Osaka and the large air structures constructed since then at the Antioch College branch campus in Maryland and at Milligan College in Tennessee were not really the beginning of the new technology. Years of development led to the breakthrough.

As early as 1917, patents had been obtained on the principles involved in using air structures as architecture—that is, as buildings. However, the earliest practical and useful air structure was an air-supported radar dome (radome) developed at Cornell Aeronautical Laboratory in Buffalo, New York, in 1946–47. It was developed under a government contract for a portable, lightweight structure without metal parts. The structure was to be used to protect sensitive radar equipment from extreme weather conditions without interfering with the operation of the radar (which a structure using metal might do). Since 1962, air-supported radomes of up to 210 feet in diameter have been erected at Telstar ground communications centers around the world. These radomes required that special equipment be already in place before they could be built. Now, however, many of the air structures used as warehouses and as coverings for tennis courts can be erected in a matter of hours by several men.

It is not even necessary for the men to have had any special training.

▶ KINDS OF AIR STRUCTURE

Technically, there are a number of types of air-supported or air-inflated structures. There is the single-walled structure—sometimes called a membrane or skin. There is a single- or double-walled structure reinforced with a network of cables. (The United States Pavilion at Osaka was built this way.) There are also air structures that use air-inflated tubes that work the way structural elements like columns, beams, or arches work in conventional buildings. And there are air structures that may use combinations of all of these approaches.

Another way of classifying air structures is by referring to the way in which they are inflated, or air supported. The interior space of the single-walled or -skinned structure is inflated till the air pressure inside is slightly higher than the outside atmospheric pressure. In the double-walled structure, the space between the two walls is pressurized at slightly more than atmospheric pressure; the occupied space is pressurized somewhat more than the area between the two walls, or skins. These pressures are maintained by air blowers that also circulate and condition the air. Air locks are provided at the doorways so that people or vehicles do not change the air pressure inside. Another kind, called the dual-walled structure, has only the space between the two skins pressurized.

All of these structures, whether or not they are reinforced with cables, are fastened to a ring made of concrete or timbers. This ring (which rests upon an earthen beam) prevents the force of the winds from changing the shape of the structure or blowing it away. The ring, then, operates as a restraining force. However, there are also three "air forces" that keep the structure stable and hold the roof up. (1) The difference between the outside atmospheric pressure and the inside pressure, which is slightly higher, keeps the air structures inflated like an automobile tire or a balloon. (2) The air inside the structure, heated by solar energy or by man-made heating equipment, rises with sufficient force to help hold up the roof. This is called thermal buoyancy. (3) Wind movement over the roof creates an area of negative air pressure on the outside surface of the roof. This produces a "lift" exactly like the force that lifts the wings of airplanes in flight.

▶ A VARIETY OF USES

Because they are simple to move and to inflate or deflate, air structures can really keep up with the modern need for change.

The First National Conference on Air Structures was held on May 23–24, 1973, at Columbia, Maryland. It coincided with the opening of the air-structure campus of Antioch College in Columbia, one of Antioch's 24 temporary branch campuses throughout the country. In this 180-foot-square air structure there were gathered over 400 architects, engineers, educational specialists, and students. They discussed how air structures could provide schools and colleges with much-needed space.

The Antioch air structure, or "bubble," was designed by Runik Ekstrom, Charles Tilford, and the Research and Design Institute of Providence, Rhode Island, with the assistance of students from Antioch and from the University of Maryland.

Although the Antioch College experiment was used to show how a whole campus could use air structures, other colleges are using air structures to take the place of single buildings or to cover large areas such as sports stadiums. Milligan College, in Johnson City, Tennessee, has a 60,000-square-foot air-supported field house. Both Harvard University, in Cambridge, Massachusetts, and Columbia University, in New York City, have also used large air structures as track-and-field facilities for several years.

The use of air structures has not been limited to education or recreation. Portable warehouses have provided manufacturers with inexpensive, temporary shelter for their products. The Goodyear Tire and Rubber Company plans to construct an air structure in Topeka, Kansas. It will cover 1½ acres.

There have also been special uses evolved

Tennis is played during all seasons under this air-supported roof.

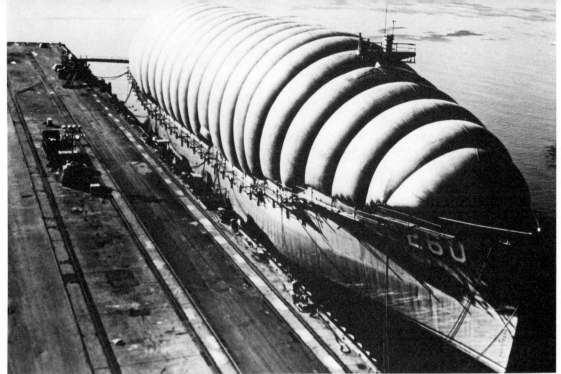

This reinforced air structure protects a mothballed naval vessel.

for air structures. A cable-reinforced membrane has been designed to be used in "mothballing" (storing) ships at the Philadelphia Naval Shipyard. A giant bubble is being used in Managua, the capital of Nicaragua, to store medical supplies and emergency relief supplies, as that city recovers from the devastating earthquake that struck in 1972.

Air structures are being used in agriculture, too. In Cranbury, New Jersey, a bubble covering somewhat more than an acre is used for large-scale, year-round rose growing. The costs of building this super greenhouse and heating it were lower than those of building and heating conventional greenhouses.

Since 1966 the University of Arizona and the University of Sonora in Mexico have been jointly operating a desert horticulture station near Puerto Peñasco, Mexico, on the Gulf of California. The air shelters there are used to protect the growing plants from the hot desert sun and to provide a highly humid environment. The air blowers that keep the "greenhouses" inflated also circulate air saturated with salt water, which is pumped from a nearby seawater well.

▶ PROBLEMS

Even with these successes, there are definite problems that must be solved before air structures can meet even more building needs. Local zoning and building codes will have to be changed to accommodate the new technology. As it is, only one or two existing air structures in the United States have been classified as "permanent structures." There is a great need to develop materials that cannot catch fire easily to use in these structures. Systems must also be worked out that would keep a structure from deflating if the air blowers stopped working.

Despite all the problems and the unanswered questions, air structures are obviously going to become very familiar to all of us. They will continue to sprout in farmers' fields and on city streets and in parks. For if there is one thing the modern world does consistently, it changes. These structures are also capable of changing with the times to meet all our needs. If you have ever seen the great inflated balloon figures that are sometimes carried in parades you have some idea of the variety of colors and shapes an air-inflated structure can take. There are really very few limitations to the things that truly creative architects can do with this wonderful new technique of building.

RICHARD KATHMANN
Co-director
Chicago River Spectacle Company

Left: Untitled work by Gail Eason, age 17, Illinois. Above: *What Is It?*, by Heather Gilason, age 17, Illinois. Below: *Breaking the Barrier*, by William Heiden, age 17, California.

YOUNG PHOTOGRAPHERS

Each year amateur photographers in grades 7 through 12 are invited to submit examples of their work to the Scholastic Photography Awards program. It is the aim of the program to recognize and encourage the creative achievement of young people. Photographs may be submitted in both color and black and white. Some of the prize-winning works of the 1973 program are shown on these pages. For the 46th year Scholastic Magazines, Inc., conducted the program, and for the 11th year Eastman Kodak Company sponsored it. A committee of national judges made the prize-winning selections. The awards were scholarships for two college-bound seniors, more than 200 cash prizes, and medallions for excellence.

Above: *The Navigator*, by Emily Payne, age 17, California.
Below: *Old Wood*, by James Visser, age 17, Pennsylvania.

Aunt Polly, her family, and the neighbors set off on the Fourth of July picnic.

TOM SAWYER

They're all back at your neighborhood movie theater—and it's cause for celebration! Tom and Huck, Muff Potter and Aunt Polly, Becky Thatcher and Injun Joe—do the names sound familiar to you? They should, because these are the principal characters of Mark Twain's classic novel *The Adventures of Tom Sawyer*. And this is the fourth time that they have stepped from the printed page to the motion-picture screen.

This latest film version, in living color and set to lively music, got a rousing reception. Critics applauded the opening of *Tom Sawyer* at New York City's famous Radio City Music Hall, and in no time crowds were forming block-long lines. By summer, the film made its way across the United States, much to the delight of the moviegoing public.

The star of this new musical extravaganza is red-haired, many-freckled Johnny Whitaker. One look at this young actor and you know he's just the boy Mark Twain had in mind when he wrote *The Adventures of Tom Sawyer* nearly 100 years ago. If the face beneath all the red hair and freckles looks familiar, there's a very good reason. For 6 years, Johnny Whitaker played the part of Jody in the long-running television series "Family Affair."

Of course the film would not be complete without Tom's friends and relatives. Newcomer Jeff East makes his movie debut as Huckleberry Finn; Celeste Holm plays Tom's Aunt Polly; and Warren Oates is Muff Potter, the comical and lovable town drunk. Jodie Foster, a little trouper who has been an actress for 6 of her 9 years, plays the role of Tom's girl friend, Becky Thatcher.

Nothing has been left out of this film version of *Tom Sawyer*. All of the characters and all of Tom's exciting adventures have been transferred from the book to the screen. Everything is there—the mighty Mississippi River; the 19th-century town of Hannibal, Missouri, with its dusty streets and scrubbed frame houses; the town characters; Muff Potter's trial; and the scary chase through the cavern, with Tom and Becky being pursued by Injun Joe. And this is the first movie musical version; Mark Twain's novel has been set to tuneful, zesty, finger-snapping music. It's also the first film version to be photographed entirely on location in the Missouri countryside.

The action gets under way as Tom, heading for school, hears the sharp blast of the steamboat whistle. This loud blast not only heralds the arrival of the majestic *River Queen,* it also signals the start of the adventures of young Tom Sawyer.

One of the funniest scenes in the film has Tom turning a punishment into a profitable business venture. He talks his friends into paying him for the "privilege" of whitewashing his aunt's fence. And his fast talk works —for a while at least.

Later Tom and his friend Huck Finn, playing pirate, "sail off" to an island in the Mississippi and are thought by the townsfolk to have drowned. The boys finally return home—just in time to attend their own funeral service! Needless to say, everyone in Hannibal is overjoyed at the sight of the two lost boys.

One of the highlights of this new musical is the Fourth of July picnic. And what a happy affair it is, with three-legged races, sack races, find-your-shoe races, tug-of-war, and horseshoe pitching—all topped off with a fireworks display. Since a picnic wouldn't be much of a picnic without food, there's plenty of that, too—sandwiches, cakes, pies, and lots of punch to wash it all down.

This is a film for the whole family, just the right thing to brighten up a rainy Saturday afternoon or a dull evening. There's enough sentiment, thrills, and laughter to keep everyone's eyes glued to the screen. So have some fun and enjoy yourselves by visiting a timeless place in the American past. Once you've seen the film, you just might hurry home to experience the fun of reading the book!

Above: Muff Potter and his little friends sample the picnic goodies. Below: Fireworks mark the end of the Fourth of July festivities.

A SONG TO SING

Aiken Drum

Happily

O there came a man to our town, to our town, to our town; There came a man to our town, And his name was Aik-en Drum. And he play'd up-on a la - dle, a la - dle, a la - dle; And he play'd up-on a la - dle, And his name was Aik-en Drum.

2. And his coat was made of good roast beef, good roast beef, good roast beef;
   And his coat was made of good roast beef, and his name was Aiken Drum.
   And he play'd upon a ladle, etc.

3. And his hat was made of good cream cheese, good cream cheese, good cream cheese;
   And his hat was made of good cream cheese, and his name was Aiken Drum.
   And he play'd upon a ladle, etc.

4. And his vest was made of pancakes, pancakes, pancakes;
   And his vest was made of pancakes, and his name was Aiken Drum.
   And he play'd upon a ladle, etc.

5. And his buttons were made of cinnamon buns, cinnamon buns, cinnamon buns;
   And his buttons were made of cinnamon buns, and his name was Aiken Drum.
   And he play'd upon a ladle, etc.

6. And his pants were made of dribs and drabs, dribs and drabs, dribs and drabs;
   And his pants were made of dribs and drabs, and his name was Aiken Drum.
   And he play'd upon a ladle, etc.

The 1973 Summer Jam rock celebration at Watkins Glen, New York.

THE MUSIC SCENE

It was Woodstock all over again. However, 1973's mammoth rock celebration took place not in Woodstock, but in Watkins Glen, New York. Billed as the Summer Jam, the event drew 600,000 rock worshipers. Many of those who attended, however, thought the festival lacked the excitement and symbolic significance of Woodstock.

During 1973, a number of new superstars exploded on the rock scene. Bette Midler, Al Green, and Gary Glitter shook up the popular music world with their distinctive styles. There were also new disc hits by old masters. John Fogerty, formerly of the Creedence Clearwater Revival; Paul Simon; George Harrison; Paul McCartney; and Art Garfunkel showed the newcomers how to make the best seller charts.

Rock music also took to television in the form of two regular series. ABC's *In Concert* and NBC's *Midnight Special* both featured performances by some of the top-ranking rock artists. Many of the performers had seldom, if ever, been seen on the home screen.

But 1973, like the preceding year, was a twilight year for pop-rock music. Many people felt that it was on its way out. What was being offered in its place was something quite different. "Bizarre" and "decadent" seemed to be the best words to describe the new sound— and look.

The most pronounced trend suggesting decadence was something known by many names, among them Vaudeville Rock, Freak Rock, Glitter Rock, Rock Theater, and Rock 'n' Rouge. The chief performers of this "new rock" were Alice Cooper, David Bowie, Edgar Winter, Mott the Hoople, and the New York Dolls. Their acts used not only outlandish costumes—men even dressed as women and vice versa—but also outrageous props, all to provoke audiences to near frenzy. "Ugly is in," wrote one commentator. Many people felt that music had been forced into the background and that sight was becoming more important than sound.

NOSTALGIA IS STILL IN

When rock music was not running to bizarre extremes, it was looking to the past. Nostalgia was still around, and 1973 proved to be a boom year for old music in new packages. Particular emphasis was placed on the artists, sounds, and hits of the 1950's. The critically acclaimed film *American Graffiti* used these ingredients as background in a story about high school days of that time. And producer Richard Nader brought his rock 'n' roll revival to the screen in *Let the Good Times Roll*. In the film Bill Haley, Jerry Lee Lewis, Little Richard, Fats Domino, and other pioneers of rock 'n' roll appeared in contrasting images of today and yesterday. A two-record LP album based on the soundtrack of the film was a best seller, as was a Dick Clark 20th anniversary album, based on Clark's television special. Two albums of the Beatles, tracing their evolution from their rise to their demise, were giant sellers.

Broadway again joined in the nostalgia craze with *Grease*. This successful musical, which opened in 1972, reproduced the songs, dress, fads, and dances of the 1950's. The show was written by Warren Casey and Jim Jacobs, and inventively choreographed by Patricia Birch. The musical, described as a "compendium of the wails, wiggles, and witlessness of the fatuous fifties," captivated audiences on a cross-country tour while the Broadway production continued to play to full houses.

Some of the year's hit single records also had the sound of yesteryear. The lyrics of the Carpenters' "Yesterday Once More" echoed with the popular "sha-na-na" refrain of the 1950's. And Johnny Rivers dug back into the past and revived a novelty oldie, "Rockin' Pneumonia and Boogie Woogie Flu." Theresa Brewer re-recorded her 1950's hit "Music, Music, Music," and found a whole new generation of fans.

The high school dance scene from the hit Broadway musical *Grease*.

Neil Diamond's *Jonathan Livingston Seagull.*

Nostalgia wasn't limited to recordings, movies, or the Broadway stage. Suddenly there was a renewed interest among the young crowd in cheek-to-cheek dancing, with the dancers actually touching each other—something unheard-of during the 1960's. Dance studios reported a demand for instruction in the waltz and the fox-trot. Amusement parks and dance halls announced that the big-band sound of the Swing Era was back and holding its own against the rock combos. It was the 1940's all over again.

▶ FILM MUSIC

Hollywood beckoned, and many of the popular music writers and performers made the trek to the West Coast to work in the film industry. Jimmy Webb of "Up, Up and Away" fame wrote the musical score for *The Naked Ape.* Joe Raposo of *Sesame Street* renown composed the music for the film *Maurie,* and Bob Dylan wrote both the songs and background music for *Pat Garrett and Billy the Kid.* Multi-talented Neil Diamond suspended all concert appearances and recording dates for a year while he composed the musical score for *Jonathan Livingston Seagull*—the film version of the best-selling book.

Paul McCartney and Curtis Mayfield also contributed their talents to motion pictures. McCartney's score for the James Bond film *Live and Let Die* yielded a hit single in the title song. And Curtis Mayfield's *Super Fly* music not only produced a hit, but signaled the beginning of a solo career for Mayfield, who was formerly with The Impressions.

Not only did motion pictures make use of the talents of the music industry, they also contributed to it. Filmdom's John Wayne recorded a spoken album entitled *America, Why I Love Her.* The success of this album proved that you don't have to be a singer to have a hit record. Another hot item was the original sound track of the film *Deliverance.* It became a runaway best-selling album and produced a hit single, "Dueling Banjos."

▶ OTHER SOUNDS

While rock continued to flounder, searching for a positive direction, new things were happening on the music scene. For a while, a sensual, Jamaican-based rhythm known as *reggae* attracted the talents of songwriter-performers. Paul Simon, Paul McCartney, and the Rolling Stones are just a few of the artists who performed songs in the *reggae* rhythm. But apart from Johnny Nash's "I Can See Clearly Now," there was no sign that *reggae* would lead to the hoped-for rejuvenation of rock.

Country music was one of the most popular sounds that seemed to be filling the void left by rock music. Indeed, it took the nation by storm. From the largest cities to the smallest towns, radio stations blasted the country sound and record buyers couldn't seem to find enough country albums.

The biggest-selling artists are those who can sing pop as well as country, like Johnny Cash, Glen Campbell, and even Elvis Presley. But many others, with nothing more than a pure country sound, have won countless fans. Tammy Wynette, Jody Miller, Loretta Lynn, Tom T. Hall, Merle Haggard, and Buck Owens are all exponents of the "Nashville Sound." Their records, as well as those by other country singers, have won many awards

Charley Pride

Loretta Lynn

Johnny Cash and his wife, June Carter.

335

Grammy Award winner Donna Fargo.

The Divine Miss M—Bette Midler.

and racked up sales of $350,000,000 a year. Donna Fargo won the 1973 Grammy Award for Best Female Country Vocal Performance with her hit recording "Happiest Girl in the Whole U.S.A." The Grammy for Best Male Country Vocal Performance went to Charley Pride for his album *Charley Pride Sings Heart Songs*.

▶ NEW VOICES

Many new recording artists emerged in 1973. The Stylistics, soul sentimentalists from Philadelphia, scored a success, as did Rita Coolidge, a contemporary torch singer who used to be a background voice for many star groups. Bobby Womack was another newcomer to the pop charts. After writing hits like "Midnight Hour" for Wilson Pickett and "It's All Over Now" for the Rolling Stones, Womack became a performer.

Another newcomer, Al Green, was the biggest award winner of the year. He was named the number-one vocalist by all the major record publications, and his disc "Let's Stay Together" was the unanimous choice as the number-one rhythm and blues record of the year. A cross between the late Sam Cooke and Otis Redding, Green was named Rock and Roll Star of the Year by *Rolling Stone* magazine.

But perhaps the biggest sensation of all was Bette Midler, the most talked-about and written-about new artist of the year. Described as shorter than Mickey Rooney, louder than Ethel Merman, longer-nosed than Barbra Streisand, and more outrageous than Mick Jagger, the Divine Miss M—as she was dubbed on her first album—was hailed as an original and a trailblazer. A superb comedienne, the dynamic redhead dismissed her work as "trash with flash." But whether it was trash or just plain good music, she mesmerized her audiences with a concert program that covered songs from the 1930's to the 1970's. Some people felt that this was a triumph for nostalgia, but others thought it was a signpost pointing toward a future of middle-of-the-road music.

▶ ALL-TIME FAVORITES

The charts were crowded with established artists who scaled new heights or managed to sustain their popularity. Chicago, Three Dog Night, Led Zeppelin, Carley Simon, Elton John, Diana Ross, and Gladys Knight and the Pips all recorded hit albums.

John Fogerty left the Creedence Clearwater Revival and reappeared as a one-man band named the Blue Ridge Rangers. Chuck Berry scored the biggest hit single of his two-decade career with "My Ding-a-Ling," which proved to be an audience rouser in personal appearances. In the album *There Goes Rhymin' Simon,* Paul Simon demonstrated that he could really make it without Art Garfunkel. One of the cuts from the album, "Kodachrome," was one of the best-selling singles of the year.

After a few years on the inactive list, Art Garfunkel, not to be outdone by Simon, returned to the recording studio. The result was *Garfunkel, Angel Clare,* and the album's arrival was proclaimed by an immediate listing on the best-selling charts.

Before he was injured in a nearly crippling auto accident, Stevie Wonder displayed his remarkable creativity and versatility in *Music of My Mind.* He wrote all the songs in the

Simon . . .

. . . and Garfunkel.

Best-selling recording artist Helen Reddy.

album and played virtually all the instruments, including the electronic synthesizer.

Roberta Flack, who headed 1973's Grammy winners with her recording of Ewan MacColl's ballad "The First Time Ever I Saw Your Face," followed its success with "Killing Me Softly with His Song." Helen Reddy of "I Am Woman" fame merged straight pop with soft rock in *Long Hard Climb,* an album of interpretative, old-style singing.

Some of the established pop-and-jazz singers also did their share of merging pop with rock in new albums. Peggy Lee recorded *Norma Deloris Egstrom from Jamestown, North Dakota;* Nina Simone came through with *Emergency Ward!;* and Barbra Streisand hit the charts with *Barbra Joan Streisand.*

All in all, it was a year of mix-and-match. Even though the bizarre joined forces with country music and nostalgia in an attempt to fill the void left by the stagnation of rock music, no new music trend was established.

ARNOLD SHAW
Author, *The Rock Revolution* and
The Rockin' 50's

1973 GRAMMY AWARDS

Record of the Year	*The First Time Ever I Saw Your Face*	Roberta Flack, artist
Album of the Year	*The Concert for Bangla Desh*	George Harrison, Ravi Shankar, Bob Dylan, Leon Russell, Ringo Starr, Billy Preston, Eric Clapton, Klaus Voormann, artists
Song of the Year	*The First Time Ever I Saw Your Face*	Ewan MacColl, songwriter
New Artist of the Year		America
Pop Vocal Performance—female	*I Am Woman*	Helen Reddy, artist
Pop Vocal Performance—male	*Without You*	Nilsson, artist
Rhythm and Blues Vocal Performance—female	*Young, Gifted and Black*	Aretha Franklin, artist
Rhythm and Blues Vocal Performance—male	*Me and Mrs. Jones*	Billy Paul, artist
Country Vocal Performance—female	*Happiest Girl in the Whole U.S.A.*	Donna Fargo, artist
Country Vocal Performance—male	*Charley Pride Sings Heart Songs*	Charley Pride, artist
Original Score for a Motion Picture	*The Godfather*	Nino Rota, composer
Score from an Original Cast Show Album	*Don't Bother Me, I Can't Cope*	Micki Grant, composer
Classical Album	*Mahler: Symphony No. 8 in E-flat major*	Georg Solti conducting the Chicago Symphony Orchestra
Recording for Children	*The Electric Company*	

1973 AT A GLANCE

JANUARY

Early in the morning on January 23, flames and smoke began rising from the island of Heimaey, 10 miles off the southern coast of Iceland. The Helgafell volcano, quiet for thousands of years, had begun to erupt. Lava, hot ash, and stones rained on the island, causing the hurried evacuation of nearly 5,000 people. They were ferried out by sea and air. Most of the island's population lives in the town of Vestmannaeyjar. Heimaey, the most important of the Vestmannaeyjar group of volcanic islands, is located in rich fishing waters. Iceland relies on Heimaey for 12 percent of the fish the country exports. The volcanic eruption lasted more than 3 weeks, threatening Iceland's economy.

Flames and billowing smoke from the volcanic eruption off Iceland.

After 10 years of negotiations, Britain joined the European Economic Community (Common Market) on January 1. Denmark and Ireland also became members. Now nine Western European nations are working for political and economic unity.

The trial of Daniel Ellsberg and Anthony Russo began on January 3. In 1971 the two men had made public the Pentagon Papers, a secret study of United States involvement in Vietnam. The men were charged with theft of government property, conspiracy, and espionage.

On January 8, the trial of seven men involved in the Watergate case began. The men were charged with burglary, and with conspiracy to wiretap and bug the Democratic Party national headquarters located in the Watergate building complex in Washington, D.C. (On January 30, two of the defendants were found guilty. The five others had pleaded guilty at the beginning of the trial.)

The U.S. Government ended its mandatory wage and price controls on January 11. Phase 3 went into effect, relying on voluntary co-operation by businesses and labor organizations.

On January 20, Richard M. Nixon and Spiro T. Agnew were sworn in as president and vice-president of the United States for their second terms.

On January 22, Lyndon Baines Johnson, the 36th president of the United States, died at the age of 64. Johnson took over the presidency after the assassination of John F. Kennedy in November, 1963, and won a landslide victory in the 1964 elections. Because of extreme pressure from antiwar activists, Johnson announced a limited bombing halt in Vietnam in March, 1968, and then declared that he would not seek to run for a second term as president.

On January 27 a cease-fire went into effect in Vietnam. The peace agreement was formally signed in Paris by representatives of all four parties engaged in the war (the United States, South Vietnam, North Vietnam, and the Vietcong). The pact provided for a halt to the fighting, for the withdrawal of U.S. troops, and for the release of all prisoners of war. An international commission, composed of Poland, Hungary, Canada, and Indonesia, was to supervise the cease-fire.

The United States announced on January 27 that it had ended its military draft and would create all-volunteer armed forces. However, the Selective Service System will continue to register and classify young men in case the draft might be reinstated.

FEBRUARY

The long-awaited release of Vietnam War prisoners began on February 12. North Vietnam released 116 United States prisoners, and another 27 were freed by the Vietcong from prison camps in South Vietnam. The South Vietnamese released 250 enemy prisoners, and 140 of their troops held by the North Vietnamese were returned the same day. This was the first phase of prisoner exchanges called for by the peace agreement signed on January 27. Nearly one quarter of the total 587 United States prisoners were released in this exchange. Most of them had been imprisoned for at least 6 years.

U.S. war prisoners, freed by North Vietnam, arrive in the Philippines.

The International Olympic Committee voted on February 4 to hold the 1976 Winter Games in Innsbruck, Austria. (The 1976 Summer Games are to be held in Montreal, Canada.)

On February 5, the International Commission of Control and Supervision (consisting of Indonesia, Polish, Hungarian, and Canadian delegates) sent out peacekeeping teams to seven sites in South Vietnam. The teams were to check for cease-five violations of the Vietnam peace agreement.

The United States announced on February 12 that the dollar would be devalued by 10 percent, the second dollar devaluation in 14 months. (This means that U.S.-made products are cheaper overseas, and foreign products are more expensive in the United States.)

On February 15, the United States and Cuba signed an agreement to curb the hijacking of airplanes and boats between the two countries. A similar pact was signed by Canada and Cuba.

Pioneer 10 safely emerged on February 15 from its 7-month, 270,000,000-mile journey through the hazardous asteroid belt. The spacecraft, which was due to arrive in the vicinity of Jupiter in December, 1973, had been launched by the United States in 1972.

Scientists have concluded that the moon has been geologically dead for some 3,000,000,000 (billion) years. The findings, announced on February 15, were based on an analysis of the orange moon soil brought back to earth by the Apollo 17 astronauts.

U.S. Secretary of Agriculture Earl L. Butz stated on February 20 that the cost of food had risen between 2 and 3 percent in January, 1973, the highest monthly rise in about 25 years.

The Laotian Government and the Communist-led Pathet Lao signed a peace agreement on February 21, ending 20 years of war.

On February 21, Israeli fighter planes shot down a Libyan jetliner that was flying over the Israeli-occupied Sinai peninsula. Israel claimed that it had not realized the plane was carrying civilian passengers, and that the pilot of the plane had ignored instructions to land. Israel said it would compensate the families of the 106 persons who had been killed.

According to the 1973 United Nations *Demographic Yearbook,* Shanghai, China, has taken the place of Tokyo, Japan, as the world's most populous city, with 10,820,000 people.

MARCH

The newest London Bridge was officially opened on March 16 by Queen Elizabeth II. The six-lane bridge, which took 5½ years to complete, is the third known bridge to have stood on this site over the Thames River. The first bridge stood for almost six centuries, and is the subject of the children's song and game "London Bridge Is Falling Down." The second bridge, opened in 1831, was unable to handle the growing traffic and was dismantled in 1968. It was shipped to the United States in pieces, and later rebuilt in Arizona as part of an international tourist village.

Queen Elizabeth II arrives for the opening of the new London Bridge.

In Sudan, an Arab terrorist group took six hostages, demanding the release of Arab prisoners from several countries. On March 2, they killed one Belgian diplomat and two United States diplomats. The terrorists later surrendered, releasing the remaining hostages unharmed.

On March 2, representatives of 12 governments (Canada, China, France, Hungary, Indonesia, North Vietnam, Poland, South Vietnam, the Soviet Union, Britain, the United States, and the Vietcong) signed an agreement guaranteeing to respect and not interfere with the Vietnam peace agreement, which had been signed in January.

Pearl S. Buck, winner of the Nobel and Pulitzer prizes in literature, died at the age of 80 on March 6. She was the author of more than 85 books. Many of them, including *The Good Earth, Sons,* and *A House Divided,* are about the life and people of China, where she spent the first half of her life.

Liam Cosgrave was sworn in as prime minister of the Republic of Ireland on March 14. The victory of the Fine Gael and Labor parties coalition in parliamentary elections had ended 16 years of rule by the Fianna Fáil Party.

On March 15, David K. E. Bruce was appointed to head the United States liaison office in Peking. Bruce had served under seven presidents, and had been the U.S. ambassador to France, West Germany, and Britain.

On March 26, the National Aeronautics and Space Administration (NASA) announced that a huge balloon carrying two scientific packages had orbited the earth twice within 5 weeks. The balloon had been sent up as part of a study of cosmic rays and radiation effects. It was the first balloon to carry scientific instruments while orbiting the globe.

On March 29, the last of the 587 United States prisoners of war were released by the North Vietnamese. On the same day, the last United States troops were withdrawn from South Vietnam. Several thousand U.S. civilian technicians remained to assist the South Vietnamese armed services.

It was announced in March that the first successful radar probe of the planet Saturn had been completed earlier in the year. The probe had produced evidence that Saturn's rings are composed of chunks of unidentified solid matter. Until then, scientists had believed that the rings were made of dust, gas, and ice crystals.

APRIL

Pablo Picasso, "the master" of modern art, died on April 8 at the age of 91 at his home near Mougins, France. Picasso was born in Spain, but he refused to return to his homeland after the Spanish Civil War, in protest against the policies of the Spanish Government. His feelings about the war were expressed in his famous painting *Guernica,* which shows the inhumanity of war. Although best known as a painter, Picasso was also very famous for his sculpture, graphics, ceramics, and collages. He had a vivid imagination and worked in a great variety of styles. His cubist paintings, such as the *Three Musicians,* are among his most well known works. Other famous paintings include *Les Demoiselles d'Avignon* and *Mother and Child.*

The *Three Musicians*, one of Picasso's cubist paintings.

India began a 6-year project on April 1 to save its tigers from extinction. Supported by the World Wildlife Fund, this project will provide sanctuaries for Bengal tigers. Forest clearing and the illegal shooting of tigers for their valuable skins have greatly reduced India's tiger population. In less than 50 years, the number of tigers has decreased from 40,000 to 2,000.

A week-long meat boycott in the United States ended on April 7. Although there was no significant decline in prices, the leaders of the boycott urged further consumer action to fight against rising meat prices.

King Sobhuza II of Swaziland announced on April 12 that he had dissolved the Constitution and had assumed full control of the African nation. The Constitution had been in effect since 1968, when Swaziland gained its independence from Great Britain.

On April 13 the *chogyal,* or ruler, of the Indian protectorate of Sikkim announced that he agreed to give up much of his power and would allow a government to be popularly elected. Chogyal Palden Thondup Namgyal and his American-born wife, the former Hope Cooke, had been placed under guard in their palace on April 6, as 15,000 protesters demonstrated against their rule.

On April 23, Henry A. Kissinger, presidential adviser on national security affairs, proposed "a new Atlantic charter" between the United States and its European allies to strengthen economic, military, and diplomatic ties. He urged that Canada and Japan play important roles in the alliance.

L. Patrick Gray 3d resigned on April 27 as acting director of the Federal Bureau of Investigation, following reports that he had destroyed documents relating to the Watergate case. (On February 17, Gray had been nominated FBI director, and he was awaiting Senate confirmation.)

In a televised speech on April 30, President Richard Nixon told the American people that he accepted responsibility for the Watergate affair. But he said that he had not been personally involved in, and had had no knowledge of, the political espionage or the attempted cover-up.

As a consequence of the Watergate case, four top Nixon administration officials resigned on April 30. They were H. R. Haldeman, White House chief of staff; John D. Ehrlichman, chief domestic adviser; John W. Dean 3d, the presidential counsel; and Richard G. Kleindienst, attorney general. Secretary of Defense Elliot L. Richardson was nominated attorney general.

MAY

On May 8, members and supporters of the American Indian Movement ended their 70-day occupation of Wounded Knee on the Oglala Sioux Reservation in South Dakota. Two months earlier, the Indians had seized the town and held 11 residents hostage to dramatize their protest against the United States Government's policies toward Indians. After many unsuccessful attempts at negotiating, the government agreed to meet with Indian representatives to discuss charges of broken treaties and lost lands. (Wounded Knee was the site of an 1890 massacre in which the United States Cavalry killed more than 153 Indians, including women and children.)

The new way: a Sioux chief and a U.S. official meet at Wounded Knee. The old way: a Sioux brave keeps vigil beside stacked rifles.

On May 7, Israel marked its 25th year as an independent nation with day-long celebrations and a military parade in Jerusalem.

Former Attorney General John N. Mitchell and former Commerce Secretary Maurice H. Stans were among those indicted by a federal grand jury on May 10. They were charged with perjury, conspiracy to obstruct justice, and conspiracy to defraud the United States—in connection with their involvement in the 1972 campaign to re-elect President Richard M. Nixon.

James R. Schlesinger, director of the Central Intelligence Agency, was nominated secretary of defense by President Nixon on May 10 to succeed Elliot L. Richardson.

On May 11, United States District Court Judge W. Matthew Byrne dismissed all charges against Daniel Ellsberg and Anthony Russo, Jr., the defendants in the Pentagon Papers trial that began on January 3. The Judge cited the disclosure of government wiretapping of one or more telephone conversations of Ellsberg and also the White House–authorized break-in of the office of Ellsberg's psychiatrist as reasons for the dismissal.

Shortly after the United States launched its first orbiting space station, Skylab, on May 14, signals from the craft revealed that it was seriously damaged. Two solar wings that were to have opened in orbit did not unfold. The wings were meant to convert sunlight into electricity. A three-man crew went up in an Apollo spacecraft 11 days later. They successfully docked with Skylab and repaired enough of the damage to continue the mission.

On May 17, the Senate Select Committee on Presidential Campaign Activities opened hearings on the Watergate affair and related charges of wrongdoing during the 1972 presidential campaign.

Climaxing the first trip ever made to West Germany by a high-ranking Soviet leader, Communist Party General Secretary Leonid Brezhnev signed three agreements with West German Chancellor Willy Brandt on May 19. The areas involved were cultural co-operation, landing rights for airlines, and a 10-year economic agreement to increase trade between the two countries.

The Canadian Government announced on May 29 that it intended to withdraw its cease-fire observers from Vietnam. Canada based its decision to leave the International Commission of Control and Supervision on the belief that its observers were not being permitted to do their job properly by other members of the commission and by the parties involved in the peace agreement.

JUNE

During the month of June the price of gold soared to more than
$125 an ounce. The rising value of this metal has brought a new
gold rush to the western part of the United States. The area around
Cripple Creek, Colorado, is believed to contain the largest, most
concentrated mass of high-grade gold ore in the world. In 1890 it
was the site of one of the last American gold rushes. Over the
next 40 years, 20,000,000 ounces of gold were mined there. Once
a boomtown of 55,000 people, today Cripple Creek has only 500
inhabitants, and several decaying buildings. But with the renewed
interest in gold mining, at least two mining companies were to
begin operations. The rush has started in other states too. Nevada
now has five major working mines, and Alaska has two. Other
areas where people are panning for gold are the Black Hills of
South Dakota, and the mining areas of California, Montana, and
Oregon. Panning is the simplest method of separating gold in
stream deposits from silt, sand, and gravel.

A whole family pans for gold in Custer State Park, South Dakota.

On June 1, the military-led government of Greece abolished the monarchy and proclaimed the country a republic. George Papadopoulos became president. He had been premier since 1967, when a military junta had taken over the government. The deposed king, Constantine II, was living in exile in Rome.

On June 3, Israel released 56 Syrian and Lebanese prisoners of war in return for 3 captured Israeli pilots. It was the first exchange of prisoners across Israel's northern frontiers in 3½ years.

President Richard Nixon named former secretary of defense Melvin R. Laird as his chief domestic adviser on June 6. He also named General Alexander M. Haig, Jr., as the White House chief of staff.

Generalissimo Francisco Franco, Spain's leader since 1939, appointed Admiral Luis Carrero Blanco as premier on June 8.

West German Chancellor Willy Brandt ended a 5-day visit to Israel on June 11. It marked the first time a German head of government had visited Israel.

Juan D. Perón returned to Argentina on June 20. His supporters urged him to seek the presidency. (Perón had been president of Argentina from 1946 until his overthrow in 1955. In 1972 he had spent a month in that country, ending a 17-year exile.)

The first crew of Skylab astronauts returned to earth June 22, after living and working aboard the first U.S. orbiting space station. Their 28 days in space set a world space endurance record.

Eamon de Valera, the world's oldest living head of state, resigned as president of Ireland on June 24 at the age of 90. The new president, Erskine H. Childers, was sworn in the following day.

Soviet Communist Party leader Leonid I. Brezhnev ended a 10-day visit to the United States on June 25. In the course of talks at the White House and at San Clemente, California, Mr. Brezhnev and President Nixon signed agreements covering a variety of subjects. The most important was a declaration of principles to speed up the Strategic Arms Limitation Talks (SALT) and to complete a new arms limitation treaty by the end of 1974.

One of the longest total eclipses of the sun, lasting 7 hours and 14 minutes, occurred on June 30. The shadow, caused by the moon's passing between the sun and the earth, moved across northern Brazil, the Atlantic Ocean, and the full width of Africa, and ended in the Indian Ocean.

JULY

Queen Elizabeth II of England ended a 10-day visit to Canada on July 5. The Queen and Prince Philip had started their tour in Toronto, where they were welcomed at the airport by Governor-General Roland Michener and Prime Minister Pierre Elliott Trudeau. The Queen, smiling and chatting, strolled through the crowds waiting to greet her. This informal "walkabout" set the tone of her visit. She later made trips to Kingston and other Ontario cities, and visited Prince Edward Island to help celebrate its 100th anniversary as part of Canada. She traveled to Saskatchewan for the 100th anniversary of the Royal Canadian Mounted Police and to Calgary for the annual stampede (rodeo).

Queen Elizabeth II and Prince Philip in Saskatchewan for the 100th anniversary of the Royal Canadian Mounted Police.

On July 1, President Richard M. Nixon signed into law two bills bearing amendments to end the bombing of Cambodia by August 15. After that date, congressional approval would be needed for any United States military action in Indochina.

On July 8, Mariano Rumor was sworn in as premier of Italy, heading the 35th government since the end of World War II. A Christian Democrat, Rumor had been premier in three previous governments.

Three centuries of British rule ended for the Bahamas on July 10, when the island nation became independent. The flag—black, aquamarine, and gold—was raised for the first time. Prince Charles, representing the British crown, presented to the prime minister the independence order and the new constitution.

United States Secretary of Defense James R. Schlesinger admitted on July 16 that the United States had conducted secret bombings of Cambodia in 1969 and 1970.

Two Canadian officers of the International Commission of Control and Supervision were freed by the Vietcong on July 15. They had been held prisoner for 17 days.

Mohammed Zahir Shah, King of Afghanistan since 1933, was deposed by a coup on July 17. A republic was proclaimed, and martial law was put into effect.

Phase 4 of the United States economic control policy was put into effect on July 18. It required compliance with a system of price and wage controls similar to those of Phase 2. The plan ended the price freeze on food and on health care that had been in effect since June 13.

France conducted the first of a series of nuclear tests over the Mururoa atoll, in the South Pacific Ocean, on July 21. The tests were taking place despite an injunction by the United Nations International Court of Justice at The Hague, and protests by nations and individuals.

On July 26, President Richard M. Nixon refused to comply with subpoenas served on him by Special Prosecutor Archibald Cox and by the Senate Watergate Committee, commanding him to release the tapes and other documents related to the Watergate case. The fact of the existence of the tapes had been made public on July 16, during the Senate Watergate hearings. President Nixon's refusal to release the tapes forced the issue into the courts.

AUGUST

On August 28, a pre-dawn earthquake shook central Mexico from coast to coast, devastating many towns and villages. The disaster area was, at its closest point, 120 miles away from Mexico City. The disaster area included 24 cities, towns, and villages. Cracks 100 yards wide ran through several communities. Measuring 5.5 to 6.5 on the Richter scale, the earthquake was Mexico's worst disaster in modern history. More than 700 people were reported dead, and more than 1,000 were injured. The earthquake added thousands to those who had already been left homeless in central and eastern Mexico by the effects of a hurricane and a month of torrential rains. The rainy season was the worst one in 30 years.

A church in Puebla, Mexico, in ruins after the August earthquake.

Government leaders of 32 nations of the former British Empire met in Ottawa, Canada, in the Conference of Commonwealth Countries. The 9-day meeting ended on August 10. Important social, economic, and political issues were discussed.

On August 13, the Justice Department announced the creation of an Office of Indian Rights, for protecting the civil liberties of the American Indians.

On August 15, United States bombing of Cambodia ceased. This marked the official end of U.S. combat in the war in Southeast Asia, in which 46,000 Americans had died since 1961.

In an address to the nation on August 15, President Richard Nixon asserted once again that he had had no prior knowledge of the Watergate break-in, and that he had been unaware of subsequent efforts to cover it up. He also defended his refusal to release the tape recordings of his meetings and telephone conversations relating to the Watergate affair. He urged that the Watergate case be left to the courts. In the course of a news conference on August 22, President Nixon's first in 5 months, he said that he would not resign.

On August 20 it was announced that a new rabies vaccine had been developed. Since the vaccine is strong enough to be effective with just one injection, rather than with the painful 14 to 21 shots usually needed, the number of deaths from rabies is expected to be greatly reduced.

On August 22, President Nixon announced the resignation of Secretary of State William P. Rogers. Henry A. Kissinger, the White House adviser on national security, was nominated to succeed him.

India and Pakistan signed an agreement on August 28 clearing the way for the release of most of the 90,000 Pakistani prisoners held in India as a result of the December, 1971, war.

On August 29, Judge John J. Sirica, chief judge of the U.S. district court, ordered that President Nixon make the tape recordings of White House conversations involving the Watergate affair available to him. The President replied that he would not comply with the court order, and would appeal the order.

August food prices in the United States made the biggest rise for a single month in 27 years. In Canada the largest monthly rise in living costs in more than 22 years occurred in August; the sharpest increase was in food prices.

SEPTEMBER

President Salvador Allende Gossens of Chile died in a violent seizure of power by Chile's armed forces on September 11, 1973. He had refused to surrender to a four-man military junta, led by army chief General Augusto Pinochet Ugarte. A fierce attack on the presidential palace took place, and Allende lost his life. It was unclear whether he had taken his own life or had been killed in the coup. Allende was the first Marxist to become the democratically elected head of a Latin-American country. After his inauguration in 1970, Allende had launched a program of sweeping reforms. This included nationalizing private businesses and land. The aim was to redistribute the country's wealth. The middle class reacted against this program, and took part in a series of massive strikes. The strikes and other severe economic problems had resulted in demands for Allende's resignation.

Presidential palace in Chile under attack in violent September coup.

On September 1, the Canadian Parliament passed emergency legislation ordering 56,000 railroad employees to end a 9-day rail strike. The nationwide strike had caused the shutdown of factories and had stopped the shipment of grain from farms for export. The day after Parliament's action the railroads were back in operation.

On September 12, the British Government announced its decision to construct a tunnel under the English Channel. The proposed 32-mile, $2,000,000,000 "chunnel," to be completed in 1980, is to run from Cheriton, England, to Fréthun, France. The French Government had approved the project earlier.

King Gustaf VI Adolf, 90-year-old monarch of Sweden, died on September 15. He had reigned nearly 23 years. His 27-year-old grandson was enthroned as King Carl XVI Gustaf.

East Germany, West Germany, and the Bahamas were admitted to membership in the United Nations, September 18, bringing the number of member nations to 135.

Bobby Riggs, a 55-year-old tennis player, set out to prove that a man plays better tennis than a woman does. But he picked the wrong woman. Five-time Wimbledon winner Billie Jean King, 29, beat him in a match in Houston, Texas, on September 20.

Juan D. Perón was elected president of Argentina for the third time, on September 23. His third wife and running mate, Isabel, was elected vice-president.

The three-man crew of Skylab III splashed down safely in the Pacific, September 25, after a record-setting 59-day space flight.

On September 29, two Soviet cosmonauts completed a 2-day test flight in a Soyuz spacecraft. Their mission was the first successful manned Soviet space flight in over 2 years.

Floods raged in southeastern Pakistan from mid-August into early September. Deaths were estimated in the thousands.

An outbreak of cholera, traced to mussels from polluted waters, occurred in Naples and Bari, Italy, late in the summer. It was the first cholera epidemic in Italy since 1911. By the middle of September more than 20 deaths had been reported.

Bicycles are the most hazardous consumer product, the Consumer Product Safety Commission, a new federal agency, reported late in September. Among the hazards of bicycles are mechanical failures and riders' catching their feet in spokes or chains.

OCTOBER

Yom Kippur is the most solemn of all Jewish religious holidays. On that day—it fell on October 6 in 1973—the prayers of the devout in Israel were interrupted by news that war had broken out. For the fourth time since May 14, 1948, when Israel became a state, it was at war with its Arab neighbors. Fighting broke out on two fronts at once. Egyptian forces crossed from the western bank of the Suez Canal to the Israeli-held eastern bank, and in the north Syrian forces struck at the Israeli-occupied Golan Heights. Fighting was fierce on both fronts, and losses of life were high. Jordan entered the war in its second week, joining Iraq and a number of other Arab states. A dramatic turn came when thousands of Israeli troops crossed to the western bank of the Suez Canal, trapping an Egyptian army on the eastern bank. In the north, Israelis held Syrians off the Golan Heights and pushed toward Damascus. The United States resupplied Israel, and the Soviet Union resupplied the Arab nations, but both major powers worked at the same time to achieve a cease-fire. On October 22 the United Nations Security Council approved a cease-fire in place. On October 25 the United States reacted to what it felt was the possibility that the Soviet Union was planning to send troops to the Middle East. The United States placed its forces around the world on a "precautionary alert." The crisis eased as the United Nations approved a resolution to establish a UN peacekeeping force in the area. By the end of October an uneasy cease-fire was in effect.

Left: Egyptian troops east of the Suez Canal. Right: Israeli troops in Syria.

Left: Spiro T. Agnew resigns. Right: Gerald R. Ford is nominated.

"I hereby resign the Office of Vice President of the United States, effective immediately." With these words, on October 10, Spiro T. Agnew gave up the nation's second highest office. His formal resignation was delivered, as the law requires, to the secretary of state. Agnew became the second vice-president in the history of the United States to resign. (The first was John C. Calhoun in 1832.) The drama that led to this startling climax had begun long before. Early in 1973 evidence was presented to a Baltimore grand jury accusing certain businessmen of paying kickbacks to Baltimore County officials. Agnew was the county executive of Baltimore County before he became Maryland's governor in 1967. The public had no idea of the investigation until early August, 1973, when the Vice-President made an announcement. He said that he was under investigation for possible violations of criminal statutes, but "I am innocent of any wrongdoing." A legal storm raged around Agnew for the next 2 months. He said he would not resign even if indicted. However, on October 10, Vice-President Agnew submitted his resignation. A short time later he appeared in Baltimore before Judge Walter E. Hoffman and pleaded no contest to income tax evasion. (No contest amounts to a plea of guilty.) The Justice Department, in return, said it would drop all the other charges, but would make public a summary of the evidence against him. According to the evidence, businesses had made payments to Agnew as county executive, as governor, and as vice-president. With Agnew's resignation House Speaker Carl Albert of Oklahoma became next in line for the presidency. On October 12, President Richard Nixon nominated House Minority Leader Gerald R. Ford of Michigan to be the 40th vice-president.

The words "Watergate" and "the tapes" were in the headlines in October as they had been for many months. On October 12 the U.S. Court of Appeals decided that the President must turn over to Judge John J. Sirica, of the U.S. District Court, White House tape recordings that might shed light on the Watergate case. (The tapes in question were recordings of conversations held by President Richard Nixon and certain aides between June 20, 1972, shortly after the Watergate break-in, and April 15, 1973.) On October 19 the President said he would not obey the court ruling nor appeal to the Supreme Court. He would give Judge Sirica and the Senate Watergate committee summaries of the contents of the tapes, verified by Senator John C. Stennis (D-Miss.). Watergate Special Prosecutor Archibald Cox said that this solution was not acceptable to him. On October 20, President Nixon directed Attorney General Elliot L. Richardson to dismiss Cox. Richardson refused and resigned. Deputy Attorney General William D. Ruckelshaus also refused to fire Cox, and he was dismissed. Solicitor General Robert H. Bork became acting attorney general and dismissed Cox. During the next few days there was talk in Congress and among the public of impeachment. But on October 23 the President made a surprise move. He informed Judge Sirica that he would give him the tapes. On October 31, however, in one more surprise twist, Judge Sirica was told that two of the White House conversations most critical for the investigation had never been recorded at all; these tapes did not exist.

Canada announced on October 5 that it had arranged a 3-year, $1,000,000,000 sale of wheat to China.

On October 5, Quebec-born Jules Léger was named to succeed Roland Michener as Canada's governor-general upon Michener's retirement in January, 1974.

On October 8 Spyros Markezinis was sworn in as Greece's first civilian premier since the military coup of 1967.

On October 10, Canada's Prime Minister Pierre Elliott Trudeau and Mrs. Trudeau arrived in China for a 7-day official visit, the first by a Canadian prime minister. On October 13 in Peking, Trudeau signed a trade agreement with Premier Chou En-lai.

On October 10 Cape Kennedy, the Florida launching site for U.S. space missions, resumed its original name: Cape Canaveral. It had been named Cape Kennedy after the assassination of President John F. Kennedy in 1963.

On October 14 Sanya Dharmasakti, a university dean, became Thailand's first civilian premier since 1953. Premier Thanom

Kittikachorn and his military government resigned after students demonstrated for a return to constitutional government.

On October 16, Maynard Jackson, 35, was elected mayor of Atlanta, Georgia. Jackson, a lawyer, thus became the first black mayor of a leading southern city.

On October 17, representatives of Arab oil-producing states meeting in Kuwait agreed to cut production of oil and reduce their exports of oil to the United States and to other nations supporting Israel in the Middle East conflict. The cutbacks would continue until Israel gave up the lands it had occupied since 1967.

Pablo Casals, 96, the most renowned cellist of his time, a celebrated conductor and composer, and a humanitarian, died on October 22 in Río Piedras, Puerto Rico. The Spanish-born musician had exiled himself from Spain upon Franco's rise to power in 1939.

On October 28, Justice William O. Douglas earned the distinction of having served on the U.S. Supreme Court longer than any other justice in history—34 years and 196 days.

Parts of an ancient city named Oplonti had been unearthed about 10 miles north of Pompeii, Italy, it was announced in late October. The city, like Pompeii, was buried by the eruption of the volcano Vesuvius in A.D. 79. A large, almost perfectly preserved villa has been excavated at the site.

THE 1973 NOBEL PRIZES

Chemistry: Ernst Otto Fischer of West Germany and Geoffrey Wilkinson of Britain, for studies of the merging of organic and metallic atoms.

Economic Science: Wassily Leontief, Russian-born Harvard economist, for the "input-output" system of economic analysis.

Literature: Patrick White of Australia, for his novels.

Peace: Henry A. Kissinger of the United States and Le Duc Tho of North Vietnam, for negotiating the Vietnam peace agreement.

Physics: Leo Esaki of Japan (working in the United States), Ivar Giaever of the United States, and Brian David Josephson of Britain, for research in the behavior of electrons in solids.

Physiology or Medicine: Karl von Frisch of West Germany, Konrad Lorenz of Austria, and Nikolaas Tinbergen of Britain, for pioneer work in ethology, the study of animal behavior.

NOVEMBER

The wedding of Princess Anne, 23-year-old daughter of Queen Elizabeth II and Prince Philip, to Captain Mark Phillips, 25, of The Queen's Dragoon Guards, took place on November 14 in Westminster Abbey. The bride wore a high-necked ivory silk princess-style dress, and the bridegroom was in scarlet and gold military uniform. Dr. Michael Ramsey, the Archbishop of Canterbury, performed the wedding ceremony, which an estimated 500,000,000 people watched on television. After a wedding breakfast at Buckingham Palace, the couple left for a Caribbean honeymoon. On their return, Captain Phillips was to take up his post as an instructor at Sandhurst, the Royal Military Academy.

Princess Anne and Captain Mark Phillips leave Westminster Abbey after their wedding ceremony.

On November 1, President Richard M. Nixon nominated Senator William B. Saxbe (R-Ohio) to succeed Elliot L. Richardson as attorney general. On the same day, Leon Jaworski, a lawyer from Houston, Texas, and a Democrat, was appointed to succeed Archibald Cox as special Watergate prosecutor.

Mariner 10, an unmanned spacecraft, was launched from Cape Canaveral on November 3 on a journey past Venus and Mercury.

On November 7, two thirds of those present and voting in the House of Representatives and in the Senate overrode the presidential veto of a war-powers resolution. The measure limits the president's power to commit armed forces to hostilities abroad without the approval of Congress.

On November 11, at Kilometer 101 on the road between Cairo and Suez city, representatives of Egypt and Israel signed a cease-fire agreement. On November 15 Egypt and Israel began the exchange of prisoners of war agreed to in the cease-fire. The exchange was expected to return about 238 Israelis and 8,400 Egyptians.

On November 16, the third and final three-man crew went up from Cape Canaveral to dock with Skylab, the U.S. space station.

On November 16, President Richard M. Nixon signed into law a bill authorizing the building of a 789-mile pipeline across Alaska from the North Slope to the warmwater port of Valdez. It was predicted that the pipeline might deliver oil by late 1977.

On November 25, Greek President George Papadopoulos, who had seized power in 1967, was removed in a military coup. He was replaced by Lieutenant General Phaidon Gizikis. Premier Spyros Markezinis, appointed in October, was dismissed.

On November 25, President Richard M. Nixon outlined unusual peacetime measures to reduce the nation's energy consumption. They included a 15 percent cut in deliveries of heating oil to homes, a 15 percent cut in gasoline production, and reduction of the speed limit for cars.

On November 26 the Senate committee investigating presidential campaign activities ended its 1973 hearings.

Arab cutbacks in oil shipments to nations supporting Israel began to cause serious problems. On November 4 the Netherlands became the first European nation to impose a ban on Sunday driving. To save gas, the Dutch, young and old, took to their bicycles. On November 16 the Japanese Government announced that industry would have to cut oil and electricity use by 10 percent.

DECEMBER

On December 3, Pioneer 10, an unmanned American spacecraft, flew within 81,000 miles of Jupiter, passing safely through the belts of intense radiation about that planet. Pioneer sent back dazzling color pictures and volumes of scientific data. The pictures showed Jupiter's brilliant bands, caused by gases flowing at different speeds, and its unexplained Red Spot, some 30,000 miles long and 7,000 miles wide. Pioneer, launched on March 2, 1972, had journeyed about 620,000,000 miles before it reached Jupiter. After a week's flyby of the planet, Pioneer continued its journey through space. By 1980, if the craft continues to function, Pioneer will become the first spacecraft ever to leave the solar system.

Closeup photo of Jupiter shows the Red Spot (*left*); the shadow of Io, one of Jupiter's moons (*right*); and atmospheric bands.

On December 1, David Ben-Gurion, one of the founders of Israel and its first prime minister, died at the age of 87 in Tel Aviv.

December 2 was the first gasless Sunday in the United States, with more than 90 percent of the service stations closed. On December 5, Norway became the eighth European country to ban Sunday driving.

On December 6, Gerald R. Ford was sworn in as the 40th vice-president of the United States.

On December 9, Carlos Andrés Pérez was elected president of Venezuela. His 5-year term was to start in March, 1974.

On December 11, Governor Nelson A. Rockefeller of New York, a Republican, resigned after 15 years in office. Lieutenant Governor Malcolm Wilson succeeded him.

On December 13, Prime Minister Edward Heath announced electricity cuts that would limit Britain's workweek to 3 days. Most of Britain's generators are run by coal, and work slowdowns in the coal industry have drastically cut supplies.

On December 15, President Richard M. Nixon signed a bill placing most of the United States on year-round daylight saving time for two years, starting January 6, 1974.

On December 18 a group of Arab terrorists attacked a U.S. airliner in a Rome airport, killing 31 people. The band then hijacked a West German airliner and flew with hostages to Athens, Greece, where one of the hostages was killed. The hijackers finally landed in Kuwait, where they gave up their hostages and surrendered.

On December 20, Premier Luis Carrero Blanco of Spain was killed when assassins bombed his car in Madrid.

On December 21 a Middle East peace conference, the first between Arabs and Israelis, opened in Geneva, Switzerland. The six participants were Egypt, Jordan, Israel, the Soviet Union, the United States, and the United Nations. Syria boycotted the meeting.

On December 25 the wife of Canadian Prime Minister Pierre Elliott Trudeau gave birth to their second child, Alexandre Emanuel. Their first son had also been born on Christmas day.

On December 26 the Soviet spacecraft Soyuz 13 landed safely in Kazakhstan with its 2-man crew after an 8-day mission.

INTERNATIONAL STATISTICAL SUPPLEMENT
(as of December 31, 1973)

NATIONS OF THE WORLD

NATION	CAPITAL	AREA (in sq. mi.)	POPULATION (estimate)	GOVERNMENT
Afghanistan	Kabul	250,000	18,000,000	Mohammed Daud Khan—president
Albania	Tirana	11,100	2,300,000	Enver Hoxha—communist party secretary Mehmet Shehu—premier
Algeria	Algiers	919,593	15,500,000	Houari Boumédienne—president
Argentina	Buenos Aires	1,072,158	24,000,000	Juan D. Perón—president
Australia	Canberra	2,967,909	13,200,000	Gough Whitlam—prime minister
Austria	Vienna	32,374	7,500,000	Bruno Kreisky—chancellor Franz Jonas—president
Bahamas	Nassau	5,380	190,000	Lynden O. Pindling—prime minister
Bahrain	Manama	240	225,000	Isa bin Sulman al-Khalifa—head of government
Bangladesh	Dacca	55,126	75,000,000	Mohammed Ullah—acting president Mujibur Rahman—prime minister
Barbados	Bridgetown	166	240,000	Errol W. Barrow—prime minister
Belgium	Brussels	11,781	9,800,000	Baudouin I—king Edmond Leburton—premier
Bhutan	Thimbu	18,000	900,000	Jigme Singye Wangchuk—king
Bolivia	La Paz	424,163	5,200,000	Hugo Banzer Suárez—president
Botswana	Gaborone	231,804	710,000	Sir Seretse Khama—president
Brazil	Brasília	3,286,478	99,000,000	Emílio Garrastazú Médici—president
Bulgaria	Sofia	42,823	8,600,000	Todor Zhivkov—communist party secretary Stanko Todorov—premier
Burma	Rangoon	261,789	28,000,000	Ne Win—prime minister
Burundi	Bujumbura	10,747	3,400,000	Michel Micombero—president
Cambodia (Khmer Republic)	Pnompenh	69,898	7,000,000	Lon Nol—president Long Boret—premier
Cameroon	Yaoundé	183,569	5,900,000	Ahmadou Ahidjo—president
Canada	Ottawa	3,851,809	23,000,000	Pierre Elliott Trudeau—prime minister
Central African Republic	Bangui	240,535	1,700,000	Jean Bedel Bokassa—president
Ceylon (Sri Lanka)	Colombo	25,332	13,100,000	William Gopallawa—president Sirimavo Bandaranaike—premier

NATION	CAPITAL	AREA (in sq. mi.)	POPULATION (estimate)	GOVERNMENT
Chad	Fort-Lamy	495,754	3,800,000	Ngarta Tombalbaye—president
Chile	Santiago	292,259	10,100,000	Augusto Pinochet Ugarte—president
China (Communist)	Peking	3,705,396	800,000,000	Mao Tse-tung—chairman Chou En-lai—premier
China (Nationalist)	Taipei	13,885	15,000,000	Chiang Kai-shek—president Chiang Ching-kuo—premier
Colombia	Bogotá	439,736	23,000,000	Misael Pastrana Borrero—president
Congo	Brazzaville	132,047	1,000,000	Marien Ngouabi—president Henri Lopès—prime minister
Costa Rica	San José	19,575	1,900,000	José Figueres Ferrer—president
Cuba	Havana	44,218	8,800,000	Osvaldo Dorticós Torrado—president Fidel Castro—premier
Cyprus	Nicosia	3,572	650,000	Archbishop Makarios III—president
Czechoslovakia	Prague	49,370	14,600,000	Gustáv Husák—communist party secretary Ludvík Svoboda—president Lubomír Štrougal—premier
Dahomey	Porto-Novo	43,483	2,900,000	Mathieu Kerekou—president
Denmark	Copenhagen	16,629	5,100,000	Margrethe II—queen Poul Hartling—premier
Dominican Republic	Santo Domingo	18,816	4,400,000	Joaquín Balaguer—president
Ecuador	Quito	109,483	6,700,000	Guillermo Rodríguez Lara—president
Egypt	Cairo	386,660	35,000,000	Anwar el-Sadat—president
El Salvador	San Salvador	8,260	3,800,000	Arturo Armando Molina—president
Equatorial Guinea	Malabo	10,830	300,000	Francisco Macías Nguema—president
Ethiopia	Addis Ababa	471,777	26,000,000	Haile Selassie I—emperor
Fiji	Suva	7,055	550,000	Ratu Sir Kamisese Mara—prime minister
Finland	Helsinki	130,120	4,700,000	Urho K. Kekkonen—president Kalevi Sorsa—premier
France	Paris	211,207	52,000,000	Georges Pompidou—president Pierre Messmer—premier
Gabon	Libreville	103,346	500,000	Albert B. Bongo—president
Gambia	Banjul	4,361	390,000	Sir Dauda K. Jawara—president
Germany (East)	East Berlin	41,610	17,100,000	Erich Honecker—communist party secretary Horst Sindermann—premier
Germany (West)	Bonn	95,743	61,900,000	Gustav Heinemann—president Willy Brandt—chancellor
Ghana	Accra	92,099	9,100,000	Ignatius K. Acheampong—head of government

NATION	CAPITAL	AREA (in sq. mi.)	POPULATION (estimate)	GOVERNMENT
Greece	Athens	50,944	9,000,000	Phaidon Gizikis—president Adamantios Androutsopoulos—premier
Guatemala	Guatemala City	42,042	5,500,000	Carlos Arana Osorio—president
Guinea	Conakry	94,926	4,100,000	Sékou Touré—president Lansana Beavogui—premier
Guyana	Georgetown	83,000	800,000	Arthur Chung—president Forbes Burnham—prime minister
Haiti	Port-au-Prince	10,714	5,100,000	Jean-Claude Duvalier—president
Honduras	Tegucigalpa	43,277	2,700,000	Oswaldo López Arellano—president
Hungary	Budapest	35,919	10,500,000	János Kádár—communist party secretary Jenő Fock—premier
Iceland	Reykjavik	39,768	210,000	Kristján Eldjárn—president Ólafur Jóhannesson—prime minister
India	New Delhi	1,266,598	565,000,000	V. V. Giri—president Indira Gandhi—prime minister
Indonesia	Jakarta	575,894	125,000,000	Suharto—president
Iran	Teheran	636,294	31,000,000	Mohammed Reza Pahlavi—shah Amir Abbas Hoveida—premier
Iraq	Baghdad	167,925	10,100,000	Ahmed Hassan al-Bakr—president
Ireland	Dublin	27,136	3,000,000	Erskine H. Childers—president Liam Cosgrave—prime minister
Israel	Jerusalem	7,992	3,200,000	Ephraim Katzir—president Golda Meir—prime minister
Italy	Rome	116,303	54,800,000	Giovanni Leone—president Mariano Rumor—premier
Ivory Coast	Abidjan	124,503	4,600,000	Félix Houphouët-Boigny—president
Jamaica	Kingston	4,232	2,000,000	Michael N. Manley—prime minister
Japan	Tokyo	142,886	108,000,000	Hirohito—emperor Kakuei Tanaka—prime minister
Jordan	Amman	37,738	2,500,000	Hussein I—king Zaid al-Rifai—premier
Kenya	Nairobi	224,959	12,100,000	Jomo Kenyatta—president
Korea (North)	Pyongyang	46,540	14,700,000	Kim Il Sung—president Kim Il—premier
Korea (South)	Seoul	38,922	32,900,000	Chung Hee Park—president Kim Jong Pil—premier
Kuwait	Kuwait	6,880	1,000,000	Sabah al-Salim al-Sabah—head of state Jabir al-Ahmad al-Jabir—prime minister
Laos	Vientiane	91,429	3,200,000	Savang Vatthana—king Souvanna Phouma—premier

NATION	CAPITAL	AREA (in sq. mi.)	POPULATION (estimate)	GOVERNMENT
Lebanon	Beirut	4,015	3,000,000	Suleiman Franjieh—president Takieddin Solh—premier
Lesotho	Maseru	11,720	1,000,000	Moshoeshoe II—king Leabua Jonathan—prime minister
Liberia	Monrovia	43,000	1,600,000	William R. Tolbert—president
Libya	Tripoli	679,360	2,100,000	Muammar el-Qaddafi—president Abdul Salam Jallud—premier
Liechtenstein	Vaduz	61	21,000	Francis Joseph II—prince
Luxembourg	Luxembourg	999	350,000	Jean—grand duke Pierre Werner—premier
Malagasy Republic	Tananarive	226,657	7,000,000	Gabriel Ramanantsoa—head of government
Malawi	Zomba	45,747	4,700,000	H. Kamuzu Banda—president
Malaysia	Kuala Lumpur	127,316	11,000,000	Abdul Halim Muazzam—paramount ruler Tun Abdul Razak—prime minister
Maldives	Male	115	112,000	Ibrahim Nasir—president
Mali	Bamako	478,765	5,400,000	Moussa Traoré—president
Malta	Valletta	122	325,000	Dom Mintoff—prime minister
Mauritania	Nouakchott	397,954	1,300,000	Moktar O. Daddah—president
Mauritius	Port Louis	720	860,000	Sir Seewoosagur Ramgoolam—prime minister
Mexico	Mexico City	761,602	52,700,000	Luis Echeverría Álvarez—president
Monaco	Monaco-Ville	0.4	24,000	Rainier III—prince
Mongolia	Ulan Bator	604,248	1,400,000	Yumzhagiyn Tsedenbal—communist party secretary
Morocco	Rabat	172,997	16,000,000	Hassan II—king Ahmed Osman—premier
Nauru		8	7,000	Hammer DeRoburt—president
Nepal	Katmandu	54,362	11,500,000	Birendra Bir Bikram Shah Deva—king Nagendra Prashad Rijal—prime minister
Netherlands	Amsterdam	15,770	13,500,000	Juliana—queen Joop den Uyl—premier
New Zealand	Wellington	103,736	3,000,000	Norman Eric Kirk—prime minister
Nicaragua	Managua	50,193	2,000,000	headed by a triumvirate
Niger	Niamey	489,190	4,400,000	Hamani Diori—president
Nigeria	Lagos	356,668	58,000,000	Yakubu Gowon—head of government
Norway	Oslo	125,181	4,000,000	Olav V—king Trygve Bratteli—prime minister
Oman	Muscat	82,030	700,000	Qabus ibn Said—sultan

NATION	CAPITAL	AREA (in sq. mi.)	POPULATION (estimate)	GOVERNMENT
Pakistan	Islamabad	310,403	65,000,000	Chaudri Fazal Elahi—president Zulfikar Ali Bhutto—prime minister
Panama	Panama City	29,205	1,600,000	Omar Torrijos Herrera—head of government
Paraguay	Asunción	157,047	2,600,000	Alfredo Stroessner—president
Peru	Lima	496,223	14,500,000	Juan Velasco Alvarado—president
Philippines	Quezon City	115,830	40,000,000	Ferdinand E. Marcos—president
Poland	Warsaw	120,724	33,400,000	Edward Gierek—communist party secretary Piotr Jaroszewicz—premier
Portugal	Lisbon	35,553	8,600,000	Americo Thomaz—president Marcello Caetano—premier
Qatar	Doha	8,500	84,000	Khalifa bin Hamad al-Thani—head of government
Rhodesia	Salisbury	150,803	5,700,000	Clifford Dupont—president Ian D. Smith—prime minister
Rumania	Bucharest	91,699	20,800,000	Nicolae Ceauşescu—communist party secretary Ion Gheorghe Maurer—premier
Rwanda	Kigali	10,169	3,900,000	Juvénal Habyalimana—president
Saudi Arabia	Riyadh	829,997	8,200,000	Faisal ibn Abdul Aziz—king
Senegal	Dakar	75,750	4,200,000	Léopold Senghor—president Abdou Diouf—prime minister
Sierra Leone	Freetown	27,699	2,700,000	Siaka P. Stevens—president Sorie I. Koroma—prime minister
Singapore	Singapore	224	2,200,000	Benjamin H. Sheares—president Lee Kuan Yew—prime minister
Somalia	Mogadishu	246,200	3,000,000	Mohammed Siad Barre—head of government
South Africa	Pretoria Cape Town	471,444	23,000,000	J. J. Fouché—president Balthazar J. Vorster—prime minister
Spain	Madrid	194,897	34,500,000	Francisco Franco—head of state Carlos Arias Navarro—premier
Sudan	Khartoum	967,497	16,900,000	Gaafar al-Numeiry—president
Swaziland	Mbabane	6,704	500,000	Sobhuza II—king
Sweden	Stockholm	173,649	8,200,000	Carl XVI Gustaf—king Olof Palme—prime minister
Switzerland	Bern	15,941	6,500,000	Ernst Brugger—president
Syria	Damascus	71,498	6,900,000	Hafez al-Assad—president Mahmoud al-Ayubi—premier
Tanzania	Dar es Salaam	364,898	14,400,000	Julius K. Nyerere—president

NATION	CAPITAL	AREA (in sq. mi.)	POPULATION (estimate)	GOVERNMENT
Thailand	Bangkok	198,456	36,300,000	Bhumibol Adulyadej—king Sanya Dharmasakti—premier
Togo	Lomé	21,622	2,200,000	Étienne Eyadema—president
Tonga	Nuku'alofa	270	90,000	Taufa'ahau Tupou IV—king Prince Tu'ipelehake—prime minister
Trinidad & Tobago	Port of Spain	1,980	1,100,000	Eric Williams—prime minister
Tunisia	Tunis	63,170	5,500,000	Habib Bourguiba—president Hedi Nouira—prime minister
Turkey	Ankara	301,381	37,100,000	Fahri Korutürk—president Naim Talu—premier
Uganda	Kampala	91,134	10,500,000	Idi Amin—president
U.S.S.R.	Moscow	8,649,512	248,000,000	Leonid I. Brezhnev—communist party secretary Aleksei N. Kosygin—premier Nikolai V. Podgorny—president of presidium
United Arab Emirates	Abu Dhabi	32,278	200,000	Zayd bin Sultan—president
United Kingdom	London	94,216	56,000,000	Elizabeth II—queen Edward Heath—prime minister
United States	Washington, D.C.	3,615,123	211,000,000	Richard M. Nixon—president Gerald R. Ford—vice-president
Upper Volta	Ouagadougou	105,869	5,700,000	Sangoulé Lamizana—president Gérard Kango Ouedraogo—prime minister
Uruguay	Montevideo	68,536	3,000,000	Juan M. Bordaberry—president
Venezuela	Caracas	352,143	11,000,000	Rafael Caldera—president
Vietnam (North)	Hanoi	61,294	22,100,000	Le Duan—communist party secretary Ton Duc Thang—president Pham Van Dong—premier
Vietnam (South)	Saigon	67,108	18,900,000	Nguyen Van Thieu—president Tran Thien Khiem—premier
Western Samoa	Apia	1,097	150,000	Malietoa Tanumafili II—head of state Tupua Tamasese Lealofi IV—prime minister
Yemen (Aden)	Madinat al-Shaab	112,000	1,600,000	Salem Ali Rubaya—head of state Ali Nasir Mohammed—prime minister
Yemen (Sana)	Sana	75,290	6,100,000	Abdul Rahman al-Iryani—head of state Abdullah al-Hagri—premier
Yugoslavia	Belgrade	98,766	21,000,000	Josip Broz Tito—president Dzemal Bijedić—premier
Zaïre	Kinshasa	905,565	22,900,000	Mobutu Sese Seko—president
Zambia	Lusaka	290,585	4,500,000	Kenneth D. Kaunda—president

DICTIONARY INDEX

A

B

Biodegradable. Capable of being easily decomposed, or broken down, by bacteria or through other natural processes into products that are usually harmless and easily disposed of. A biodegradable detergent, for example, is one that can be worked on by bacteria, which break it down into substances that are carried away in sewage without causing pollution of the soil or streams.

Burnout. In space travel, the point at which a jet or rocket engine stops operating, either because it is shut off or because there is no further fuel for it to operate with.

C

D

De facto. A Latin phrase meaning in reality or in fact; actual, regardless of legal or moral sanctions. De facto school segregation is that which is created not by law but by housing or neighborhood patterns. If certain neighborhoods in cities are largely or entirely white and others are largely or entirely nonwhite, the schools serving such neighborhoods will show actual, or de facto, segregation. (Schoolchildren are sometimes bused to schools outside their neighborhoods to eliminate such de facto segregation.) De facto devaluation of a currency is that which comes about when the currency "floats" down to a lower level though it has not been intentionally lowered by the government issuing the currency. See also De jure; Float.

De jure. A Latin phrase meaning according to law, or by right. De jure school segregation, which existed in some parts of the United States before 1954, put whites and nonwhites in separate schools in keeping with state or city laws or with official actions by school authorities. De jure devaluation of a currency is that brought about intentionally by the actions of a government or group of governments in the world exchange market. See also De facto.

Deliverance, film 334
DeMont, Rick, American athlete 294
Deneb, star 60, 61
Denmark 341
Desalination see Water desalting
Design for the Seventies, Boys' Clubs' program 235
Designs, poem 190
De Valera, Eamon, Irish president 351
Diamond, Neil, American musician 334
Diana Ross Presents Jackson Five, record album 225

Dirty tricks. Unfair actions during a political campaign that are intended to harm the chances for election of an opposing candidate. Some of the actions are illegal. They are always what most citizens would judge to be clear violations of fair play in an election contest. Some examples of dirty tricks are hiring pickets and hoodlums to break up political rallies, and distributing false information about a candidate to newspapers and broadcasters.

Distemper, disease 119
Distillation 56
Dog shows 285
Dollhouse 170–173
Dorrie and the Goblin, book 184
Douglas, William O., American judge 361
Douglass, Frederick, American reformer 211
Draft, military 341
Drug abuse 232
Dry ice 80
Dry.rice 33
Dubhe, star 60
Dylan, Bob, American musician 334

E

Earthquake 354
East, Jeff, American actor 328
Eastland, James O., U.S. senator 47
Eclipse, astronomy 351
Eco-Action, Girl Scout program 240
Eggs 68, 69
Egypt
    Israel 163
    October war 358
Ehrlichman, John D., American official 347
Eiffel Tower, Paris 137, picture 136
Electricity 91, 92
Electrodialysis 57
Elephant, animal 28, 29, 103
Elizabeth II, British ruler 352, picture 344
Ellsberg, Daniel, American conspiracy defendant 341, 349
Emmy award, television
    Thomas, Richard 227
    The Waltons 314

Endangered species. A species of animal that has become steadily smaller in number, usually as a result of being hunted and killed by human beings. It is in danger of being wiped out entirely, or made extinct. The polar bear and the wolf are often classed as endangered species.

Ender, Kornelia, American athlete, picture 294
Energy crisis 11, 90–95, 363, 365

Canada 95
Great Britain 365
English Channel 357
Erickson, Stephen J., American mayor, picture 223
Ervin, Sam, U.S. senator 44
Escape velocity, physics 76
Eskimos 215, 216
European Economic Community 341
Evaporation 56
Evert, Jeanne, American tennis player, picture 297
Executive privilege, American politics 44, 45
Expanded Food and Nutrition Education Program, 4-H Clubs 238
Explorer, Boy Scouts 232
EXPO'70, Osaka, Japan 322

Extended family. A family that includes, in addition to parents and their children, other close relatives, all living in the same household. The term for the small family unit consisting only of parents and their children is "nuclear family." If grandparents, aunts, uncles, or other close relatives are added to a nuclear family, the result is an "extended family."

F

Fargo, Donna, American singer 336
Fertilizer, organic 255
Field lacrosse, sport 309, 311
Fine Gael, Irish political party 345
Finn, Huck, literary character 329
First Amendment, U.S. Constitution 43
First Associate Holding Company, Junior Achievement 244
First National Sales Company, Junior Achievement 244
Flack, Roberta, American singer 338

Float. In economics, said of a currency that has its value determined by the law of supply and demand. In the world exchange market, the currency (paper money) of a given nation is said to float when it finds a level of value based on the free operation of supply and demand. A floating currency has no artificial influence such as support by government banks to keep the exchange rate at a particular level. Currency that floats finds its own level. And a nation that floats its currency permits it to find such a level in uncontrolled trading on the market.

Flood 357
Flowers 50–55
Fogerty, John, American musician 337
Food 64–69
    prices 343, 355
Football 286–288
Ford, Gerald R., U.S. vice-president 11, 46, 47, 359, 365
Foreman, George, American boxer, picture 284
Forsyth, James, American officer 200
Fossil fuels 92, 95
Foster, Jodie, American actress 328
4-H Clubs 238
Fourteenth Amendment, U.S. Constitution 201, 202, 211
France
    child's Paris 136–143
    coin collecting 273
    nuclear tests 353

G

H

Habitat. The place where a plant or animal normally lives and grows. In modern science the term is also used for a structure containing a controlled environment that enables people to live normally amid surrounding hostile conditions. An undersea habitat, for example, is usually a steel capsule in which the scientists, called aquanauts, can live and conduct undersea research for 30 days or more.

I

Inner city. The part of a large city that includes the main business district and adjacent residential areas. These residential areas are usually the city's oldest. In the United States they are populated largely by families of low average income, who are often members of minority groups. Because the buildings are old and the people living in them have little money, these areas are generally run down. They also have more crime and other social problems than do the outlying residential sections and suburbs, where more prosperous families live.

J

K

L

O

Oakland Athletics, baseball team 277
Oakland Raiders, football team 286
Oates, Warren, American actor 328
October war (1973) 11, 163, 164, 358
   cease-fire 363
   peace conference 365
Ohio State, football team 286
Oil, fuel
   Alaska pipeline 363
   Arabs 361
   Canada 95
   energy crisis 90–95
Oil pipeline
   Alaska 93, 363
   Canada 95
Olympic Games 343
O'Neal, Tatum, American actress, picture 221

Open classroom. A method of teaching in which students learn by doing and by individual experience, rather than by the formal method of group instruction followed by examinations. The student is encouraged to make his or her own investigation of the subject and to find the answers without help or, when that is impossible, through discussion with classmates and teachers. Open-classroom instruction stresses self-education. This method of teaching and learning, also called "open corridor," is being used in certain elementary schools in North America and Britain.

Operation Amigo, Canadian Boy Scout program 233
Orange Bowl, football 286
Organic food 64–69, 254–259
Organic garden 254–259
Orion, constellation 61, 62
Ottawa, Canada 355
Oxygen, element 82

P

Paiute Indians 194, 195
Pakistan
   flood 357
   prisoners of war 355
Palden Thondup Namgyal, Sikkim ruler 347
Palestine, region, Asia 162
Palestinian Arab refugees 163
Palmer, Jim, American baseball player 278
Panthéon, Paris 137
Papadopoulos, George, Greek president 363
Paper Bag Players, theater 318
Paris, France 136–143
Park, Bob, Canadian actor 317

Pass-fail. A system of grading students under which the only marks given are "pass" (to those who have completed their work satisfactorily) and "fail" (to those who have not). Among those who receive "pass," there is

no further grading to indicate whether the student is excellent, average, or barely passable. Some educators believe that this system focuses the student's attention on learning rather than on competing for number grades or marks.

Patty Cake, gorilla 101
Pavlova, Nadya, Russian ballerina, picture 223
Pegasus, constellation 61
Pentagon Papers 44, 341, 349
Peréz, Carlos Andrés, Venezuelan politician 365
Perihelion, astronomy 75
Perón, Juan, Argentine president 351, 357
Phad, star 60
Philip, Prince, Duke of Edinburgh, picture 352
Philippines, Republic of the 17
   clothes 30, 31
   rice terraces, picture 15
Phillips, Mark, British officer 362
Phobos, astronomy 77, 78
Phoenicia, ancient region, Asia 73
Photography 326, 327
Picasso, Pablo, Spanish artist 346
Pinochet Ugarte, Augusto, Chilean president 356
Pioneer 10, U.S. spacecraft 343, 364
Piscis Austrinus, constellation 61
Plains Indians 146
Planetoids, astronomy 77, 78
Planets, astronomy 59
   Jupiter 343, 364
   Mars 74–81
   Saturn 345
Plant press 51
Plants 50–55
   Mars 81
Pleiades, astronomy 62

Plumber. A slang term for a member of an undercover group working within the White House in the early 1970's. The group's job was to stop "leaks" of U.S. military and diplomatic secrets to the press, radio, and television; hence the nickname "the plumbers." Just as a plumber stops leaks in a household, a security "plumber" tries to stop leaks of secret or sensitive material.

Pluto, planet 59
Polar caps
   Mars 79, 89, picture 80
Polaris, astronomy 60
Pollux, astronomy 62
Pontiac's Rebellion 309
Population statistics 366–371
   Shanghai 343
Postal Service, U.S. 245
Preah Khan, temple, Cambodia 25
Presidency, American politics 42, 44, 45
Press, American 43
Price and wage controls 353
Pride, Charley, American singer, picture 335
Prisoners of war
   Israel-Egypt 363
   Pakistan 355
   Vietnam war, 11, 342, 345
Procyon, star 62
Project Identification, Junior Achievement company 243
Proposition Theater for Children 319
Puppet shows
   France 140
   Indonesia 34, 35
   United States 320

R

Rabies, disease 119, 355
Racing
   auto racing 276
   ballooning 299
   horse racing 292
Raffles, Stamford, British official 41
Rail strike 357
Randall, Juliet, Canadian actress 317
Rangers, Girl Scouts 241
REACH, Boy Scout program 232
Reconstruction, U.S. history 201
Reddy, Helen, American singer 338
Redgate, Steven, FFA award winner 239
Red Planet 75
Red Spot, Jupiter 364
Red trillium, plant 50
Reed, Willis, American athlete 283
Reggae, music 334
Regulus, star 62
Republican Party, U.S.
   Andrew Johnson's impeachment trial 201–204
Rice 65, picture 15
   Laos, 32, 33
Richardson, Elliot L., American official 43, 45, 347, 360
Riddle, A, poem 191
Riddles 266
Riel, Louis, Canadian rebel leader 147
Riggs, Bobby, American tennis player 295, 357
Ringling Bros. and Barnum & Bailey Circus 150, 151

Rip off. To cheat a person or to steal something from him. This slang expression is also used as a noun, written "rip-off" or "ripoff." As a noun it means an act of robbing, stealing, cheating, or similar dishonesty. Or the noun can refer to a person who steals from or cheats another. The expression probably comes from some instances of stealing or robbing in poor districts, where doors or windows are actually ripped off hinges or out of frames by thieves.

Rockefeller, Nelson A., American governor 365
Rock music 332–338
Rodeo 302–307
Rogers, William P., American official 355
Rose, Jack, FFA award winner 239
Rose Bowl, football 286
Ross, Edmund G., U.S. senator 204, 205
Rossetti, Christina, English poet 191
Royal Canadian Mounted Police 144–149
   stamps 250
Ruckelshaus, William D., American official 45, 360
Rumor, Mariano, Italian premier 353
Russo, Anthony, American conspiracy defendant 341, 349
Ryan, Nolan, American baseball player 278

S

Sacré-Coeur, church, Paris 137
Saddle bronc riding, rodeo 307

Sainte Chapelle, chapel, Paris 141
Saint Roch, Canadian ship 148
Saline Water, Office of 57
Salt 65
Samals, Philippine people 31
San Diego Zoo 105
San Pasquale Wild Animal Park, California 105
Sanya Dharmasakti, Thai premier 360
Saturn, planet 59, 345
Saxbe, William, U.S. senator 363

Scatter-site housing. Low-income housing projects located in middle-income neighborhoods. The purpose of such projects, which are usually run by city governments, is to enable people with low incomes to move away from inner-city ghettos. The long-range goal is to help low-income and minority groups reach the living standards of their new neighbors and become part of the middle-income community.

Schiaparelli, Giovanni, Italian astronomer 74
Schlesinger, James R., American official 349
Schmelzer, Menahem, American scholar 71
Science experiments 82, 83
Scorpius, constellation 61
Scouting 77, Canadian Boy Scout program 233

Scrambler. An attachment for a telephone or radio that turns the sound into a blur of static or meaningless noise. It is often used by the armed forces or government agencies as a security measure to prevent secret or confidential messages sent by telephone, walkie-talkie, or shortwave radio from being overheard by persons for whom they are not intended. A similar device at the receiving end of the conversation can turn the blurred sound into something recognizable, making it clear and understandable to the person for whom it is intended.

Sculpture 264
Sea salt 65
Seaver, Tom, American baseball player 278
Secretariat, horse, picture 292
Seeds 67
Seine, river, France 141
Separation of powers, political science 42
Shanghai, China 343
Short Bull, American Indian leader 197
Sikkim, Indian protectorate 347
Silver 272
Simon, Paul, American musician 337
Simpson, O. J., American athlete 286, picture 287
Sinai Peninsula, Egypt 163, 164
Singapore 18, 39
Singapore, University of, Singapore 40
Sioux Indians 196–200
   Royal Canadian Mounted Police 146
Sirica, John, American judge 42, 43, 45, 355, 360, picture 44
Sirius, star 61
Sitting Bull, American Indian leader 198–200
   Royal Canadian Mounted Police 146
Six-Day War (1967) 163
Skiing, sport 293
Skunk, animal 118–121
Skylab, U.S. spacecraft 84–87, 349, 351, 357, 363, picture 48, 49
Slavery 206, 211
   Black Codes 202
Snow-White and the Seven Dwarfs, book 185
SOAR, Boy Scout program 232
Sobhuza II, Swazi king 347

Terracide. Destroying or spoiling the earth and the air and water surrounding it by pollution. The air we breathe is poisoned when we burn such fuels as soft coal and lead-containing gasoline. Lakes, rivers, and the oceans are polluted when waste materials are dumped into them, and some of these wastes kill fish and other marine life and even cause lakes to dry up and become marshes. Land is destroyed or eroded by strip mining, for instance. All these practices are examples of terracide.

U

Unisex. Used by or suitable for both sexes, or making no distinction or difference as to sex, and so including both sexes. For example, unisex fashions or hair styles are those worn by both sexes, sometimes making it difficult to distinguish the wearer's sex. A unisex gathering is one for both sexes.

United Nations 357
  Israel 162, 163
  October war 358
United States
  Andrew Johnson impeachment trial 201–204
  Cuba 343
  energy crisis 91–93
  October war 358
  prisoners of war 342
  Southeast Asia 12
  Sudan 345
  Watergate affair 11, 42–45, 341, 347, 349, 353, 355, 360
  women, status of 206–211
Uranus, planet 59
Ursa Major, constellation 60
Ursa Minor, constellation 60

Van Courtland House, dollhouse 170
Vega, star 60, 61
Vegetables 254
Vegetarianism 176, 177
Venus, planet 59
Vietcong, Vietnam communist guerrillas 353
Vietnam, North 12, 19, pictures 18, 19
  prisoners of war 342
Vietnam, South 12, 19, pictures 18, 19
  International Commission of Control and Supervision 343, 349
  prisoners of war 342
  U.S. troops 345
Vietnam war 11, 12, 19, 341
  peace agreement 345
  prisoners of war 342
Viking, U.S. spacecraft 81
Virgo, constellation 62
Volcano 340
  Mars 79

Wage and price control 341
Waite, Ralph, American actor 315
Walt Disney stamps 250
Walton, Bill, American athlete 282
Waltons, The, TV show 227, 314–316
Warm-blooded animals 125
Warren House, dollhouse 171
Water
  Mars 78, 81
Water desalting 56

Watergate affair 11, 42–45, 341, 347, 349, 353, 355, 360
Watkins Glen, New York 332
Weed 258
Weiskopf, Tom, American golfer 289
Weitz, Paul J., American astronaut 85
Westminster Kennel Club 285
Wetland farming 33
What Is Pink?, poem 191
Wheat 360
Wheat germ 66
Whitaker, John, American actor 328
White House tape recordings 44, 45
Whitside, Samuel, American officer 200
Wildflowers 50–55
Wilson, Malcolm, American governor 365
Wimbledon tournament, tennis 295
Wingate Memorial Trophy, lacrosse 310
Wire sculpture 264, 265
Womack, Bobby, American singer 336
Women of the West, American history 206–211
World Hockey Association 290
World population 366–371
World Series, baseball 277, 278

Worry beads. A string of beads used by an adult as a plaything, usually as something to relax with after doing work that causes mental strain or worry. Worry beads were first known in the Arab countries and other parts of the Middle East.

Wounded Knee, South Dakota 200, 348
Wovoka, American Indian leader 194, 195, 197, 198, picture 196
Wyoming Trek, Girl Scout program 240

Yogurt 66
Yom Kippur War (1973) 11, 163, 164, 358
  cease-fire 363
  peace conference 365
Youth Art Exhibit (1973) 228–231

Zahir Shah, Mohammed, Afghani king 353

Zero population growth (ZPG). Growth of population that does not increase the population's overall size, but merely keeps it at an existing level. When there is zero population growth, the number of live births exactly replaces the losses caused by the death rate.

Zoo 102–109
Zoology
  cold-blooded animals 123
  elephant 28, 29
  skunk 118–121
  warm-blooded animals 125

ILLUSTRATION CREDITS AND ACKNOWLEDGMENTS

The following list credits or acknowledges, by page, the source of illustrations and text excerpts used in THE NEW BOOK OF KNOWLEDGE ANNUAL. Illustration credits are listed illustration by illustration—left to right, top to bottom. When two or more illustrations appear on one page, their credits are separated by semicolons. When both the photographer or artist and an agency or other source are given for an illustration, they are usually separated by a dash. Excerpts from previously published works are listed by inclusive page numbers.

10 Peter Arnold; Courtesy of Raven Industries, Inc., Sioux Falls, South Dakota; California Museum of Science and Industry; The Royal Canadian Mounted Police; From the collection of Joel Skodnick; James Ford Bell Museum of Natural History; NASA
12 Frank Schwarz—Lee Ames Studio
13 Michael Charles; Banyan Productions, Singapore
14 Erickson—De Wys, Inc.
15 FPG
16 Alan Band Associates; Tomas D. W. Friedmann—Photo Researchers
17 Thailand Tourist Organization; FPG
18 Marc Riboud—Magnum Photos, Inc.; Hiroji Kubota—Magnum Photos, Inc.
19 Marc Riboud—Magnum Photos, Inc.; Rene Burri—Magnum Photos, Inc.
21 Vietnam Council on Foreign Relations
23 P. W. Holzgraf—Monkmeyer Press Photo Service
24 P. W. Holzgraf—Monkmeyer Press Photo Service
25 P. W. Holzgraf—Monkmeyer Press Photo Service
26 Harrison Forman
27 New York Public Library Picture Collection
28 M. Durrance—Photo Researchers
29 Peter Arnold Agency
30 Randolph King
31 Randolph King
32 Carl Purcell
33 Carl Purcell
34 Indonesian Tourist Office
35 Indonesian Tourist Office
37 New York Public Library
39 Walter Hortens
40 Fujihira—Monkmeyer Press Photo Service
41 David Muench
42 UPI
43 UPI
44 UPI
46 UPI
48– NASA
49
50 Falk—Monkmeyer Press Photo Service
52 Hal Hinds
53 Hal Hinds
57 Publishers Graphics
58 Robert Little—Celestron Pacific
60 Robert Little—Celestron Pacific
61 Robert Little—Celestron Pacific
62 Robert Little—Celestron Pacific
63 Fawcett Publications, Inc.
64 Randolph King, courtesy Pete's Spice and Everything Nice, New York City
65 Randolph King
66 Randolph King
67 Randolph King
68 Randolph King
69 Randolph King
70 The New York Times
71 Hugh and Suzanne Johnston
72 From The Harrison Collection, Bridwell Library, Southern Methodist University

73 American Friends of the University of Haifa
74 W. S. Tinsen—Republic Observatory, Johannesburg; Miller Pope
75 U.S. Geological Survey
76 Miller Pope; Lowell Observatory Photo
77 Miller Pope
78 Jet Propulsion Laboratory—NASA
79 The New York Times, © 1969, reprinted by permission; NASA
80 Lowell Observatory Photo; NASA
81 NASA
82 Copyright © 1968 by D. C. Heath & Co., reprinted by permission of the publishers
83 Copyright © 1970 by D. C. Heath & Co., reprinted by permission of the publishers
84 NASA
85 The New York Times
86 NASA
87 NASA
88 NASA
89 Science World magazine
90 Wide World Photos
91 Randolph King
93 Jacques Chazaud
94 Pacific Gas & Electric Company
95 Imperial Oil Limited
96– Luis Villota
97
98 New York Daily News Photo; The New York Times
99 New York Daily News Photo; UPI; The New York Times
100 UPI; reprinted by permission of Nature magazine; UPI
101 UPI; New York Daily News Photo
102 Dennis Yeandle
103 Lion Country Safari, Kings Dominion
104 Robert Scott Milne
105 Busch Gardens
106 Lion Country Safari
107 Robert Scott Milne; Busch Gardens
108 Busch Gardens
109 Busch Gardens
111 New York Public Library Picture Collection
112 New York Public Library Picture Collection
114 James Ford Bell Museum of Natural History
115 James Ford Bell Museum of Natural History
116 James Ford Bell Museum of Natural History
117 James Ford Bell Museum of Natural History
118 Don Bender for J. B. Lippincott Co.
119 David Wertheimer
120 David Wertheimer
121 David Wertheimer
122 Ray Atkeson—DPI
124 Edmund Appel
126 Jules Zalon—DPI
127 Richard Weiss; Dr. E. R. Degginger
129 Barbara K. Deans—National Audubon Society

130– From Kalu and the Wild Boar, text ©
133 1973 by Peter Hallard; illustrations by W. T. Mars, © 1973 by Franklin Watts, Inc. Reprinted by permission of the publishers
134– Circus World Museum
135
136 Francis Bannett—DPI
138 Don Morgan—Photo Researchers
139 Jean Lambert
140 Michel Simonet—Rapho Guillumette Pictures; Cooke—Photo Researchers
142 J. Alex Langley—DPI
143 Walter S. Clark
144 The Royal Canadian Mounted Police
145 The Royal Canadian Mounted Police
146 The Royal Canadian Mounted Police
147 The Royal Canadian Mounted Police
148 The Royal Canadian Mounted Police
149 The Royal Canadian Mounted Police
150 Circus World Museum
151 Circus World Museum
152 Circus World Museum
153 Circus World Museum
154 Poster by Lino Piccoli
155 Richard Tedeschi
157 Francesco Liuzzi; Richard Tedeschi
158 Francesco Liuzzi
159 Richard Tedeschi
160 British Tourist Authority
161 The Academy of Applied Science; British Tourist Authority
162 Tomas D. W. Friedmann—DPI
163 Dankwart von Knobloch—Lenstour Photos
164 Louis Goldman—Rapho Guillumette
165 Hank Greenberg—DPI
166 Louis Goldman—Rapho Guillumette; Georg Gerster—Rapho Guillumette
167 Louis Goldman—Rapho Guillumette
168 Louis Goldman—Rapho Guillumette
169 Louis Goldman—Rapho Guillumette; Sidney Glatter—DPI
170 Randolph King
171 Courtesy Museum of the City of New York
172 Courtesy of Essex Institute, Salem, Mass.; Historical Society of Delaware
173 Courtesy Milwaukee Public Museum
174 Barbara T. Blair
176 Barbara T. Blair
177 Bernard Silberstein—Monkmeyer Press Photo Service
178– From the book The Funny Little
179 Woman by Arlene Mosel. Illustrated by Blair Lent. Text © by Arlene Mosel; illustrations; © 1972 by Blair Lent. Published by E. P. Dutton & Co., Inc., and used with their permission
180 Courtesy of Holt, Rinehart and Winston, publishers of Anansi the Spider, Copyright © 1972 by Landmark Production, Inc.
181 Courtesy of Harper & Row, Publishers, Inc., publishers of No Kiss for Mother, © 1973 by Tomi Ungerer

182 Courtesy of E. P. Dutton & Co., Inc., Publishers of *The Funny Little Woman*. Text © 1972 by Arlene Mosel; illustrations © 1972 by Blair Lent

183 Courtesy of Harper & Row, Publishers, Inc., publishers of *Julie of the Wolves*. Text © 1972 by Jean Craighead George; illustrations © 1972 by John Schoenherr

184 Courtesy of Lothrop, Lee & Shepard Co., publishers of *Dorrie and the Goblin*, © 1972 by Patricia Coombs

185 Courtesy of Farrar, Straus and Giroux, publishers of Snow White and the Seven Dwarfs. Translated by Randall Jarrell; illustrations © 1972 by Nancy Ekholm Burkert

186 Arvis Stewart—Helen Wohlberg, Inc.

188 Arvis Stewart—Helen Wohlberg, Inc.

190 Christian John Dauer

191 Christian John Dauer

192– From *It's Raining Said John Twaining*,
193 © 1973 by N. M. Bodecker. A Margaret K. McElderry Book, used by permission of Atheneum publishers.

194 Smithsonian Institution, National Anthropological Archives, Bureau of American Ethnology Collection

196 Smithsonian Institution, National Anthropological Archives

199 Culver Pictures, Inc.

202 The New York Public Library Picture Collection

204 The Granger Collection

206– From *Women of the West*, by Dorothy
211 Levenson, © 1973 by Franklin Watts, Inc. Reprinted by permission of the publishers

207 Library of Congress

210 New York Public Library Picture Collection

212 The Public Archives of Canada

214 The Public Archives of Canada

217 The Public Archives of Canada

218– Chris Sheridan
219

220 Chris Sheridan; *The New York Times*; Wide World

221 UPI; UPI; *The New York Times*

222 *The New York Times*; UPI

223 Sovfoto; Westinghouse Electric Corp.; UPI

224 UPI

225 Jackson Five, Inc.

226 CBC Television Network

228 California Museum of Science and Industry

229 California Museum of Science and Industry

230 California Museum of Science and Industry

231 California Museum of Science and Industry

232 Boy Scouts of America

233 Boy Scouts of Canada

234 Camp Fire Girls, Inc.

235 Boys' Clubs of America

236 Boy Scouts of America; Girl Guides of Canada; Girl Scouts of the U.S.A.

237 4-H Clubs; Future Farmers of America

238 4-H Clubs

239 Future Farmers of America

240 Girl Scouts of the U.S.A.

241 Girl Guides of Canada

242 Junior Achievement

243 Junior Achievement

244 Junior Achievement

245 Junior Achievement

246– Reprinted from *Instructor,* © Febru-
247 ary, 1973, by the Instructor Publications, Inc., used by permission

251 From the Collection of Joel Skodnick

252 From the Collection of Joel Skodnick

253 From the Collection of Joel Skodnick

254 Maplevale Organic Farm

256 Reprinted by permission from *Ranger Rick's Nature Magazine*, February, 1973, published by the National Wildlife Federation

258 Maplevale Organic Farm

259 Maplevale Organic Farm

260 Randolph King, courtesy of Adventures in Crafts, New York City

261 Sybil C. Harp

262 Sybil C. Harp

263 Sybil C. Harp

264 Reprinted by permission of Van Nostrand Reinhold Company from *Building with Wire* by John Lidstone, photographs by Roger Kerkham

265 Reprinted by permission of Van Nostrand Reinhold Company from *Building with Wire* by John Lidstone, photographs by Roger Kerkham

266 From *Child Life,* © 1973 by Review Publishing Co., Inc.

267 From *Child Life,* © 1973 by Review Publishing Co., Inc.

268 Fingerprint drawings by Lydia Stein

269 From *Child Life,* © 1973 by The Saturday Evening Post Company, Inc.; from *Child Life,* © 1973 by Review Publishing Co., Inc.

270 From *Child Life,* © 1972 by Review Publishing Co., Inc.

271 From *Child Life,* © 1973 by Review Publishing Co., Inc.

272 Krause Publications, Inc.

273 American Revolution Bicentennial Commission; Krause Publications, Incorporated

274– Corson Hirschfeld—*Cincinnati* Maga-
275 zine

276 UPI; Wide World Photos

277 *Sports Illustrated* photo by Herb Scharfman, © Time Inc.

278 *Sports Illustrated* photo by Walter Iooss, Jr., © Time Inc.

280 UPI

281 UPI; Vannucci Foto-Services

282 *Sports Illustrated* photo by Sheedy and Long, © Time Inc.

283 UPI

284 Wide World Photos

285 *Chicago Tribune* photo; UPI

286 *Sports Illustrated* photo by Neil Leifer, © Time Inc.

287 *Sports Illustrated* photo by Walter Iooss, Jr., © Time Inc.; *Sports Illustrated* photo by John Iacomo, © Time Inc.

288 Wide World Photos

289 UPI

290 *Sports Illustrated* photo by James Drake, © Time Inc.

291 Wide World Photos

292 Wide World Photos

293 Wide World Photos; UPI

294 UPI

295 Wide World Photos; UPI

296 Wide World Photos

297 Wide World Photos

298 UPI

299 From *Up, Up and Away* by Jim Webb (© 1967 by Johnny Rivers Music)

300 Courtesy of Raven Industries, Inc., Sioux Falls, South Dakota

301 Courtesy of Raven Industries, Inc., Sioux Falls, South Dakota

302 Colin Lofting—Rodeo Cowboy Association

303 Louise L. Serpa

304 *The New York Times*

305 Rodeo Cowboy Association

306 Colin Lofting—Rodeo Cowboy Association; Colin Lofting—Rodeo Cowboy Association; Little Britches Rodeo

308 Corcoran Gallery

310 Willard R. Bonwit

311 Canadian Lacrosse Association

312– 1973 Scholastic–Kodak Photography
313 Awards

314 CBS Television Network

315 CBS Television Network

316 CBS Television Network

317 Canadian Broadcasting Corporation

318 City Center Young People's Theater, photographs by Ann Raychel

319 The Paper Bag Players; The Little Theatre of the Deaf

320 The Meri Mini Players

321 Bil Baird Marionette Theater; Children's Theatre Company of the Minneapolis Society of Fine Arts

322 Randolph King—courtesy of Wright Nurseries, New Jersey

323 Robert Wang—Courtesy of Educational Facilities Lab

324 Richard Kathmann

325 Birdair Structures, Inc.

326– 1973 Scholastic–Kodak Photography
327 Awards

328 Courtesy of *Reader's Digest*

329 United Artists Corporation

330 Reprinted by permission of Harcourt, Brace Jovanovich, Inc., from *A Cat Came Fiddling and Other Rhymes of Childhood*, adapted and made into songs by Paul Kapp and Irene Haas, © 1956 by Paul Kapp and Irene Haas

331 Reprinted by permission of Harcourt, Brace Jovanovich, Inc., from *A Cat Came Fiddling and Other Rhymes of Childhood*, adapted and made into songs by Paul Kapp and Irene Haas, © 1956 by Paul Kapp and Irene Haas

332 Christopher Little—Camera 5

333 Betty Lee Hunt Associates

334 Columbia Records

335 RCA; MCA; Columbia Records

336 DOT Records; Atlantic Records

337 Columbia Records

338 Capitol Records

340 Rosemary Reid Cronin

342 UPI

344 UPI

346 Collection, The Museum of Modern Art, New York, Mrs. Simon Guggenheim Fund

348 UPI

350 UPI

352 UPI

354 UPI

356 UPI

358 Wide World Photos; UPI

359 UPI; Wide World Photos

362 UPI

364 NASA